Charlottesville Wine & Country™ Weddings

Volume 1

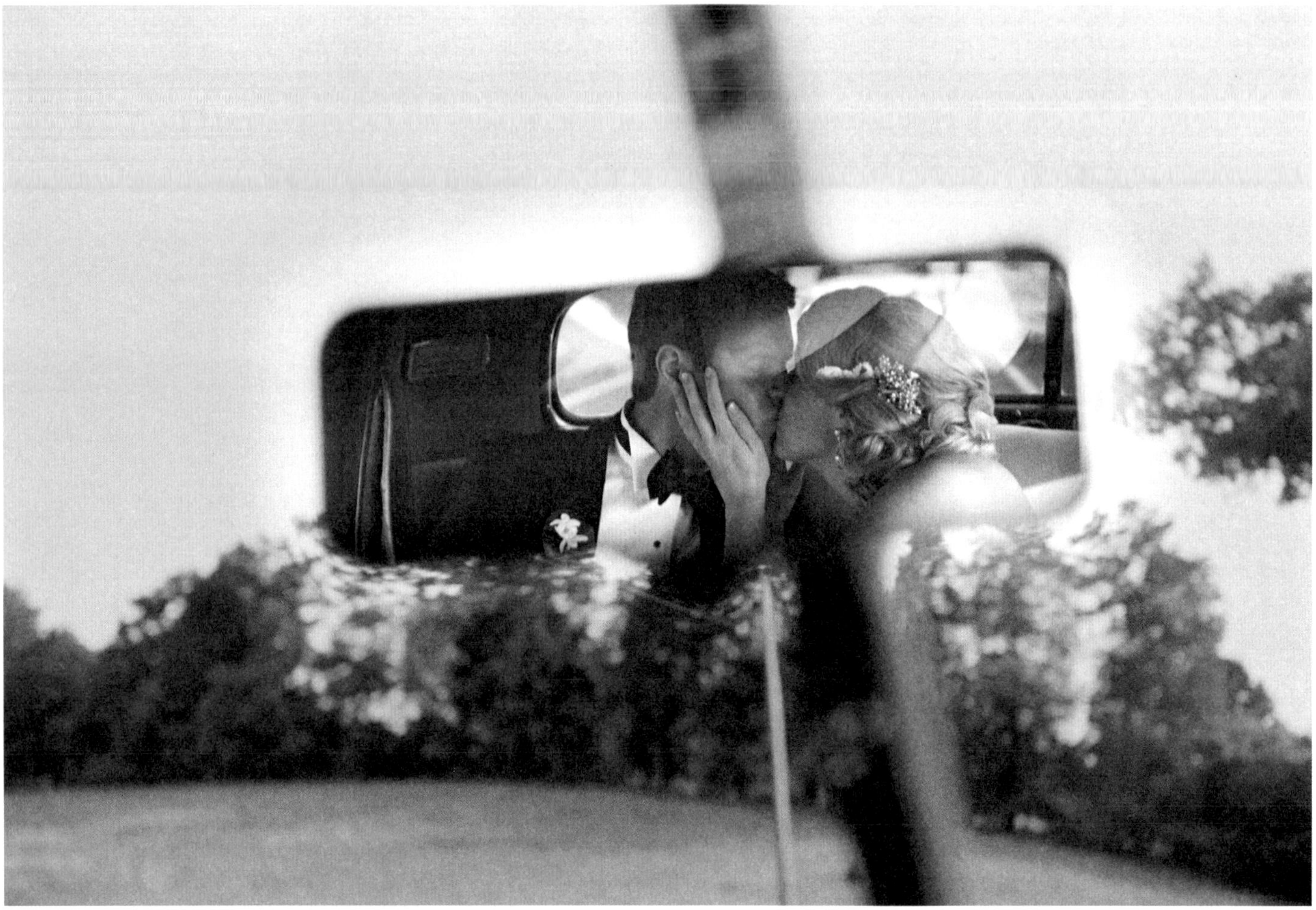

You and me together, WE COULD DO ANYTHING

— DAVE MATTHEWS

HERE'S TO *Love...*

With lovely pastoral views and nestled in the beautiful Blue Ridge Mountains, Charlottesville is a very special place. People from all over the globe gather here to study at the University of Virginia and immerse themselves in the history of Thomas Jefferson, as well as the trendy scene embodied by our local musicians gone big, the Dave Matthews Band. We do it all here—art, music, history and culture, along with a passion for nature, gardening and living in a way that embraces the beauty of the countryside and the hip vibe of our downtown. Virginia is for lovers as they say—and Charlottesville seems the perfect place to begin any love story.

Our idea for Charlottesville Wine & Country Weddings came out of our love and adoration of this place. In our curated collection of portfolios we feature our town's many talented wedding professionals, you will find not only beautiful craftsmanship, but also people who love love—people you can trust to inspire you as you dream about and embark on one of the biggest days of your life. These amazing artisans have come together from around the world and some are home-grown right here in Virginia to create an industry that is growing in joyful leaps and bounds and is committed to a level of quality that couples will find on par with cities from New York to Beverly Hills.

Jefferson is said to have found his enlightenment in Paris, and in similar fashion he influenced our region to adopt many of the same passions from winemaking and sophisticated farm-to-table cuisine to a love of architecture. The beauty of our area and the work of our many amazing wedding artisans are capturing attention in regional and national wedding publications. As a result, couples are coming here to enjoy the stunning views and elegant styles of those who make it all happen for our brides and grooms with grace and down-to-earth hospitality.

Just as new romance can feel simultaneously exciting and a little bit scary, we found ourselves similarly engrossed with each and every detail of Wine & Country Weddings' first issue. We lingered over every photograph, perfected every word—but the time has come at last to send it out into the world. Along the way, we've been blown away by the responses from our contributors. We expected only a dozen or so advertisers' portfolios and found ourselves with more than 50—and we are smitten with each one! We have made new friends and have met so many talented photographers, wedding planners, bakers and more—and we can't wait to introduce them to you.

We invite you now to explore the passions and special talents of our wedding community here in Jefferson's Virginia.

A *hug* AND THANKS TO

A hug and a thanks to everyone who helped us to create this beautiful, beautiful book.

From start to finish, it was a pleasure to work closely with the very talented Jen Fariello. Not only does she have an amazing eye behind the lens, but she is also warm, funny, generous, creative and a true joy to collaborate with. This book wouldn't be all that it is without her. Though her humble nature will not allow us to call out all of her work, her many years of experience shine through the images that grace our editorial pages.

And, a big resounding kudos to our amazing staff, who worked long hours creating each page with love, especially our sweet portfolio designer, Erin Hughes, who poured her whole heart into this project with great patience, endurance, and an inspired talent. To Barbara whose quiet, but immensely valuable, support kept us going. To our sales team who tirelessly supported this book from every angle. And to our administrative team, who patiently covered for those of us immersed in wedding. For waking up in the night with great ideas. For the families who let us work weekends.

We are so grateful to our portfolio advertisers, each and every one. They took the leap of faith that we could truly create the vision we all had for an artful, curated book that would embody the elegant country wedding in Jefferson's Virginia. They have trusted us with their art and presentation, their storytelling, and we could not have asked for better support.

To our writers, who generously shared their knowledge and creativity—we are truly grateful for the revisions and love you poured into your charming contributions. We owe much praise to the talented Catherine Twomey who pressed on against the clock to finish the lovely vineyard paintings in time to grace our pages. To all of the gifted photographers, who shared their images to make each page beautiful, we thank you. Blessings to all the wedding planners who shared their inspirations and ideas, shepherding us gently as they would a bride and groom. Thanks, also, to our darling calligrapher, Jen Maton, who waited patiently, then waited patiently a little while longer, for us to settle on final titles and quotes for her inspired pen.

We also give warm thanks to all those who shared their ideas and visions throughout the process, from the biggest idea to the littlest—your generosity of spirit is much appreciated. Most of all, we are grateful for all the new friendships we've made and to that end, we toast all the creatives in the Charlottesville wedding community who make each wedding celebration beyond beautiful, and we also raise a glass to you, our new friends, our readers.

We hope you enjoy our work of love as much as we do.

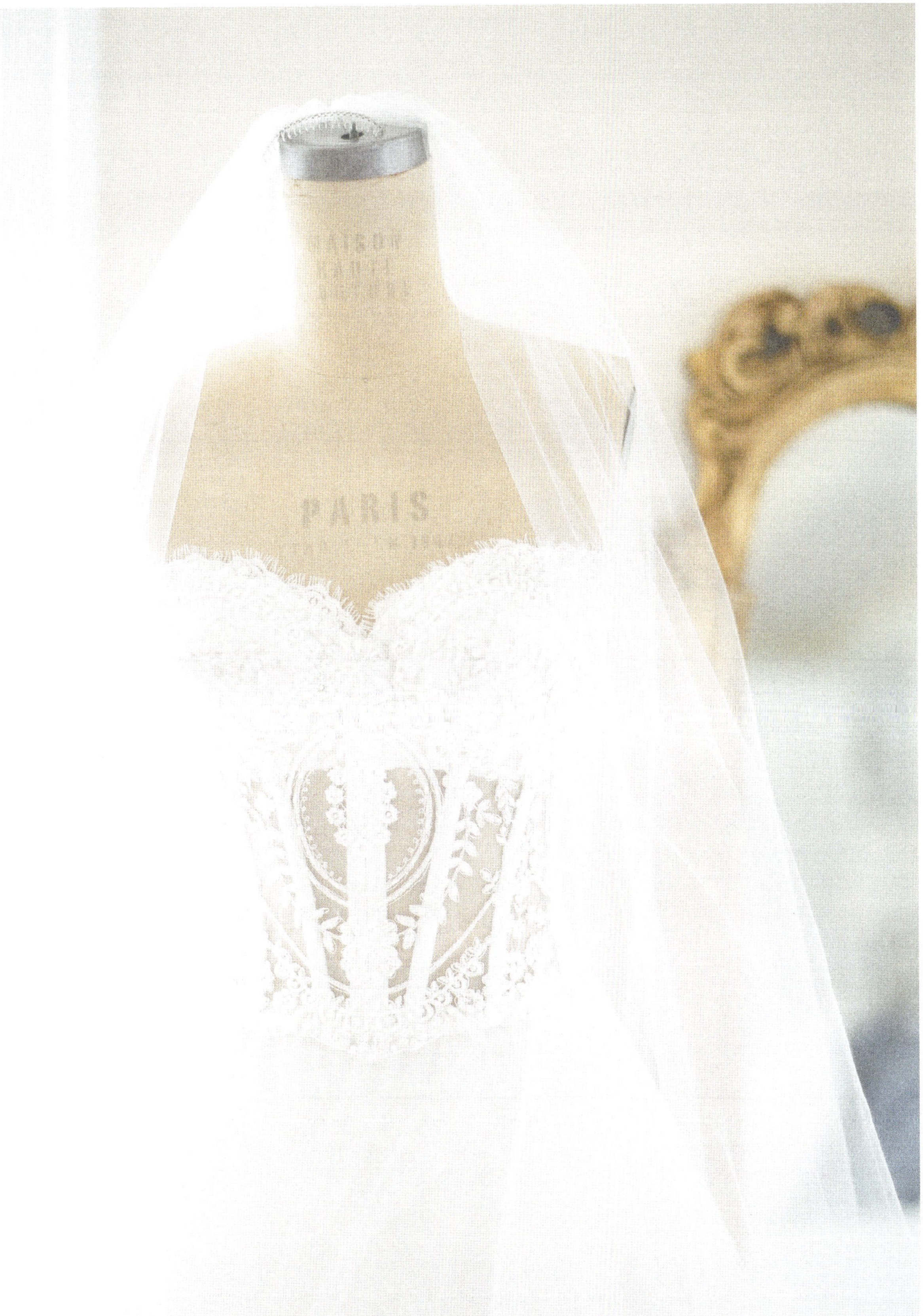
PARIS

OUR FAB TEAM

PUBLISHERS | *Robin Johnson-Bethke, Jennifer Bryerton*

CREATIVE DIRECTOR | *Robin Bethke*

EDITOR-IN-CHIEF | *Jennifer Bryerton*

CREATIVE CONSULTANT | *Jen Fariello*

TECHNICAL DIRECTOR | *Peter Bethke*

GRAPHIC DESIGN | *Erin Q. Hughes, Barbara Tompkins*

EDITORIAL PHOTOGRAPHY | *Adam Barnes, Jen Fariello, Rachel May*

WRITING & EDITING | *Sarah Crossland, Celia Dentz, Adam Donovan-Groves, Caroline Hirst, Jody Hobbs Hesler, Nicole Perrier, Meghan Streit*

CALLIGRAPHY | *Jen Maton, If So Inklined*

ARTIST | *Catherine Twomey*

SALES MANAGER | *David Valcich*

SALES CONSULTANTS | *Karrie Bos, Lindsay Lopez, Susan Powell, Jenny Stoltz, Brandi Washburn*

ADMINISTRATIVE MANAGER | *Amy Duprey*

ADMINISTRATIVE ASSISTANT | *Caitlin Morris*

DISTRIBUTION | *Ray Whitson*

Our lovely inside cover art of Barboursville Vineyard and Grace Estate Winery were painted by internationally-acclaimed local artist, Catherine Twomey.

Charlottesville Wine & Country Weddings™ is an art book published in print annually by Ivy Publications, LLC and has a companion website and social media. Editorial and curated advertiser portfolios are designed to reflect the refined and artistic aesthetic of the elegant wedding in Jefferson's Virginia. Although every effort has been made to present correct information, we do not in any way accept responsibility for the accuracy of information or for the performance or goods of businesses and organizations presented herein. No portion of this publication may be reproduced in part or in whole without the express written consent of the publisher.

Ivy Publications, LLC is proud to work with a Certified Green Press. Charlottesville Wine & Country Weddings™ is printed on recycled content paper with up to 10% post-consumer waste (PSW) using only soy-based ink and supporting responsible forestry. You can find our paper-free digital edition online as well at CharlottesvilleWineandCountryWedding.com, and please do recycle.

Printed in the United States of America.

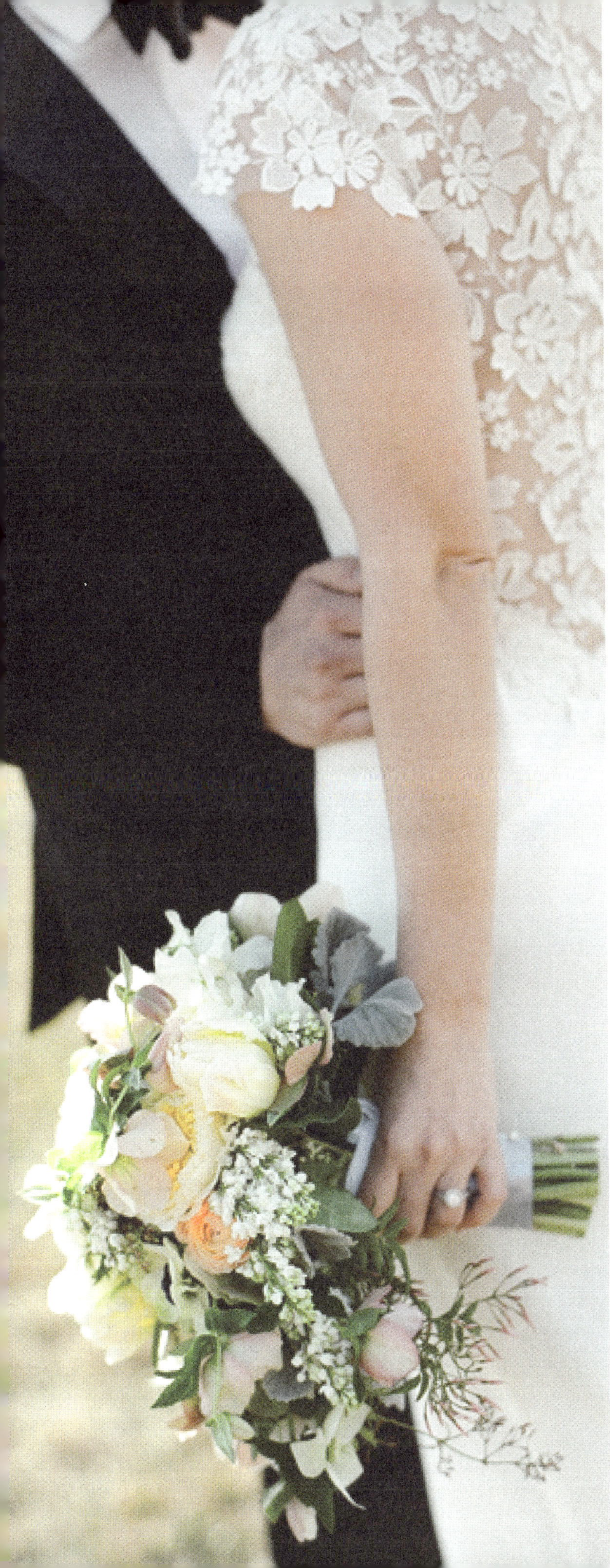

where it's at

Stay in touch! |

Weddings@IvyPublications.com

CharlottesvilleWineandCountryWeddings.com

A RICH SPOT *of Earth*

WRITTEN BY JENNIFER BRYERTON

If heaven had given him a choice, Thomas Jefferson once wrote he would have wished for a "rich spot of earth" to express his passions for all things related to our region's beautiful land. He certainly found that perfect spot here where he built his home at Monticello, spending his days in the garden with his family or studying quietly while enjoying the sweeping Blue Ridge Mountain views. He later founded the University of Virginia, bringing to Charlottesville a culture that not only reveres academia but also has a sophisticated appreciation for the arts. The combination of romantic countryside, elegance, vineyards, history and the creative people who are drawn to live here, have made Charlottesville one of the East Coast's most popular wedding destinations.

Winemaking was one of Jefferson's many passions and he dreamed that our region would someday produce wines that could rival those of Europe. As the birthplace of American wine, today we compete for and win prestigious awards around the world. With each unique vineyard pouring its own delicious wines in an array of sumptuous settings, it's no wonder

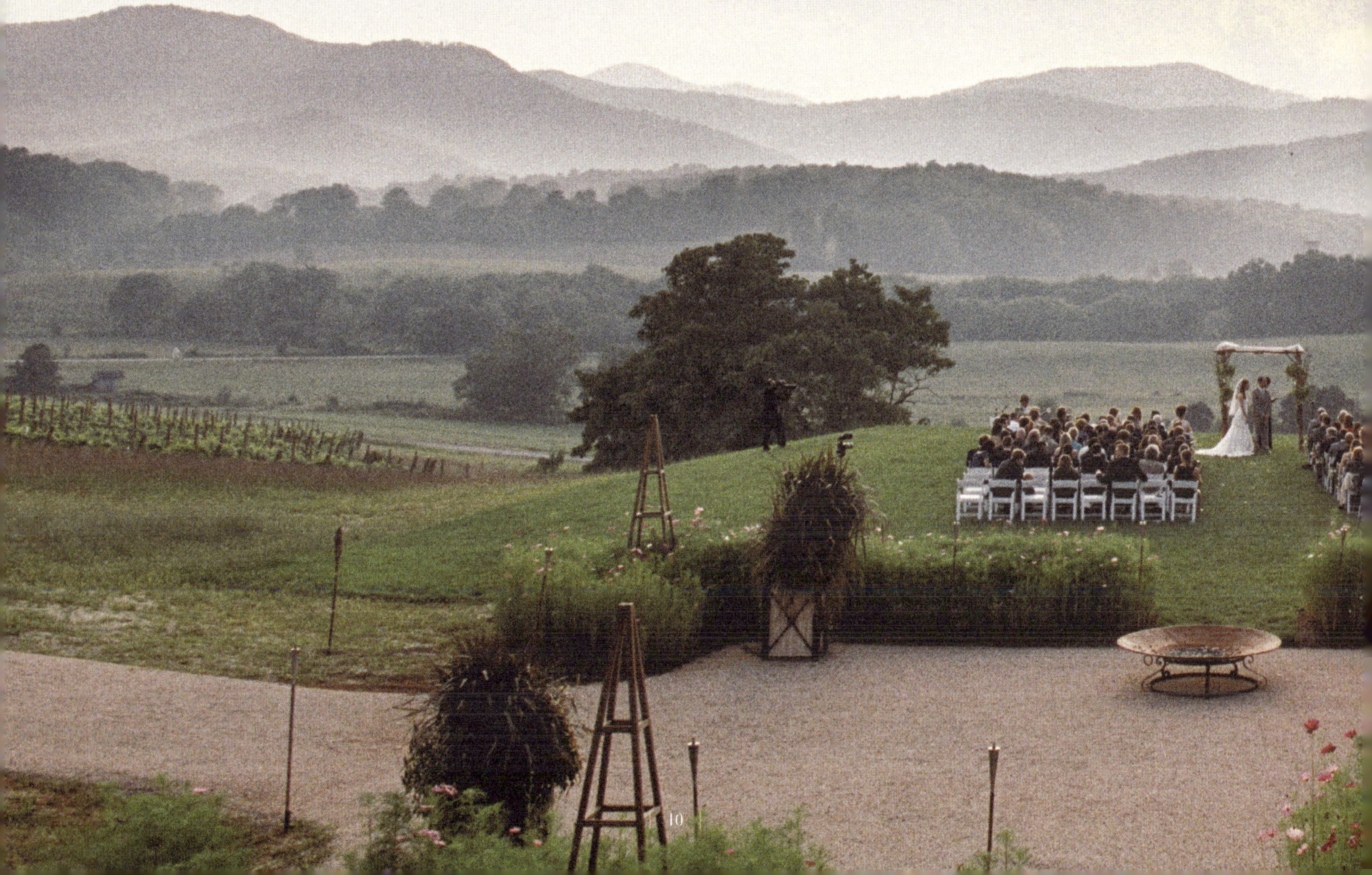

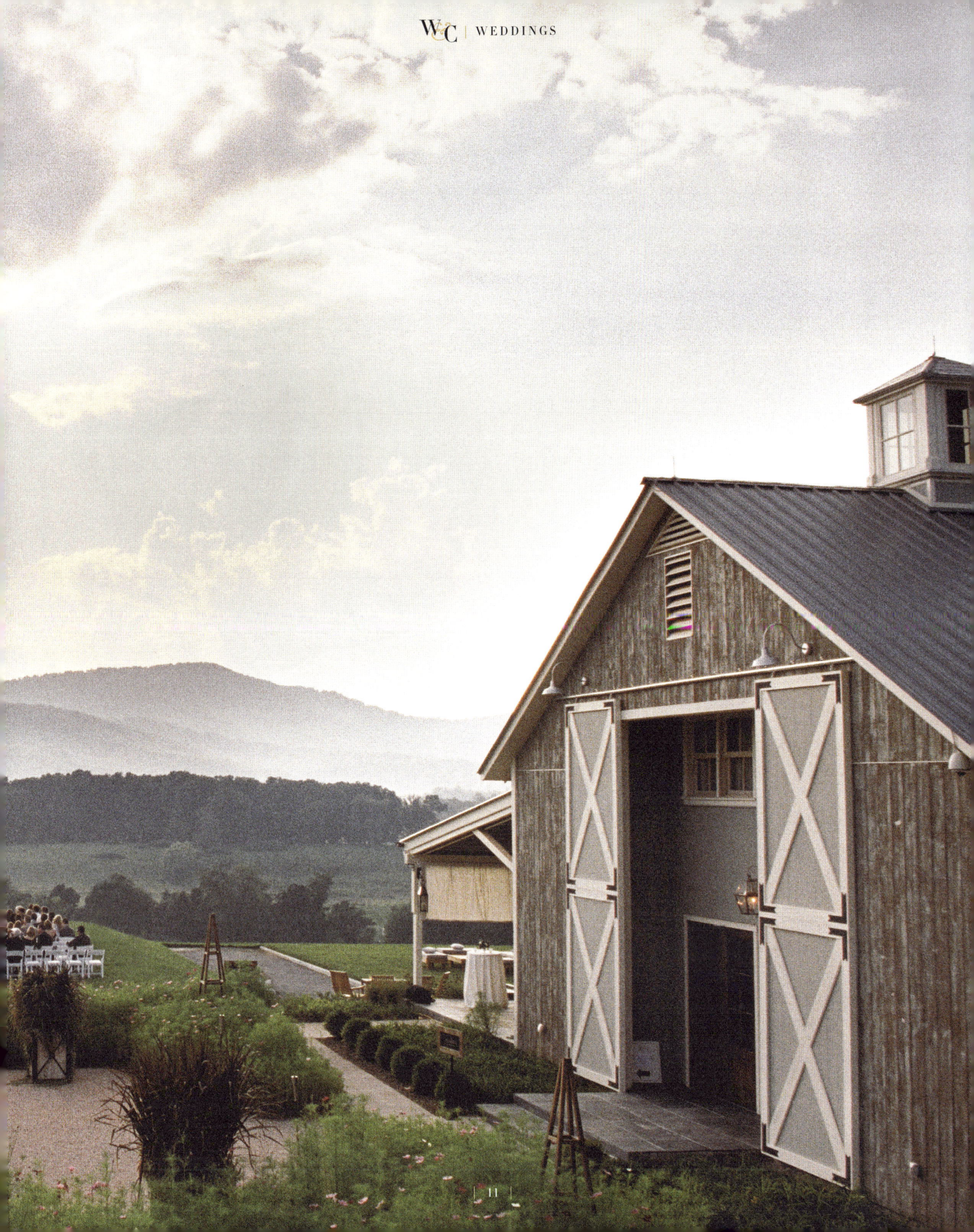

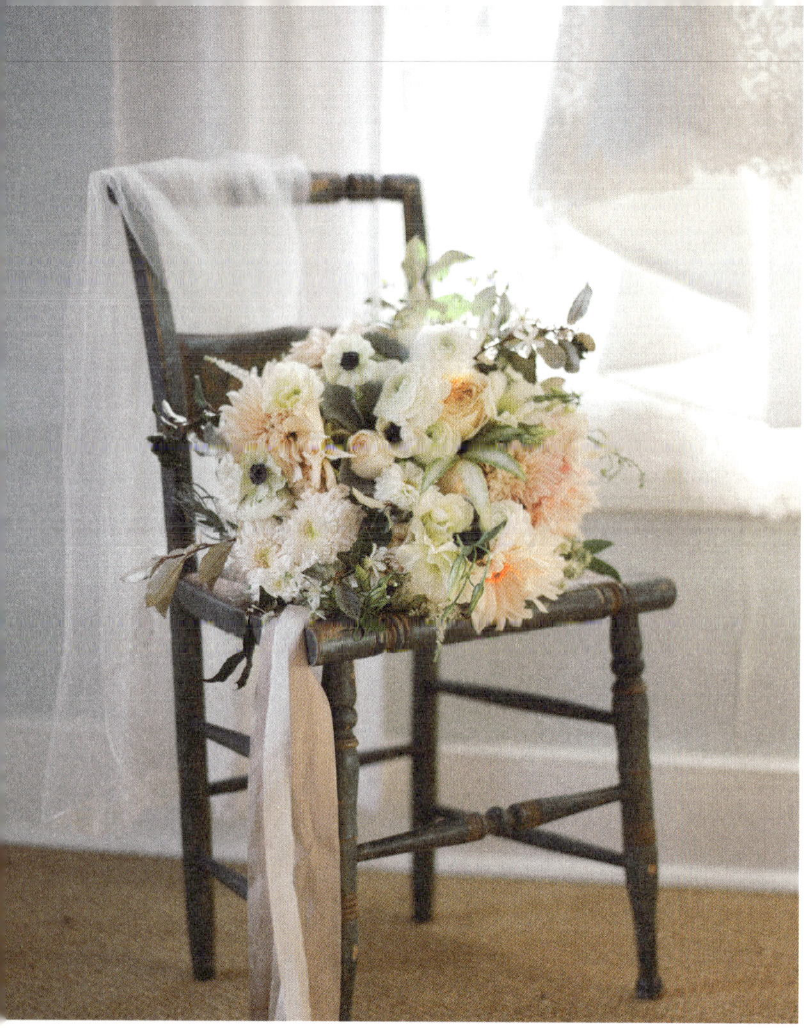

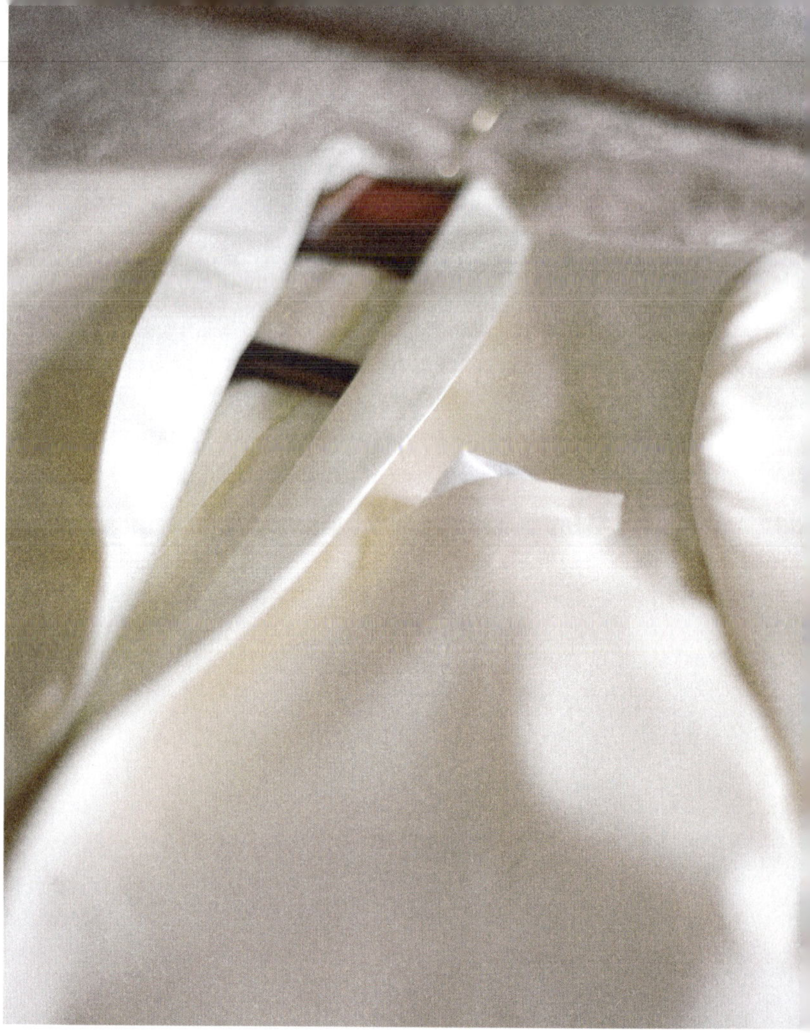

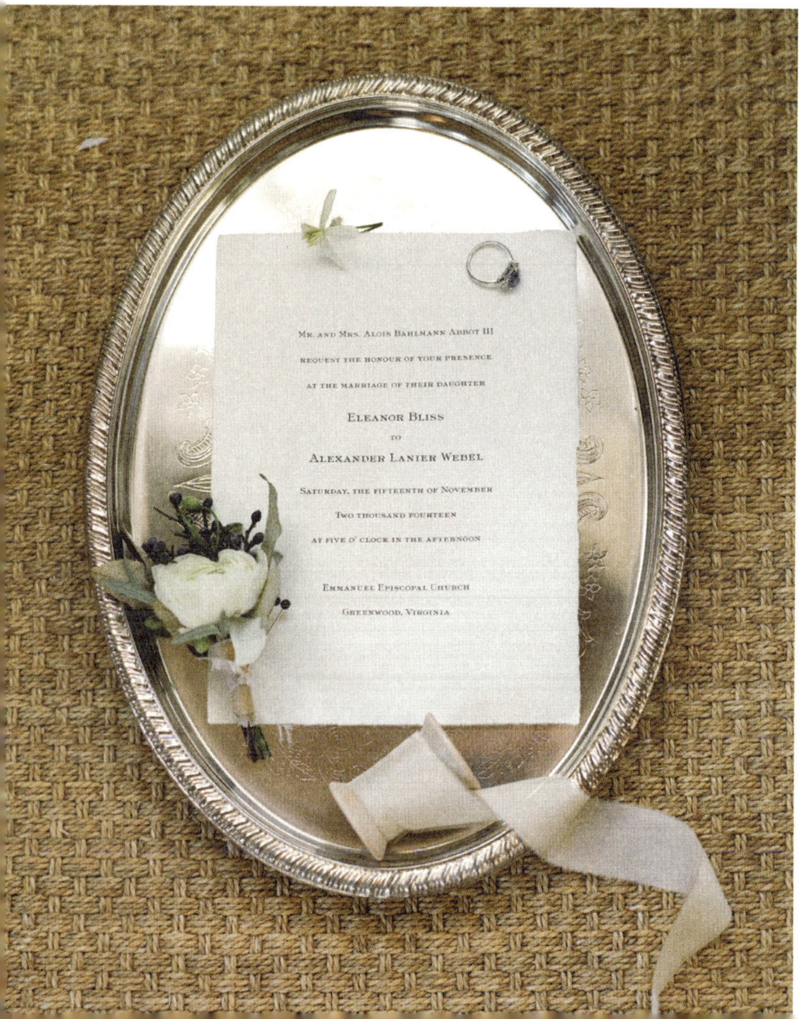
Mr. and Mrs. Alois Bahlmann Abbot III
request the honour of your presence
at the marriage of their daughter
Eleanor Bliss
to
Alexander Lanier Webel
Saturday, the fifteenth of November
Two thousand fourteen
at five o' clock in the afternoon
Emmanuel Episcopal Church
Greenwood, Virginia

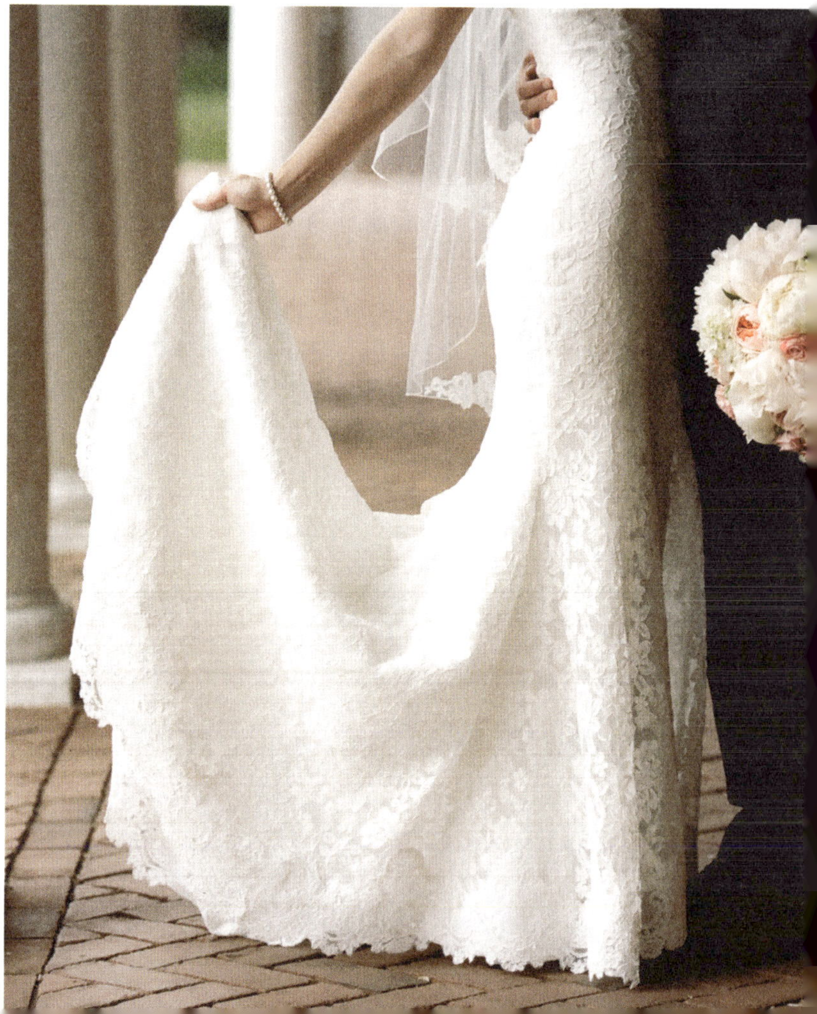

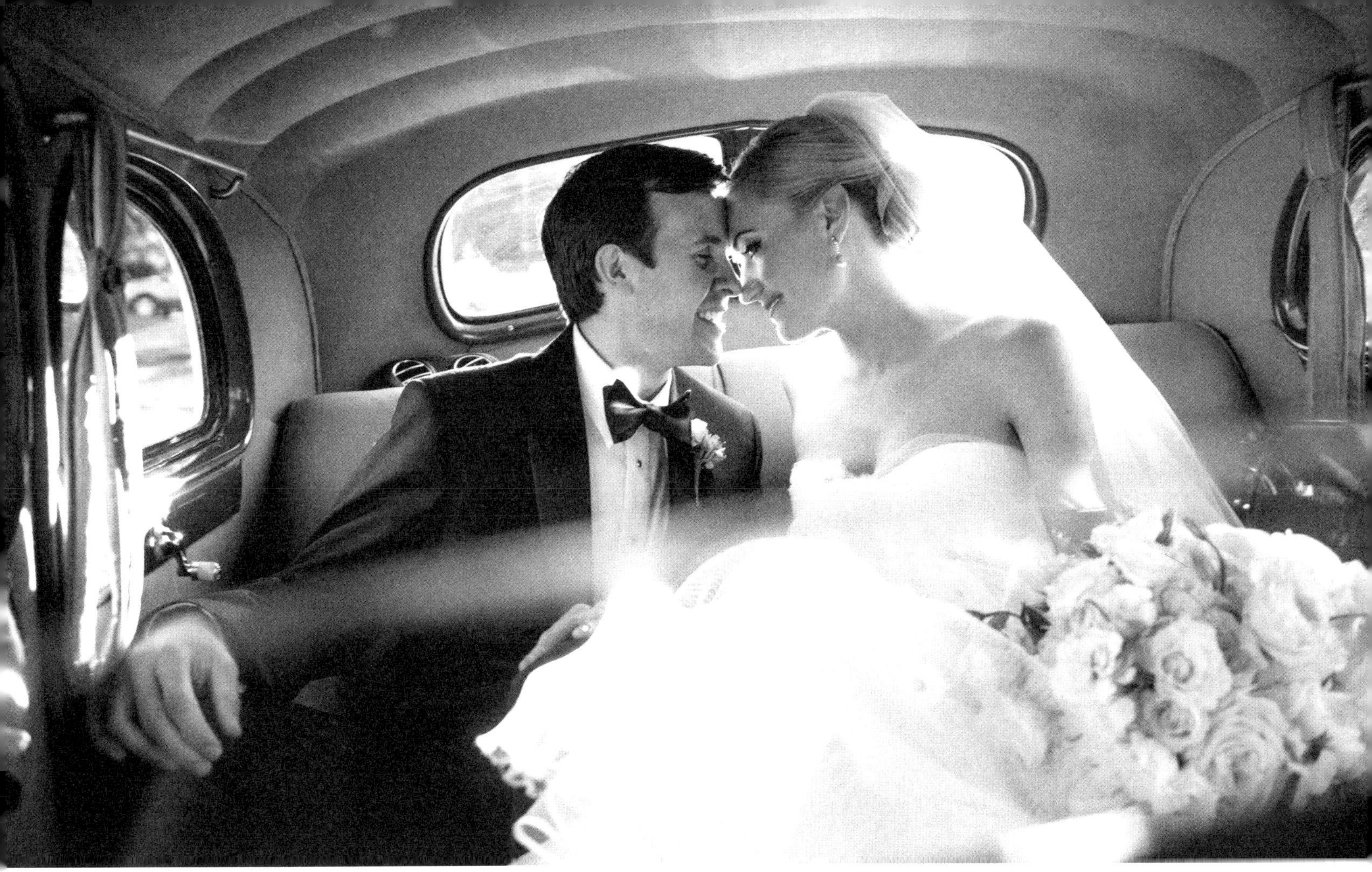

that Charlottesville has been called the Provence of the South. As a result, our enchanting vineyards and historic properties are the perfect fairytale setting for couples wanting to create a refined and intimate event. With over 40 vineyards, couples getting married here are undoubtedly spoiled for choice.

As you search for the perfect venue for your wedding, be sure to stroll the brick walkways of the University of Virginia's neoclassical Pavilion Gardens pictured at left, consider holding your ceremony at the University's immensely popular chapel or shop and dine at Charlottesville's chic downtown where the Dave Matthews Band got their start.

Our region is no stranger to celebrity. World-renowned author and local resident John Grisham recently hosted what may have been our most stunning wedding yet for his daughter at the family's country home. The charming couple on the next page is sharing a special moment at Trump Winery owned by Eric Trump, son of the well-known businessman, Donald Trump. Combine our perfect mountain views with a locally grown menu and enchanting personal touches, and the stage is set by our talented local wedding professionals for the celebration of a lifetime that will rival events held in cities from New York to Los Angeles.

For the modern couple, our trendy university town makes the guest outings, rehearsal dinner and bachelor party every bit as hip as the wedding is beautiful. The farm-to-table movement here includes much more than wine and has inspired area chefs to create innovative menus for our food-loving community brimming with local specialties—asparagus, greens, meats, eggs, cream, candies, pastries and more. Whether yours is a refined gastro-perfect palette or if you are looking for the best Southern barbecue you have ever tasted created by classically trained chefs who have left the upscale world of gastronomy to create fabulous down-to-earth Southern fare instead, you will find plenty of fresh, delicious and unique cuisines here.

At your reception, enjoy one of our craft microbrews or local hard ciders before dinner, then complement your meal with the perfect wine pairing and finish the evening by toasting with any of the growing number of locally distilled spirits. Jefferson was fond of making his own beer and cider too. Within Charlottesville's lively foodie scene, you are sure to

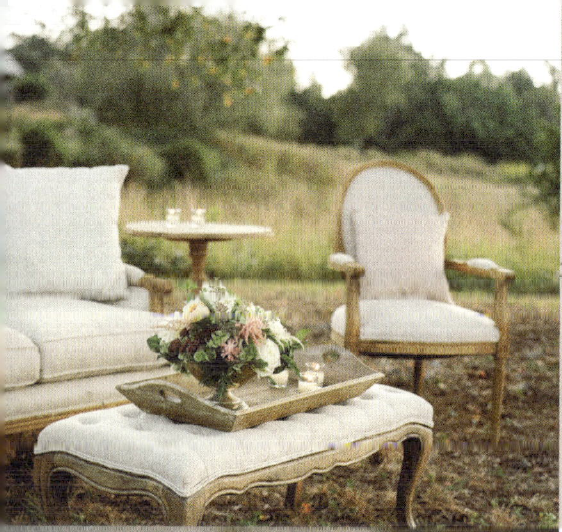
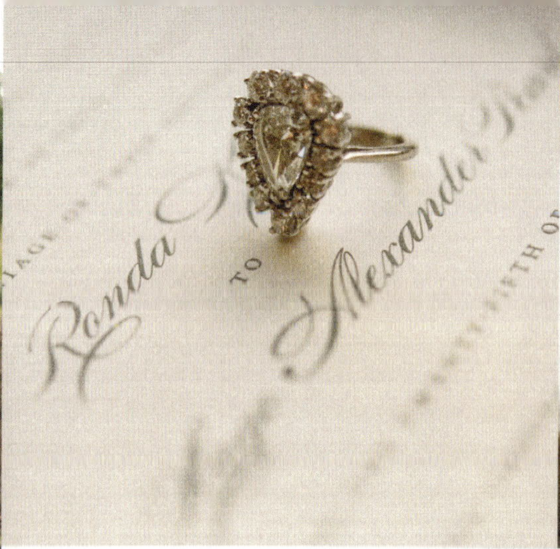
Ronda
TO
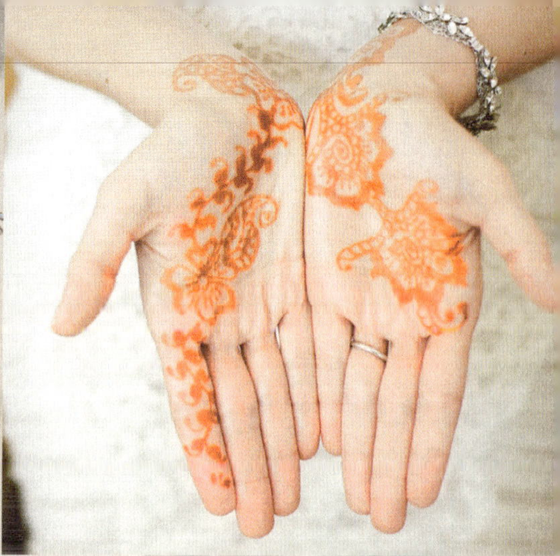
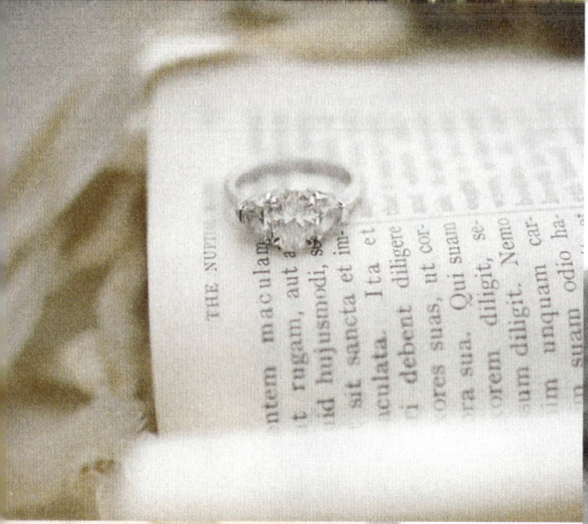
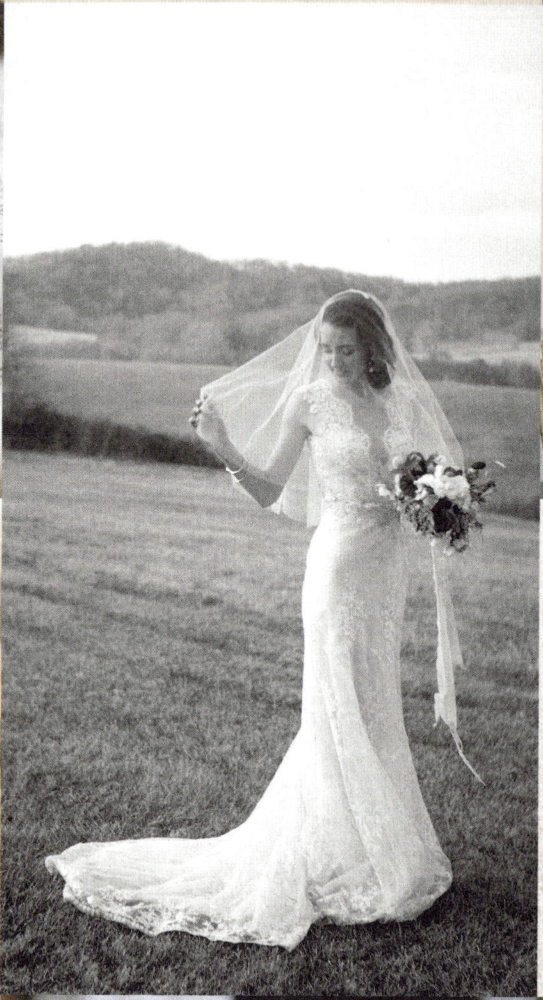
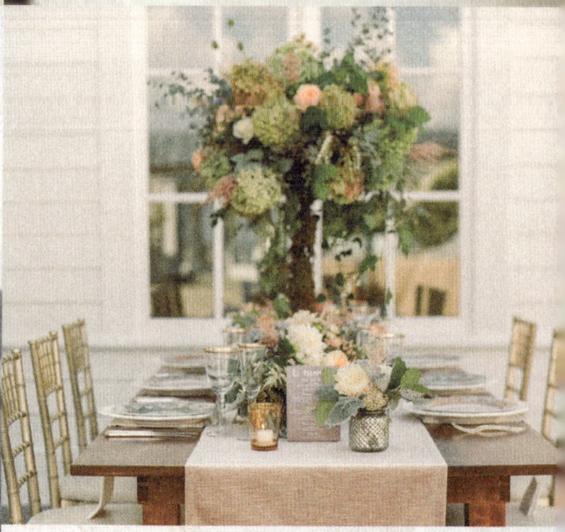
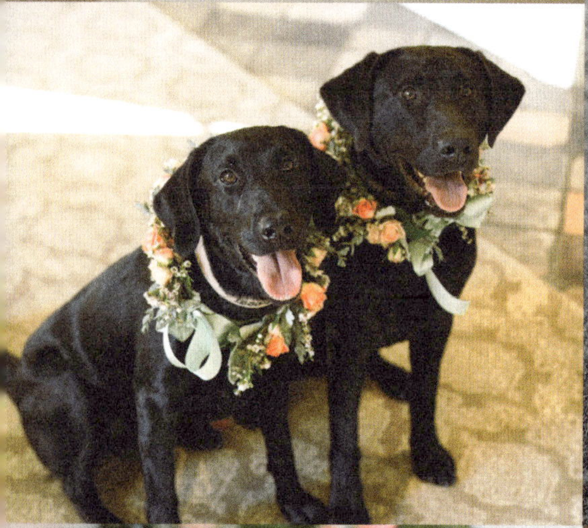
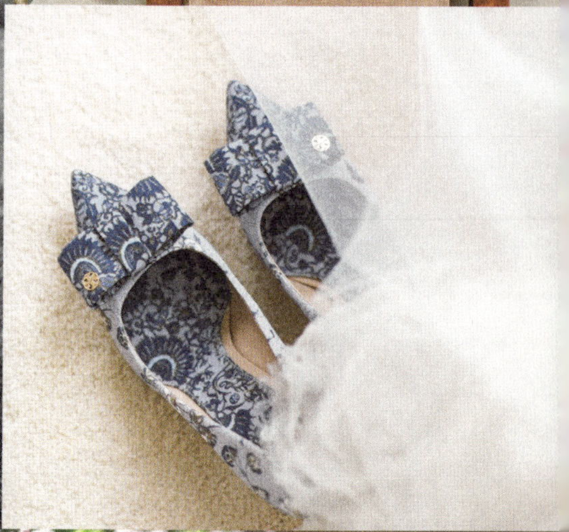
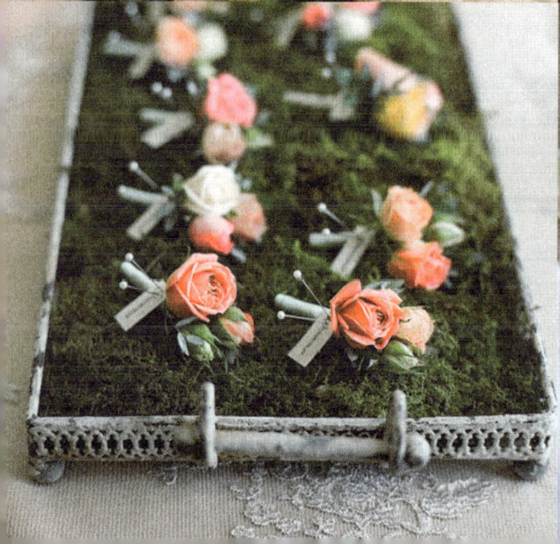
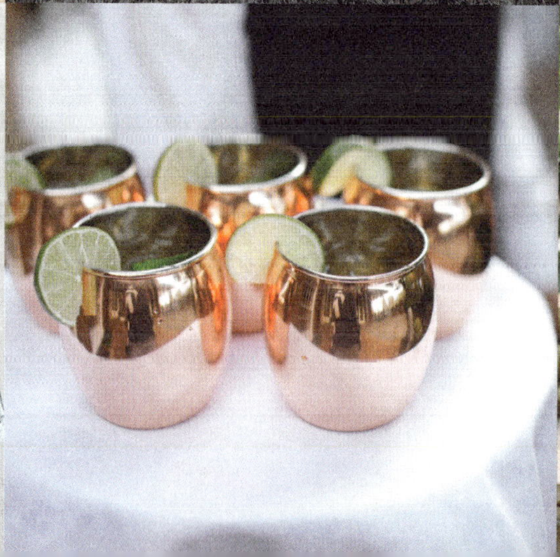
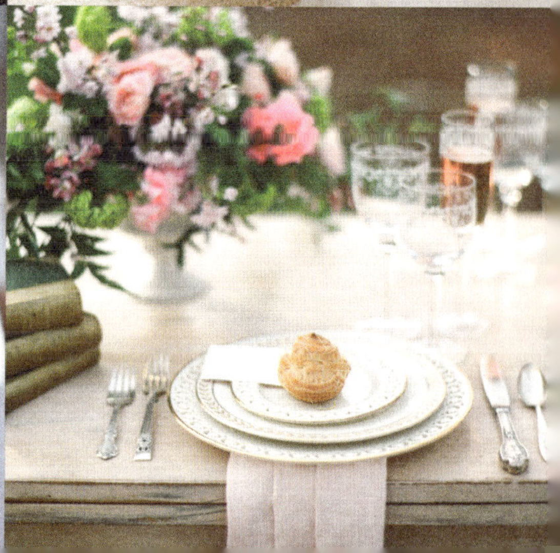

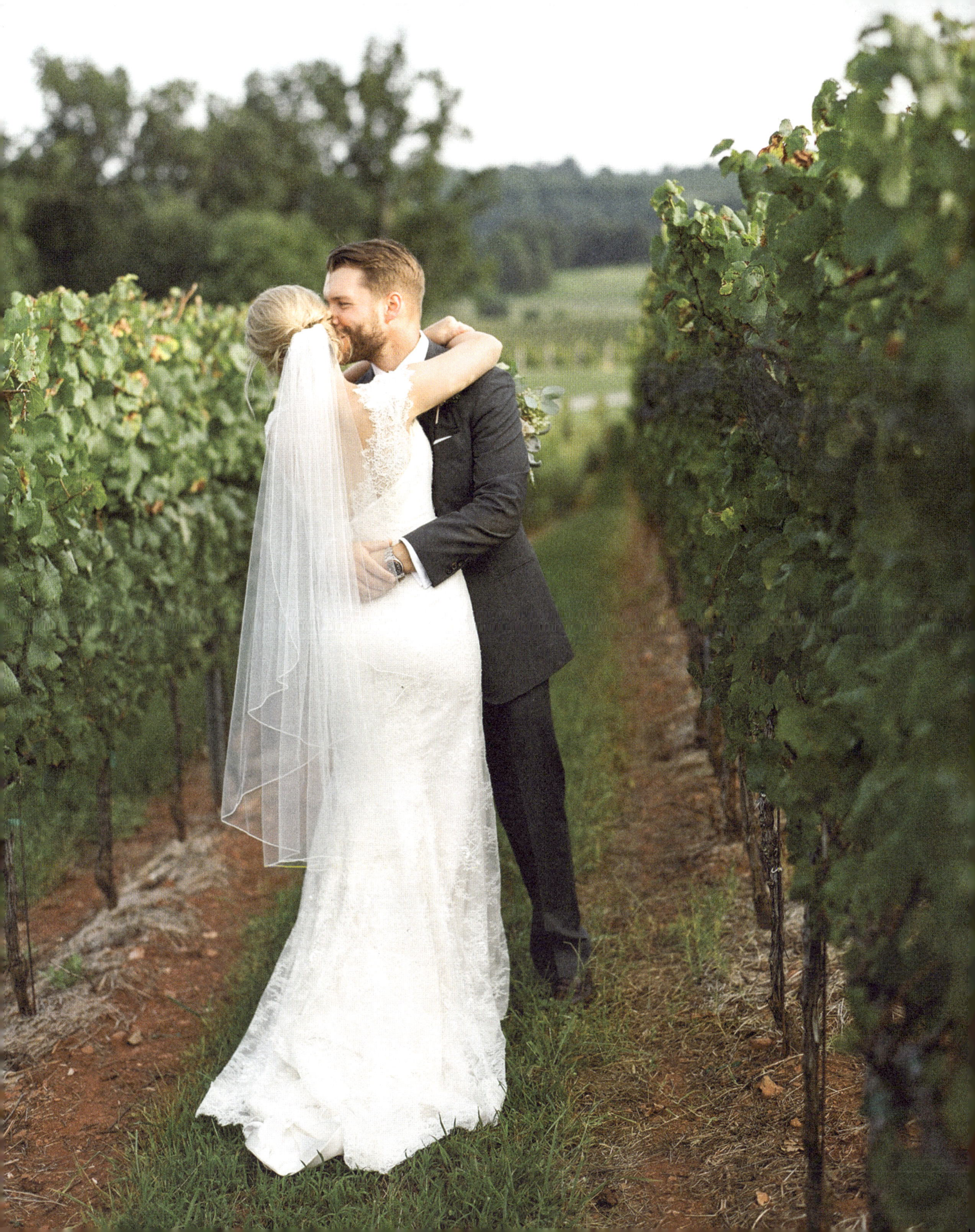

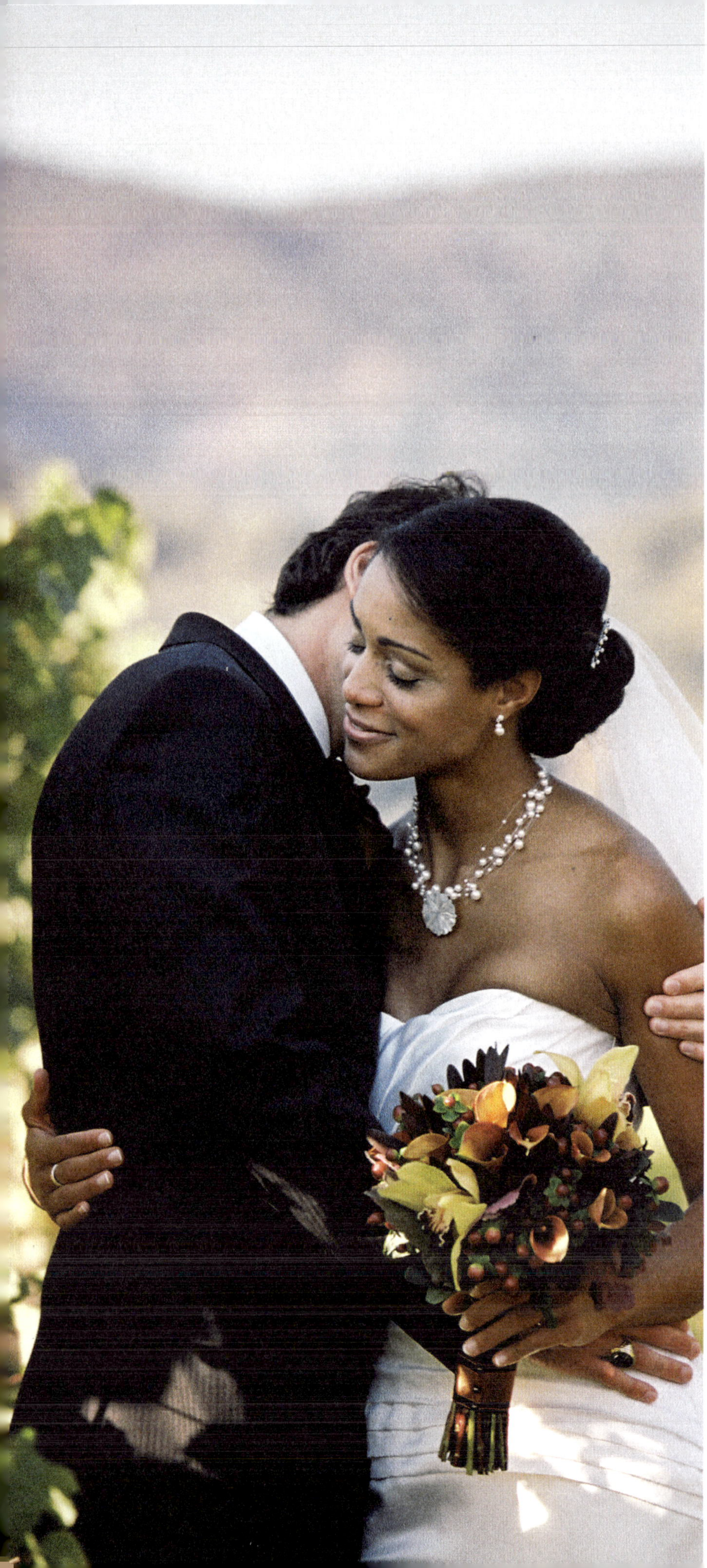

find the perfect chef caterer to suit tastes from the most classic and refined to the most trendy and adventurous.

Whatever your wedding dreams, you're sure to find the perfect venue amongst our many splendid choices. The King Family Vineyards, shown on this page, is the picturesque backdrop for this couple's sweet moment. On the page at right, the gorgeous rustic barn at top left is situated at Panorama Farms where this lovely bride and groom tied the knot. And for a grand country estate, historic Keswick Hall, top right, envelops guests in every luxury you would expect from this 5-star resort. The stunning Pippin Hill Farm & Vineyards, bottom right, is always an elegant choice for exchanging vows. Enjoy the centuries of history and charming architecture, which make a handsome backdrop for our thriving arts and music community downtown. Old Metropolitan Hall, bottom left, has it's tables dressed up and candlelit for a rehearsal dinner.

For the little touches that make your event personal and intimate, place your trust in the abundant talent of our beloved wedding community. From vintage letterpress accents and elegant tablescapes to signature cocktails and cake artistry, all the timeless beauty and intricate details of your dream wedding are within reach. For our artisans, creating amazing, one-of-a-kind weddings is a passion—they love bringing couples' wedding visions to life, and their delight for their craft shines through in the many extraordinary weddings they've created.

Just as Jefferson married here centuries ago on his "rich spot of earth", today couples can celebrate in and around Charlottesville—a town steeped in history and culture and a countryside filled with beauty—to create the perfect setting that will mark the beginning of your very own love story.

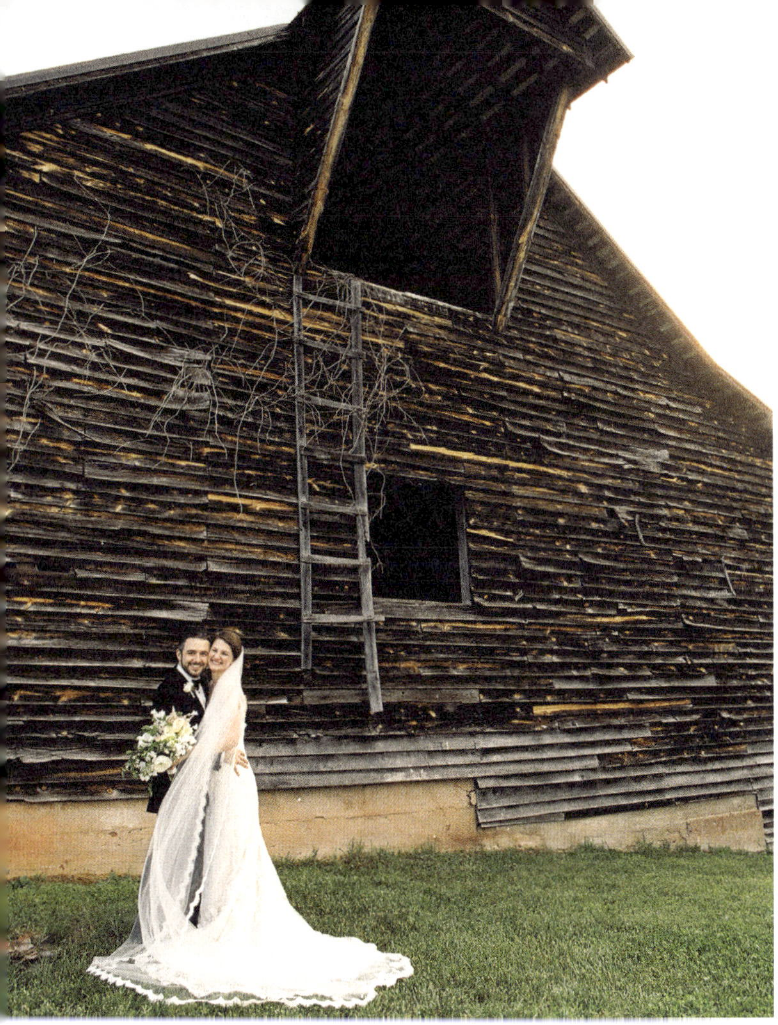

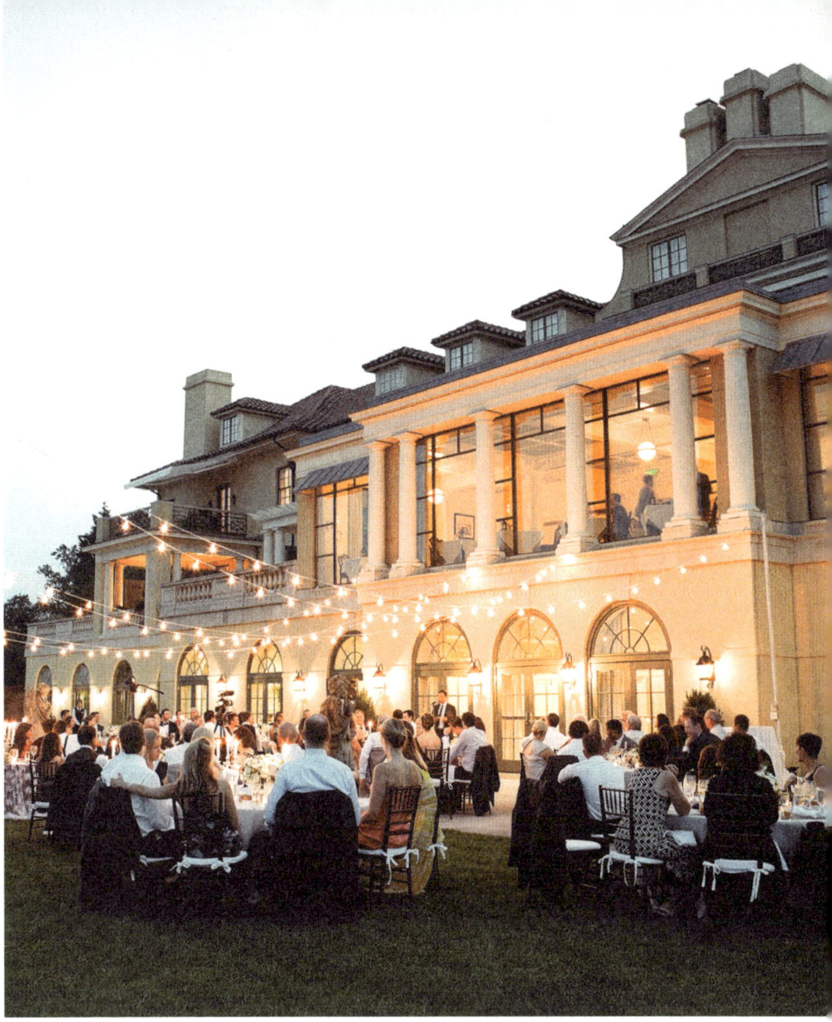

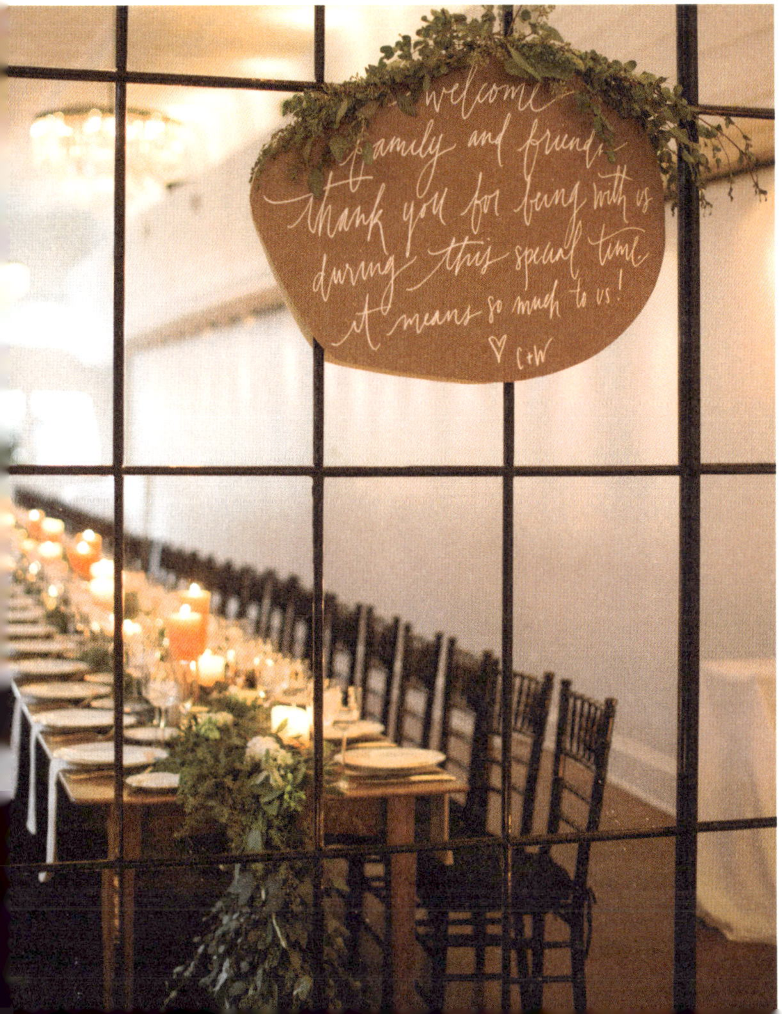
welcome
family and friends
thank you for being with us
during this special time
it means so much to us!
C+W

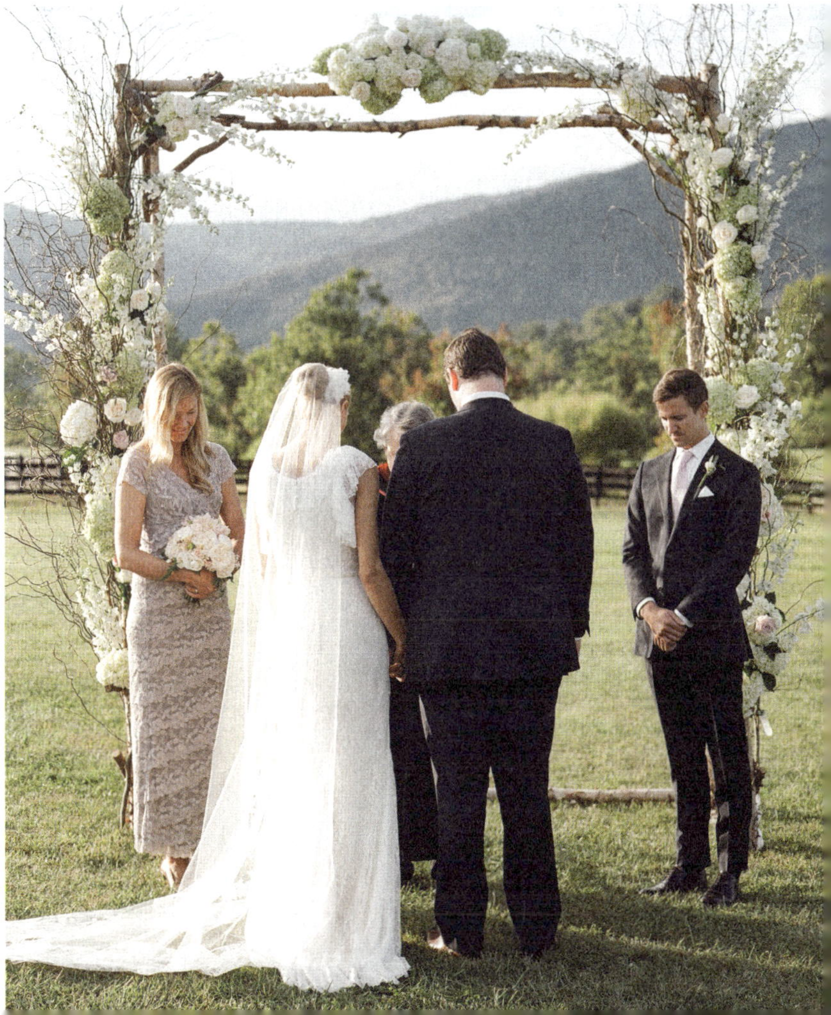

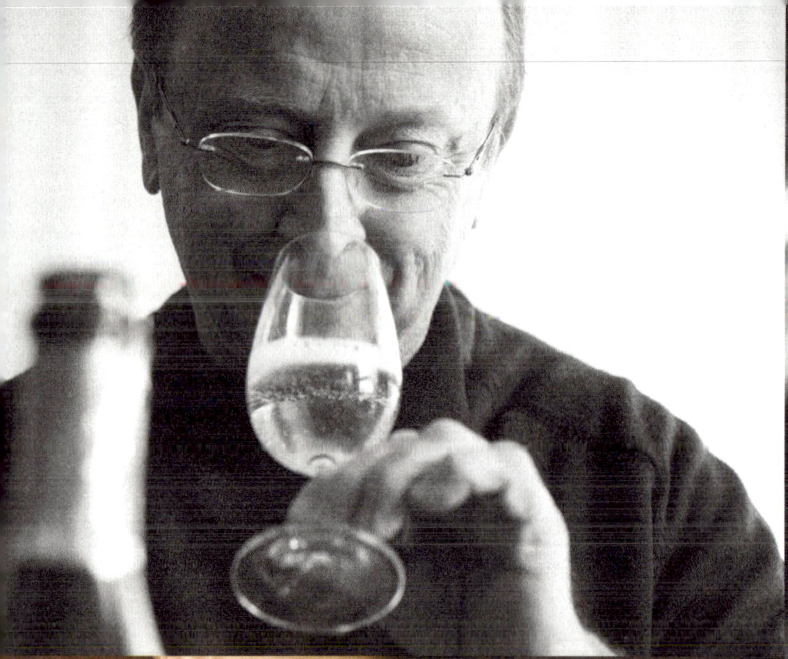

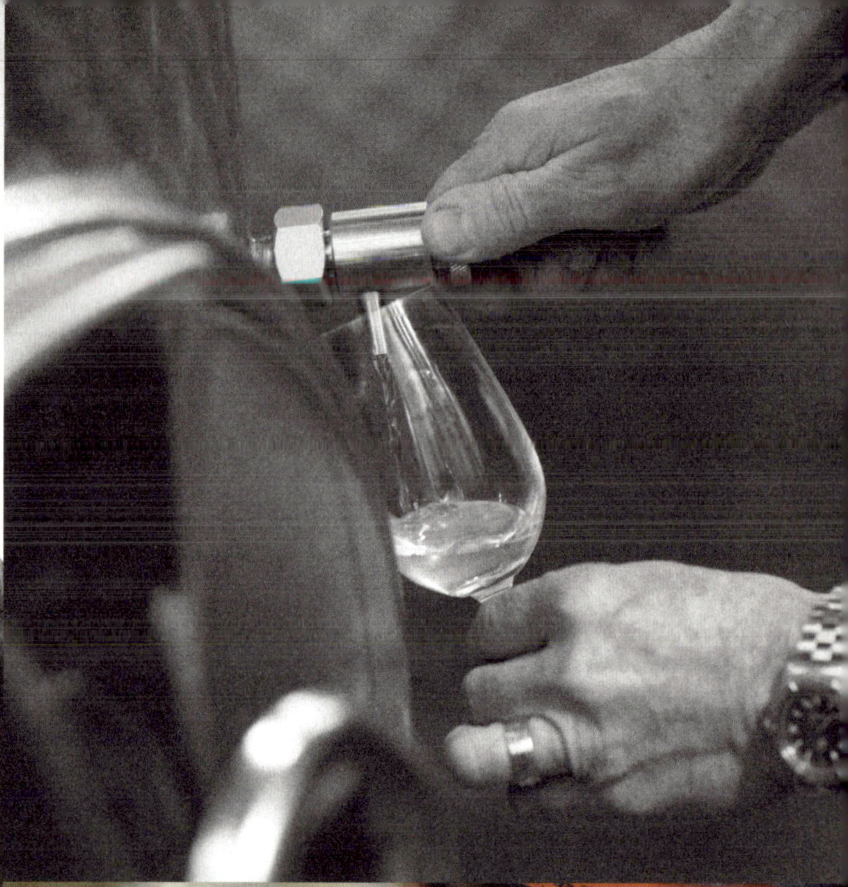

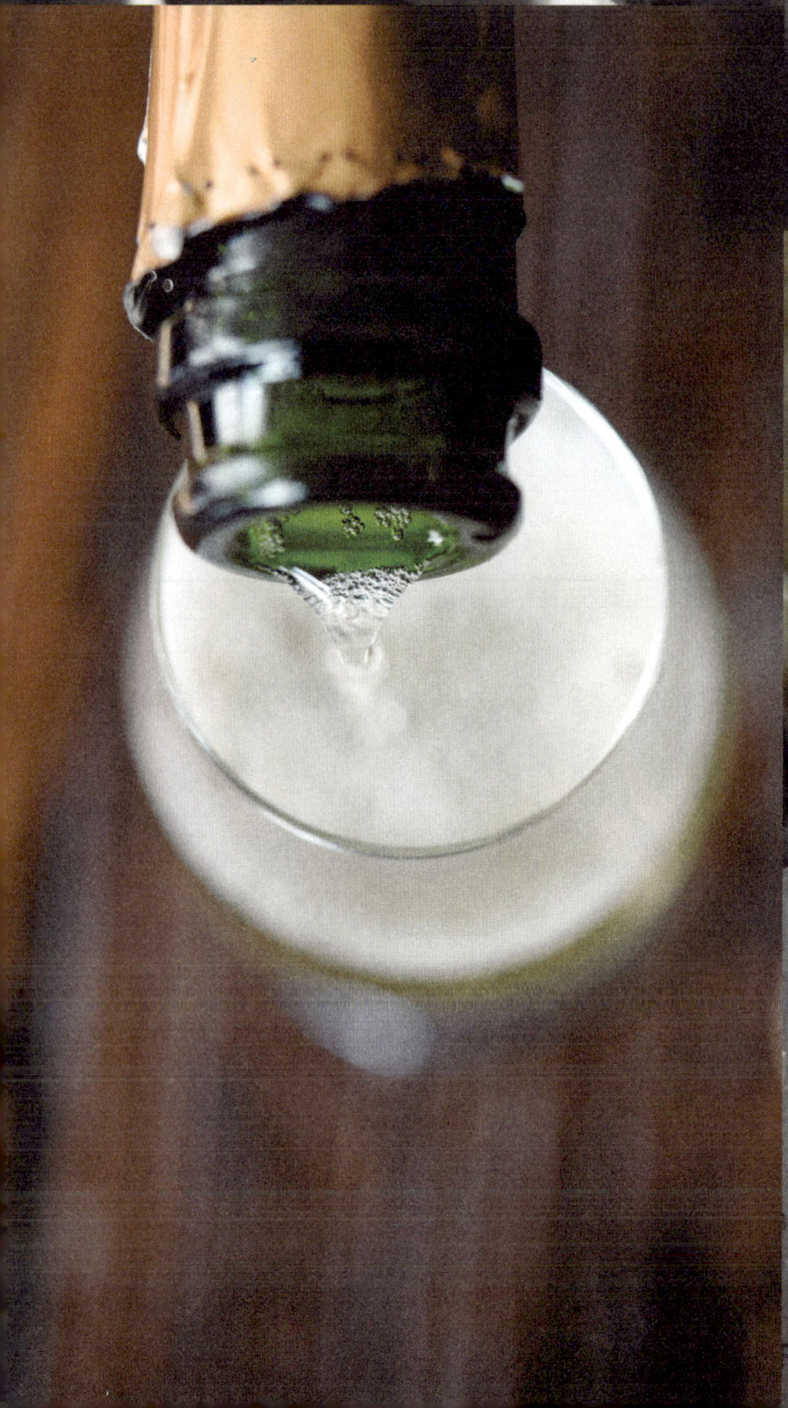

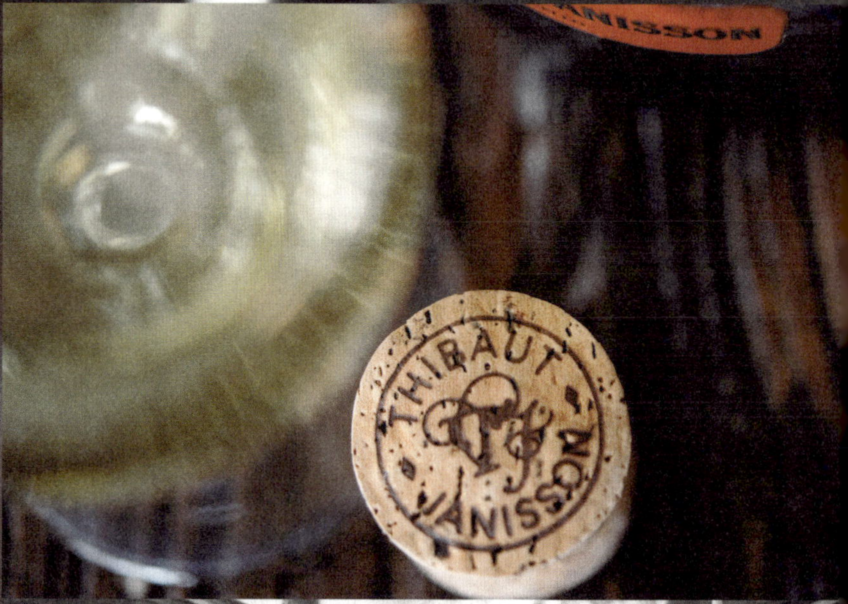
THIBAUT JANISSON

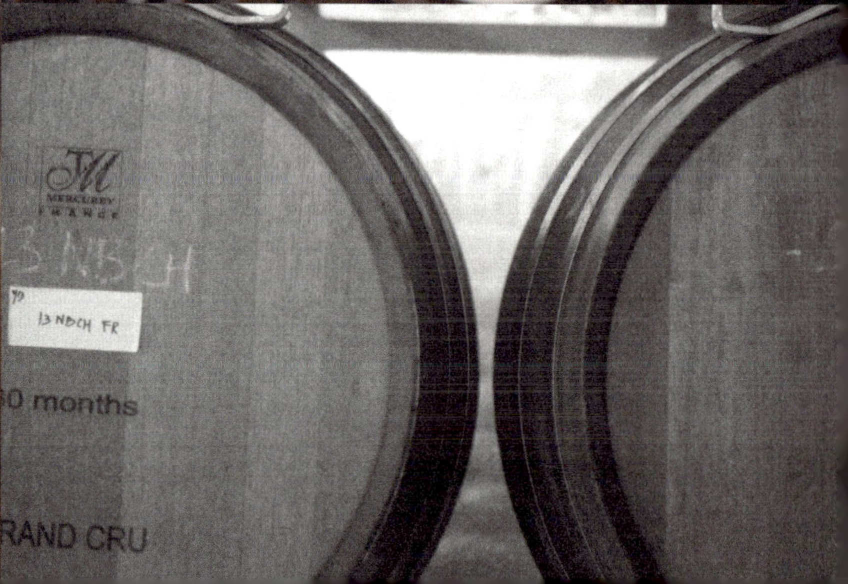

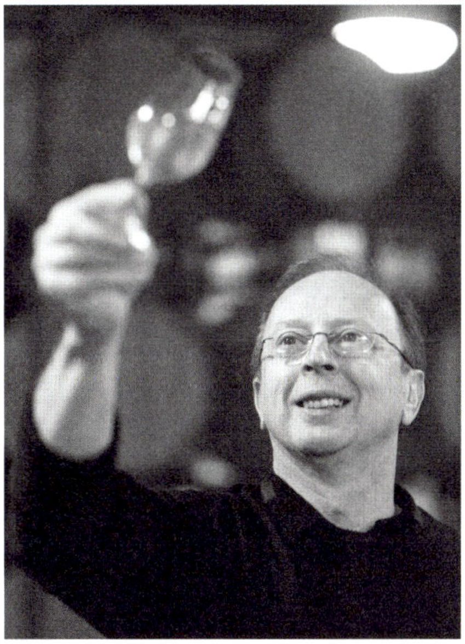

ARTISAN *Portrait*

CLAUDE THIBAUT

sparkling winemaker

Claude smiles warmly as he fills a delicate glass with Thibaut-Janisson sparkling wine, the golden bubbles a sea of shining gems celebrating their emergence into the open air. Claude lifts his glass and slowly savors the wine's radiant fragrance—notes of apple, white peach and hazelnut.

This vibrant sparkling wine is one of many lovingly produced by Thibaut-Janisson Winery, a partnership between esteemed French winemakers Claude Thibaut and Manuel Janisson based just outside of Charlottesville. While each classically trained in the art of winemaking in France's Champagne region from a young age, Claude and Manuel united behind the vision of creating an original sparkling wine together. Drawn to the Virginia countryside, they found the rolling hills of Charlottesville to be the ideal landscape to bring their vision to fruition.

The Thibaut-Janisson label is endearingly abbreviated as T-J, a sweet reference to Charlottesville's beloved Thomas Jefferson, lover of winemaking and all things French. Following in Jefferson's footsteps, Claude and Manuel's labor of love and passion for outstanding wine has yielded an impressive collection of critically acclaimed sparkling wines—Blanc de Chardonnay, Virginia Fizz, and Virginia Xtra Brut.

The grapes used by Claude and Manuel are locally grown, ensuring that each bottle perfectly captures the quaint, playful spirit of the Charlottesville countryside. Couples seeking an authentic farm-to-table wedding experience will go "ooh, la la!" for locally crafted Thibaut-Janisson sparkling wines. Guests also will be delighted by the way that the joyful, effervescent notes and French elegance perfectly complement the day of ultimate celebration.

WRITTEN BY NICOLE PERRIER

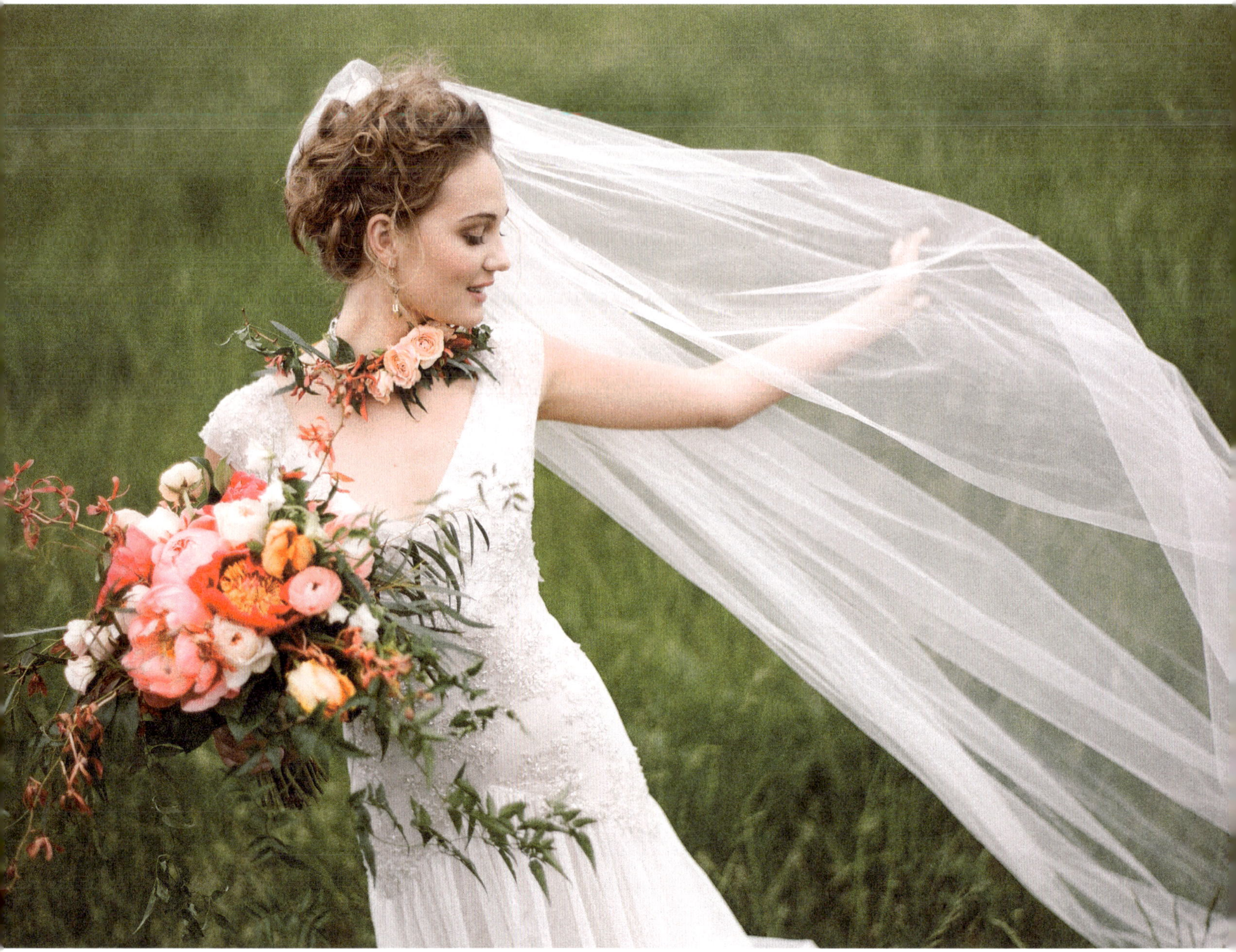

SIMPLE *Beauty*

WRITTEN BY MEGHAN STREIT | PHOTOGRAPHY BY JEN FARIELLO

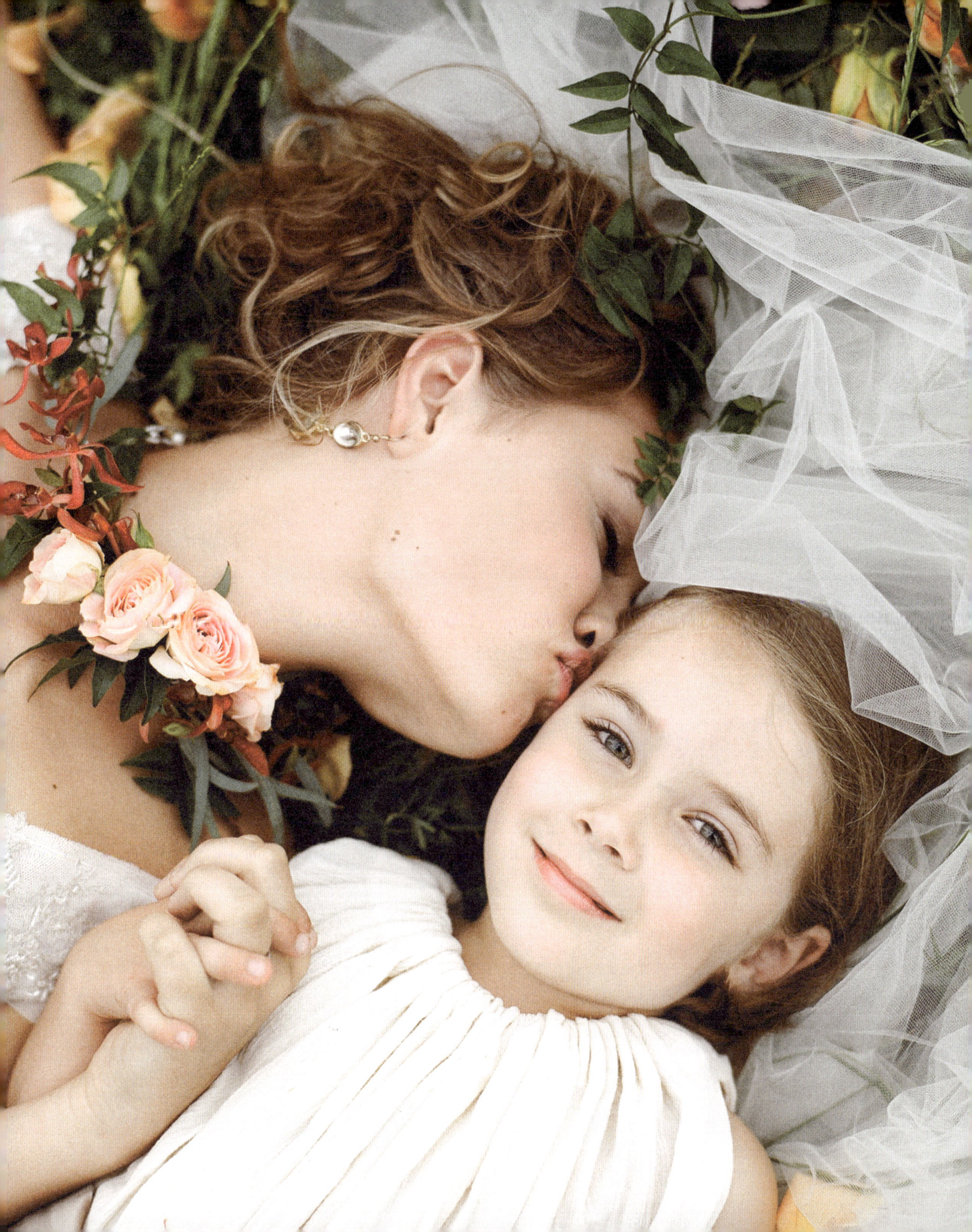

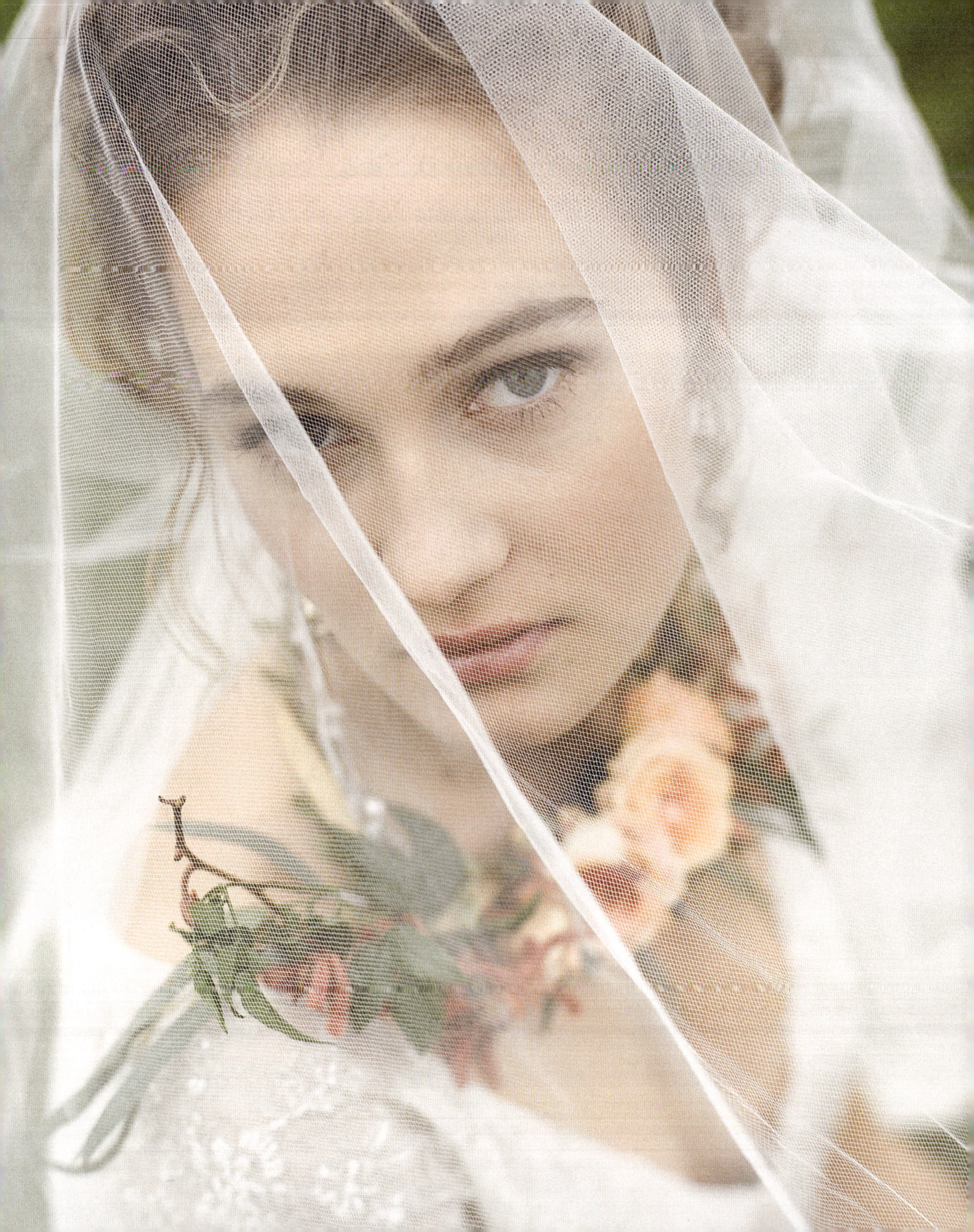

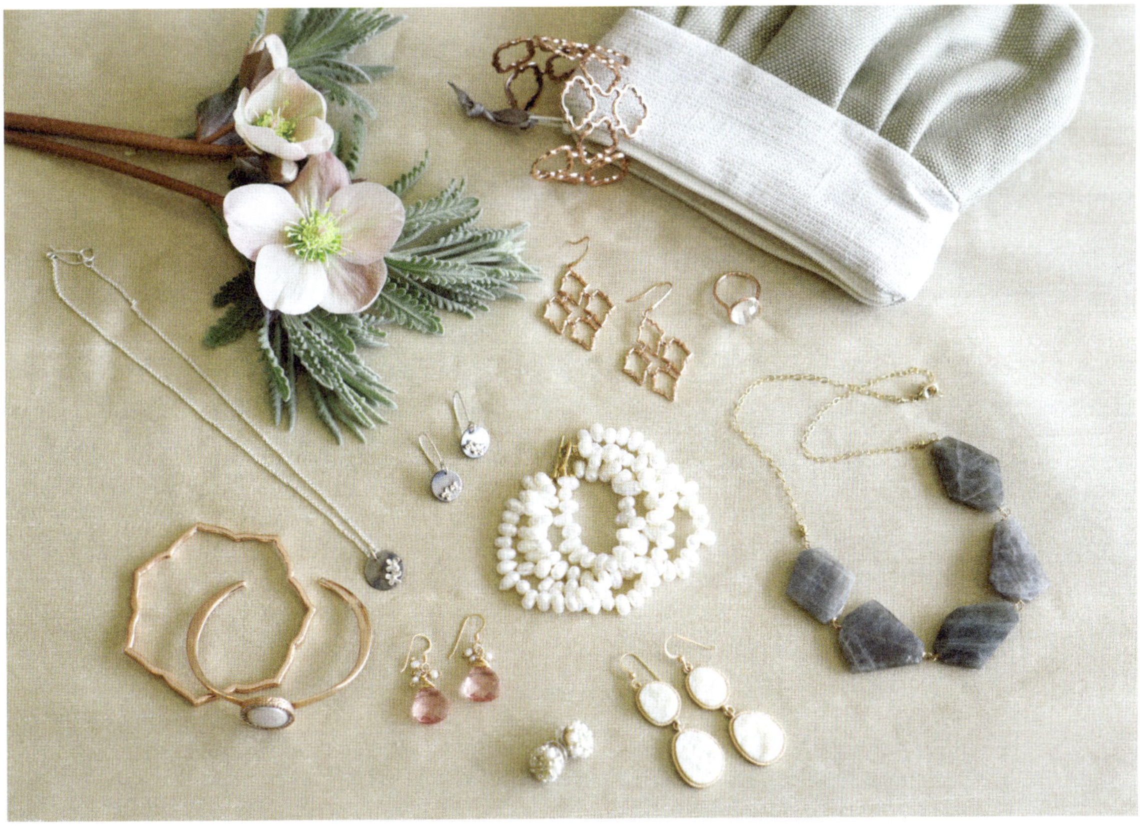

The most highly anticipated moment of every wedding is the first glimpse of the bride at the top of the aisle—a moment full of meaning, importance, and beauty.

For the celebration featured here, the inspired floral designers at Southern Blooms followed a modern romantic trend. Balancing both tradition and innovation, the bride not only carries fresh flowers but also incorporates them into her wedding day ensemble as eye-catching accessories. Look beyond wearing flowers in your hair and create captivating botanical jewelry or sashes for a decidedly fashionable and feminine style. These wearable blooms are floral works of art allowing the bride to move between several different versions of adornment throughout the celebration, switching between a floral crown to necklace to sashed garland.

A dramatic strand of petals graces this bride's neckline, creating a cultural focal point even once she's handed her bouquet over to her maid of honor. The choice of Coral Charm peonies in a palette of pinks, from fuchsia to blush, with creamy hints of gold creates a cascading informal look that seems pulled directly from the beautiful abundance of the surrounding Blue Ridge Mountains.

The tiniest (and sweetest!) wedding attendants deliver genuine affection and joy to the occasion—and often spontaneous surprises, too! To ready them for the day, think both in terms of style and comfort. On the previous page, this flower girl's simple gown sweetly complements the bride's romantically soft and elegant Sarah Janks gown and natural styling.

Once you have dreamed up your perfect wedding day look, let local artisans and designers help you bring your vision to life. Carry your little essentials in a hand-sewn bag, like this one from Just A Little Ditty shown above. It is a thoughtful way to incorporate meaningful fabric, perhaps an heirloom bridal gown, into your special day. Choose Erin McDermott's earrings, made with freshwater pearls, seed beads, and crystal, or her White Lace Druzy Earrings to pull the color from your gown. Consider this lovely crafted gold set from Suz Sumersall, inspired by the Marrakech sunset, which includes bracelets and earrings reminiscent of Moroccan tiles. The drop earrings in sparkling pink are made by Meg Hannon and come in a rainbow of colors.

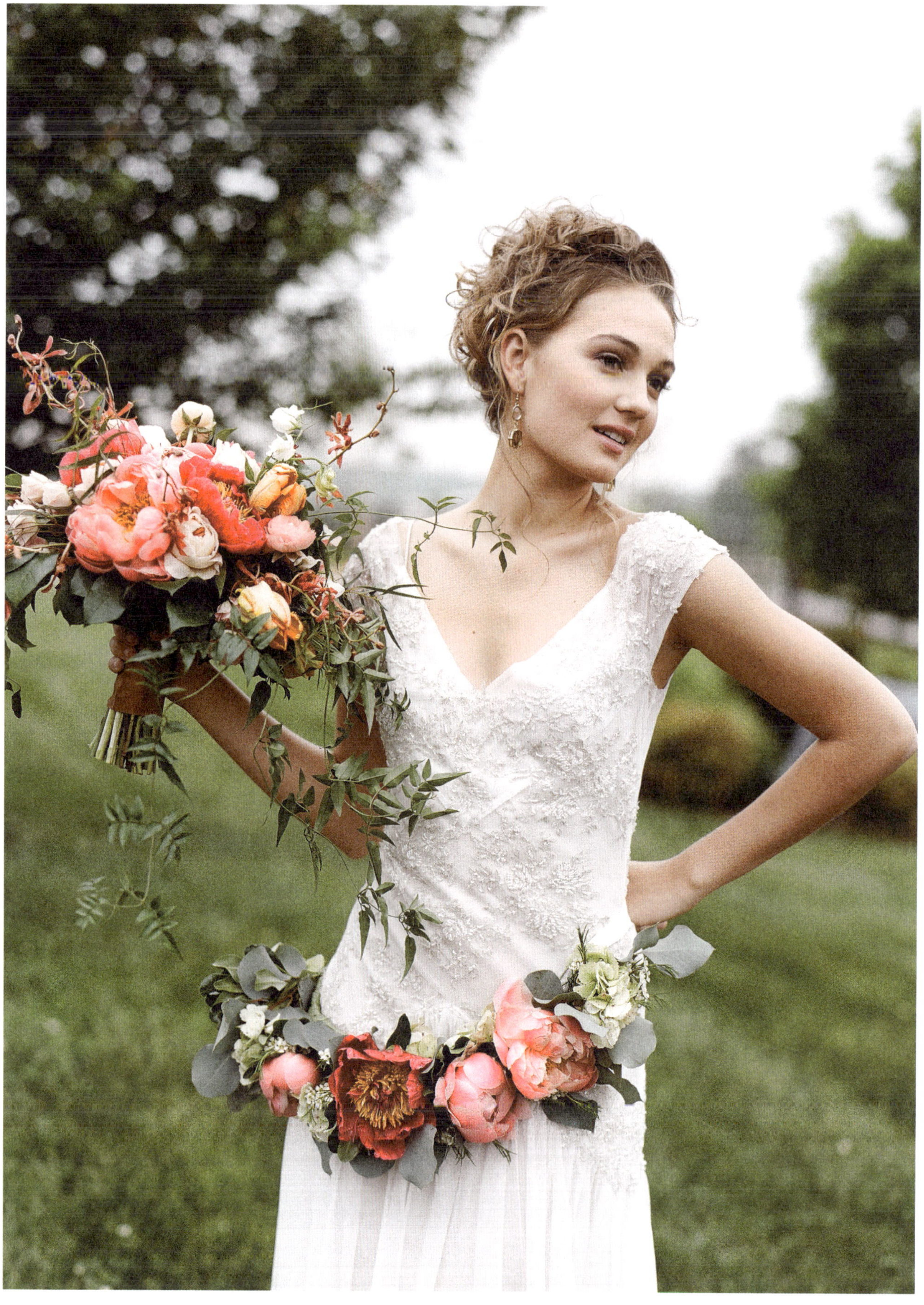

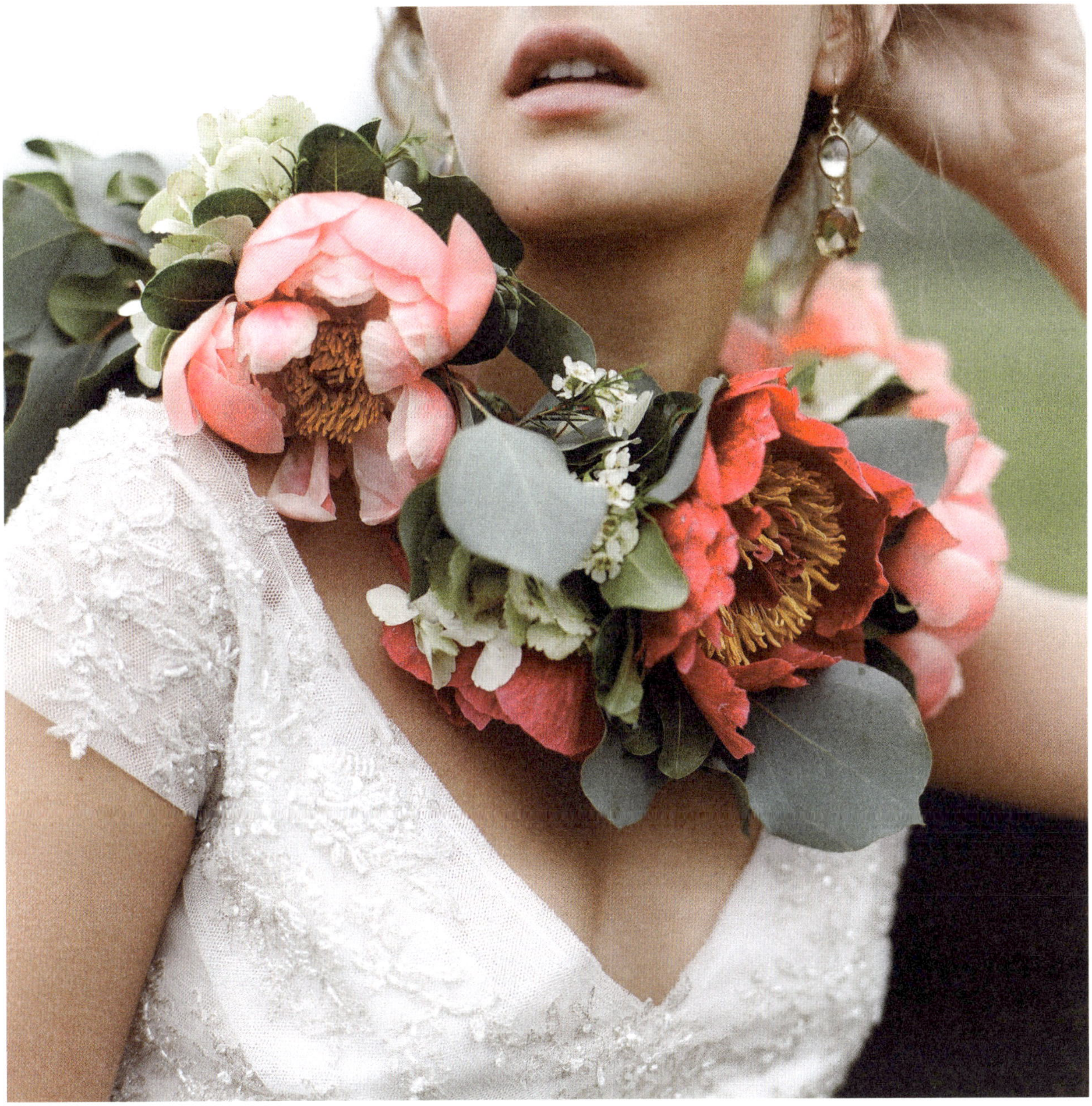

She also designed the stunning bracelet made of ivory teardrop pearls and the lustrous labradorite necklace. Or go with Tavia Metal's Midnight Blooming ensemble, a necklace and earrings set made of airy sterling silver flowers, highlighted by their titanium backdrops with a patina reminiscent of the night sky. All of these would look elegant on you as well as make delightful gifts for your bridal party.

The breathtaking landscapes of the region provide plentiful inspiration for brides seeking to create a cohesive wedding palette. Let the beauty of the area inspire you! And have fun exploring different ways to wear floral elements as memorable artful accessories for touches of color and drama that blend your style with the natural wonder around you.

Photography: Jen Fariello Photography | **Bridal Styling:** Jeannine Lalonde Smith of Be Loved PR | **Venue:** Mount Ida Farm | **Florals:** Southern Blooms by Pat's Floral Designs | **Model:** Catherine Hedrick | **Creative Direction and Styling:** Shindig Weddings & Events | **Dress:** Sarah Janks | **Veil:** Jorge Manuel Weddings | **Rings:** Norman Silverman Diamonds from Fink's Jewelers | **Hair:** Erica Haskins-Crutchfield of Top Knot Studio | **Makeup:** Linda Livernois of Rouge 9 Make Up Studio

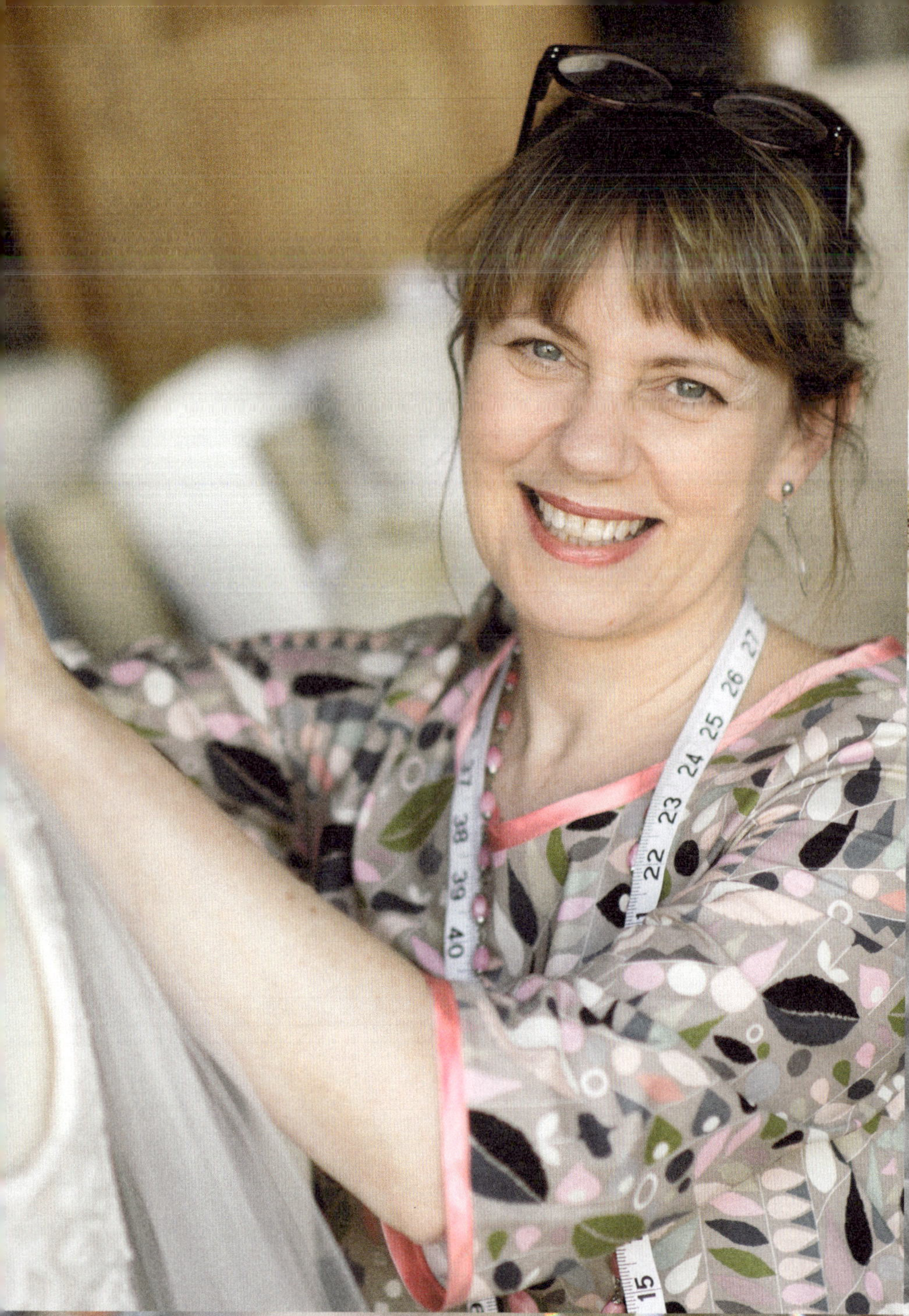
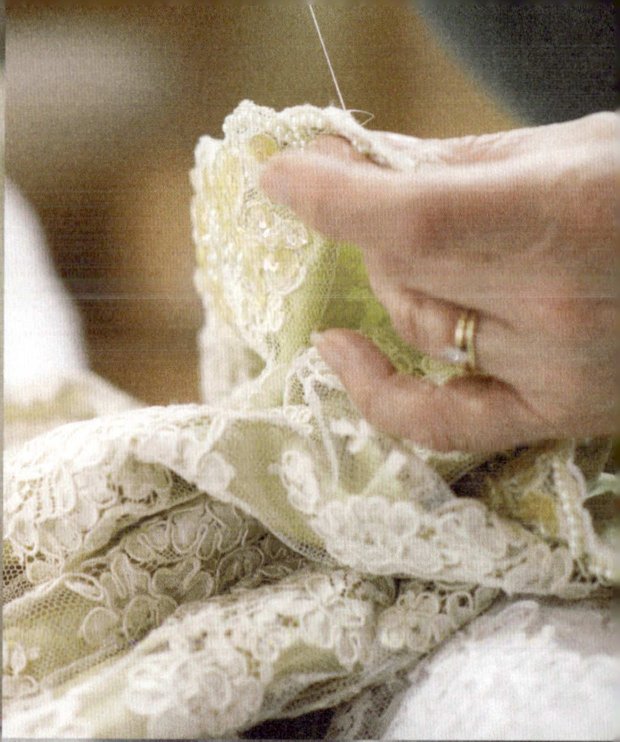
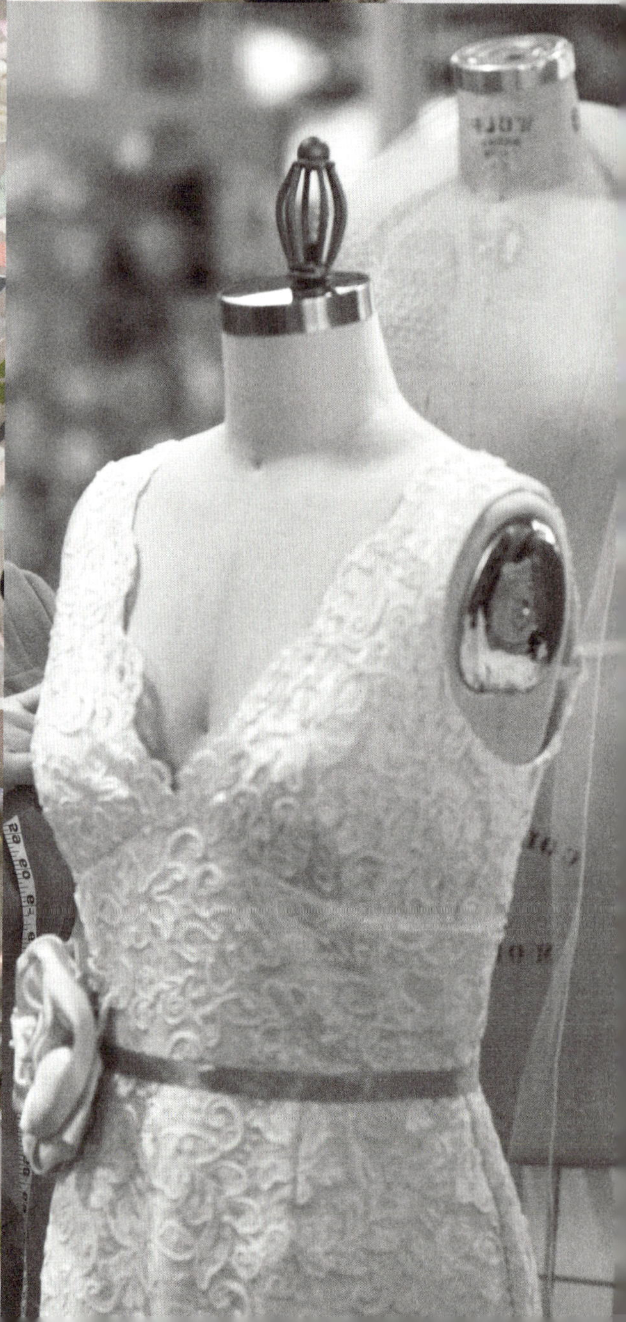
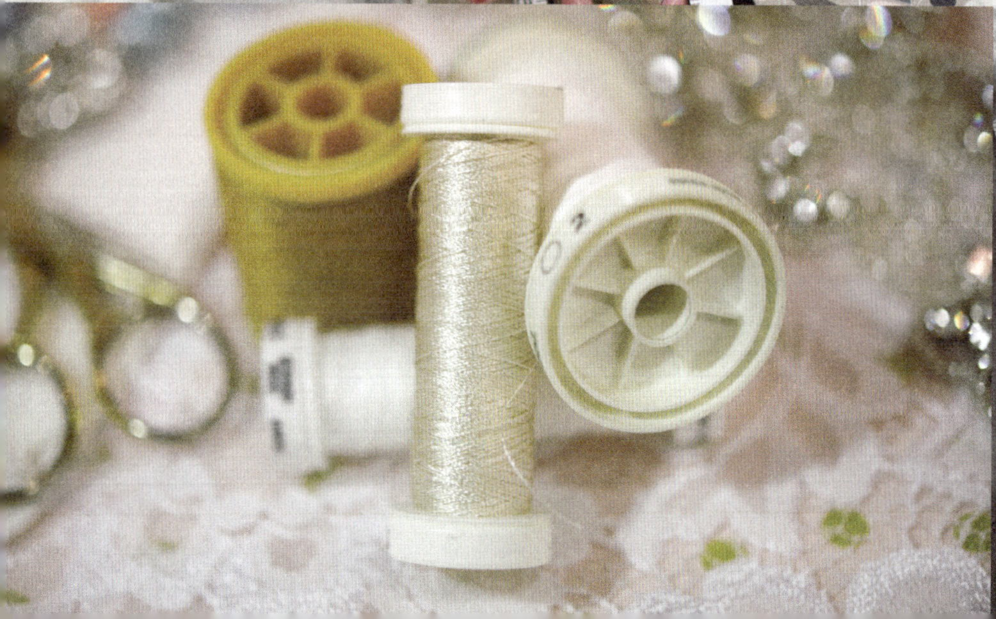

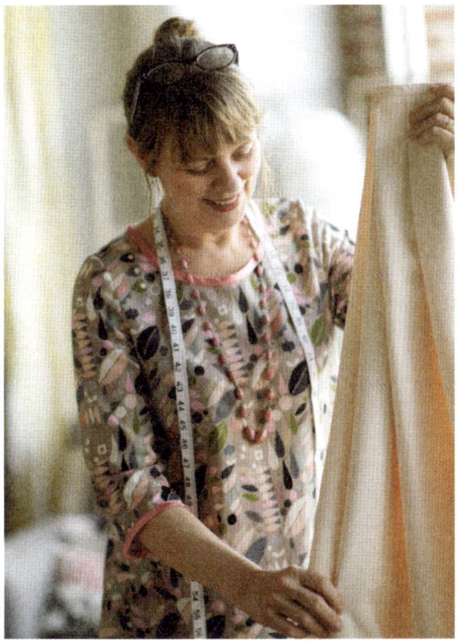

ARTISAN *Portrait*

CARLA QUENNEVILLE

seamstress

Carla Quenneville swoons for silk as she sits on her handcrafted settee in her charming downtown bridal boutique, Les Fabriques. Reminiscing about the sewing artistry she learned as a child from her mother, she exudes passion for art, style and beauty.

Constantly developing her talent as an artist, Carla is influenced and inspired by her mother's traditional tastes and interests as well as her two artistic daughters' modern flair. Vintage and delicate designs, lacy romantic textures, soft silky fabrics and wholesome colors also kindle her inspiration when working with future brides.

Her interests, along with her love of romance and fairytale endings, make Carla the ideal design collaborator for brides. Happily married to her own sweetheart for 39 years, she enthuses, "it brings me great joy to guide brides to the gown that signifies the first day of the rest of her life."

Clients usually bring their ideas and desires to Carla—photos of dresses, favorite fabrics and collections of patterns for the bodice and train—so that designing a dream dress is a collaborative effort. Some brides even bring in their own dresses for her to alter and embellish to convey their own unique sense of style.

Consulting with brides-to-be and designing gowns and bespoke accessories for flower girls, bridesmaids and mother-of-the-brides in Charlottesville since 1985, Carla esteems the charming town as, "just enough historic, just enough earthy and just enough artistic fiber for locals and visitors alike."

Les Fabriques caters to each and every bride's desires, from where to place the delicate French lace sash to how to position the intricate beadwork for the perfect sparkling finish. Carla takes pride in her talent and uses her passion to create an impeccably luxurious experience for her brides.

WRITTEN BY CELIA DENTZ

FOR THE *Gents*

WRITTEN BY ADAM DONOVAN-GROVES

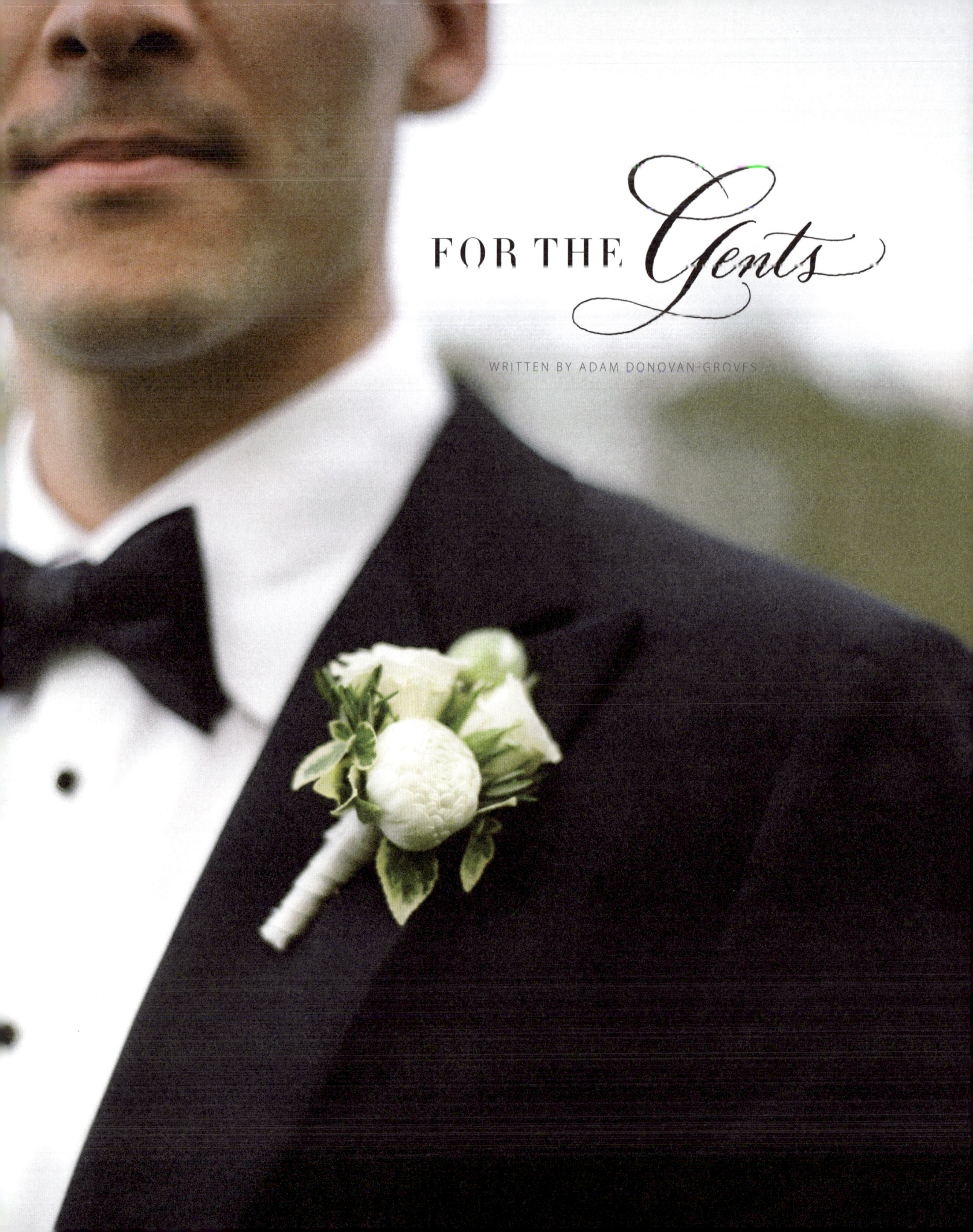

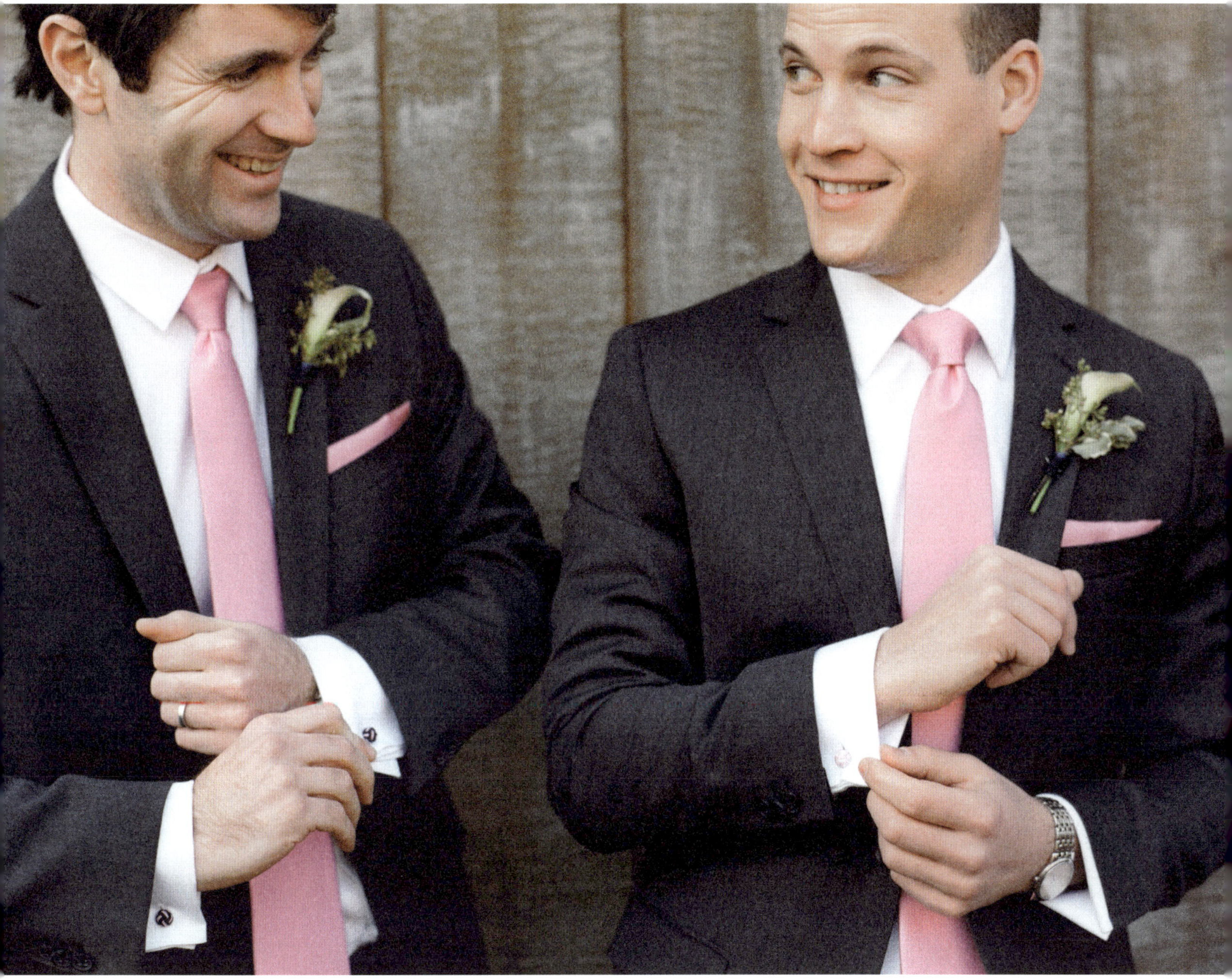

The modern groom is a man who understands what it means to wear his father's cuff links and his grandfather's pocket watch on the day of his wedding. This blend of vintage charm with personal meaning will remind you of the men who helped shape you into the man you are, the man worthy of marrying your bride. With a fresh haircut, fitted tuxedo, crisp shirt and polished shoes, you will be ready to confidently wait for your soon-to-be wife as she comes down the aisle, a vision of loveliness.

While you get ready for the ceremony, relax! Enjoy this meaningful occasion with close friends and family. Make sure to embrace these final serene moments before the wedding festivities and all the excitement begins. Take the guys out golfing, hike Shenandoah National Park, grab dinner on the UVA Corner or enjoy a concert the night before everyone gets into town. Plan a relaxing breakfast before the events start so you and the guys can share nostalgic stories. Take a few minutes

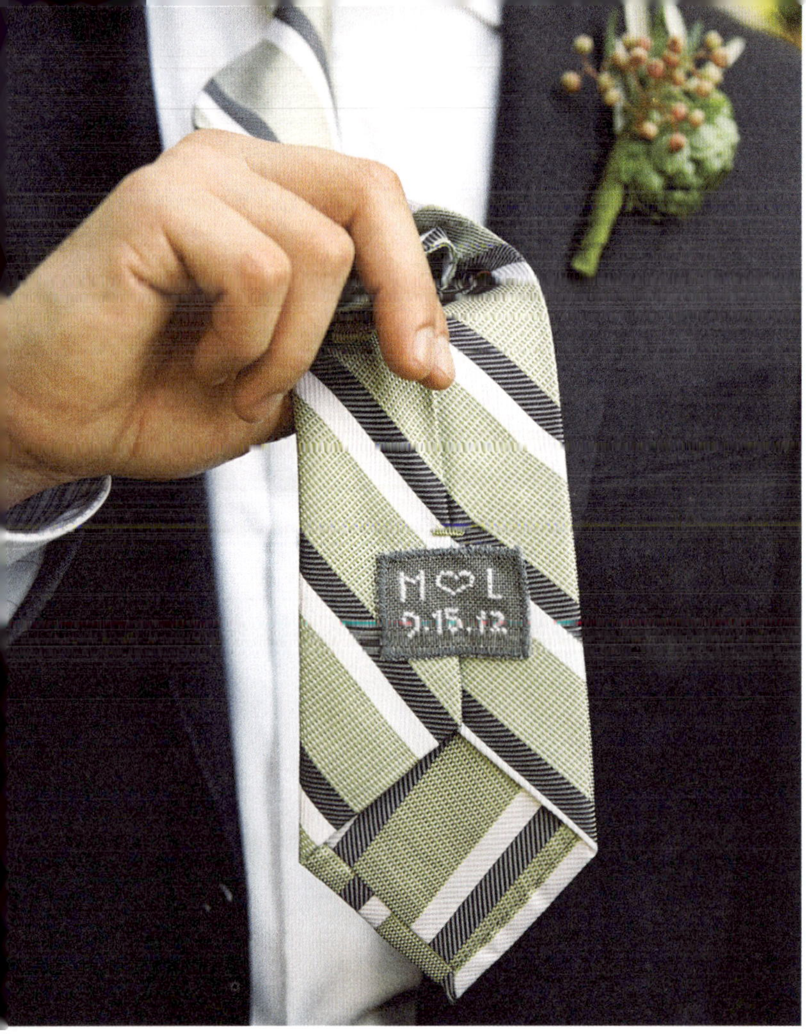

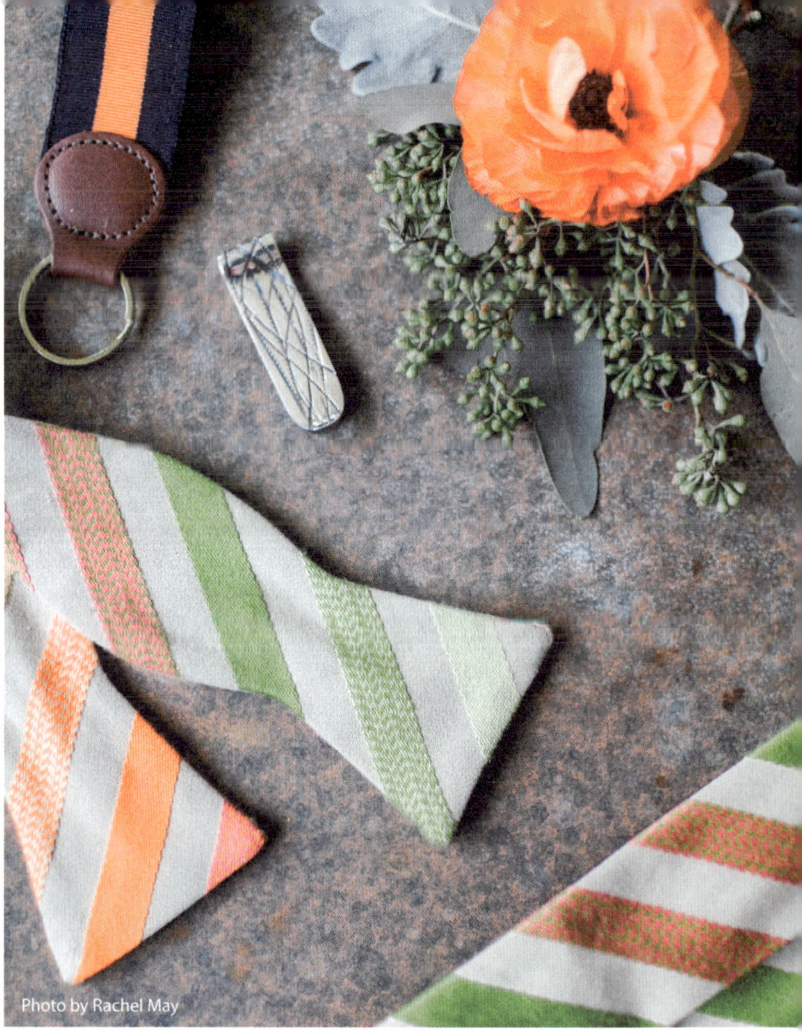

Photo by Rachel May

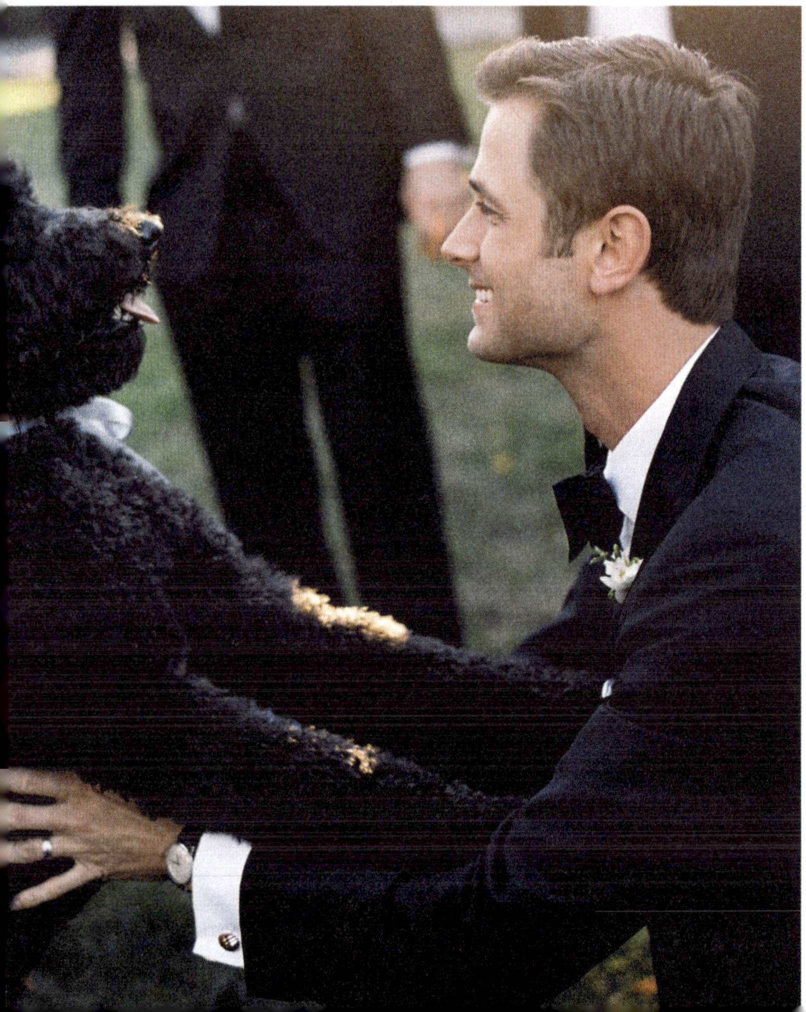

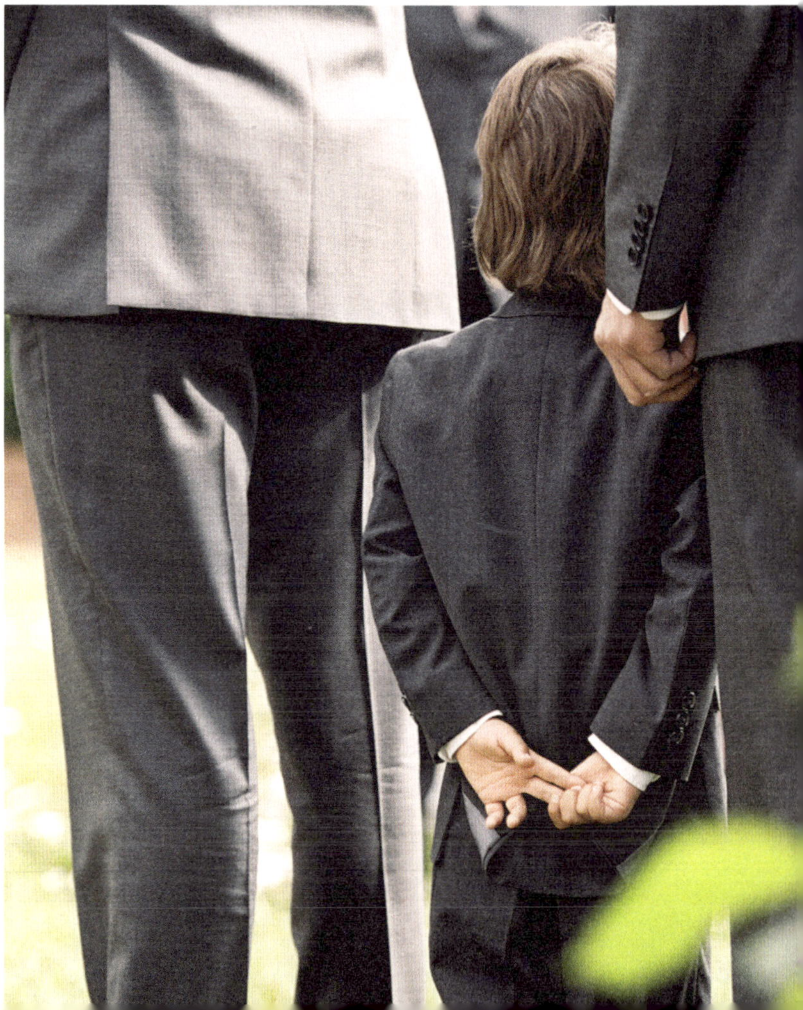

then to review details (like who has the rings), and practice those speeches. This is your chance to have fun with the people who mean the most to you.

Personal touches, like custom-embroidered ties, will help make the day unforgettable. Thank your groomsmen with a little gift—after all, you've shared a lot of adventures, and they're about to help see you off on your biggest adventure yet. Matching cuff links are a classic way to add personality to your wedding party attire and are a tried-and-true gift for groomsmen. Not exactly your style? Choose from a wide array of leather goods from the Charlottesville artisans seen on the next page, Barrons-Hunter. Leather-tabbed braces, personalized belts, and grosgrain key fobs to match your wedding palette or school colors are all great ideas. Or, toe the line of tradition with an elegant money clip, like the latest design pictured here from local jeweler Jason McLeod.

The modern groom also knows what it means to give a thoughtful gift to his bride. Don't underestimate the power of a small but significant gift. Whether it is a family heirloom passed down through the generations, a set of earrings she has been eyeing, or something that only she will understand, it is the kind of detail she will not forget, and it will serve as a lasting reminder of the love and commitment celebrated on your wedding day.

Take a few moments to remember why you're here today, and drink in the view out your window. You've found the woman of your dreams and done everything you can to prepare, so set the tone for the rest of your lives together by loving every moment! And now, you may kiss your bride.

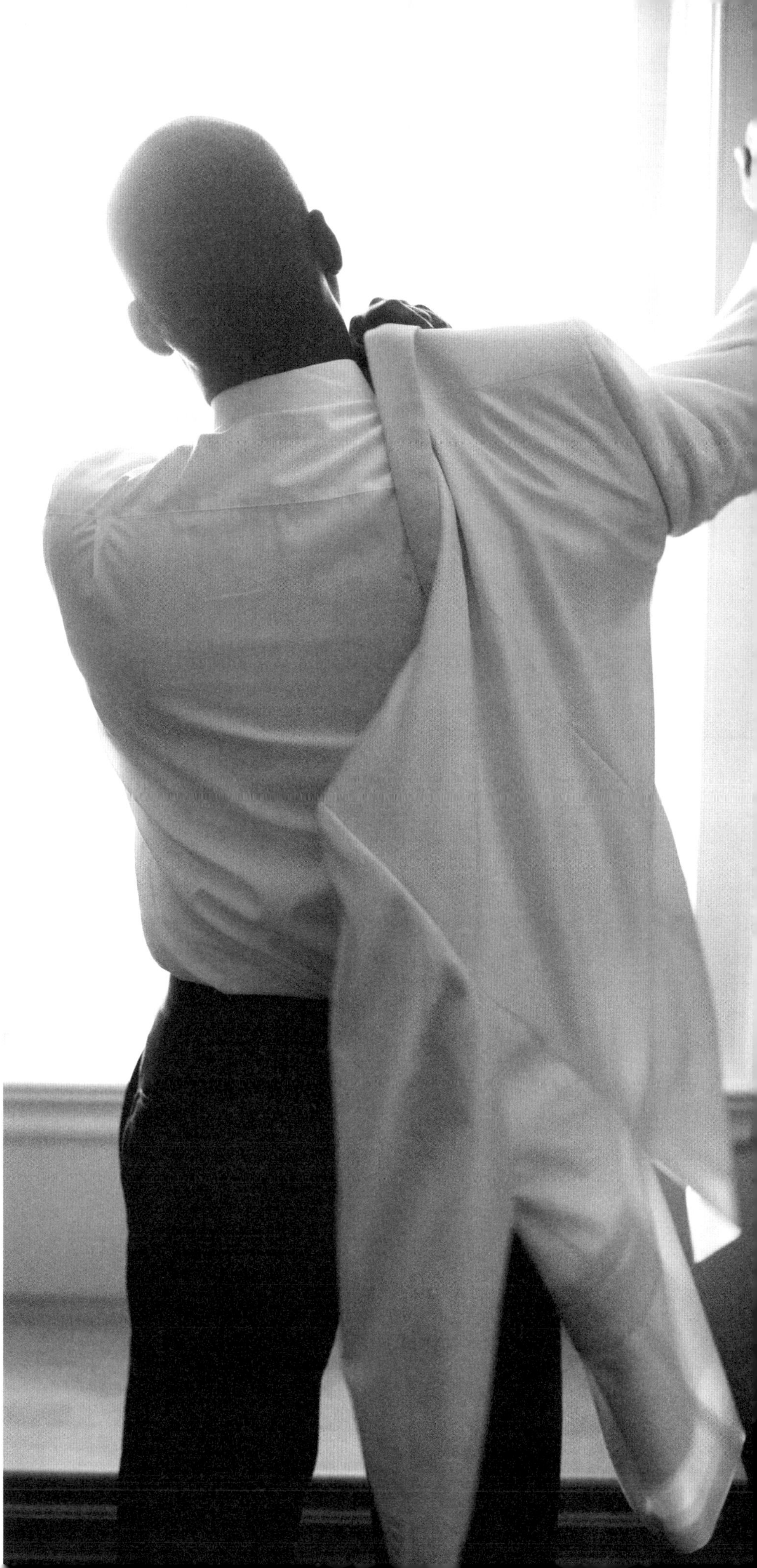

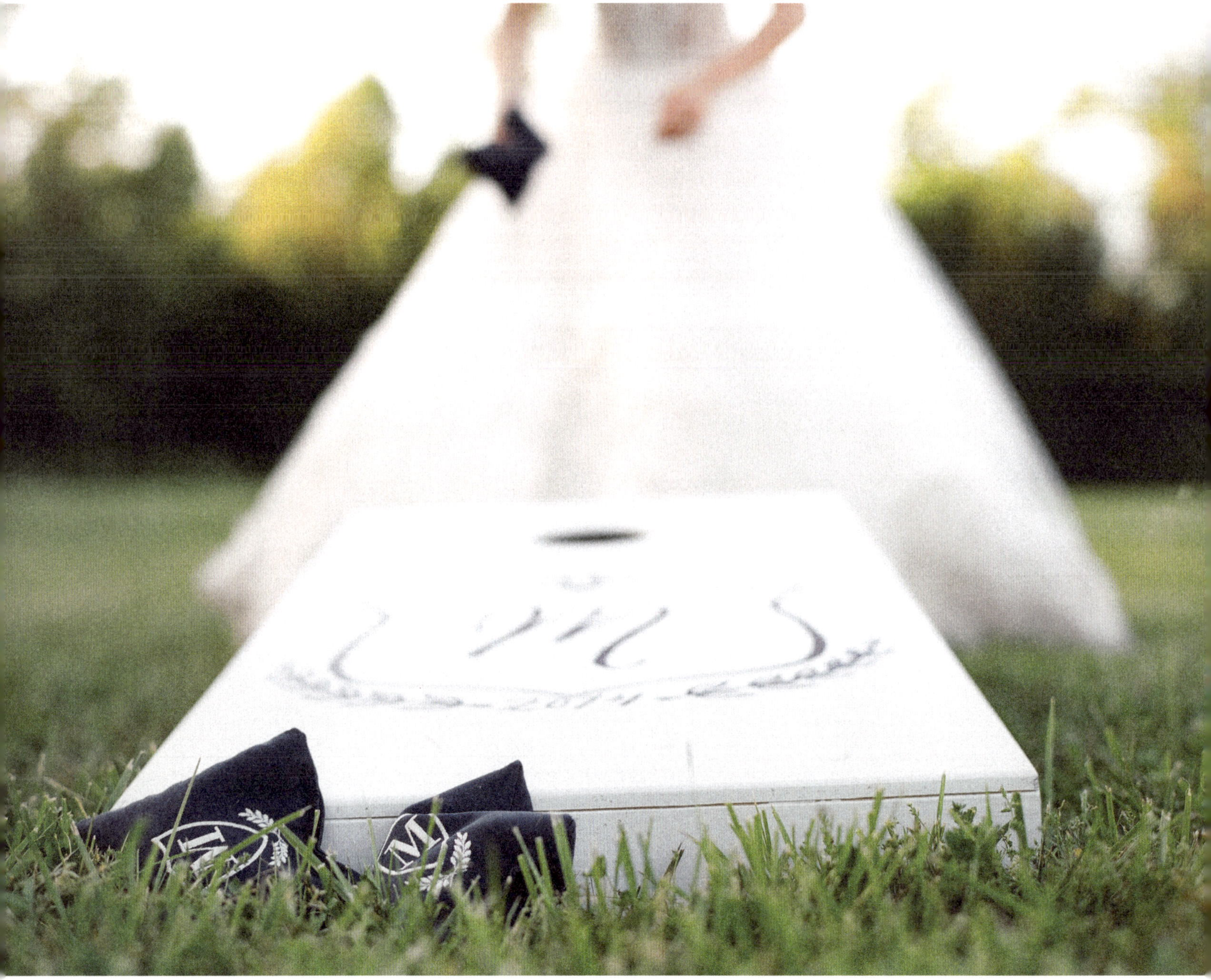

PERSONAL *Touches*

WRITTEN BY JENNIFER BRYERTON

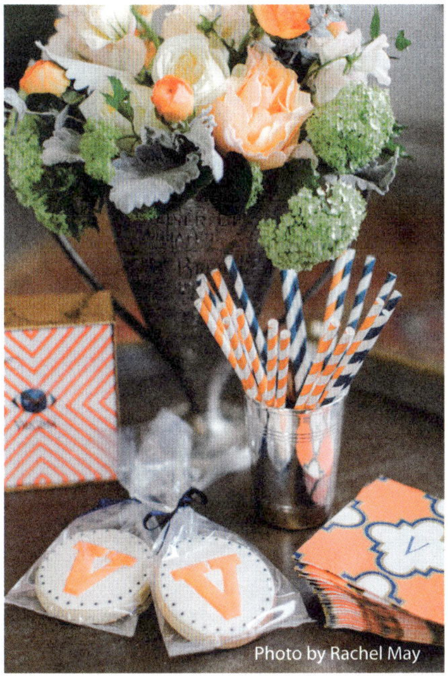

Photo by Rachel May

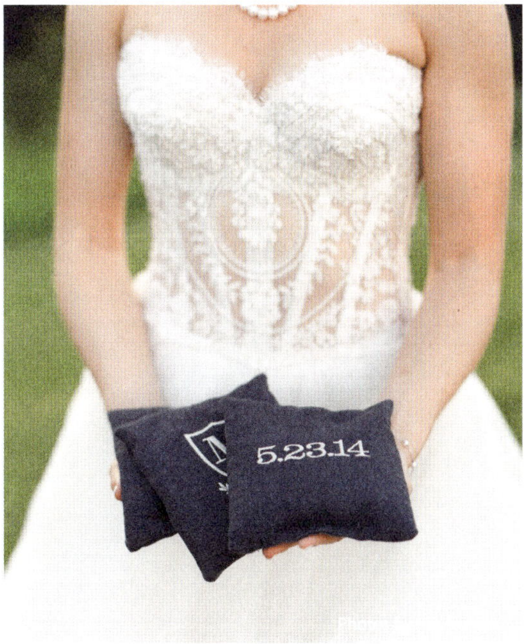

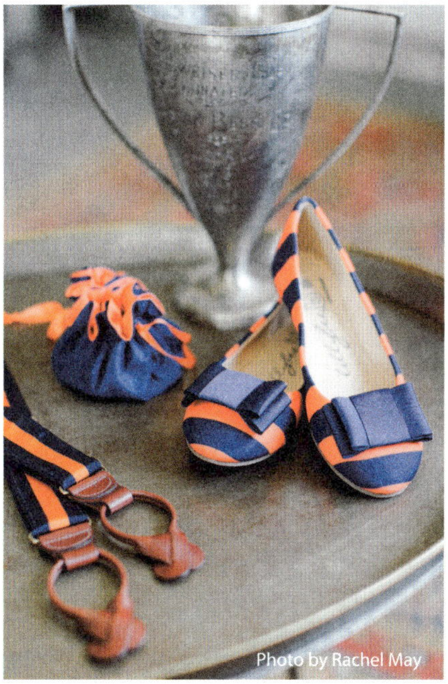

Photo by Rachel May

Little details go a long way to make yours a one-of-a-kind wedding that radiates both your personality as a couple and the beauty of your surroundings. The vibrant Charlottesville artisan community offers plenty of original ideas that are perfect for adding memorable touches to your celebration.

Fun lawn games like this cornhole at left, personalized with elegant calligraphy, add a touch of whimsy at your cocktail hour and get your guests playing together as they enjoy the scenic views.

Above, set a table worthy of Wahoos with eco-sensitive paper straws handmade in Charlottesville by Beve. Add napkins from Caspari, with design shops in Paris and of course, Downtown Charlottesville, then finish off with handmade treats by Kelly Trout of One Creative Cookie. At top right, UVA alumni can easily add their 'something blue' along with some cheerful orange with these accessories. Festive pieces like this jewelry bag, handmade in nearby Stuarts Draft and available at The Virginia Shop, are perfect for the bride who can also dance the night away in these pretty ballerina flats that wink at UVA style. Bespoke braces made by Barrons-Hunter in Charlottesville, subtle under jackets, are a fun way for the gents to sport some collegiate style. Groomsmen can each wear the colors of their alma mater for a sweetly thoughtful touch.

On the following page at top left and clockwise, a hand-painted directional sign, like this one by MakeWells, is a thoughtful way to pay homage to locations significant to you. With a groom about to be deployed by the Department of Defense to Abu Dhabi, this couple had more than a handful of geographic points to reference at their wedding! The beribboned rings shown next are a beautiful way to incorporate heirlooms and represent people close to you who can't attend the wedding. The charming personalized wine bottle below was created by the bride with the help of friends who kindly saved bottles for her custom designed labels thanking her guests.

Hearken to Jefferson's Virginia by using the stunning bowl at bottom left also on the next page, handcrafted by Fred Williamson from a felled tree at TJ's Monticello home, as a dramatic focal point for your celebration filled with blossoms, for collecting cards or adorning the dessert table. For lovers of Dave Matthews, the sophisticated wood candle holder

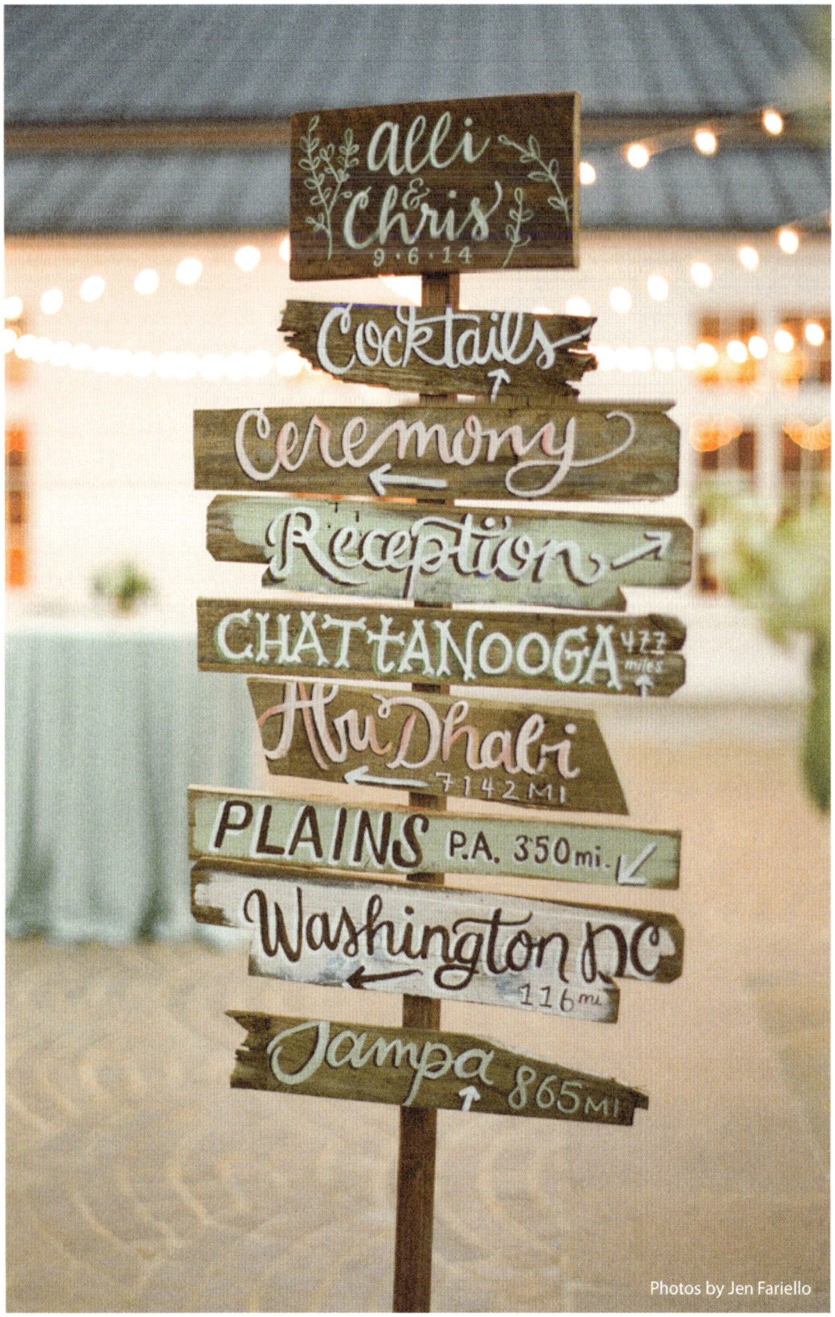

Photos by Jen Fariello

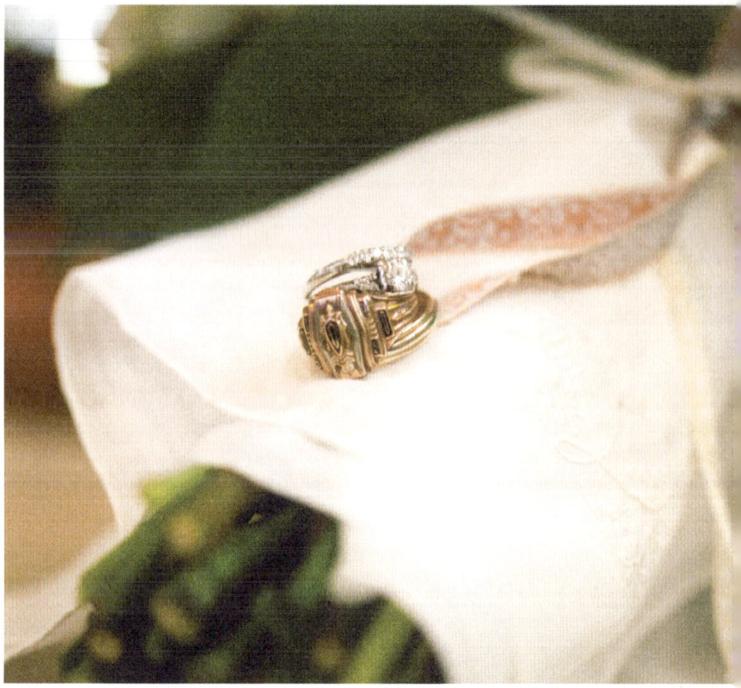

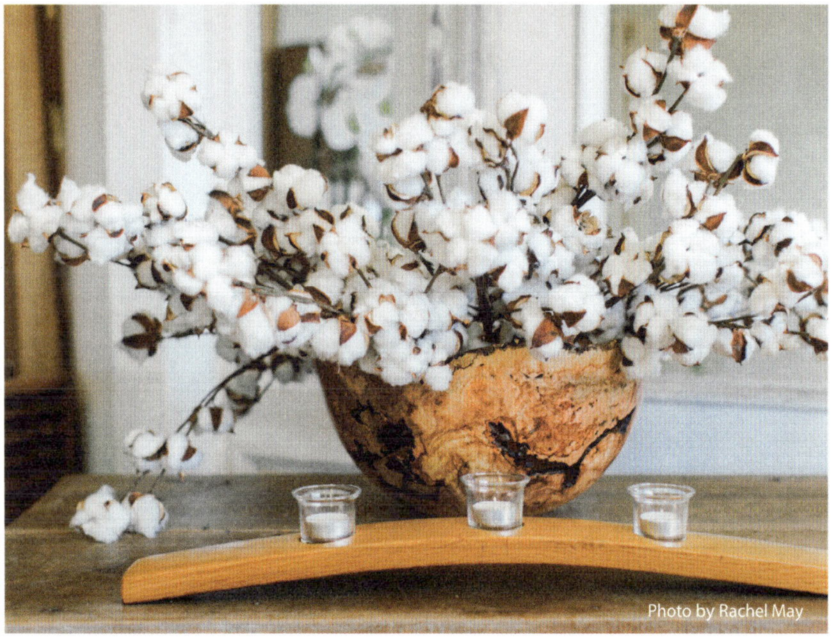

Photo by Rachel May

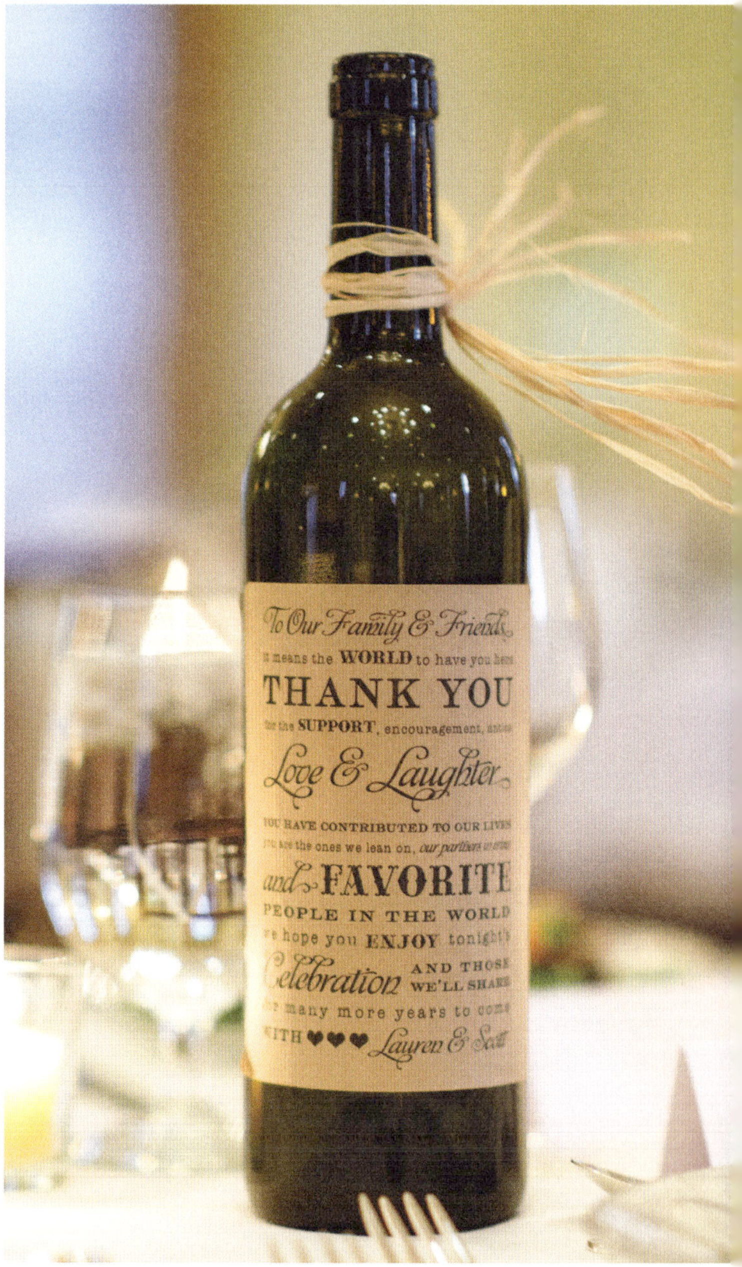

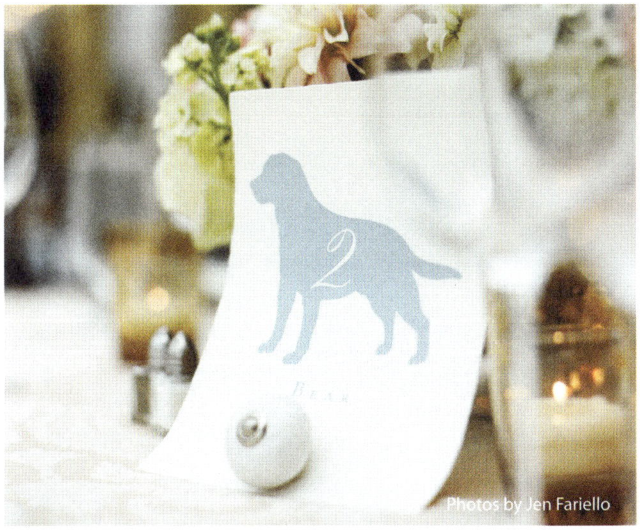
Photos by Jen Fariello

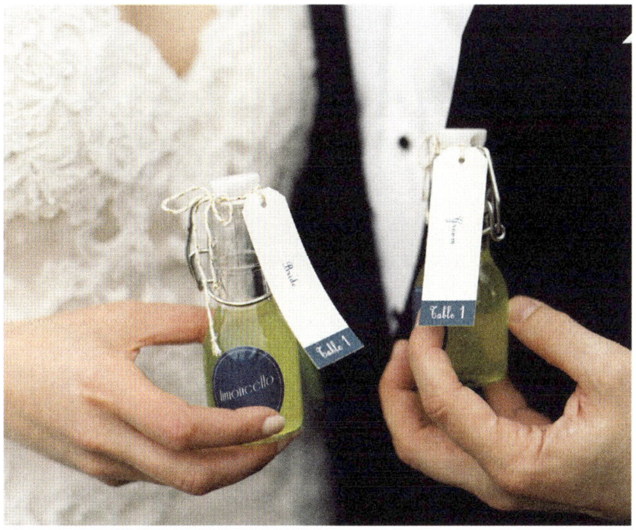

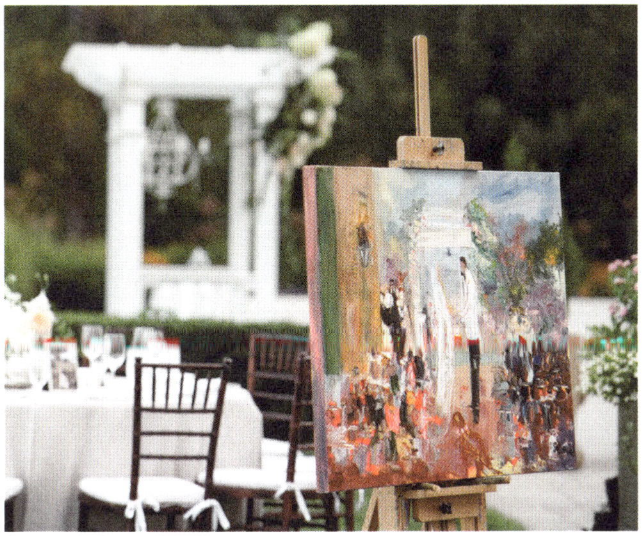

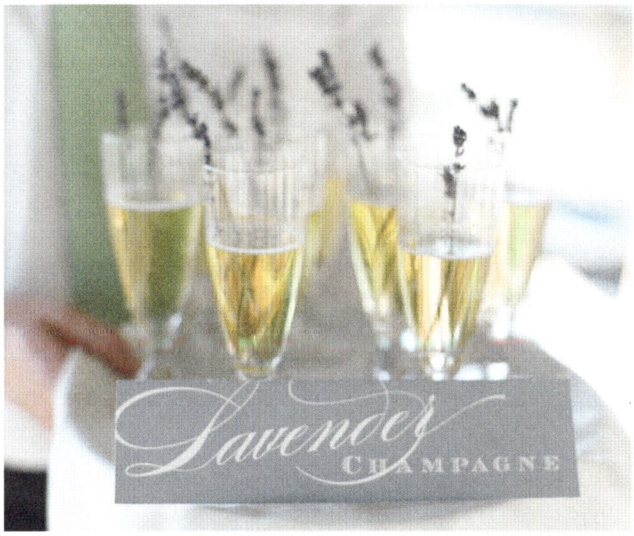

shown with the bowl, is handcrafted at Red Fox Workshop, and made from recycled French oak wine barrels used at Matthews' Blenheim Vineyards. If you stop by for a tasting you could also take home a bottle adorned with original art that Dave creates for each vintage. These wooden pieces will later serve as timeless mementos to display in your home.

The fun table numbers above left picture this couple's beloved dog, Bear, and all the reception tables featured other family pets in silhouette. These sweet bottles above right were works of love with papers designed by the bride and filled with the groom's family recipe for a delicious limoncello. It was served in over 100 bottles for the reception and doubled as favors and escort cards. Regional lavender paired with Pippin Hill Farm and Vineyards' sparkling wine above was born from the bride's love for this favorite bloom and is the perfect signature cocktail for a springtime celebration of love. For a fresh perspective on your most cherished wedding day moments, document your ceremony en plein air, inviting a live event painter like this groom did as a gift for his bride, creating both a surprising enjoyment for guests and also a precious souvenir to bring home to your newlywed nest.

Your wedding day is all about the two of you and beginning your life together, so you want to thank the many people who helped you get to this day and who will be there to support you in the years to come. It will be the special thoughtful touches, the love in the details, that help your guests feel honored and make your wedding a truly unforgettable experience, not just for you and your partner but also for your guests.

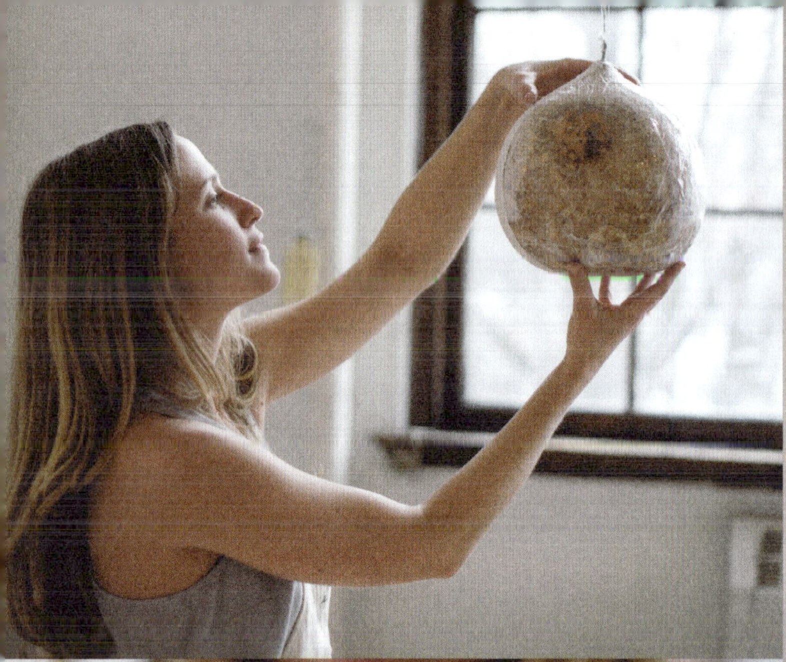
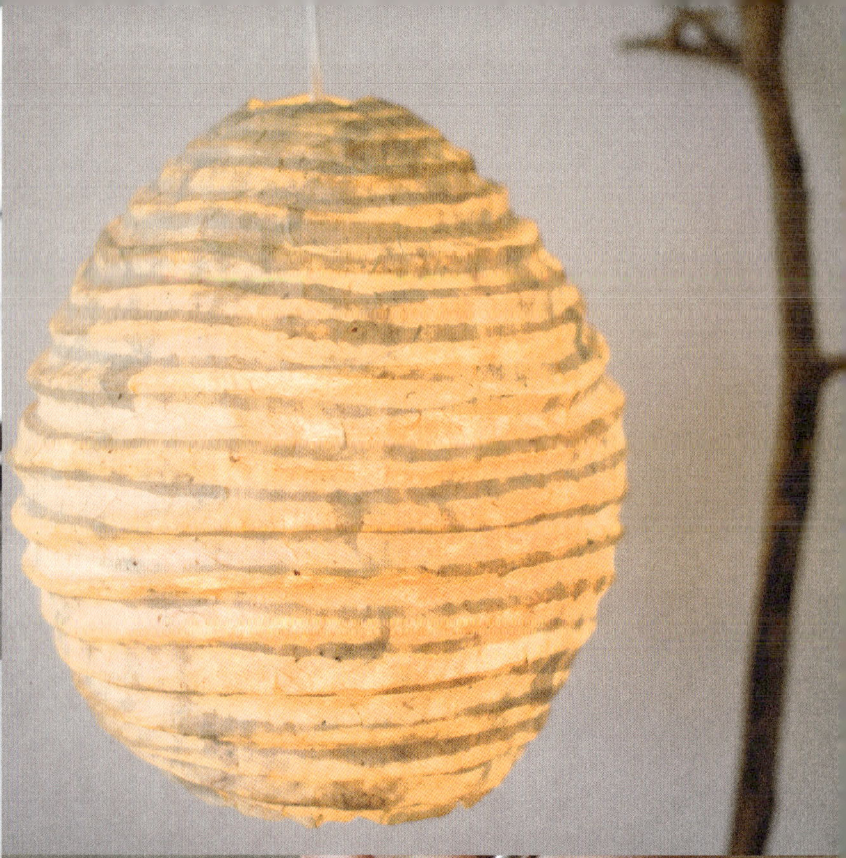
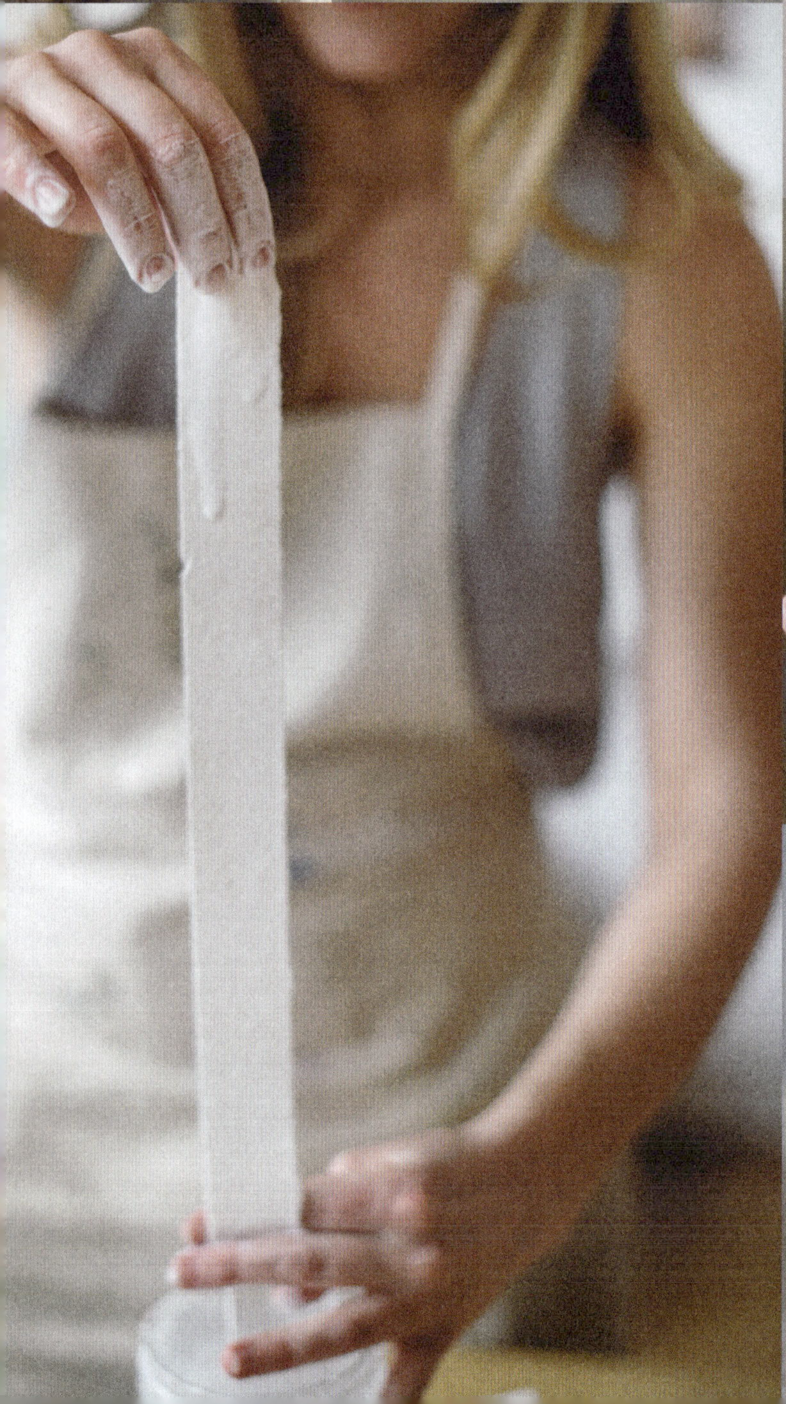
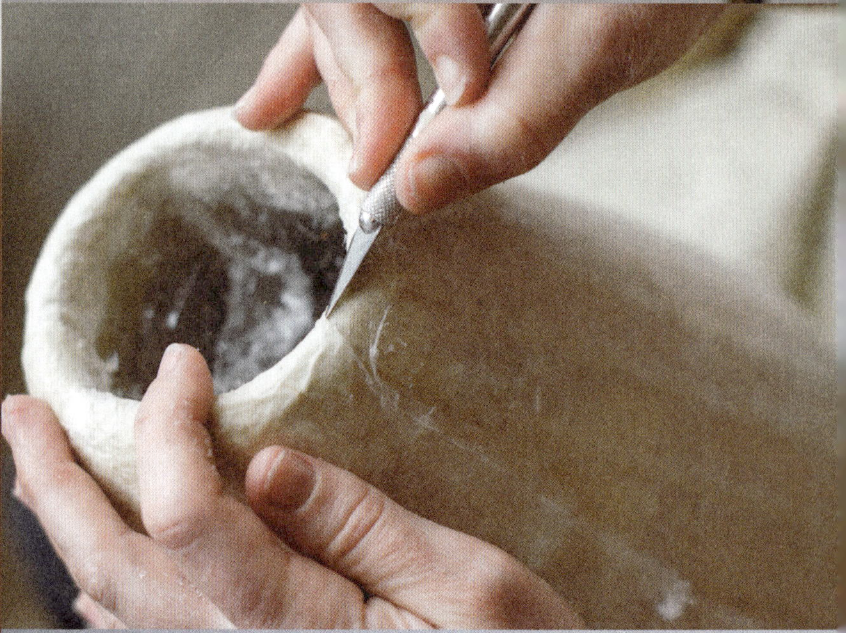
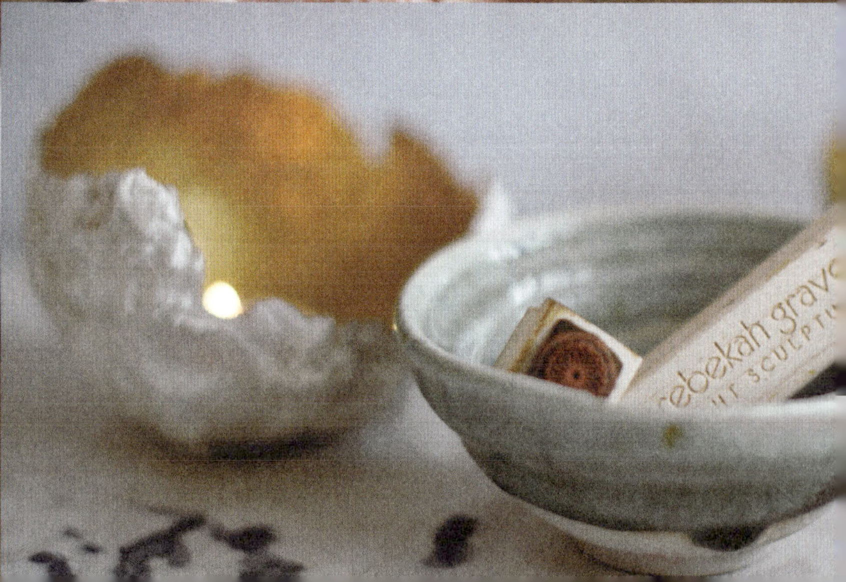

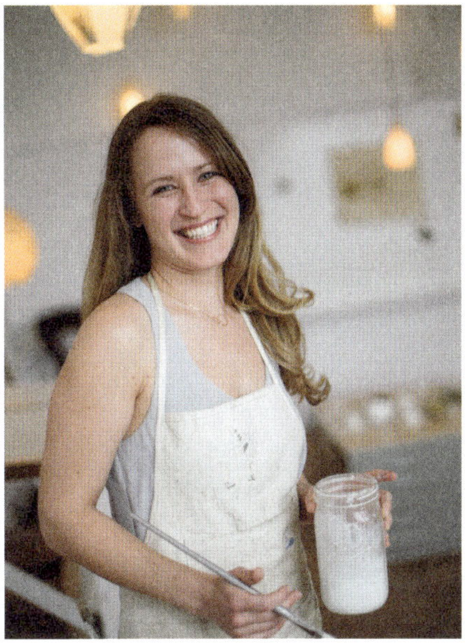

ARTISAN *Portrait*

REBEKAH GRAVES

sculptor

Luminous pendants strung from ivy-garlanded arbors. Hand-crafted, candle-filled bowls, as dainty and fragile as eggshells, floating on water. Strings of paper-shelled lights lining paths or lighting tables. Rebekah's light sculptures shine with a warm glow and grace their surroundings with a peaceful, mystical ambiance.

Rebekah has always been enamored with light and nature. Growing up on a farm, she loved playing with red clay mud and catching lightning bugs on summer nights and watching them shimmer in glass jars. As a student of environmental science and architecture at the University of Virginia, a bookmaking class led her to experiment with papermaking. "I fell in love with the way handmade paper warmed light and lent such supple texture," she says.

Combining her love of natural texture and light, Rebekah began to experiment with creating delicate light fixtures. Along her creative path, she found that a lighting piece "weighs ounces but holds such weight in beauty."

Working from her studio at McGuffey Art Center, a historic school made over as a cooperative for nearly 50 resident artists and the hub of our vibrant downtown arts scene, Rebekah sculpts in porcelain, fires the vessel, then casts it with handmade papers. The result is a light "soft and muted, in shapes pure and organic."

Rebekah's lighting enchants its surroundings, indoors or out. "Part of what brings me joy in this work is seeing a person's face when they enter an installation," she says. "People are drawn to their warmth and natural form and the ethereal way they sway in a breeze."

Her lighting is available for private installations, purchase or rental for special occasions and weddings. "My work transforms space into a warmly illuminated atmosphere that has a comforting ambiance and resonates intimately the beauty in nature," she says.

WRITTEN BY JODY HOBBS-HESLER

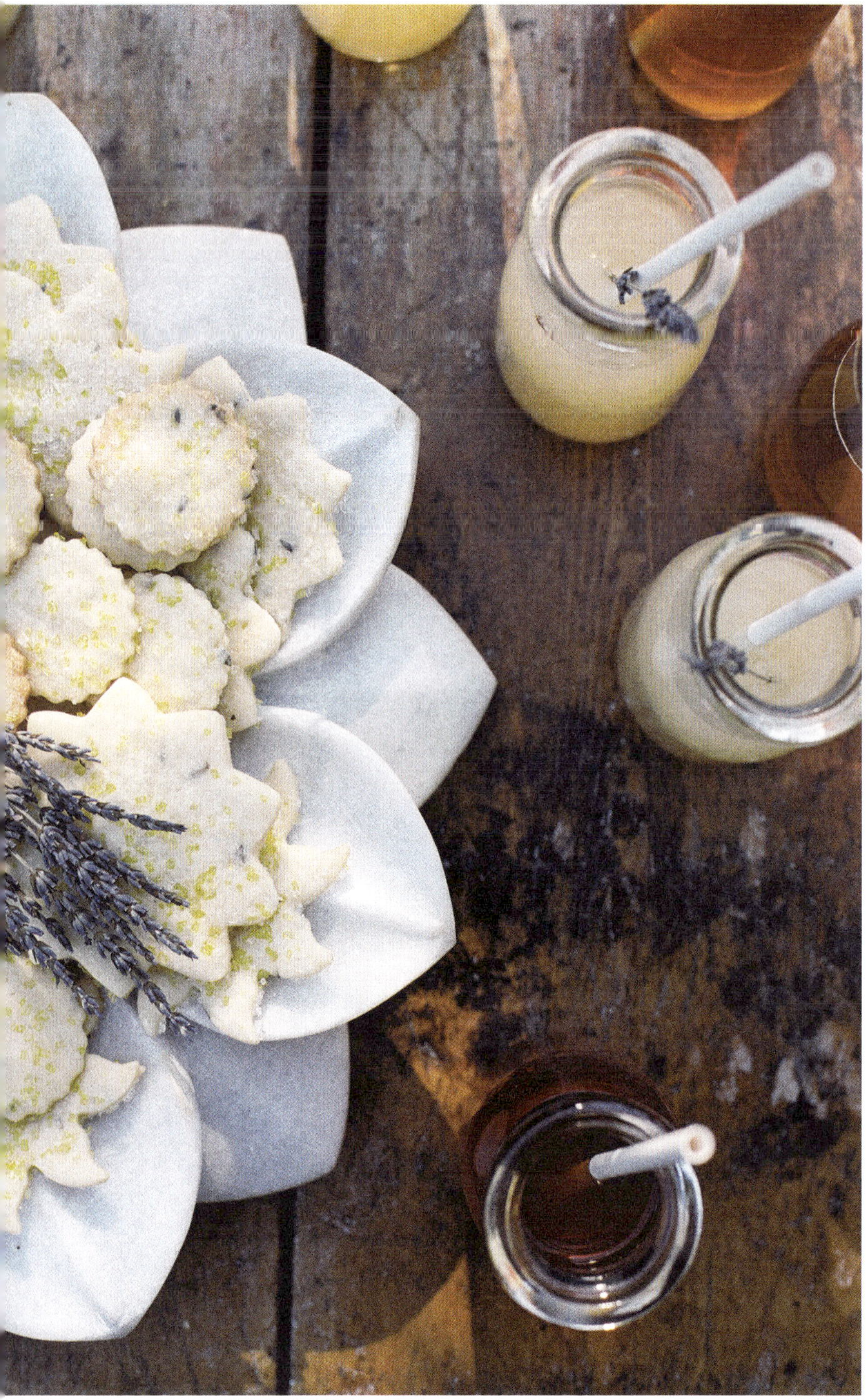

Nestled in wine country, you're at the center of the farm-to-table movement thanks to our region's seemingly endless acres of surrounding farms. *Wine Enthusiast* names the area one of "America's 5 New Foodie Cities," while *Esquire* dubs us "The food region of 2014." Eating real food, grown almost within walking distance, is now part of our everyday life and key to how we entertain and celebrate. Local food adds one more delectable detail for couples who want celebrations rich in both style and significance.

With local, craft-cuisine, caterers joining ranks with Charlottesville brides and grooms, the "locavore" wedding is no longer reserved for only the most gourmet or "foodie"-esque couples; everyone can have a menu that features local elements, to whatever degree is desired! Infusing a wedding menu with locally sourced produce, cheeses and meats heightens the level of deliciousness and creates a meaningful meal with friends and family.

Our cocktail hours showcase delightful sips, like refreshing lemonade and sweet tea, which bartenders fragrantly infuse with local lavender. This is not to mention our award-wining array of microbrews, wine, cider and

ELEGANT *Farm to Table*

WRITTEN BY JENNIFER CARROLL

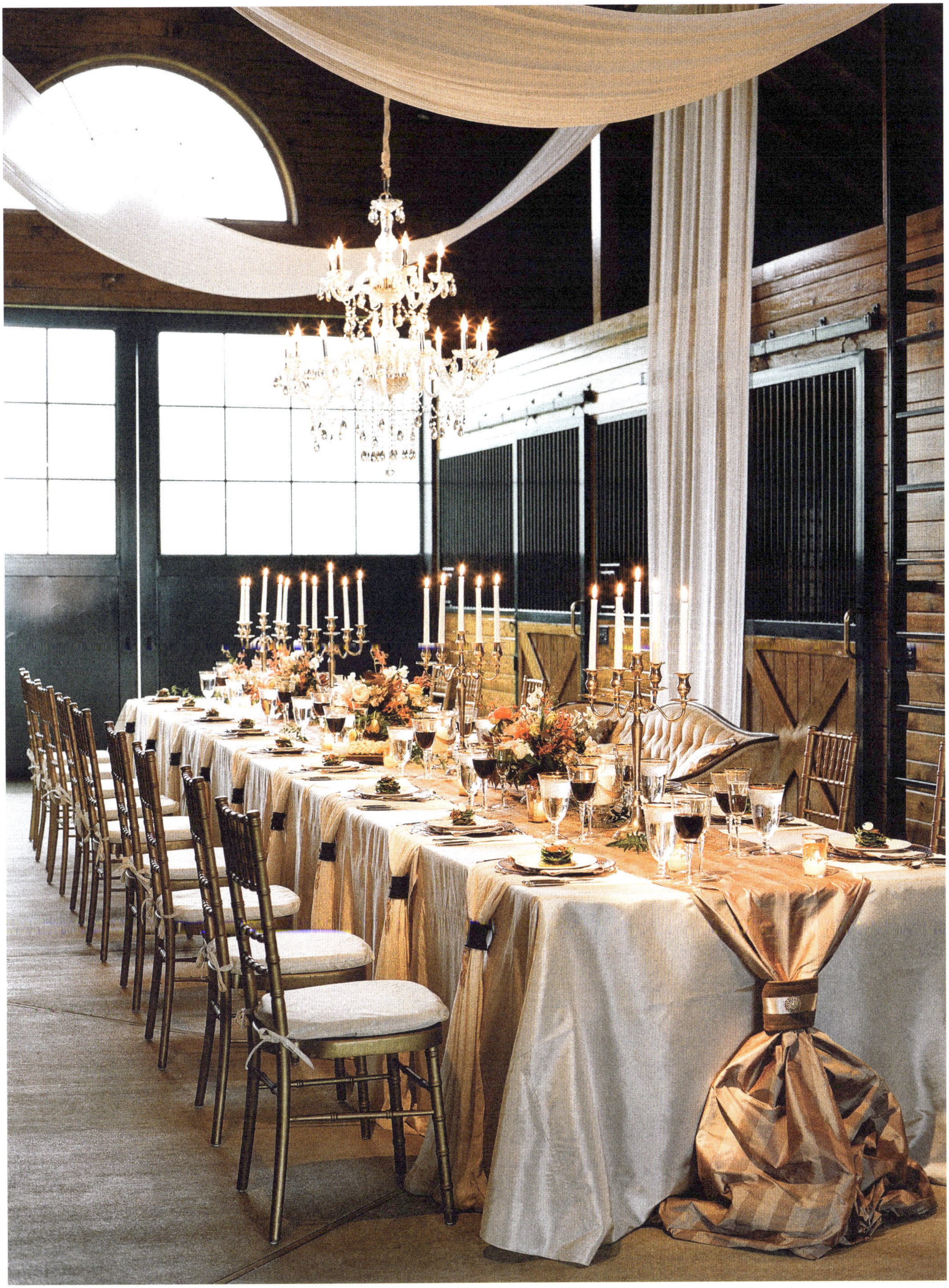

other spirits proudly concocted in our region. Our pride and joy is a traditional mint julep with fresh mint transplanted straight from Jefferson's original garden at Monticello.

The food revolution is also shaking up dinner menus. Chefs all around town specialize in local meats and produce, adding fresh savor and flair to every dish. Guests can step up to design-your-own-barbeque stations, allowing you to customize your meal from sweet to savory.

More and more couples are choosing to design their wedding receptions with a "food first" approach, seeking out what is fresh, locally available and in season on their wedding day.

For the more devoted "foodie" brides and grooms, their wedding menus even serve as inspiration for the aesthetic of their wedding by creating tablescapes that have expanded beyond the traditional floral elements. Think stunning spreads of in-season produce, delicately arranged among garlands of green, providing beautiful color—and conversation starters—for guests. Incorporating tiny pots of local honey, small crystal bowls of dried fruits and vintage canning jars with bright, locally made jams provides not only delicious accoutrements for a wedding feast, but also incredibly beautiful décor.

The use of dinner service is also reflecting a unique and telling trend in the area. More and more couples are opting for a stationed dinner as opposed to serving plated entrees or asking guests to proceed through a traditional buffet. The benefit of a stationed dinner is not only the atmosphere and vibe it creates for the reception (less formal with more opportunities for guest interaction and movement), but also the freedom and creativity it allows for the menu. Instead of having to select just a few entrees to offer guests, couples have the opportunity to create a wholly unique meal at each station—and most weddings feature four or five. Each station becomes its own story. While the growing station trend certainly centers around Virginia favorites, such as a "biscuit bar," more unique stations featuring Thai food or sushi are also cropping up at local receptions.

But the tastiest dish of all is the crowning glory of the wedding feast—the cake. With its unstructured style, the timeless English sponge cake, or Victoria cake, only has icing between its layers, rather than on its top and sides. This beautifully simple style has recently been gracing many dessert buffets. Easily prepared with farm-fresh ingredients and bedecked with local blooms, this cake is a perfect match for farm-to-table weddings.

The ready availability of such bounty has revitalized the concept of farmhouse weddings. While many couples are relishing the simplicity of getting back to basics with beautiful farm tables constructed from reclaimed wood, there is a growing group of brides and grooms who are fusing the luxurious and rustic.

Barns are being transformed or built into trendy

Cookie Bar p.38: **Catering:** A Pimento Catering. || *Tablescape* p.39: **Photography:** Jen Fariello Photography | **Creative Direction and Styling:** Shindig Weddings and Events | **Venue:** Mount Ida Farm | **Florals:** Southern Blooms by Pat's Floral Designs | **Sofa and Whiskey Barrel Bar Rentals:** Paisley & Jade | **Linen, Chairs and Tabletop Decor:** Festive Fare | **Chandelier, Draping and Lighting:** Blue Ridge AV and Lighting | **Catering and Bar:** The Catering Outfit | **Embroidered Napkins:** Beloved Thread | **Paper Goods and Calligraphy:** Joie de Vivre Calligraphy. || *Opposite, at top right and clockwise* p.41: *Image 1:* **Appetizers:** A Pimento Catering | **Design and Decor:** Beehive Events | **Venue:** Fat Cat Farm || *Image 2:* **Wine:** Veritas Vineyard & Winery || *Image 3:* **Salad:** The Catering Outfit | **Event Styling:** Shindig Weddings and Events || *Image 4:* **Cake:** Favorite Cakes | **Creative Direction and Styling:** Easton Events | **Venue:** Pippin Hill Farm & Vineyards || *Barbeque Station* p.42: **Design and Decor:** Beehive Events | **Food:** Barbeque Exchange Catering | **Venue:** Fat Cat Farm || *Place Setting* p.43: **Floras:** Southern Blooms by Pat's Floral Designs | **Event Planning:** Shindig Weddings and Events | **Rentals:** Festive Fare | **Catering:** The Catering Outfit | **Venue:** Belle Haven

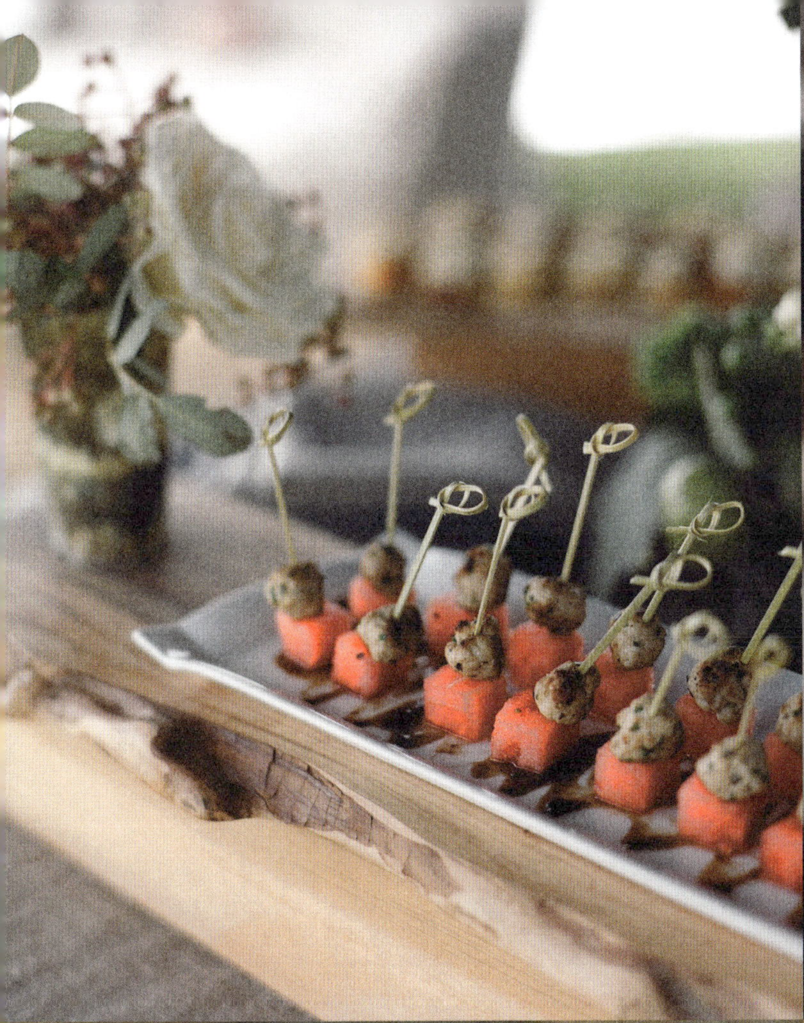
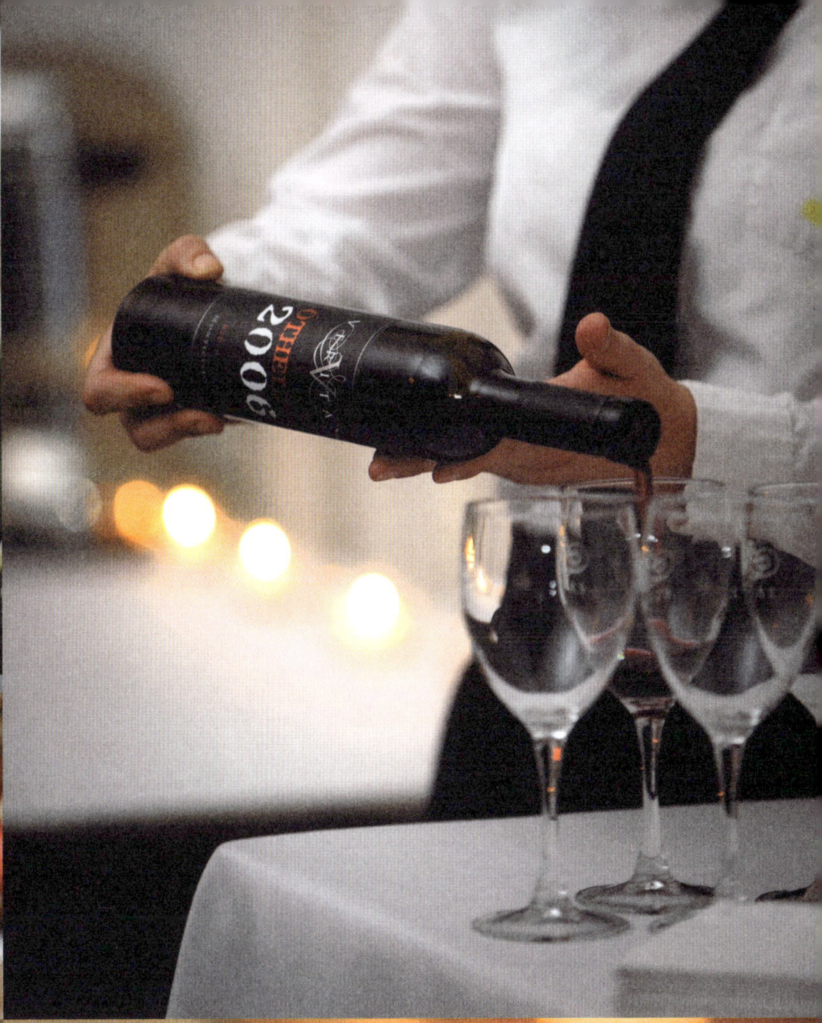
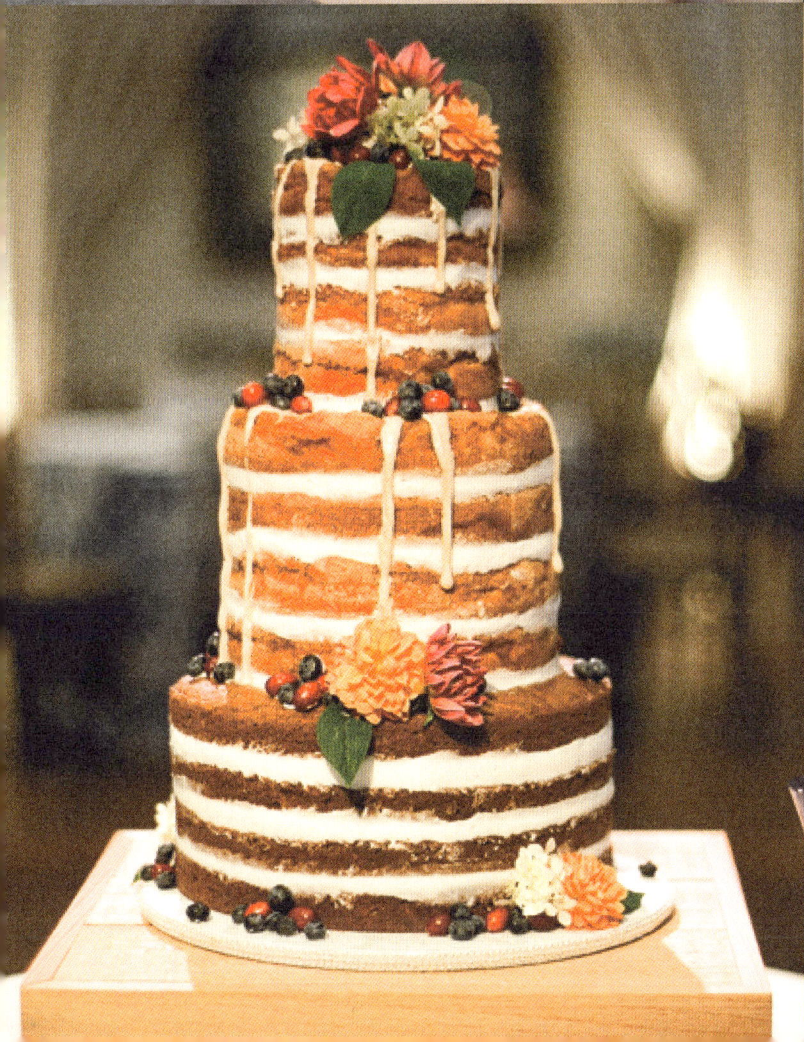
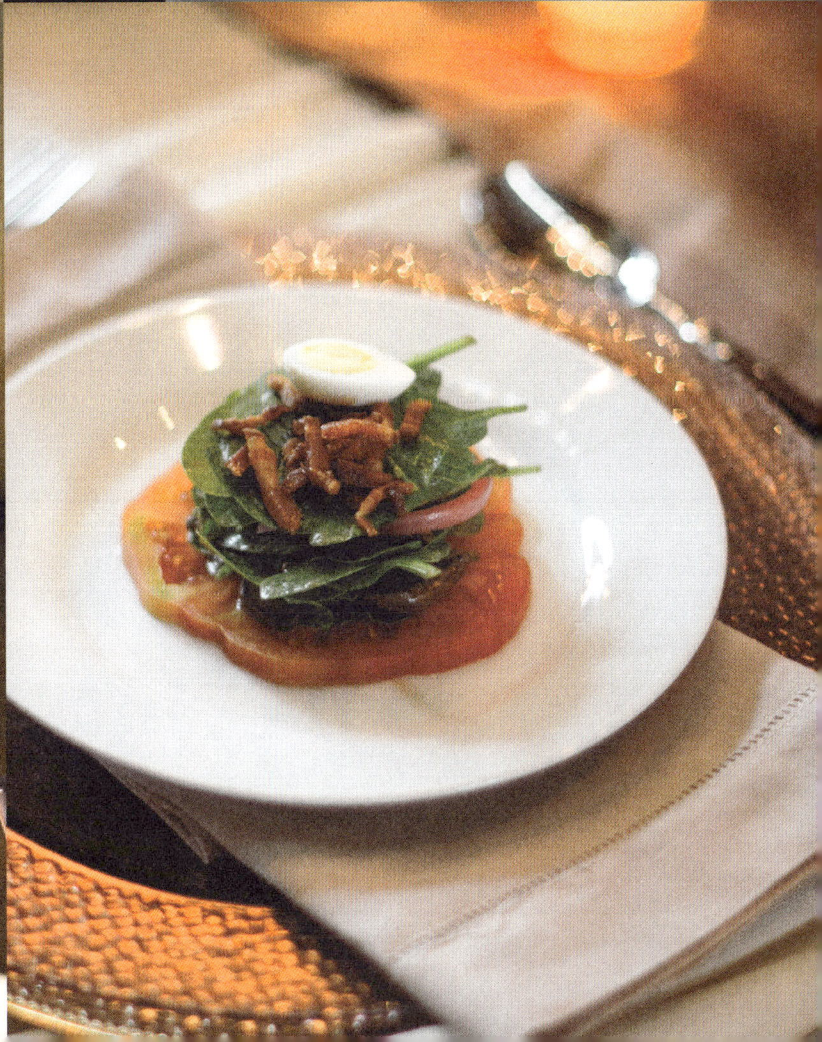

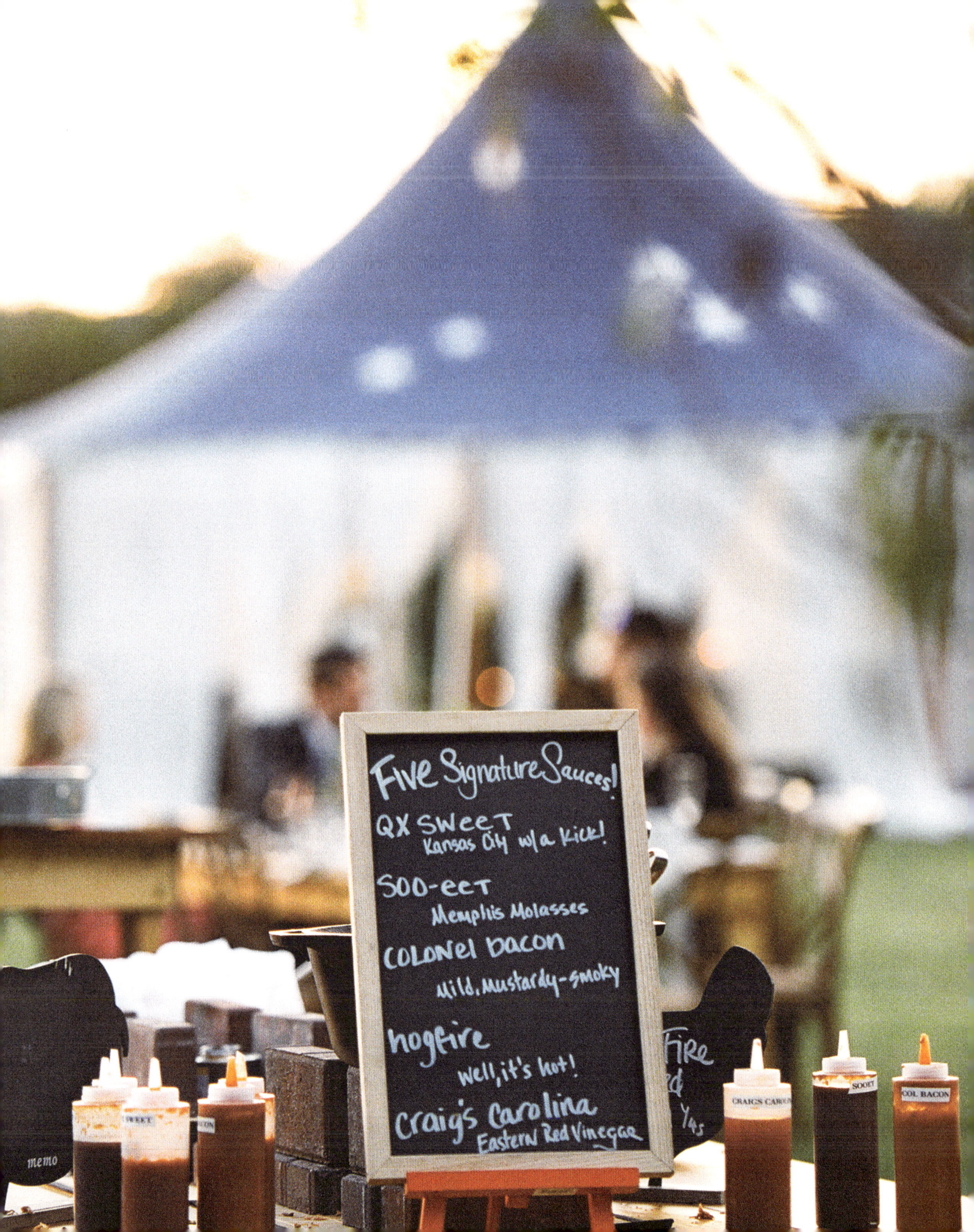
Five Signature Sauces!
QX SWEET
Kansas City w/a Kick!
SOO-EET
Memphis Molasses
COLONEL bacon
Mild, Mustardy-smoky
hogfire
Well, it's hot!
Craig's Carolina
Eastern Red Vinegar

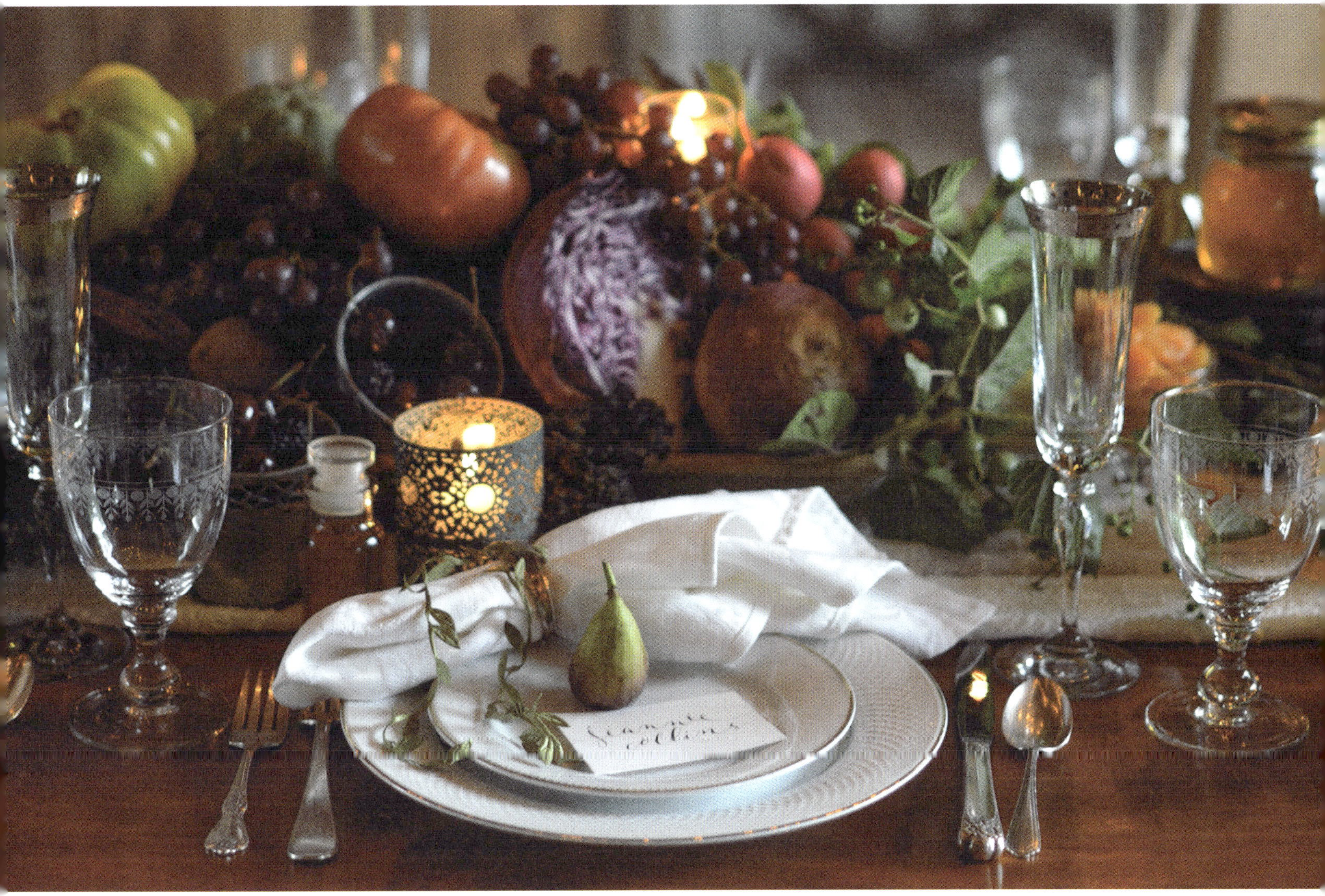

spaces, fitted with twinkling crystal chandeliers and cascades of sumptuous chiffons, silks and velvets. Rustic doors become idyllic backdrops for wedding feasts. These luxuries, typically reserved for the ballroom, are all taking pride of place in the countryside, and surprisingly, looking right at home and super chic.

Scenes such as these were once only possible for the elite, but today they are viable options for any bride and groom who want to step out into the verdant fields of the stunning properties in and around town. Fruit orchards have joined the ranks of wedding venues, too, often offering mountaintop vistas, and certainly showcasing the freshest picks of sun-warmed peaches, fresh-picked blueberries, crisp apples and juicy plums — all depending on the season of your celebration.

The abundance of farm-fresh goods in our local area allows couples to seamlessly weave local produce and products into their celebration. And now, not only can you tell your guests that their food is local, you can actually entertain them at the source. With new venues opening each year, the possibilities in our growing wedding market are amazing.

So as you and your spouse-to-be are navigating the waters of wedding planning, and learning the fine art of how to compromise in your relationship, consider applying that same theory to your wedding theme. By both thinking and stepping "outside the box," you just might open yourself up to an unforgettable event that exquisitely blends the best elements of a country club ballroom with the rustic charm that only a farm can offer. Your guests are sure to be dazzled and you will certainly never look at a barn the same way again.

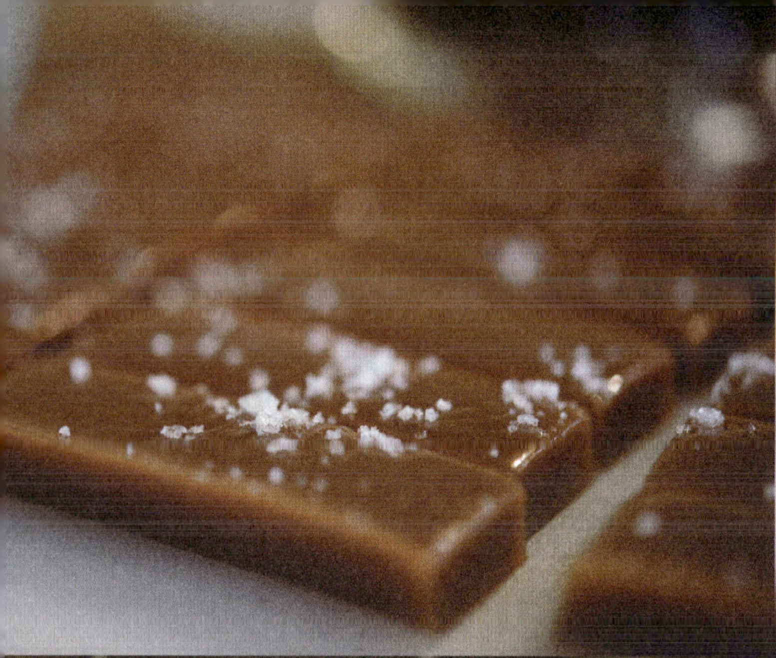

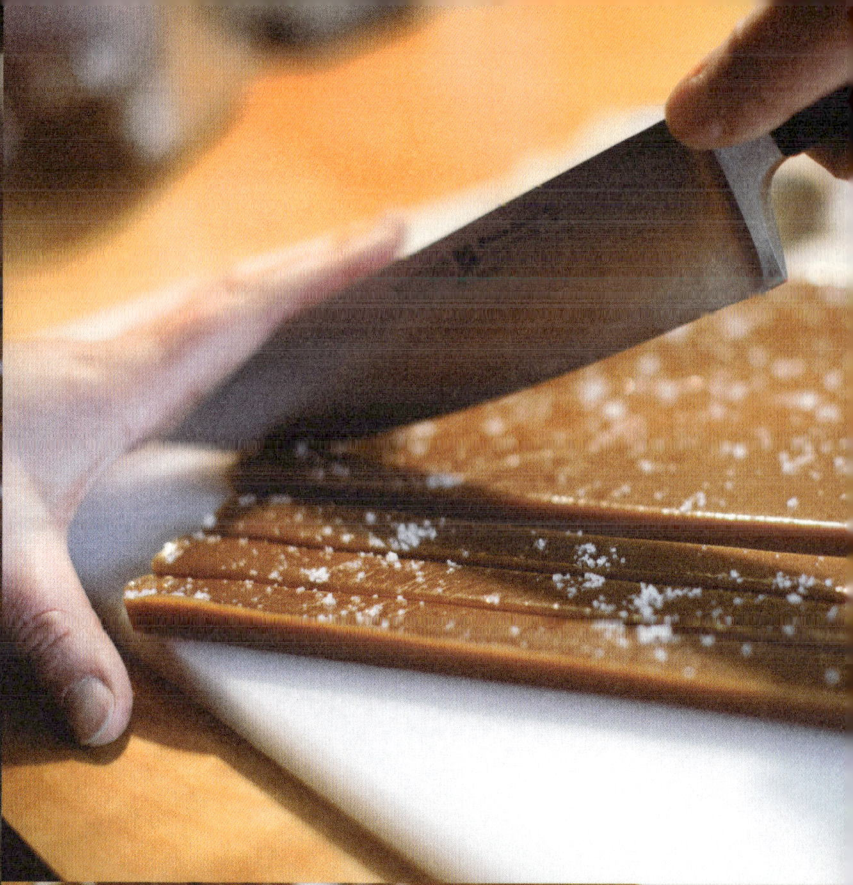

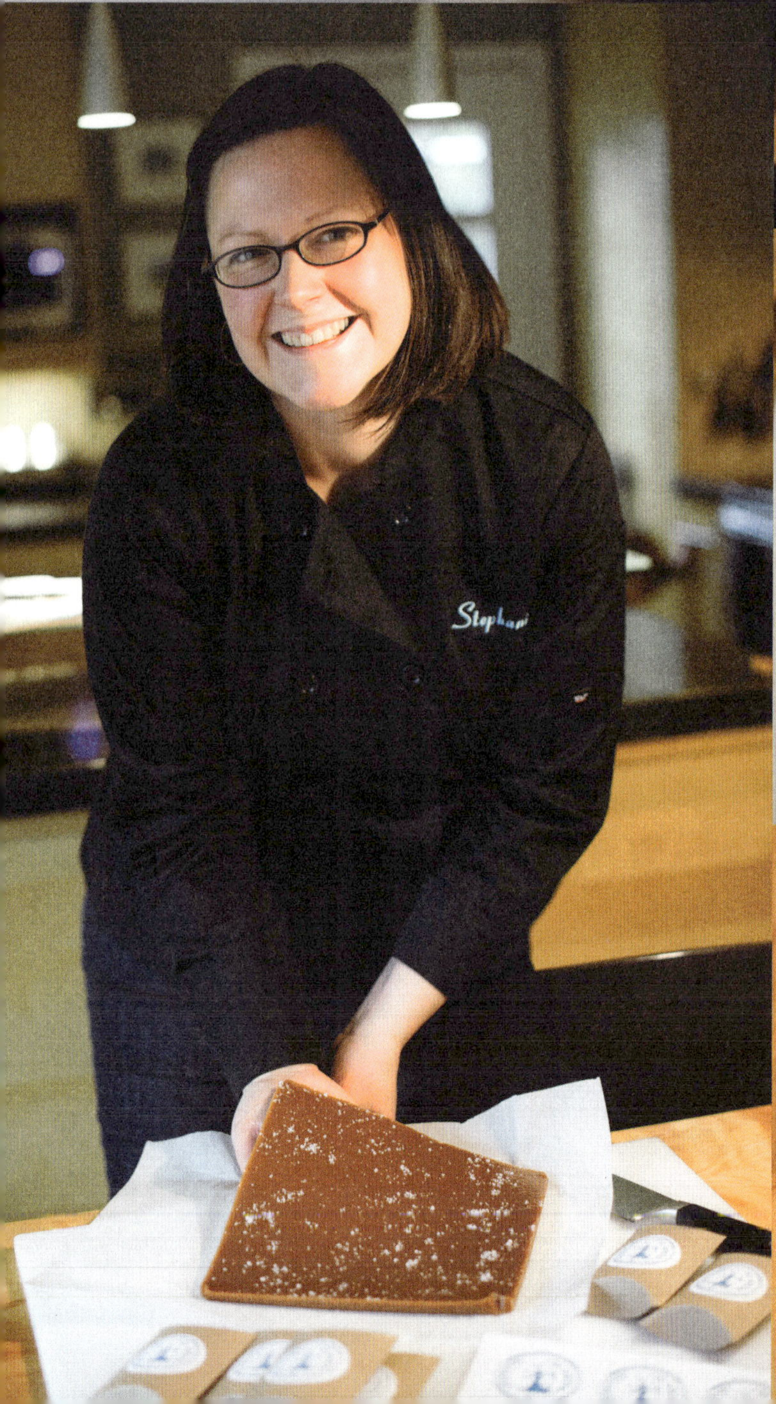

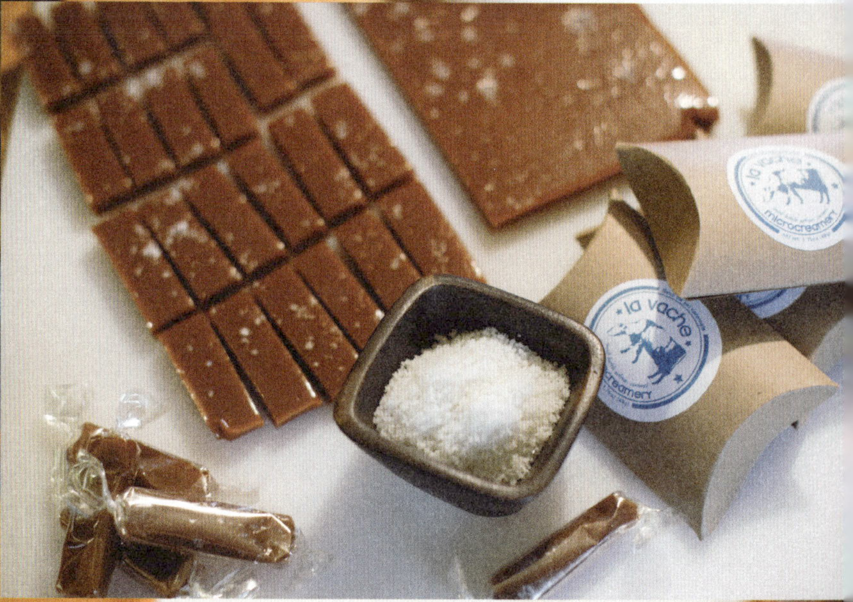
la vache
microcreamery

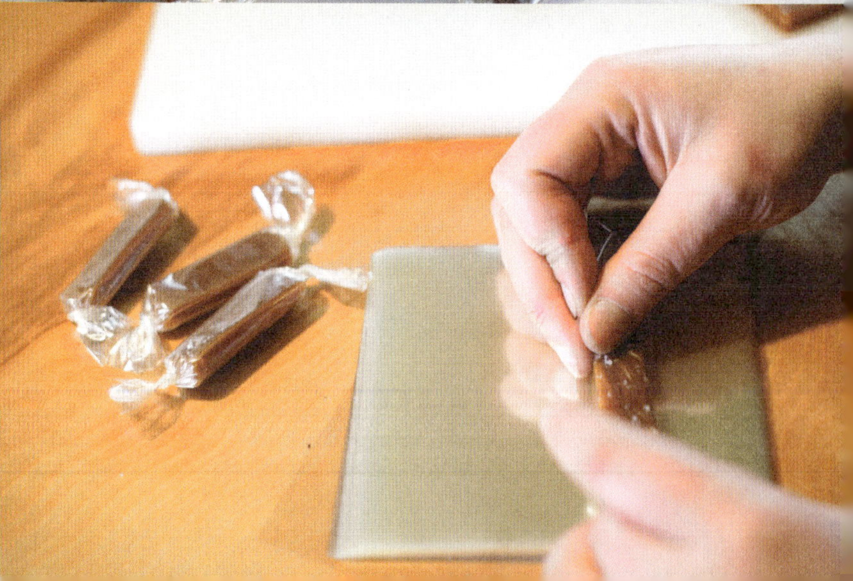

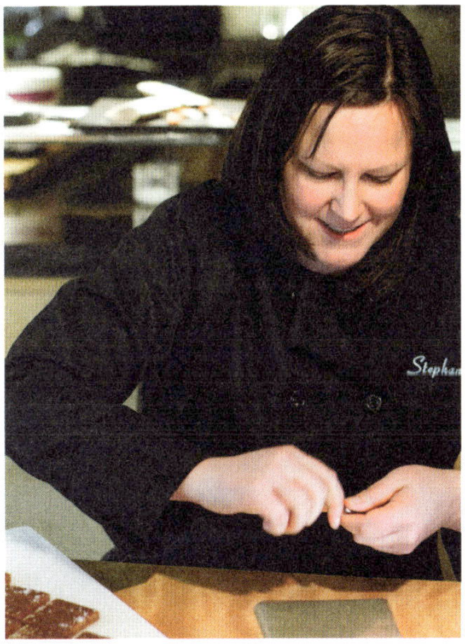

ARTISAN *Portrait*

STEPHANIE WILLIAMS

confectioner

After the economic bust of 2008, not every architect turned to artisanal caramel-making as a new career venture, but Stephanie Williams of La Vache Microcreamery did. She already enjoyed complicated cooking projects, having experimented at dinner parties with homemade candies and ice creams just for fun. "Food intimidation is what challenges me," Williams says. "Making caramel is a very tenuous process, very scientific. It's one of those things that I felt like I needed to conquer."

Before minting her own caramel-making business, Stephanie had already developed a keen interest in the local craft food movement. When she was ready to bring her caramels to market, she knew her handmade creations would be right at home in the Charlottesville community.

Stephanie's passion for the local food movement compels her to obtain as many ingredients locally as possible—including cream, honey and lavender. But her fleur de sel, with its coveted mild flavor, comes straight from France, where it is harvested by hand.

Williams brings artistic affinity and expertise to the custom label options she offers. "I think it goes back to the architect in me," she says, "which is just constant design and wanting to make something look beautiful, wanting people to feel really special, wanting to make some kind of design that fits their personality."

Caramel involves a lot of dedication and attention. "Everything is hand-packed, hand-poured. There's not a piece of caramel that my hand has not touched," Williams says. "It has love in it from beginning to end."

When people include this well-loved candy in their wedding celebrations, "that's what's really gratifying for me," Williams says. "I love that someone thinks enough of my product to give it to the people that they love the most in the world on the best day of their lives."

WRITTEN BY JODY HOBBS-HESLER

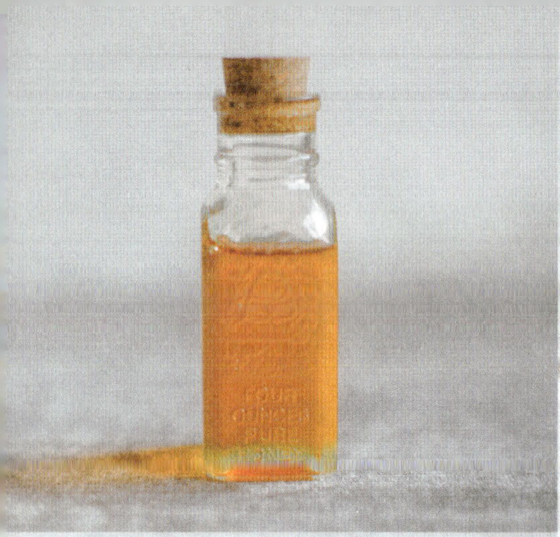

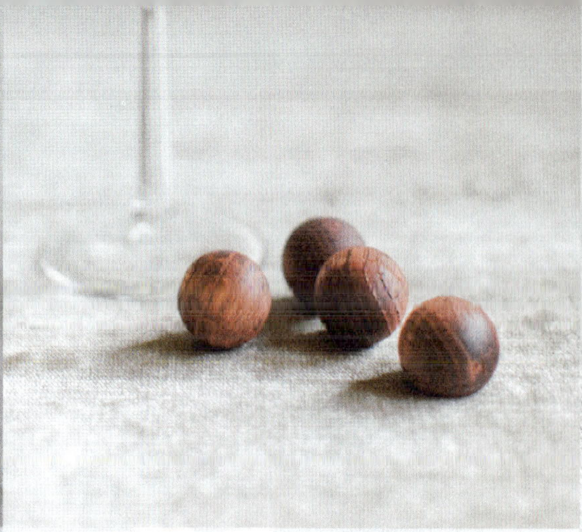

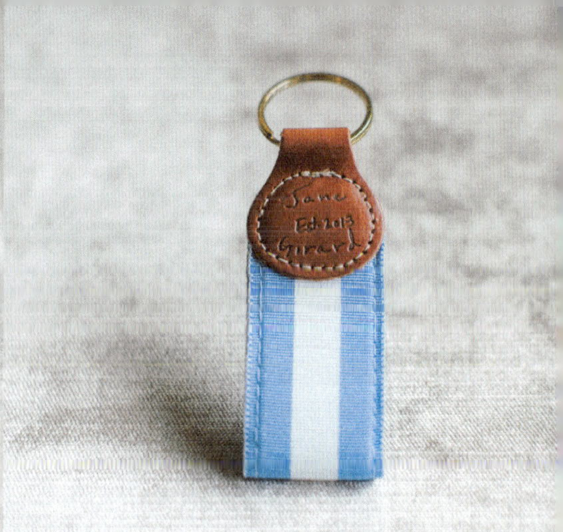

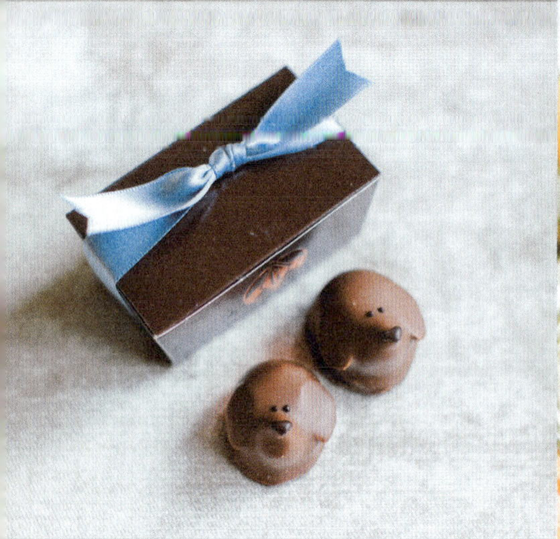

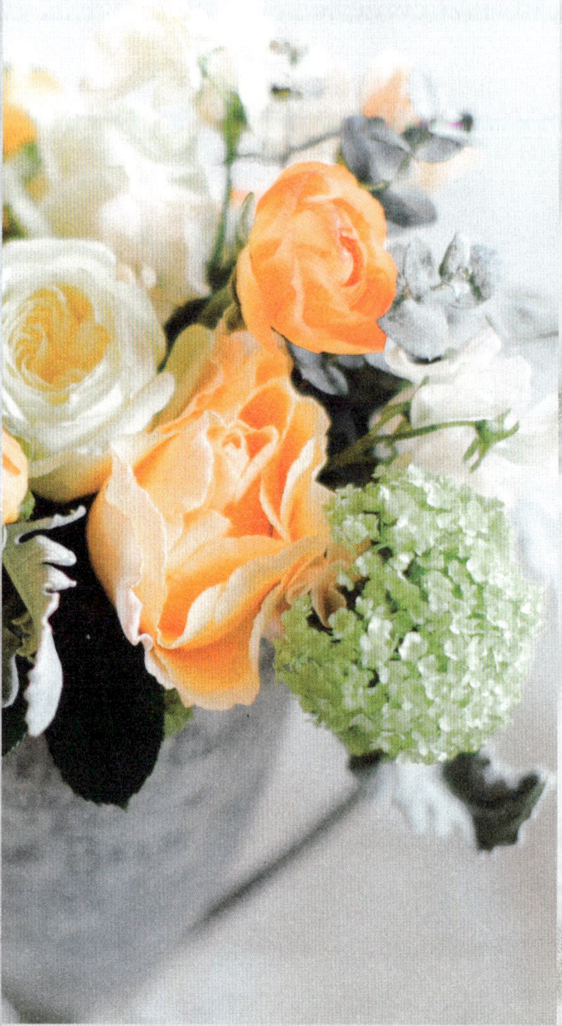

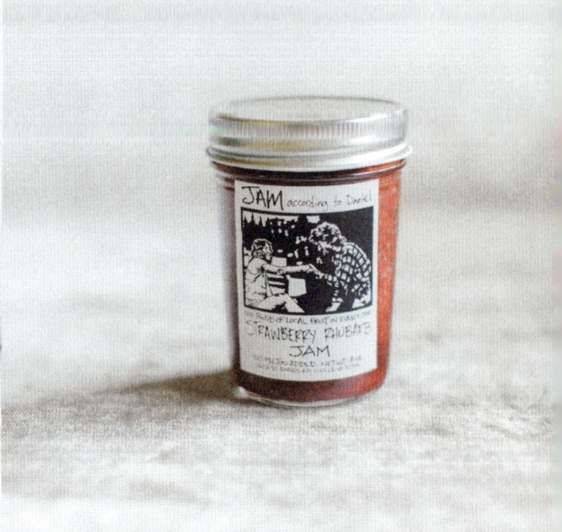

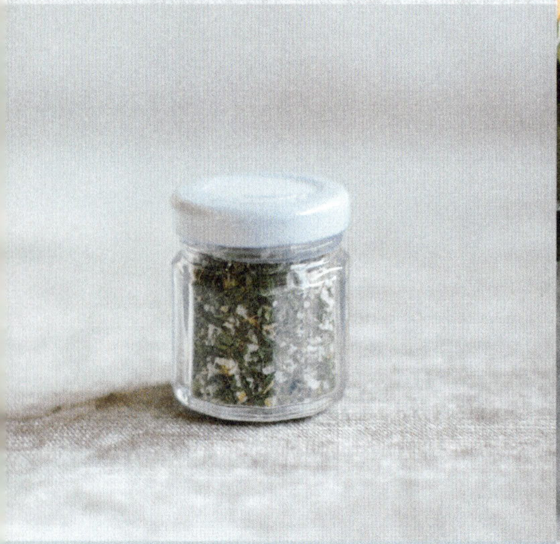

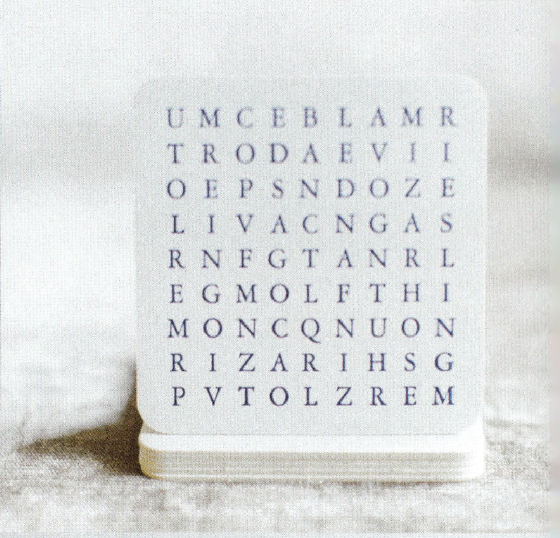
U M C E B L A M R
T R O D A E V I I
O E P S N D O Z E
L I V A C N G A S
R N F G T A N R L
E G M O L F T H I
M O N C Q N U O N
R I Z A R I H S G
P V T O L Z R E M

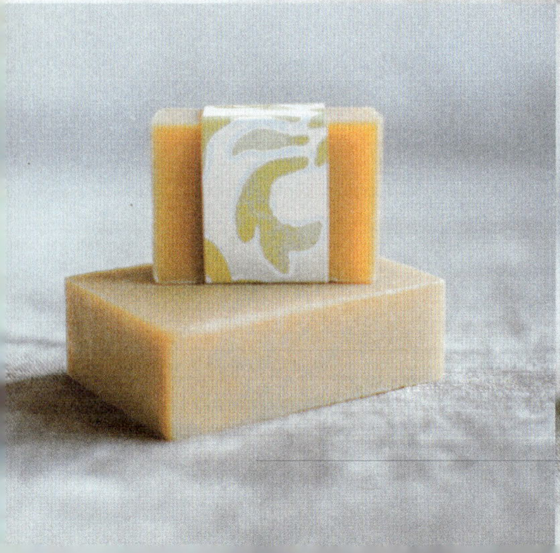

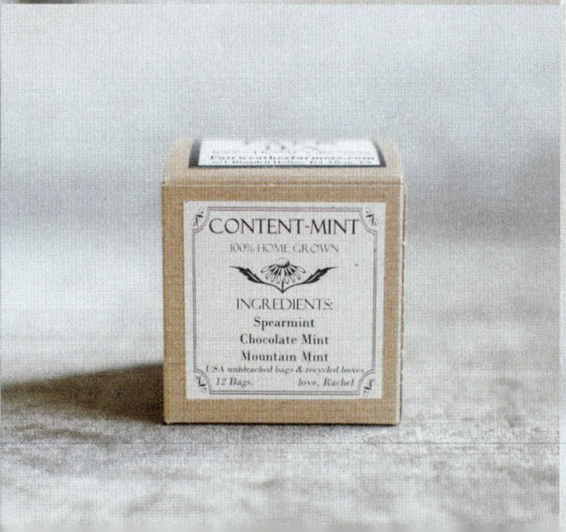
CONTENT-MINT
100% HOME GROWN
INGREDIENTS:
Spearmint
Chocolate Mint
Mountain Mint
USA unbleached bags & recycled boxes
12 Bags.
love, Rachel

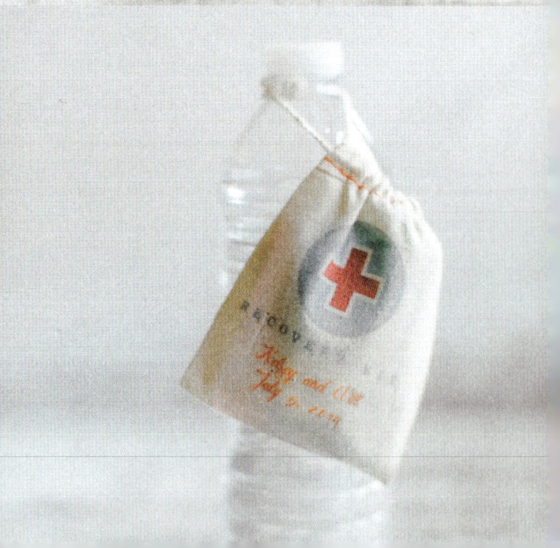

Local FLAVORS

PHOTOGRAPHY BY RACHEL MAY

Many couples want to treat their guests to a little keepsake or treat to remember their day by, especially one that is locally made and expressive of the region they loved enough to celebrate their marriage in. These lovely gifts are also the perfect items to add to welcome baskets, along with a bottle of local wine of course, for a touch of true hospitality and the special charm that is unique to Charlottesville.

From top left going clockwise we've gathered up some of our favorites: Sourwood Farm honey harvested in the fields of the Blue Ridge is as lovely as its sweet bottle. Wine-soaked oak balls are great for flavoring your grill from the barrels at First Colony Winery—they smell amazing! A preppy key fob from Barrons-Hunter with the leather custom engraved is super trendy. Jam According to Daniel is a favorite at our popular farmer's market each Saturday. A word-search wine coaster made by St Brigid's Press where time-honored processes stamp the letters is charming. A hand-screened emergency bag, made by local artist Jenny Cummins, is filled with a few over-the-counter meds, the perfect antidote for the travel weary or the late partier. Fairweather Farm Tea, with their adorable names, is 100% home-grown right here in the Piedmont, the freshest thing short of taking a cup of hot water out to the field and dropping herbs in it. Naturally moisturizing Wynott Goat Milk Soaps is made with love and available with custom labels for your event in an assortment of heavenly scents. A seasoning blend based on an old family recipe, Peg's Salt can also symbolize eternal unity. Peanut Butter Chocolate Pups, the latest creation from local chocolatier Tim Gearhart (President Obama and the French prime minister enjoyed chocolates from Gearhart's last year so you will be in fine company!). Lastly, shown at right is an on-trend treat from One Creative Cookie that just couldn't be more personal. She will transform your photo, even one taken on your special day, to make this delicious favor.

These items are just a few of the many Charlottesville-made goodies you can order from artisans and boutiques around town like The Happy Cook, Foods of All Nations, Greenwood Grocery, Feast! Market and The Virginia Shop. Lest you think this list is not long enough, these shops are stocked with more local ideas for treating your guests such as Starr Hill Brewery's Love Beer with it's super cute label, or you can spice things up with Brazen Heat BBQ sauce by Bone Doctors'—made by a couple of UVA surgeons!

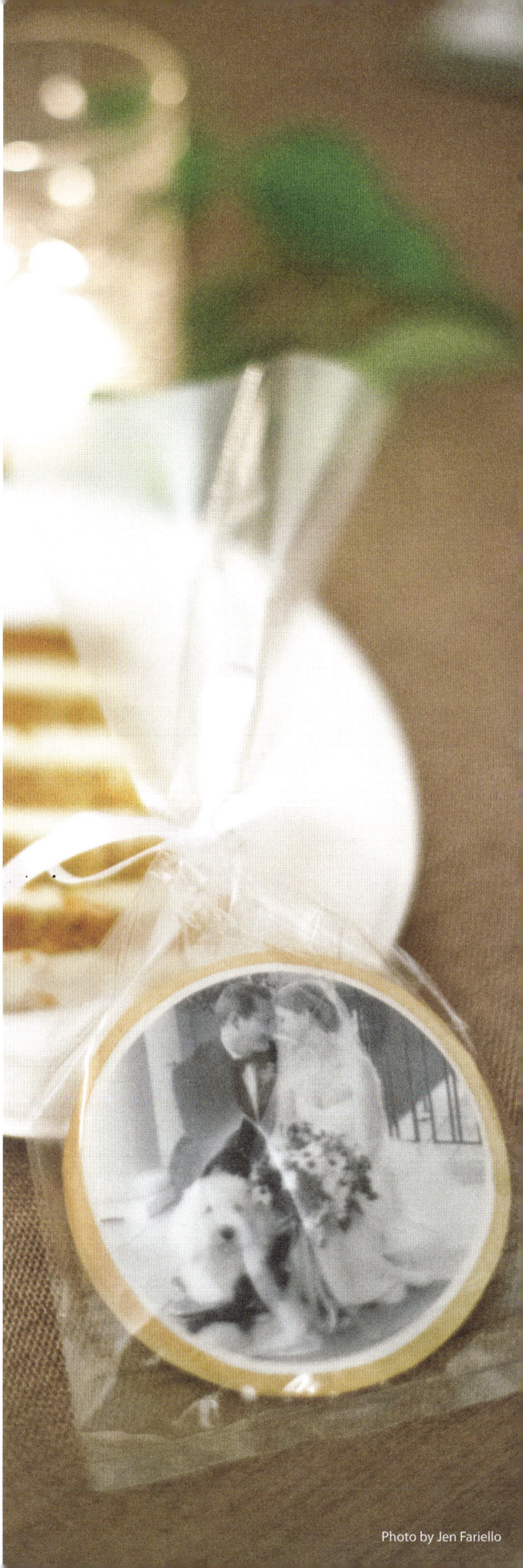

Photo by Jen Fariello

WEDDING OF THE *Year*

ELLEN & CHRIS SWEET

WRITTEN BY SARAH CROSSLAND | PHOTOGRAPHY BY ADAM BARNES

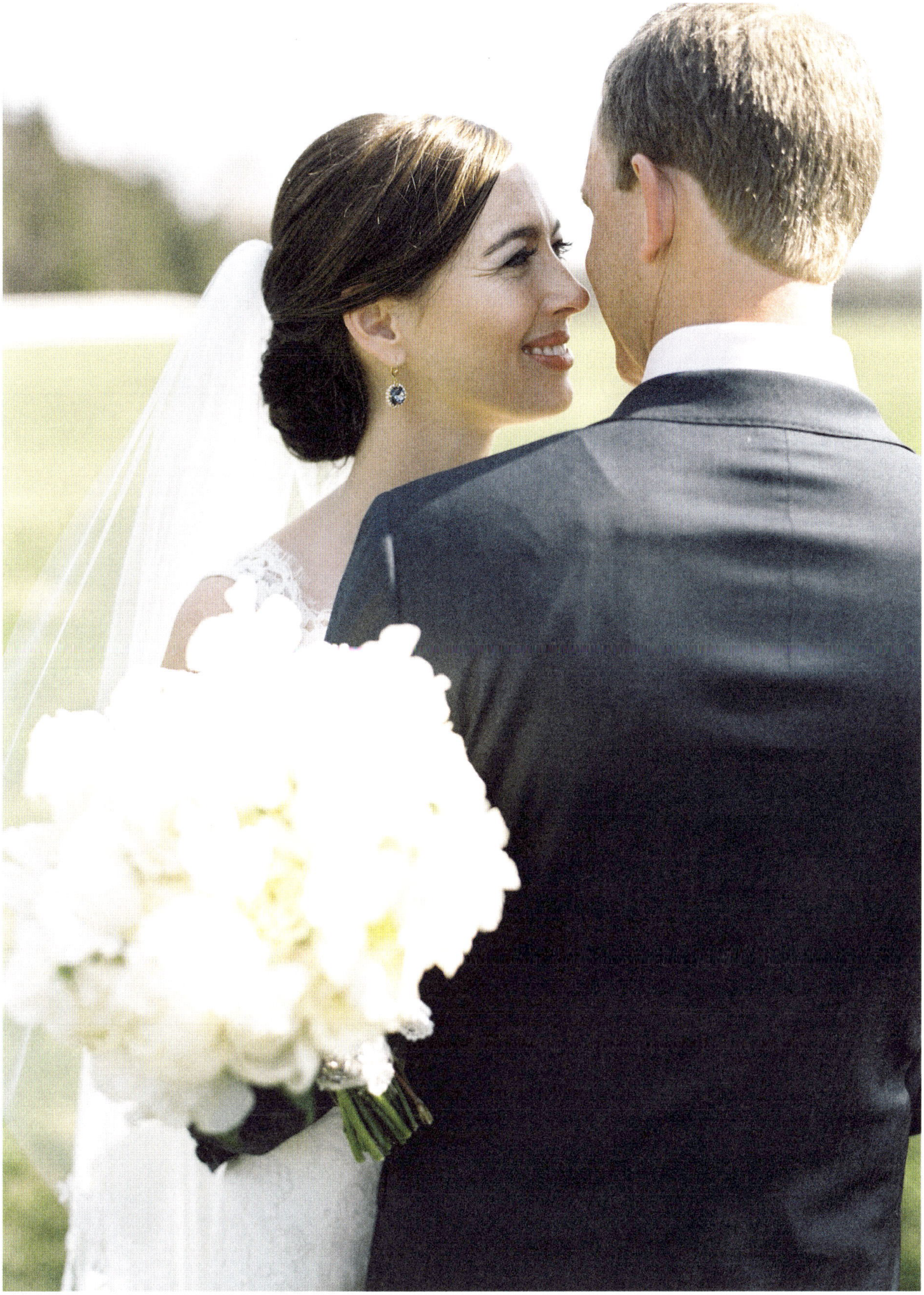

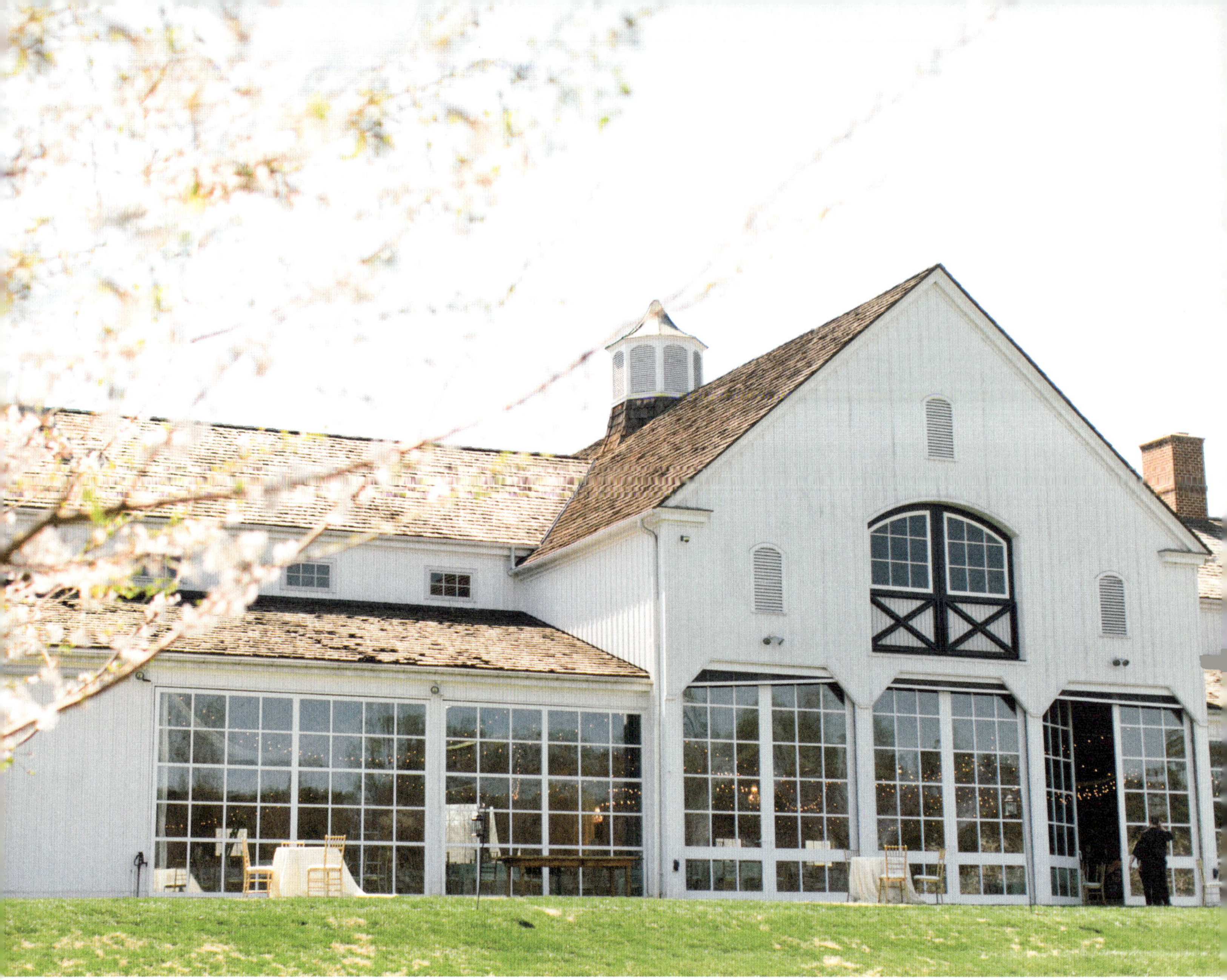

Among so many gorgeous weddings submitted this year, one emerged to win the popular vote and our selection committee couldn't agree more. Sometimes the greatest loves are the ones that take their time. Ellen first met Chris, who was visiting from New York, at a dinner in DC with friends—but it was years of chance meetings before they began to realize there was something more to their friendship.

Finally they decided a long-distance relationship was worth the risk, and soon Chris and Ellen found themselves traveling back and forth across the East Coast to see each other. Two or three times a year, they would return to Chris's alma mater, UVA, where he studied economics and played baseball. In the bold lights of the baseball stadium, Ellen and Chris fell deeper and deeper in love.

Nine years later, they joined hands on the picturesque grounds of Castle Hill Cider to recite their vows and officially declare their lifelong dedication to one another. Ellen, standing in a full lace gown by Alvina Valenta with asymmetrical tiers and a cascade of buttons down the back, couldn't believe how far they'd come.

With its gilded cupola, wide barn doors, latticed

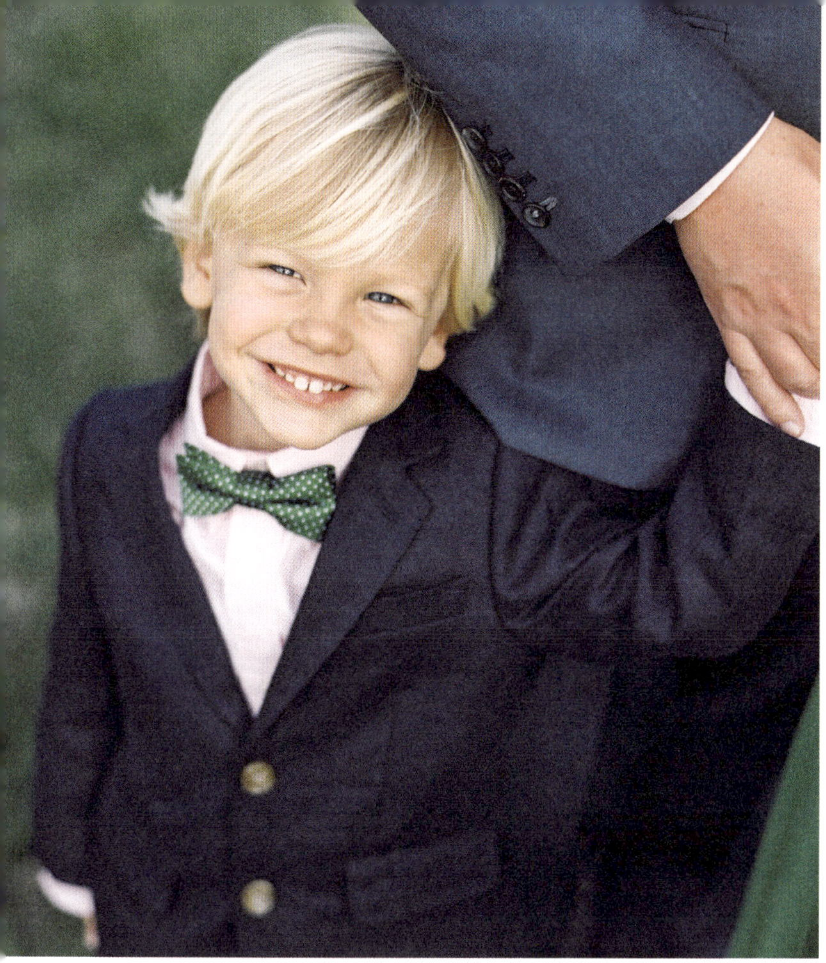
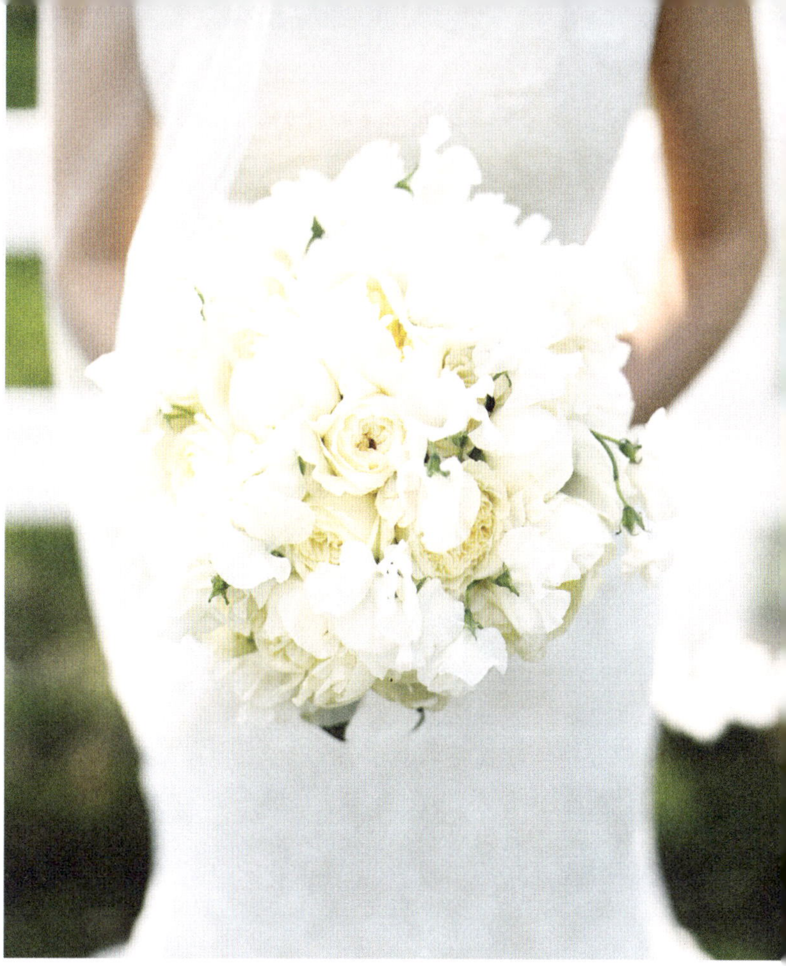
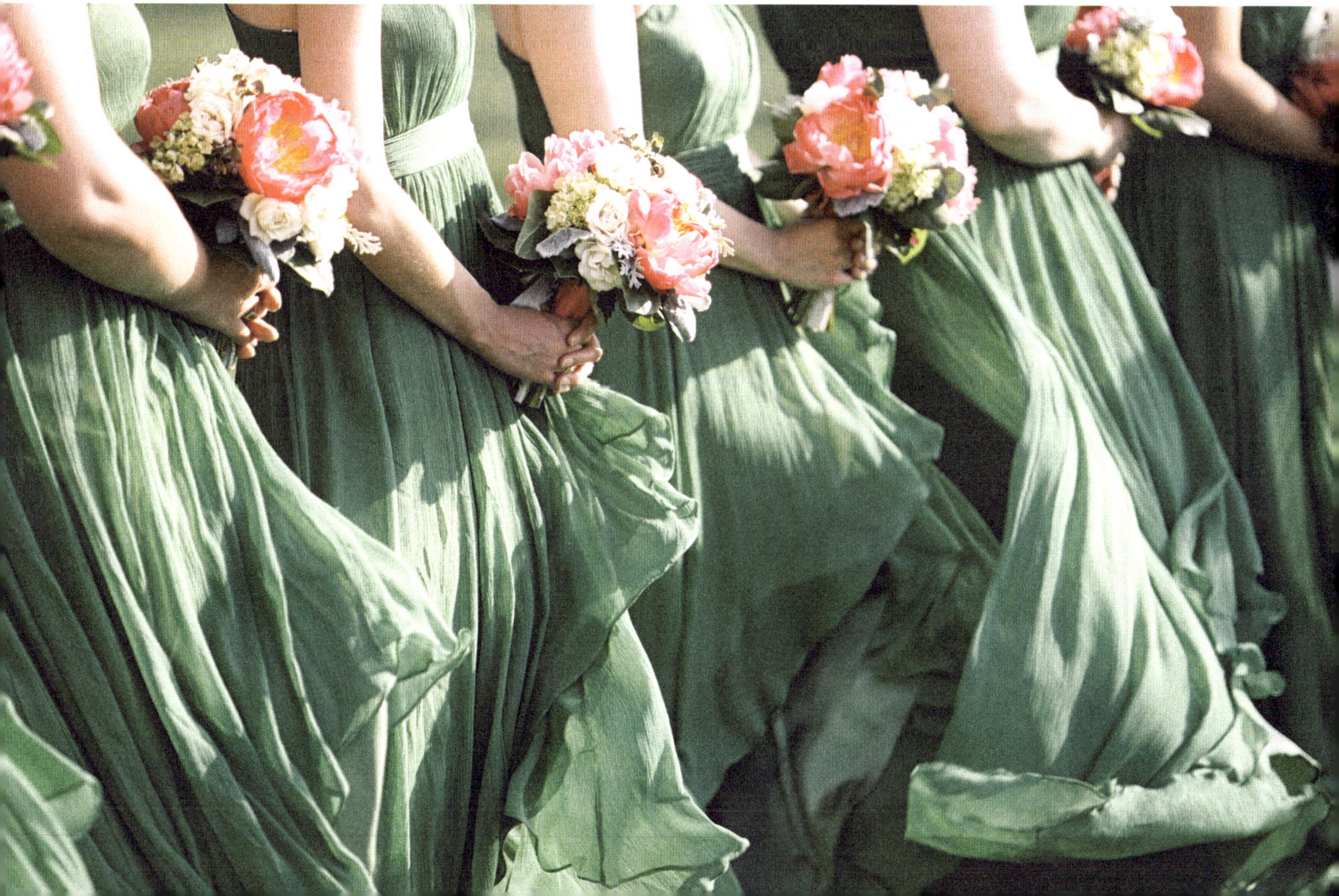

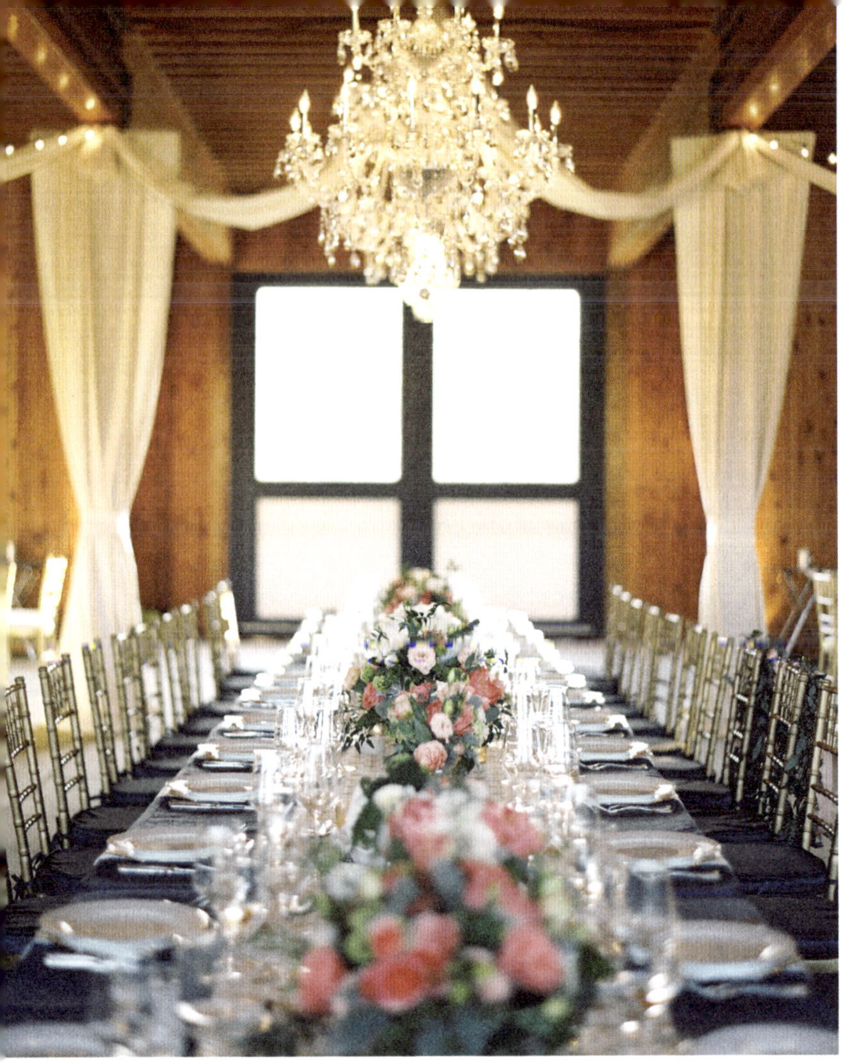

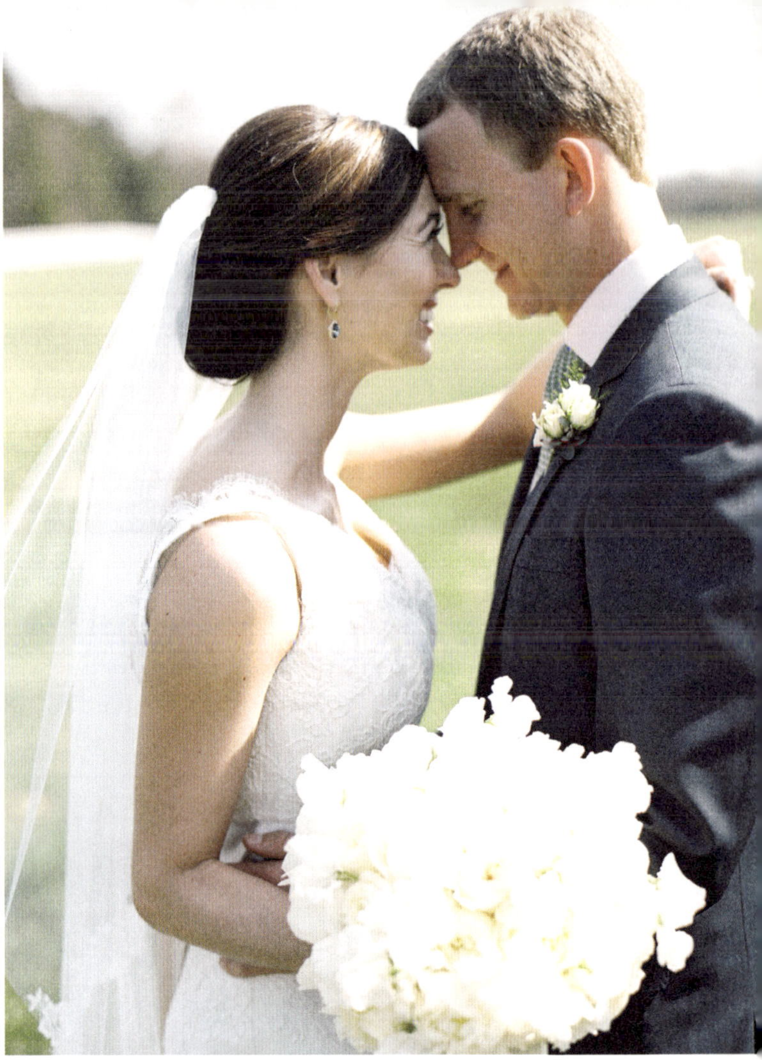

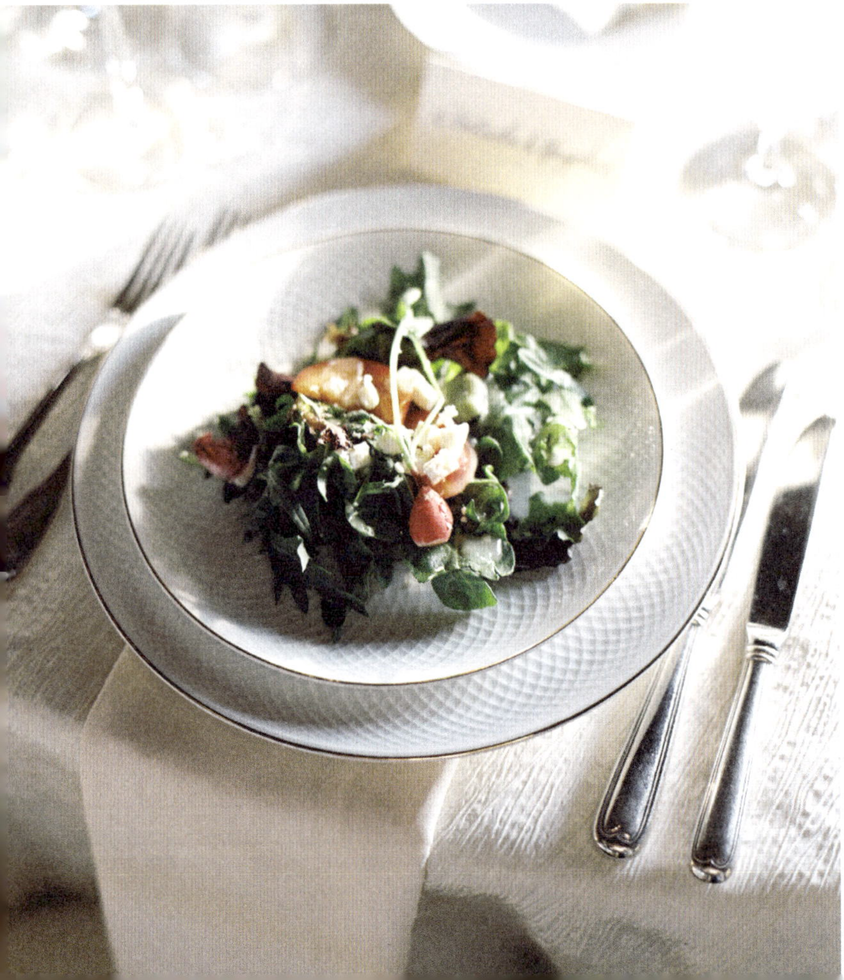

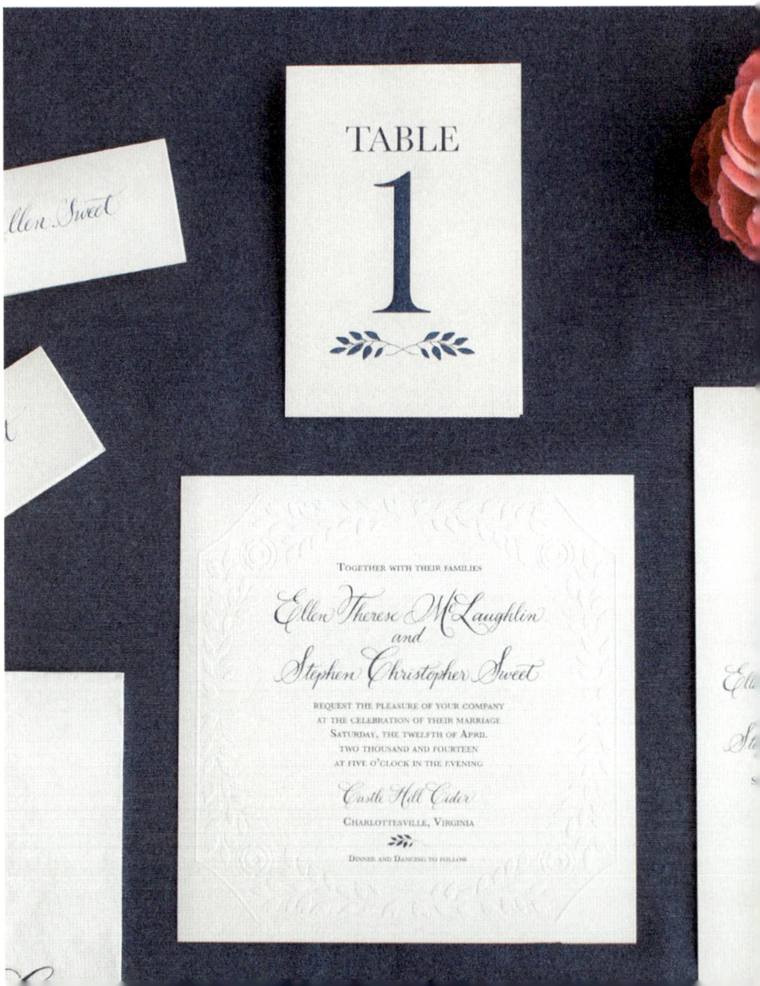
TABLE
1
Together with their families
Ellen Therese McLaughlin
and
Stephen Christopher Sweet
request the pleasure of your company
at the celebration of their marriage
Saturday, the twelfth of April
two thousand and fourteen
at five o'clock in the evening
Castle Hill Cider
Charlottesville, Virginia
Dinner and Dancing to follow

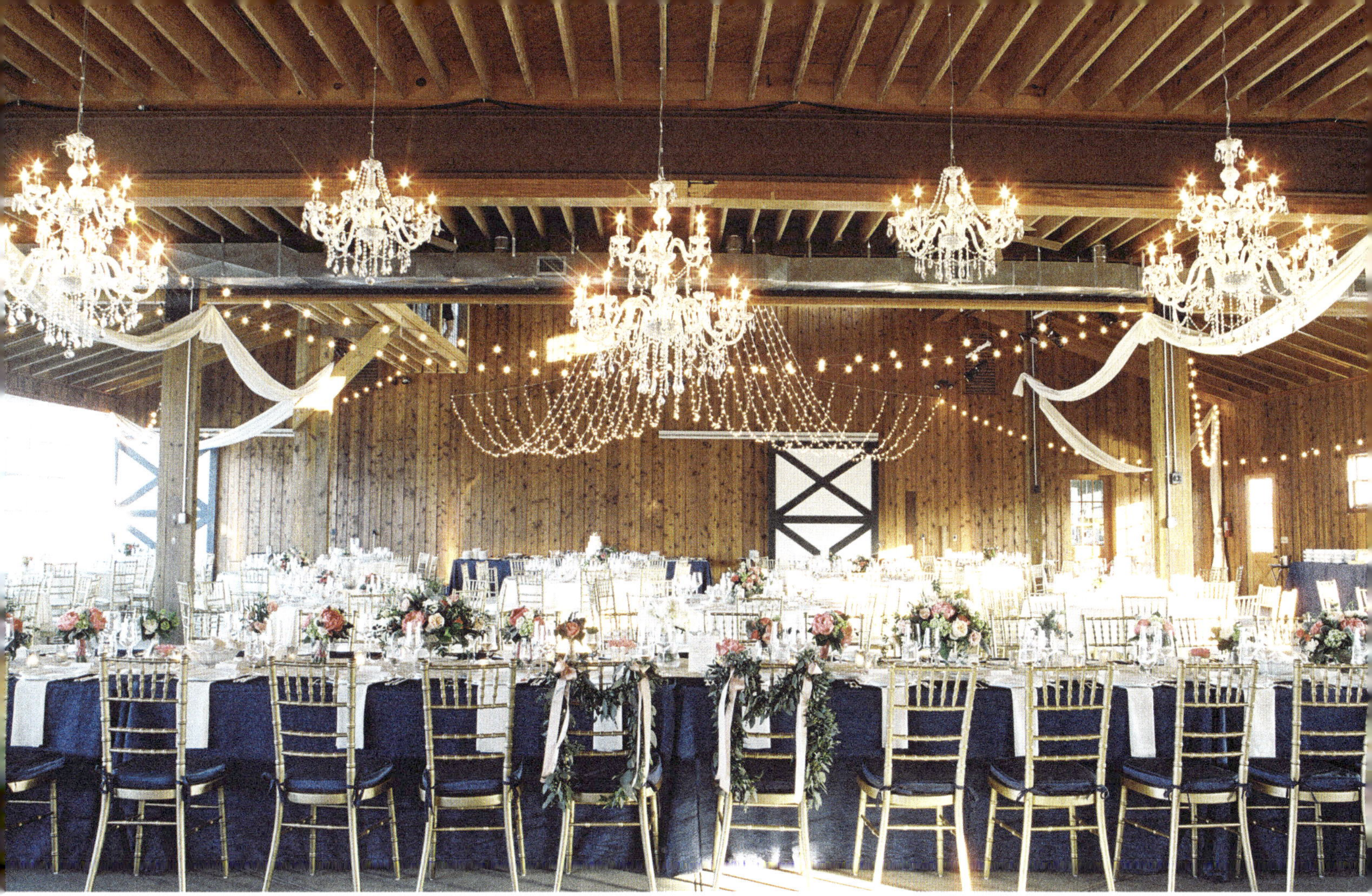

windows and walls of knotty pine, the barn at Castle Hill Cider provided a fabulous backdrop for the celebration of their marriage. In this rustic setting, surrounded by a hanging row of glittering chandeliers they chose themselves, Ellen and Chris shared their first meal as husband and wife.

Every detail reminded them of the places that they loved, from the tiny chicken-and-waffle appetizers from The Catering Outfit reminiscent of Chris's deep Southern roots in Texas to the gift boxes of See's Candies Ellen treasured from her parents' native California. But no memories shined as bright as the times they spent together on the weekend getaways as their romance budded in Virginia.

"It's just so beautiful and meaningful," Ellen said. When you fall in love in a particular place, you also fall in love with the place itself. Ellen and Chris thought a lot about their ties to Virginia and knew they wanted to showcase local artisans and businesses from the Charlottesville area.

From the all-white fondant cake decorated with the four different patterns of their formal china—prepared in a labor of love by Kathy Watkins of Favorite Cakes—to the delicate place settings and invitations designed and printed by Jen Maton of If So Inklined, all the finishing touches shined with the spirit of the Virginia countryside.

Everything brought Ellen and Chris back to those first early days, soon after they started dating, when it seemed like the world around them was suddenly enchanted. There are memories we keep, and memories that grow with us – Ellen and Chris knew that there was no other place where they wanted to begin the memories of their marriage than here, in the majestic foothills of the Blue Ridge Mountains.

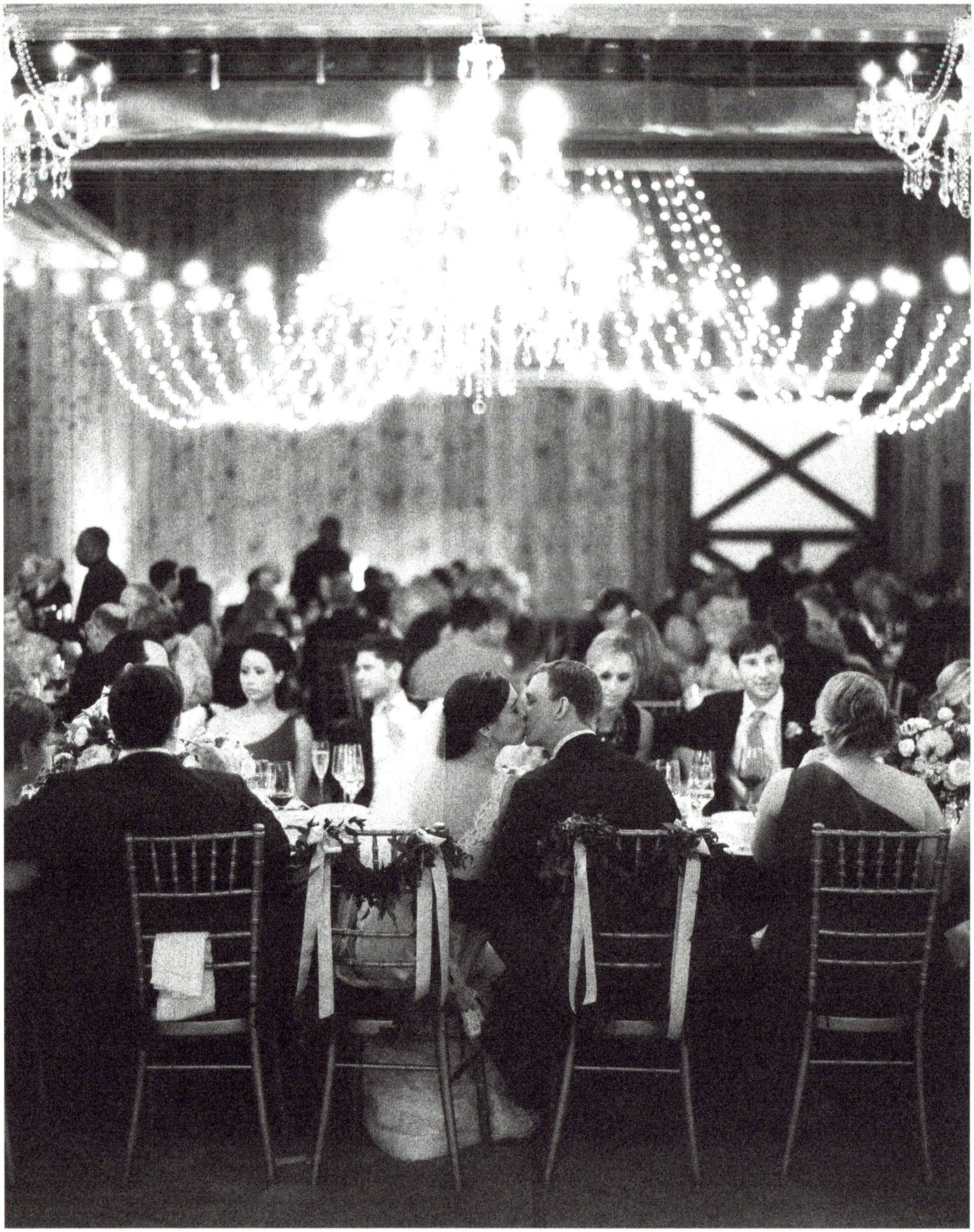

Venue: Castle Hill Cider | **Event Planning and Styling:** Shindig Weddings & Events | **Photographer:** Adam Barnes Photography | **Videographer:** Shaking Hands Productions | **Officiant:** Gay Lee Einstein | **Caterer:** The Catering Outfit | **Cake:** Favorite Cakes | **Florist**: Southern Blooms by Pat's Floral Designs | **Rental Companies:** Festive Fare, Southern Blooms by Pat's Floral Designs, Stonegate Event Rentals | **AV and Lighting Company:** Blue Ridge AV & Lighting | **Stationary:** If So Inklined | **Bridal Dress:** Alvina Valenta | **Jeweler:** Custom from I. Friedman & Son | **Beauty and Hair Stylist:** Virginia Glenn | **Transportation:** Camryn Limousine | **Ceremony Music:** Encore Quartet | **Cocktail Hour and Reception Music:** Liquid Pleasure

Portfolios

PIPPIN HILL FARM
& vineyards

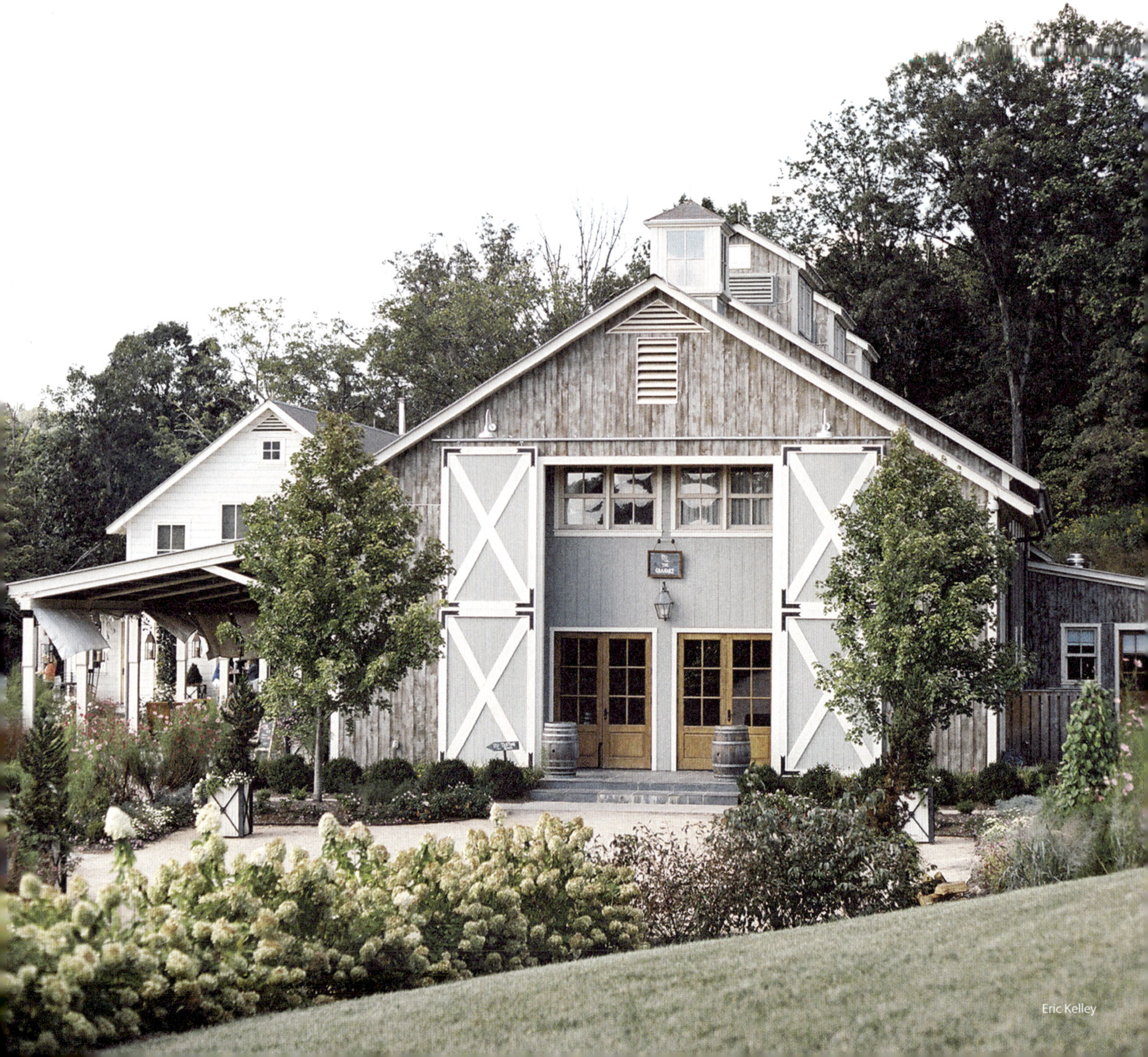

Eric Kelley

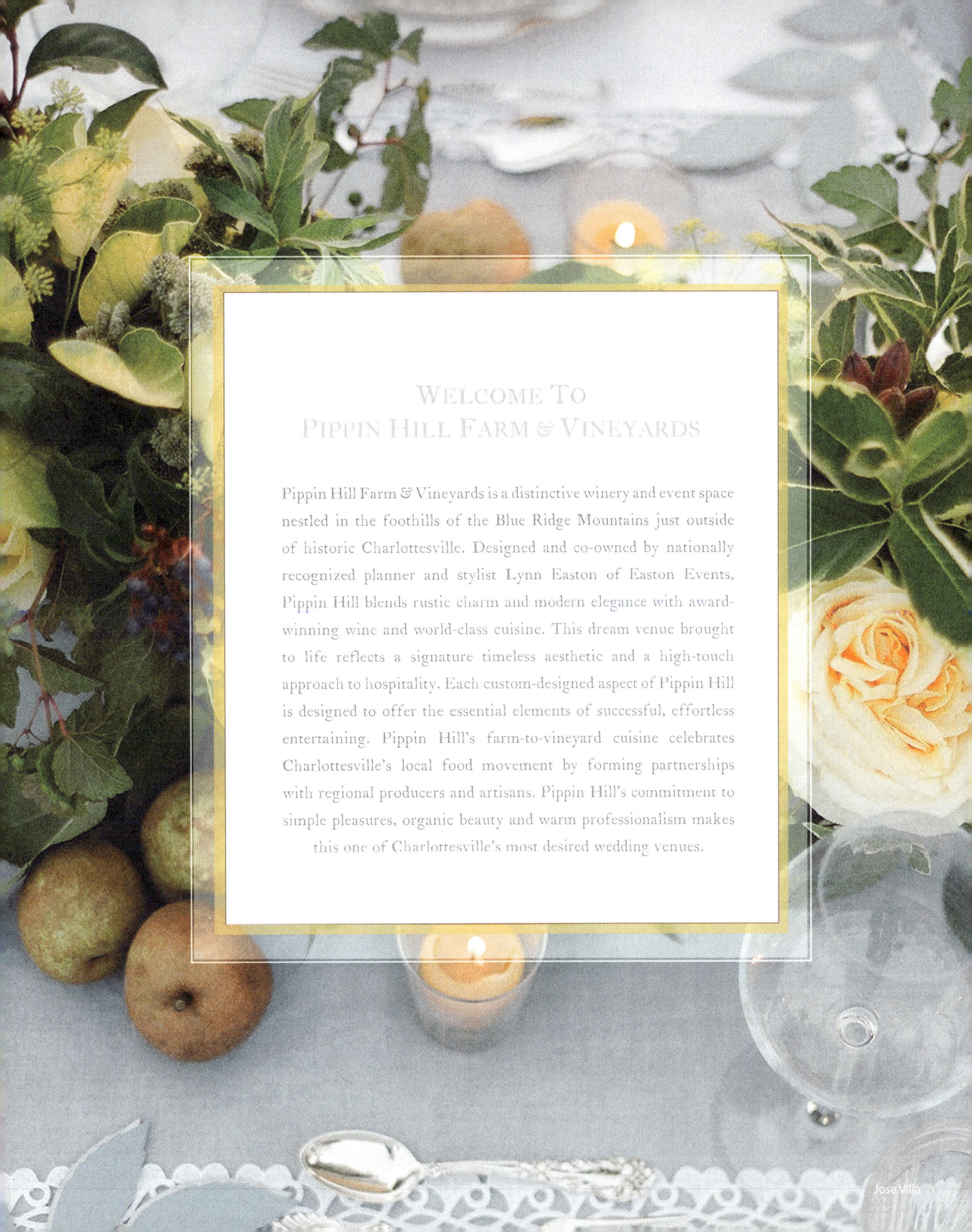

Welcome To Pippin Hill Farm & Vineyards

Pippin Hill Farm & Vineyards is a distinctive winery and event space nestled in the foothills of the Blue Ridge Mountains just outside of historic Charlottesville. Designed and co-owned by nationally recognized planner and stylist Lynn Easton of Easton Events, Pippin Hill blends rustic charm and modern elegance with award-winning wine and world-class cuisine. This dream venue brought to life reflects a signature timeless aesthetic and a high-touch approach to hospitality. Each custom-designed aspect of Pippin Hill is designed to offer the essential elements of successful, effortless entertaining. Pippin Hill's farm-to-vineyard cuisine celebrates Charlottesville's local food movement by forming partnerships with regional producers and artisans. Pippin Hill's commitment to simple pleasures, organic beauty and warm professionalism makes this one of Charlottesville's most desired wedding venues.

Jose Villa

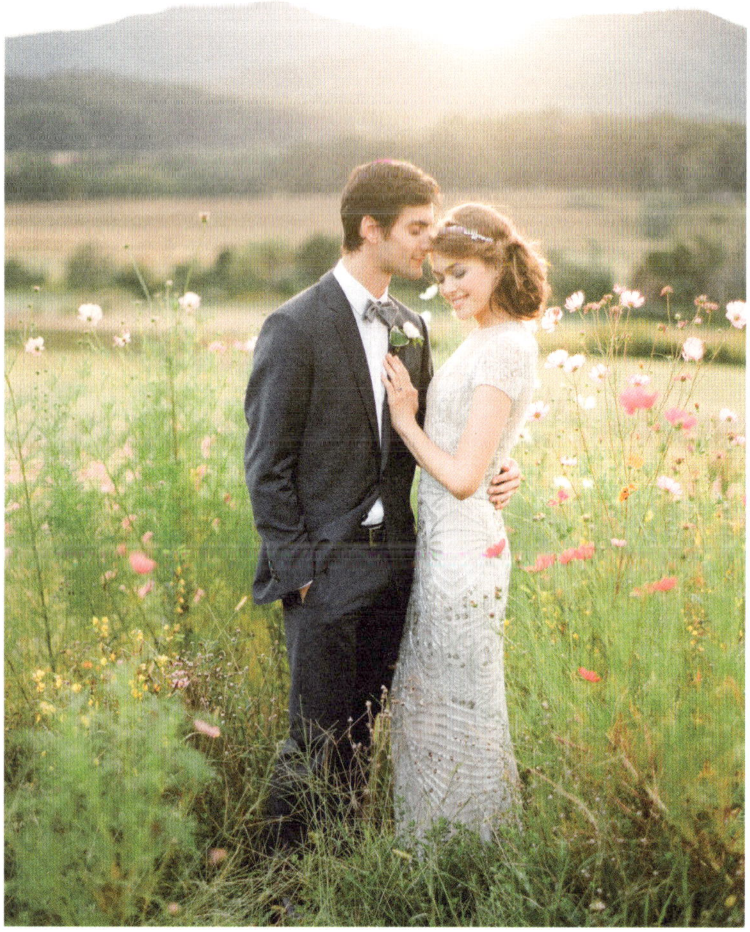

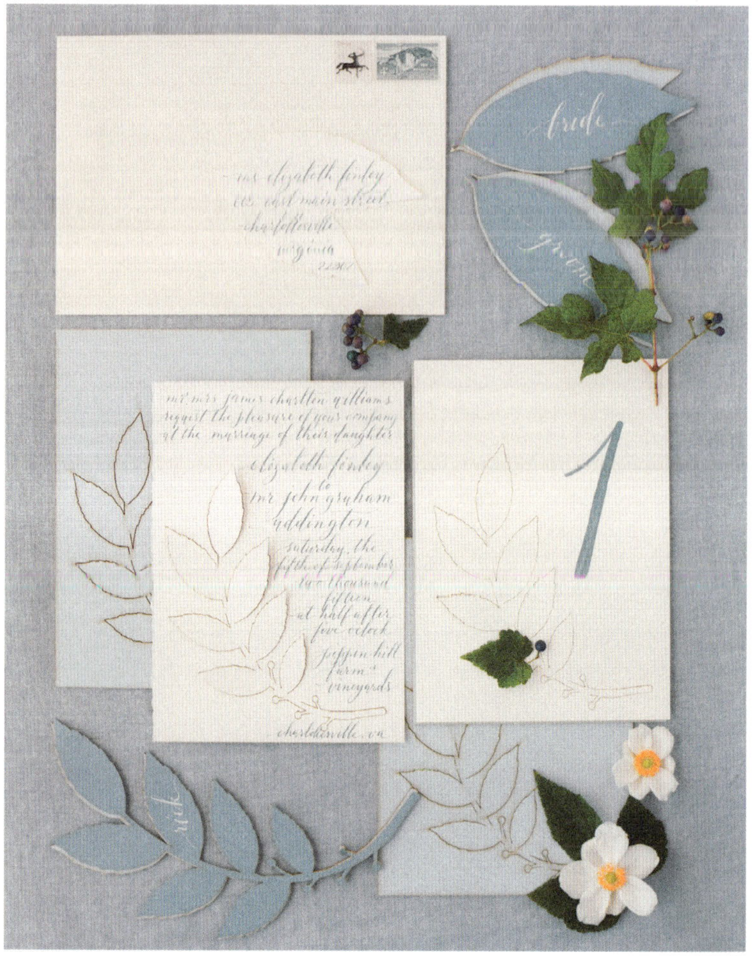

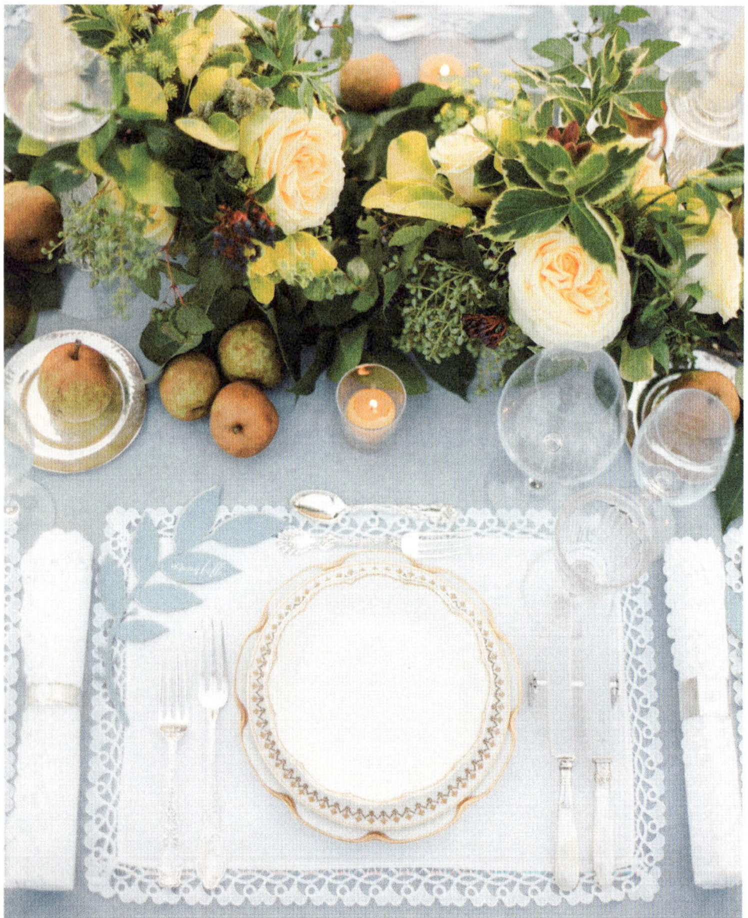

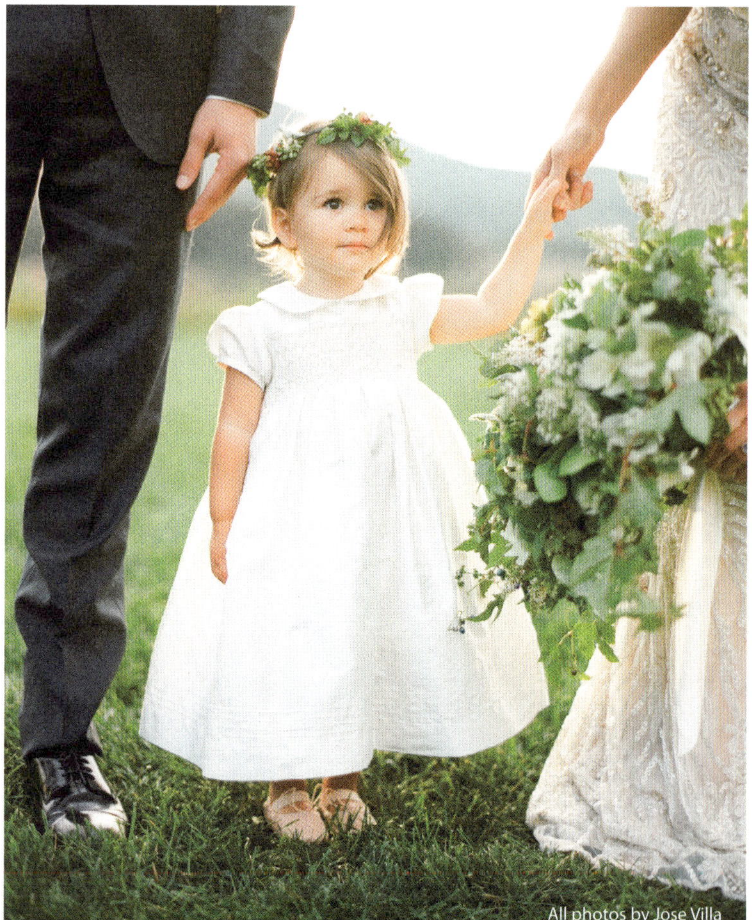

All photos by Jose Villa

Named Top 50 Most Romantic Venues
by BRIDES MAGAZINE

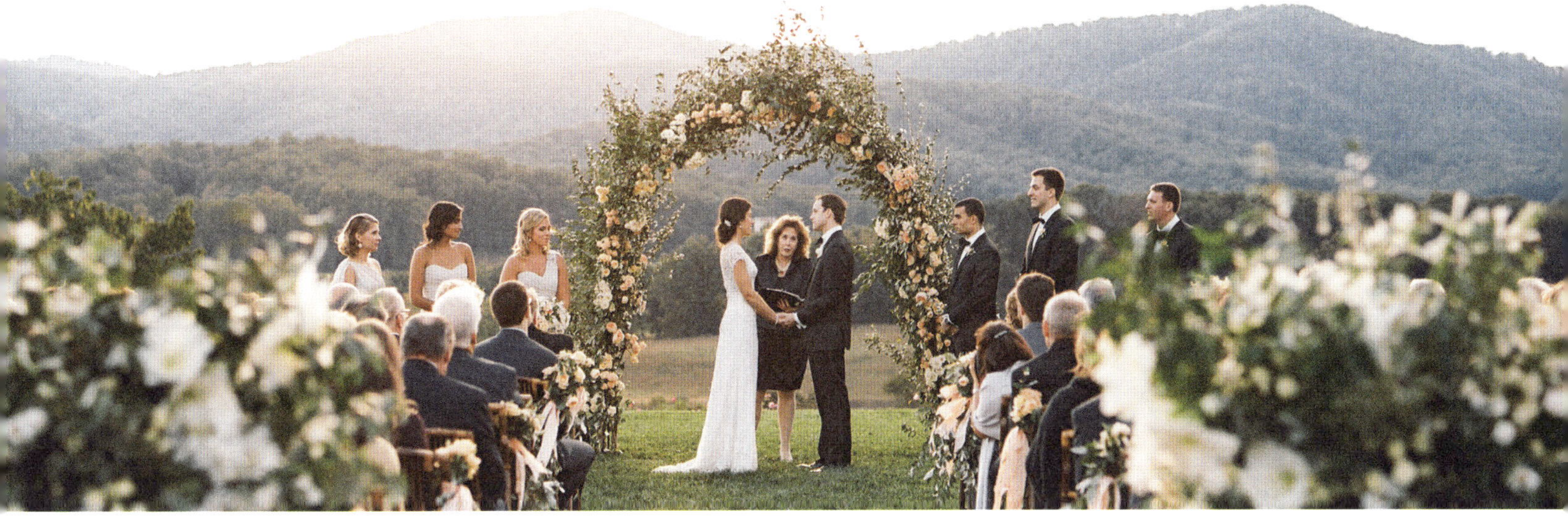

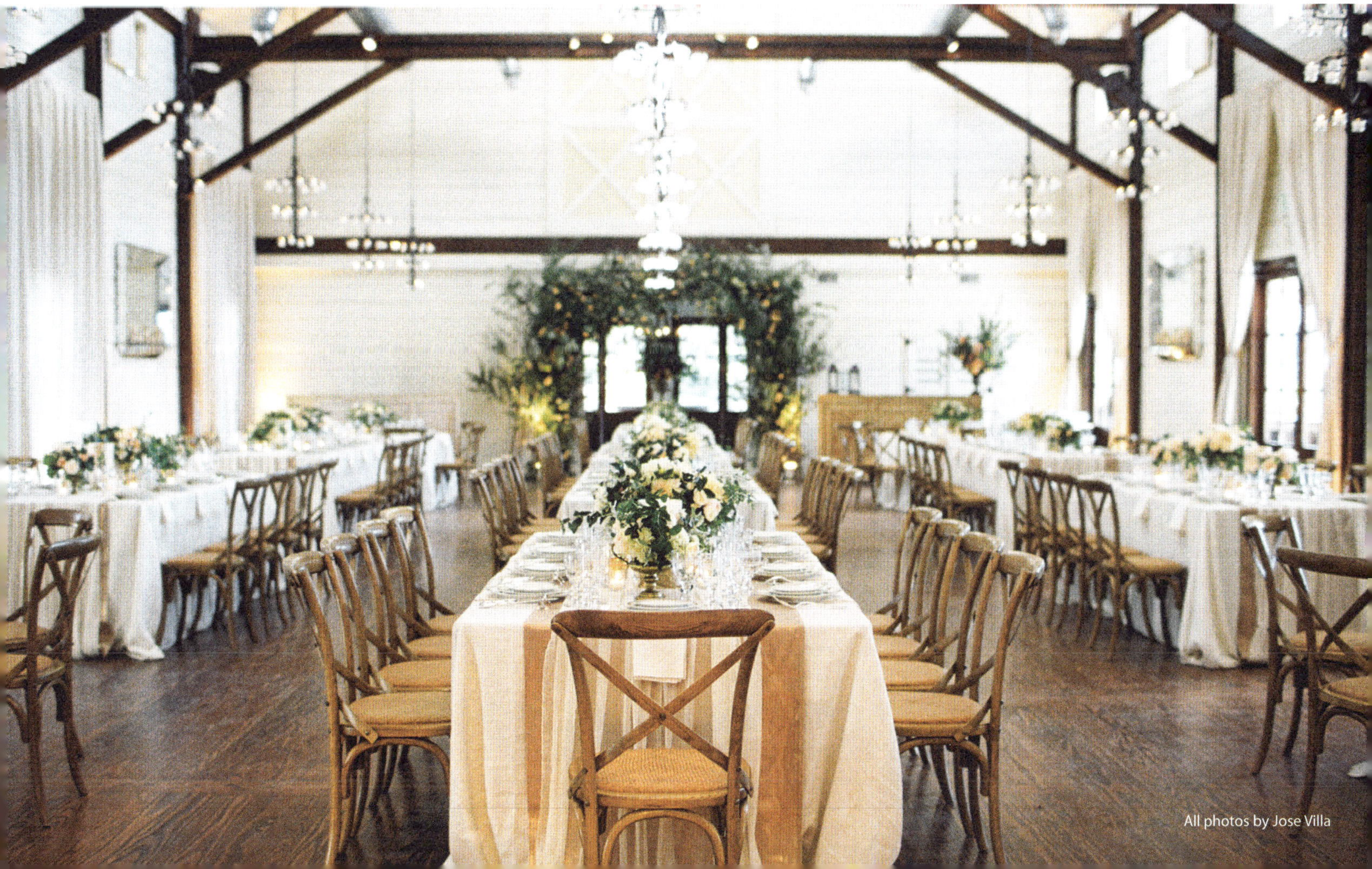

All photos by Jose Villa

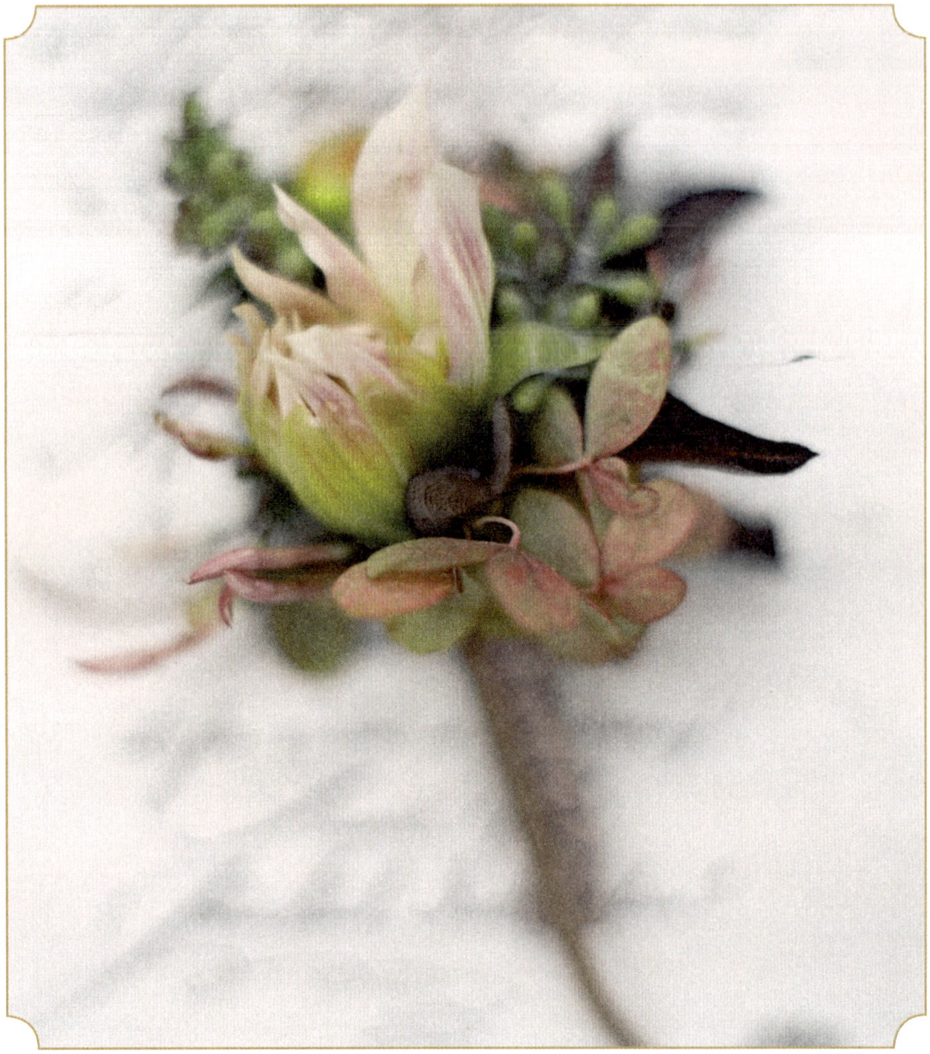

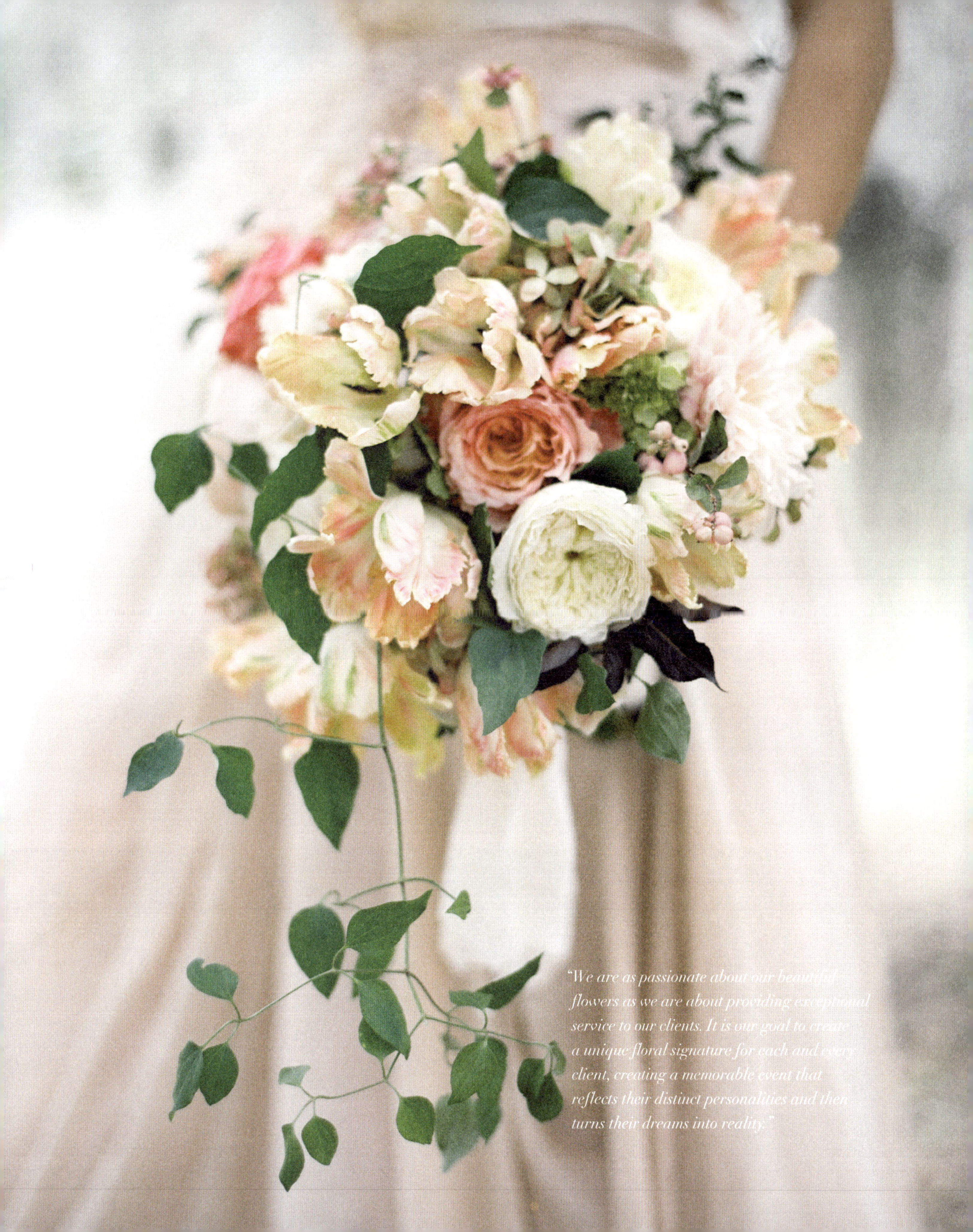

"We are as passionate about our beautiful flowers as we are about providing exceptional service to our clients. It is our goal to create a unique floral signature for each and every client, creating a memorable event that reflects their distinct personalities and then turns their dreams into reality."

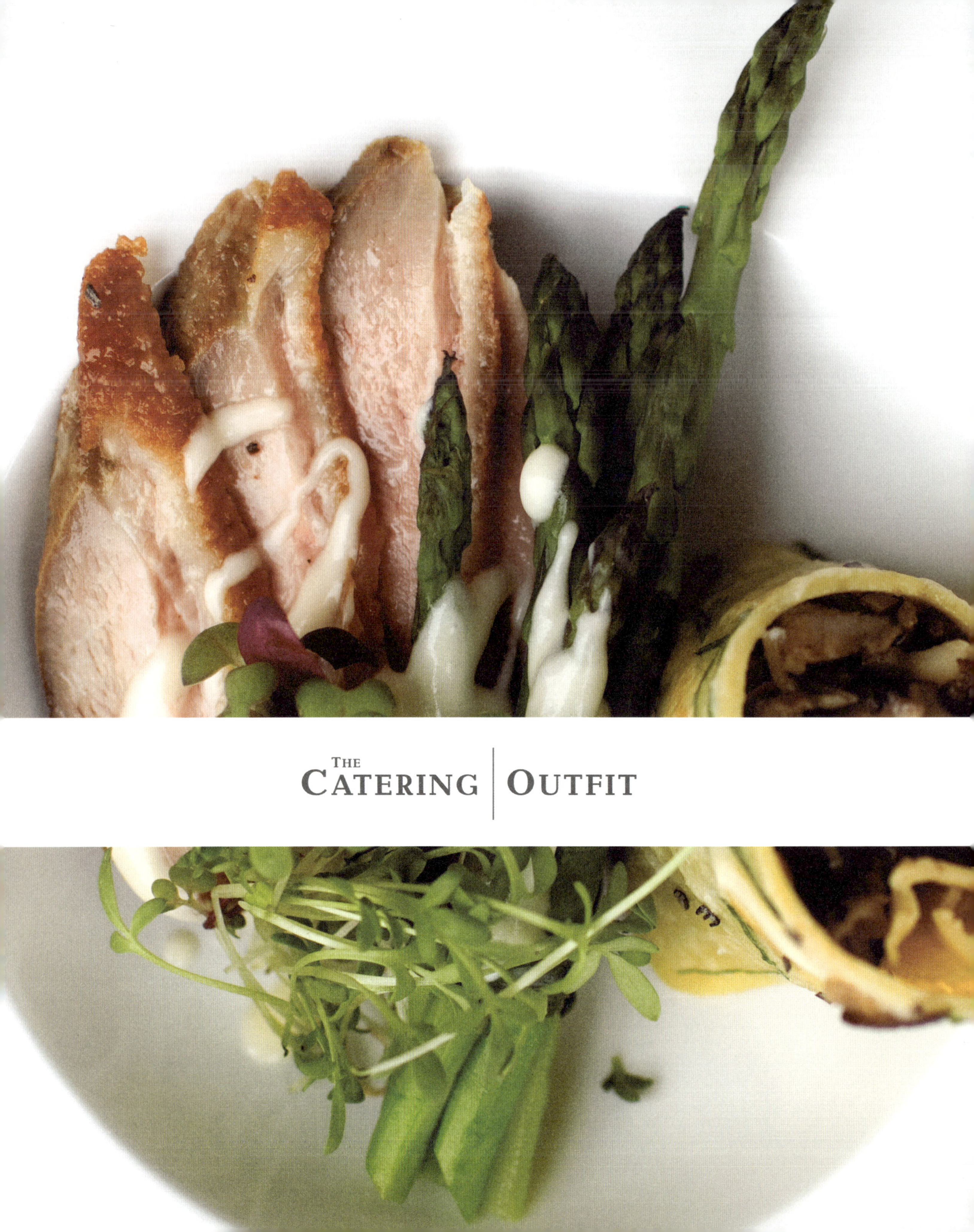
THE
CATERING | OUTFIT

The Catering Outfit was founded in 1999 by Walter TX Slawski. Extensive travel in Europe, Australia, Africa and Central America ignited a passion not only for exquisite culinary experiences but also a desire to resurrect the impossible magnificence of colonial entertaining. After graduating from The University of Virginia, Walter embarked on a different sort of travel: creation of a unique outfit specializing in craft cuisine and production. Seasonally available, locally sourced and visually stunning ingredients are only part of what we do. We believe in the old adage "it takes a village to throw a wedding," and we have carefully chosen our village. Working with the finest local industry talent and venues, we travel the path from engaged to forever with our clients, creating an exciting planning experience worthy of the final production.

Almost exclusively serving only one wedding client a day or even weekend remains the bedrock of our philosophy. Our culinary offerings prepared in collaboration with our clients and planners consider overall vision and are designed to make sense. We refuse to dilute our talents. We maintain impeccable service standards and bring a la carte quality cuisine to the catered platform. Our events are featured regularly in regional and national publications as a direct result of our desire to accept the challenge of your unique wedding.

PASSION. DEDICATION. HUNGER.

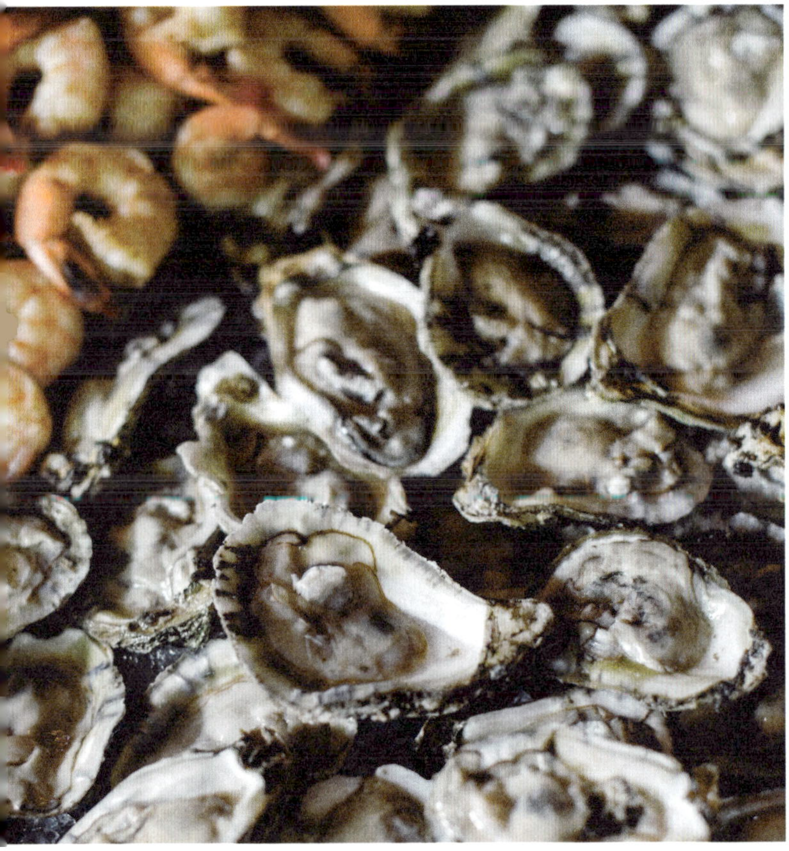
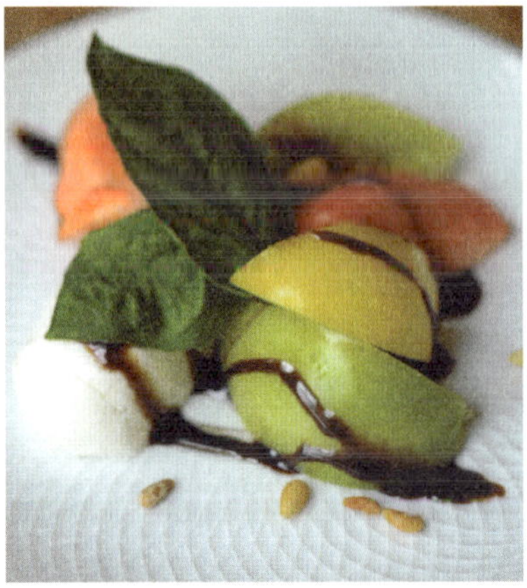
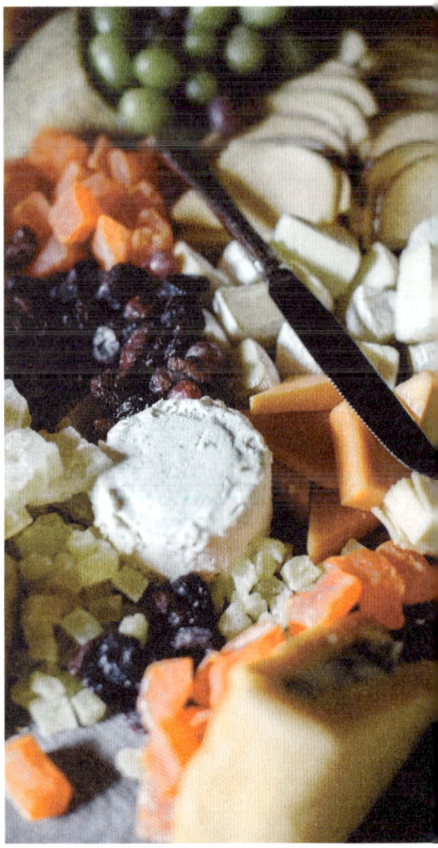
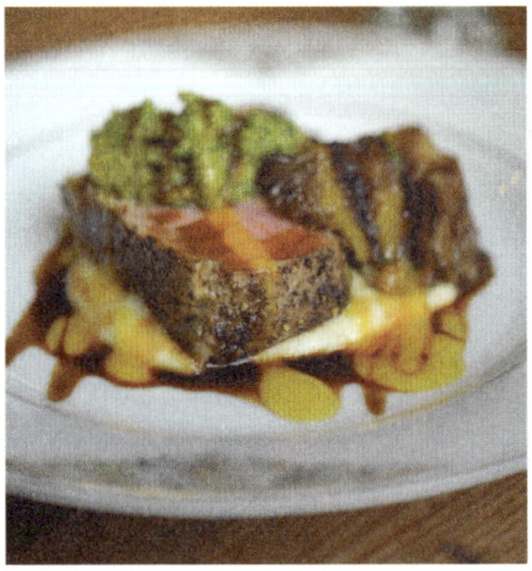

"Thank you so much! Everyone raved about the food - both the appetizers during cocktail hour and the dinner buffet – all night at the wedding. We're continuing to hear positive feedback from family and friends too. All in all, it was exactly what Andy and I were looking for and, on a personal note, we loved the staff and bartenders who made the night even more fun!"

– Lisa and Andy

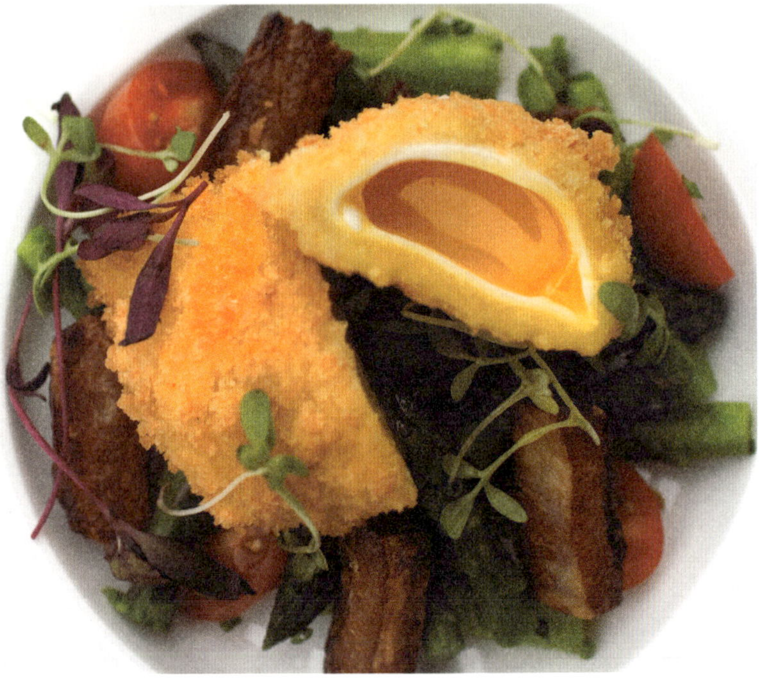
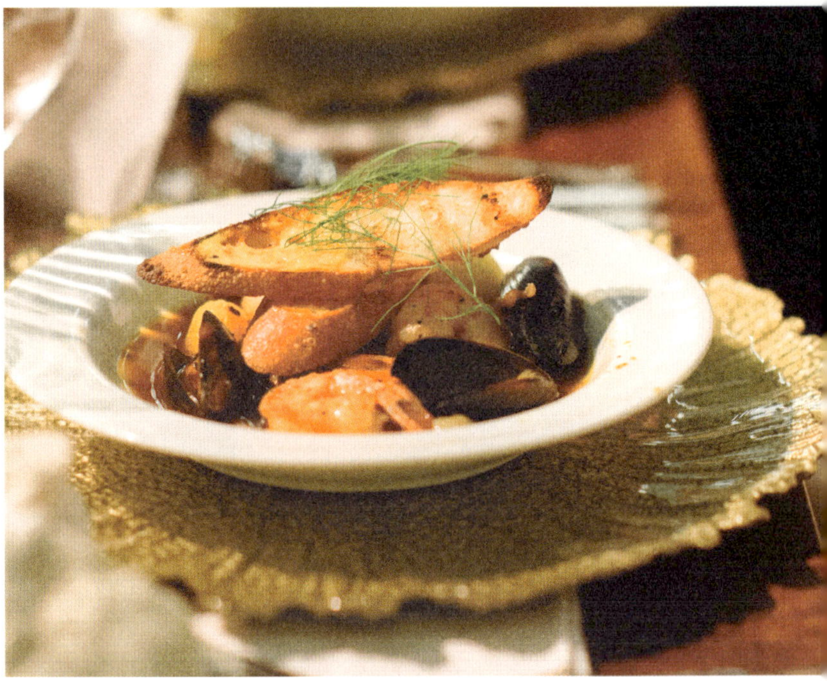

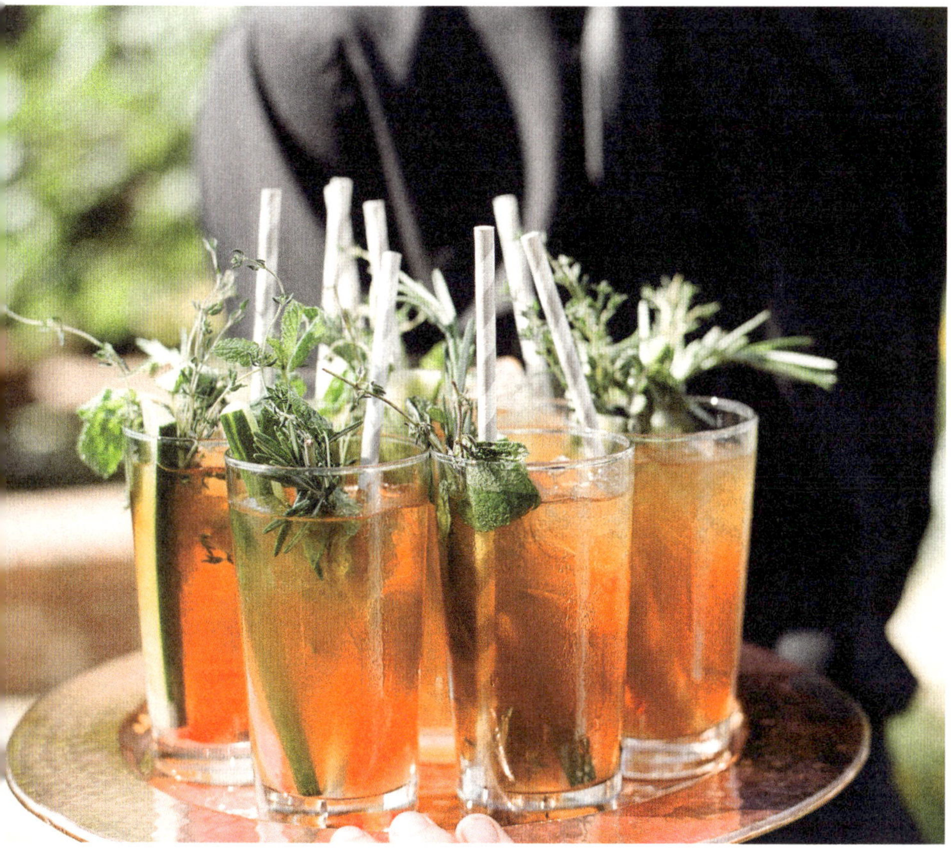
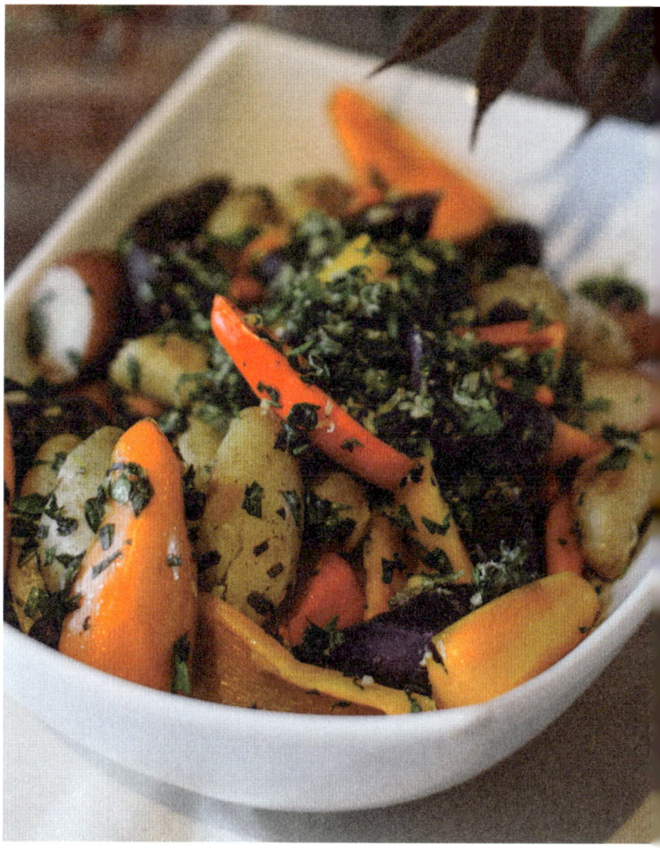

THE
CATERING | OUTFIT

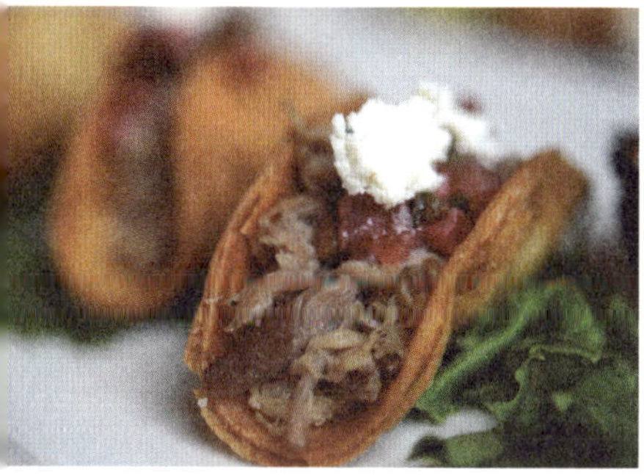
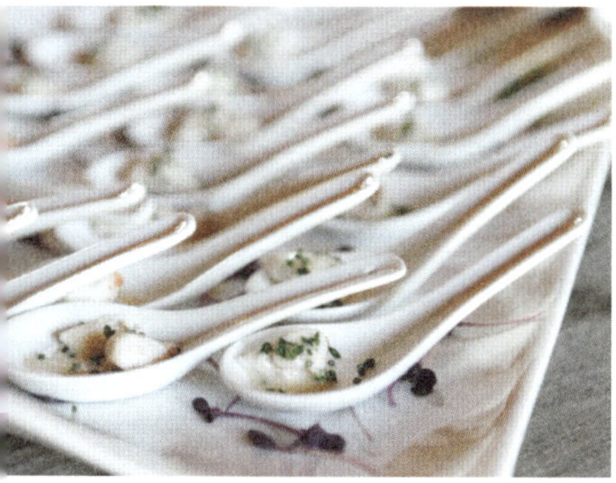
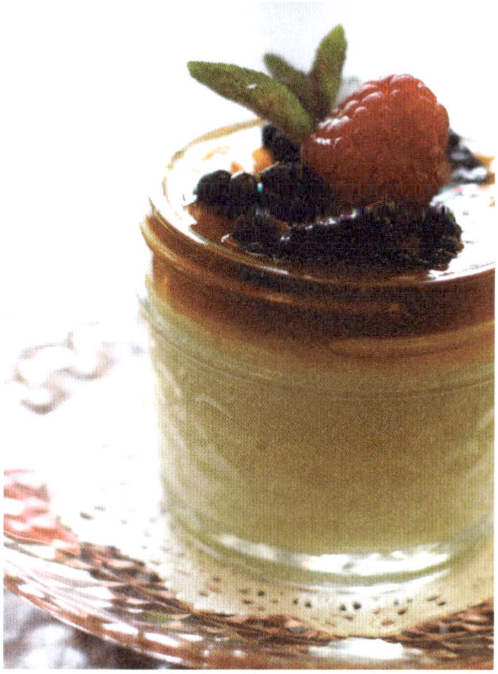
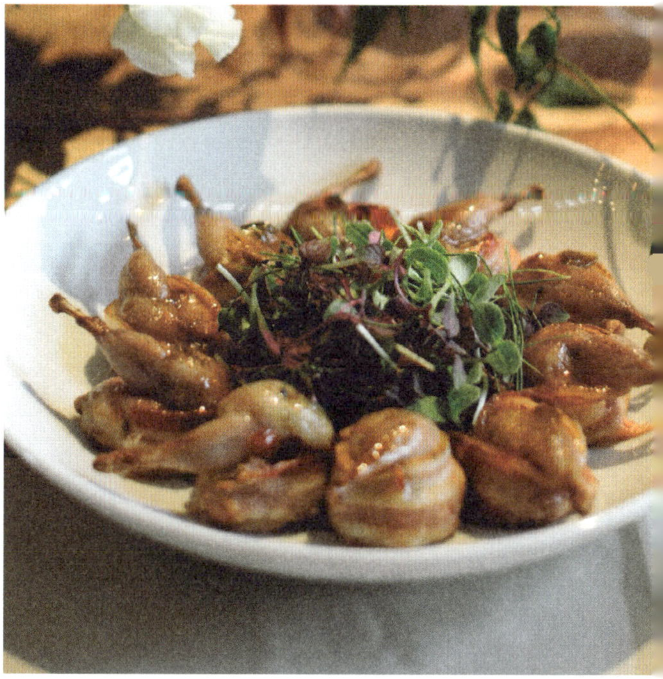

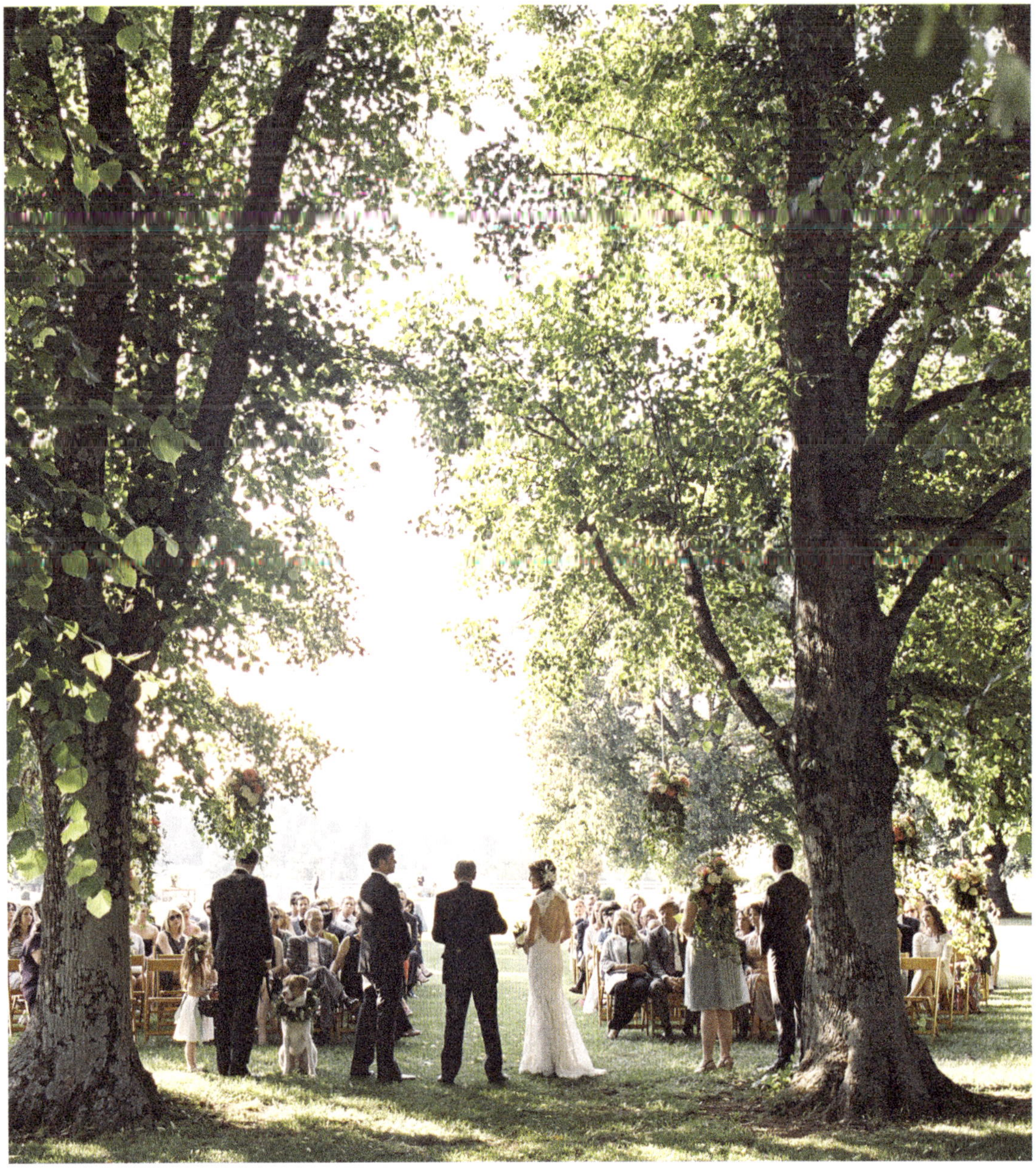

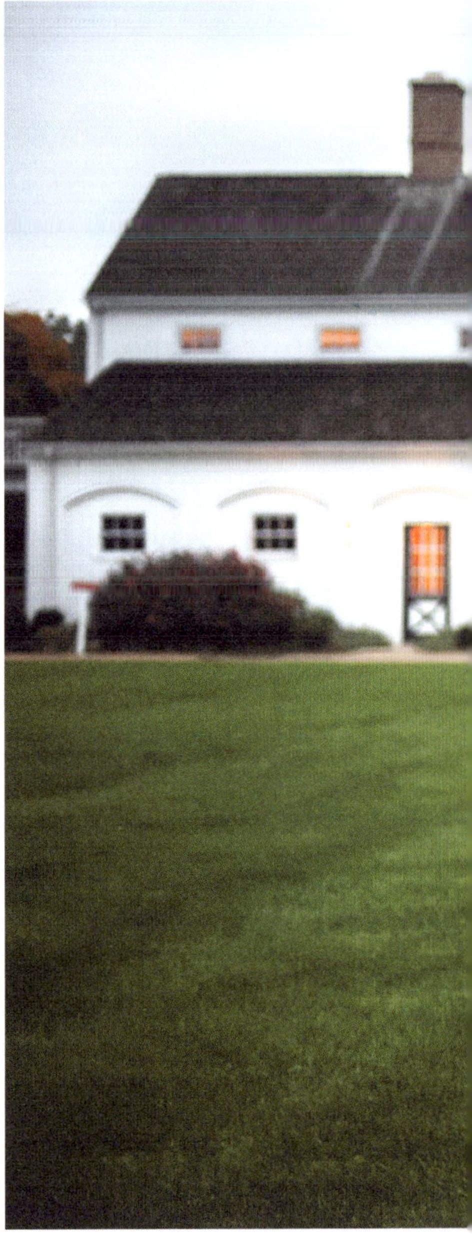

Make history at one of Virginia's most romantic settings.

Located in Keswick's horse country just miles from Charlottesville. Castle Hill Cider's many indoor and outdoor sites offer endless possibilities from the intimate to the incredible. The Cidery Barn shares the crest of a verdant knoll with a linden tree grove. Artfully arranged below are apple orchards, a two-acre lake and custom-designed pergolas framing beautifully terraced lawns perfectly suited for lawn games during cocktail hour.

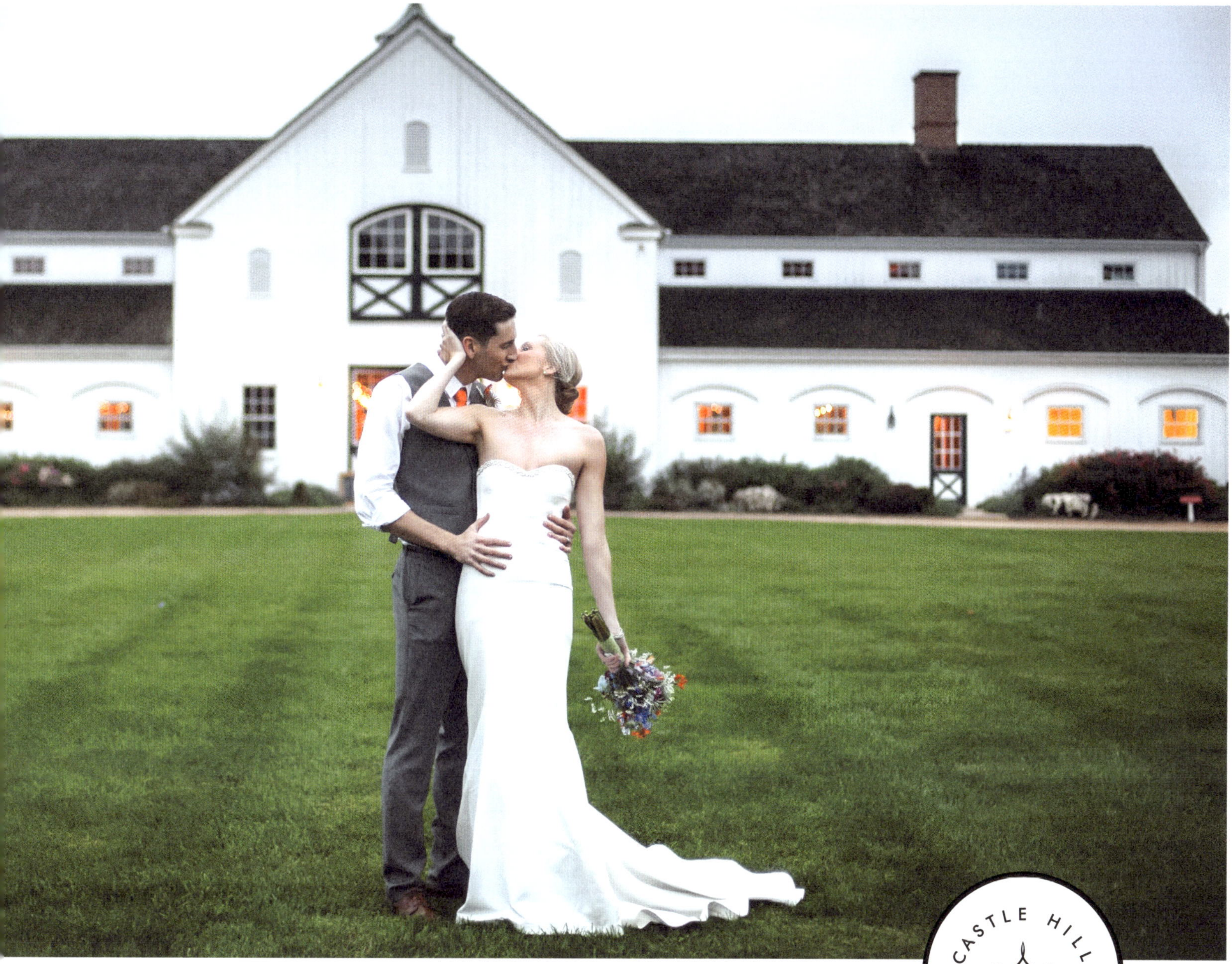

Elizabeth WOODSON

After decades spent in Manhattan art directing national food magazines, Food & Wine and Eating Well, I've returned to my native Virginia and refocused my design expertise and passion for food on creating exceptional, artfully tailored gift baskets.

ELIZABETHWOODSON.COM

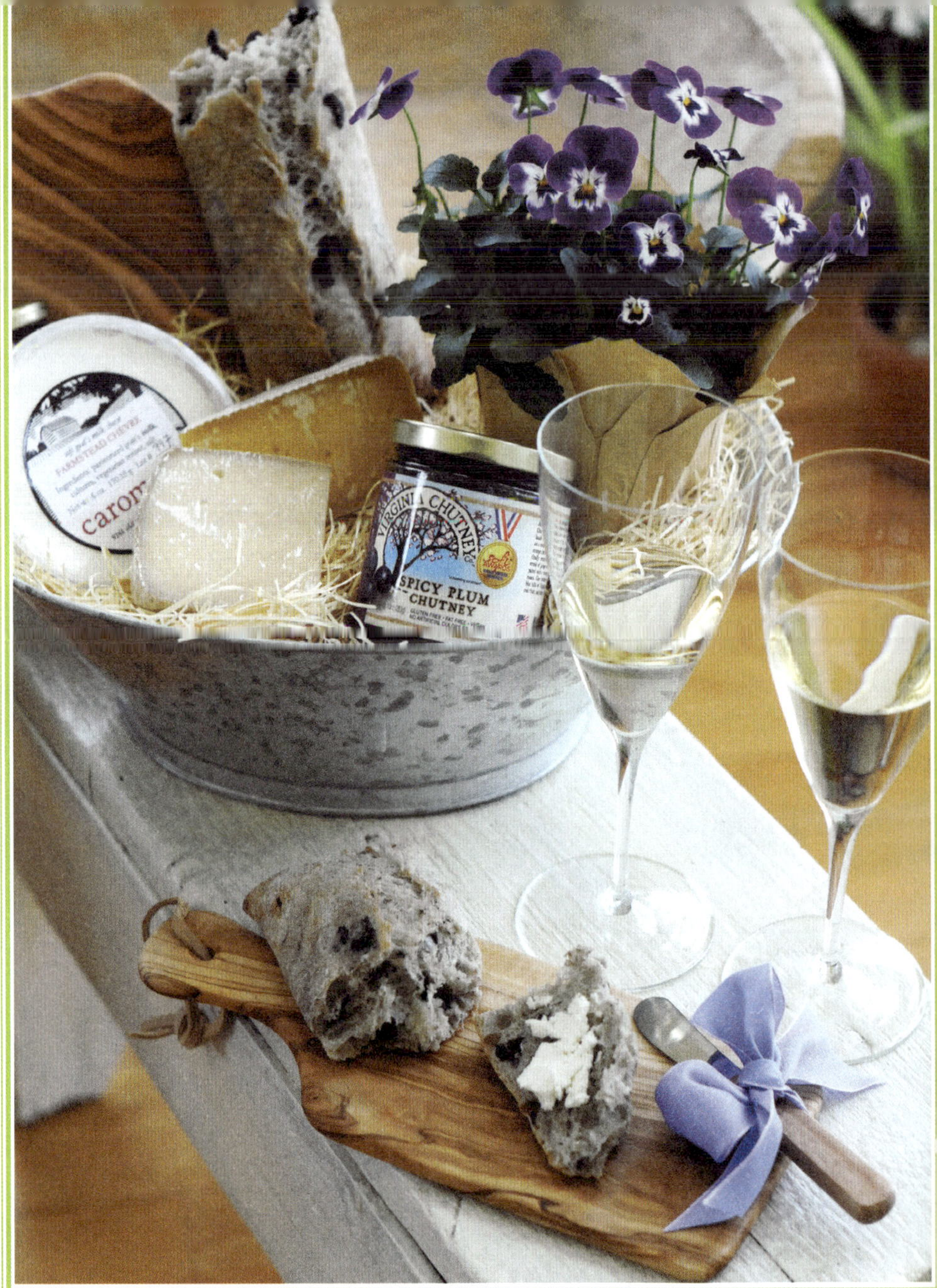

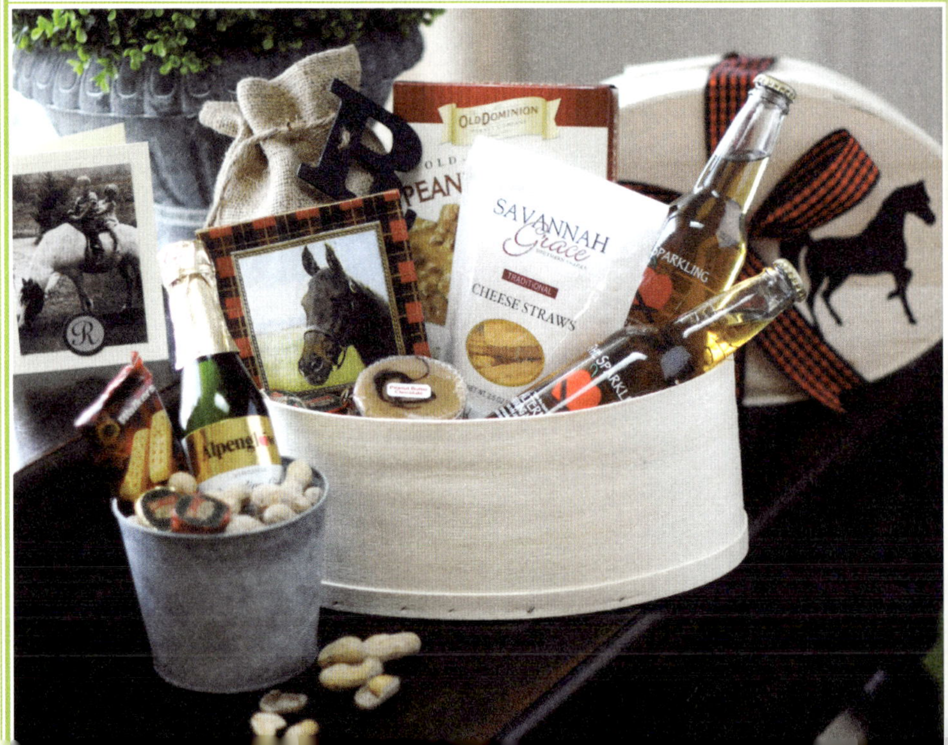

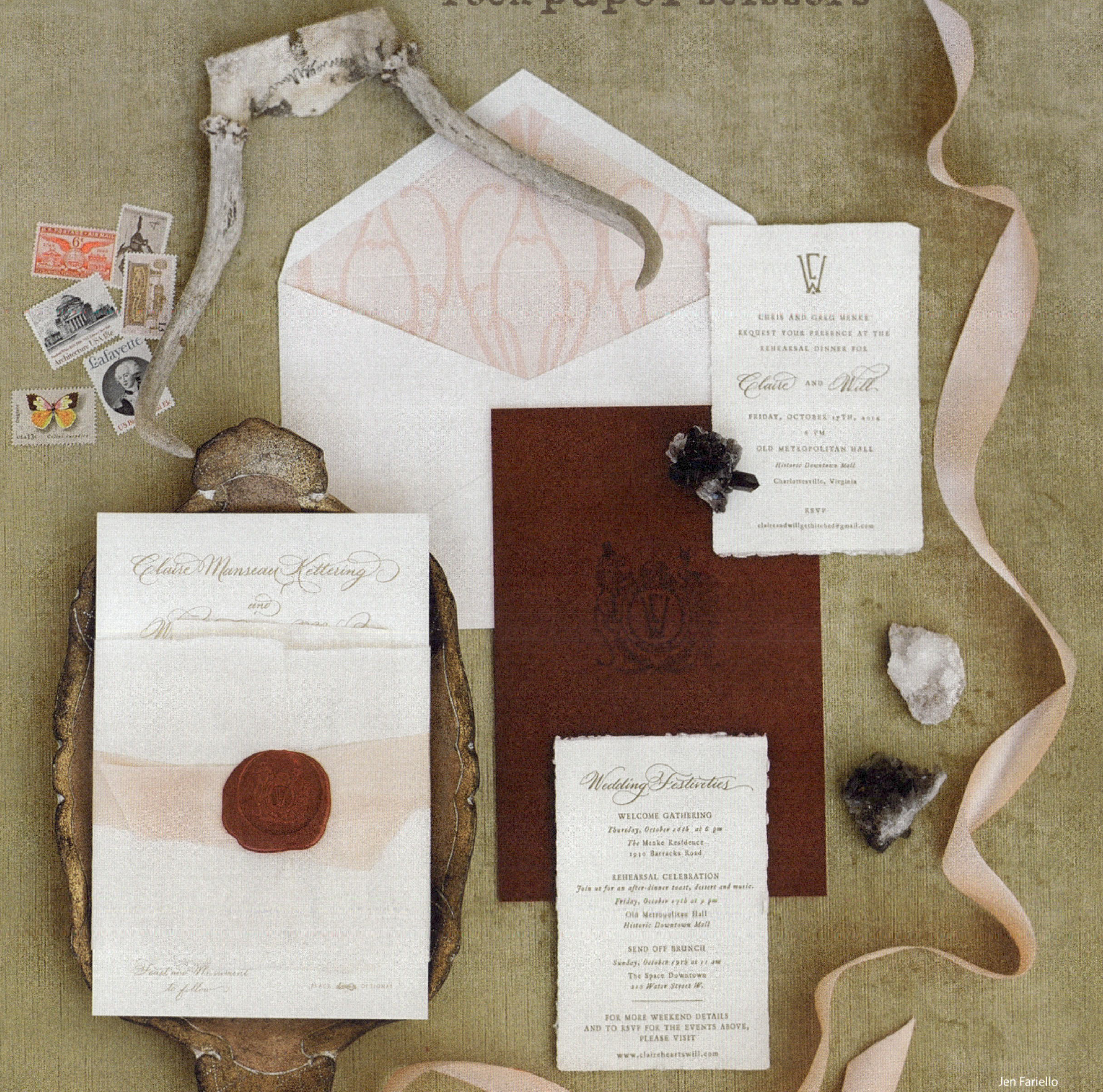

Jen Fariello

Co-owners and friends Heather Haynie and Dani Antol took over the RPS helm in 2010. Heather heads up the retail side of the business and also works closely with brides who order from their many custom albums (such as Arzberger, Haute Papier, and Page Stationery, to name a few). She helps clients navigate the etiquette waters, word-smithing even the most challenging situations. Consider her like a project manager, helping you stay on time and on budget. Her counterpart, Dani, is the creative director and lead designer who thrives on branding weddings. She is able to translate a bride's vision onto paper with stunning detail, creating a luxurious suite that is uniquely theirs. Many of her designs have been featured in *Martha Stewart Weddings, The Knot, Southern Weddings,* and *Weddings Unveiled* magazines, not to mention countless blogs!

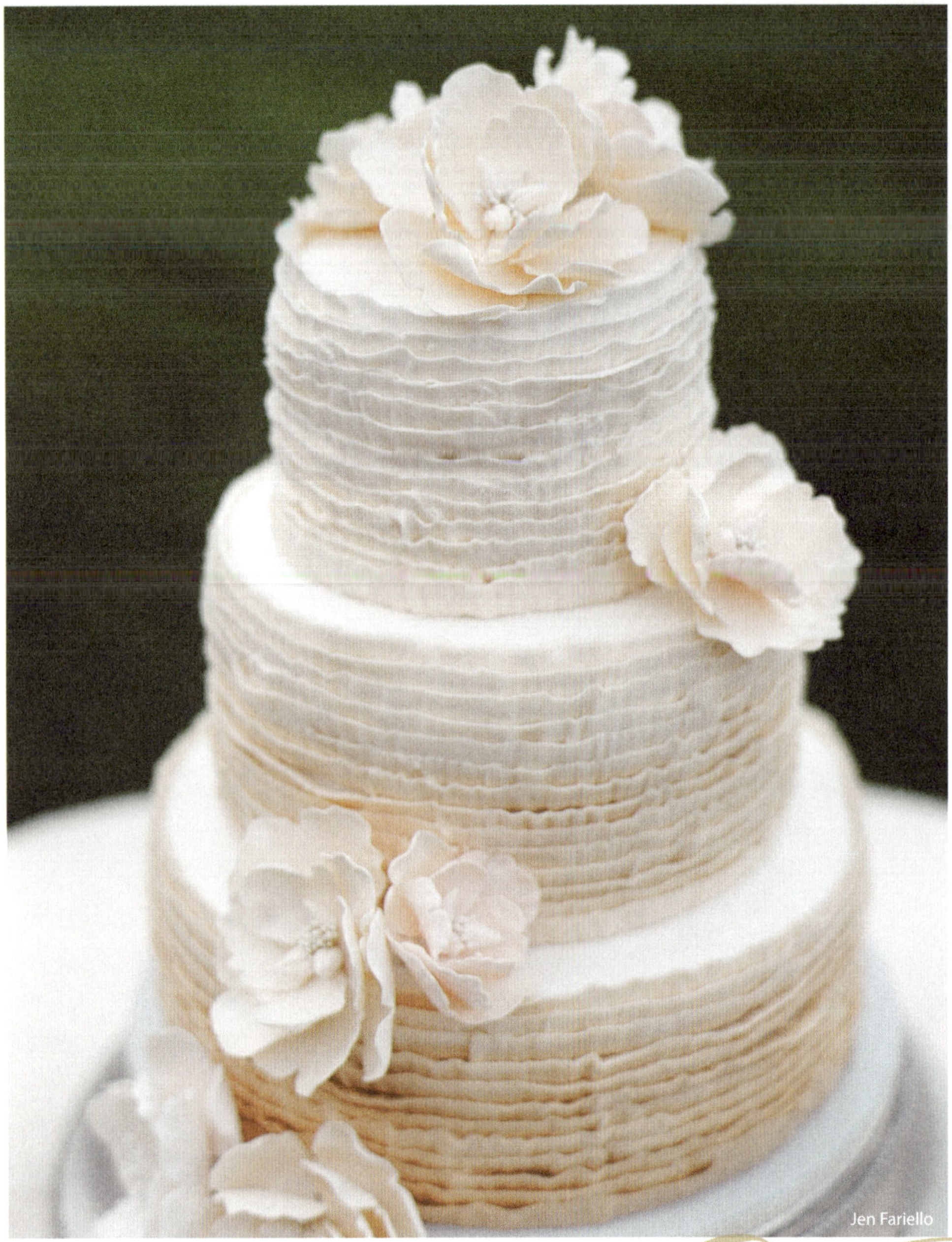

Jen Fariello

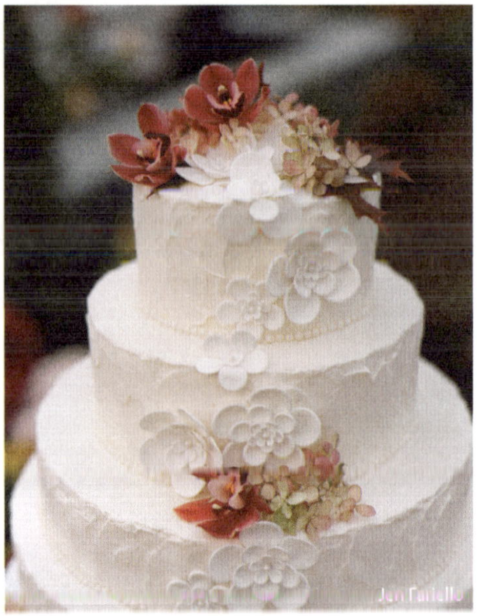

Jen Fariello

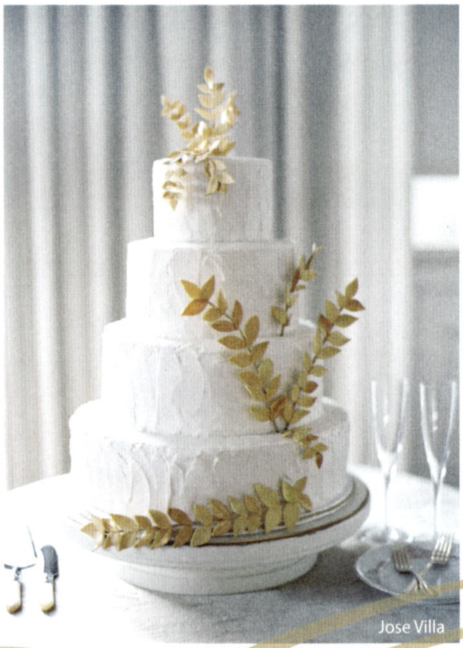

Jose Villa

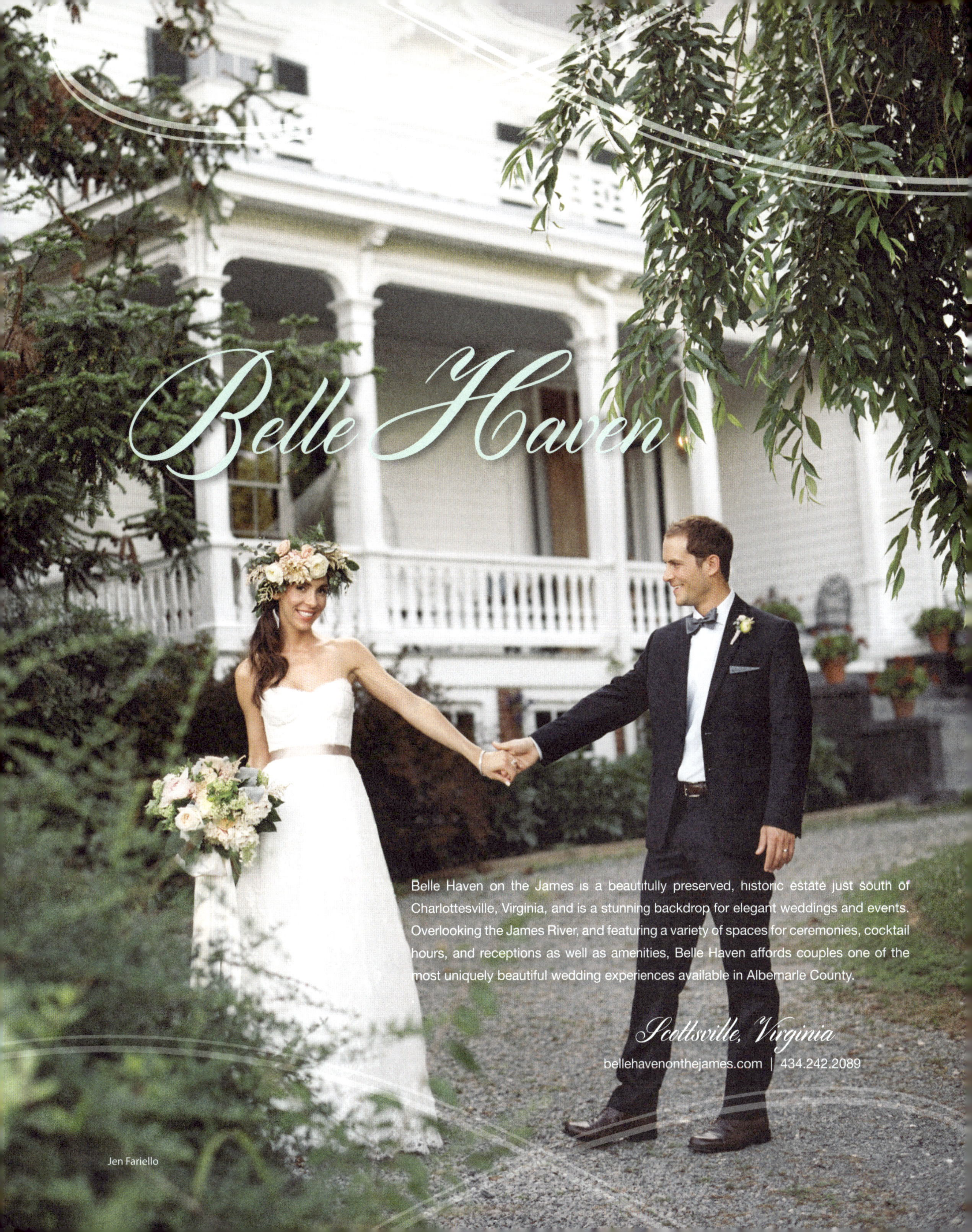

Jen Fariello

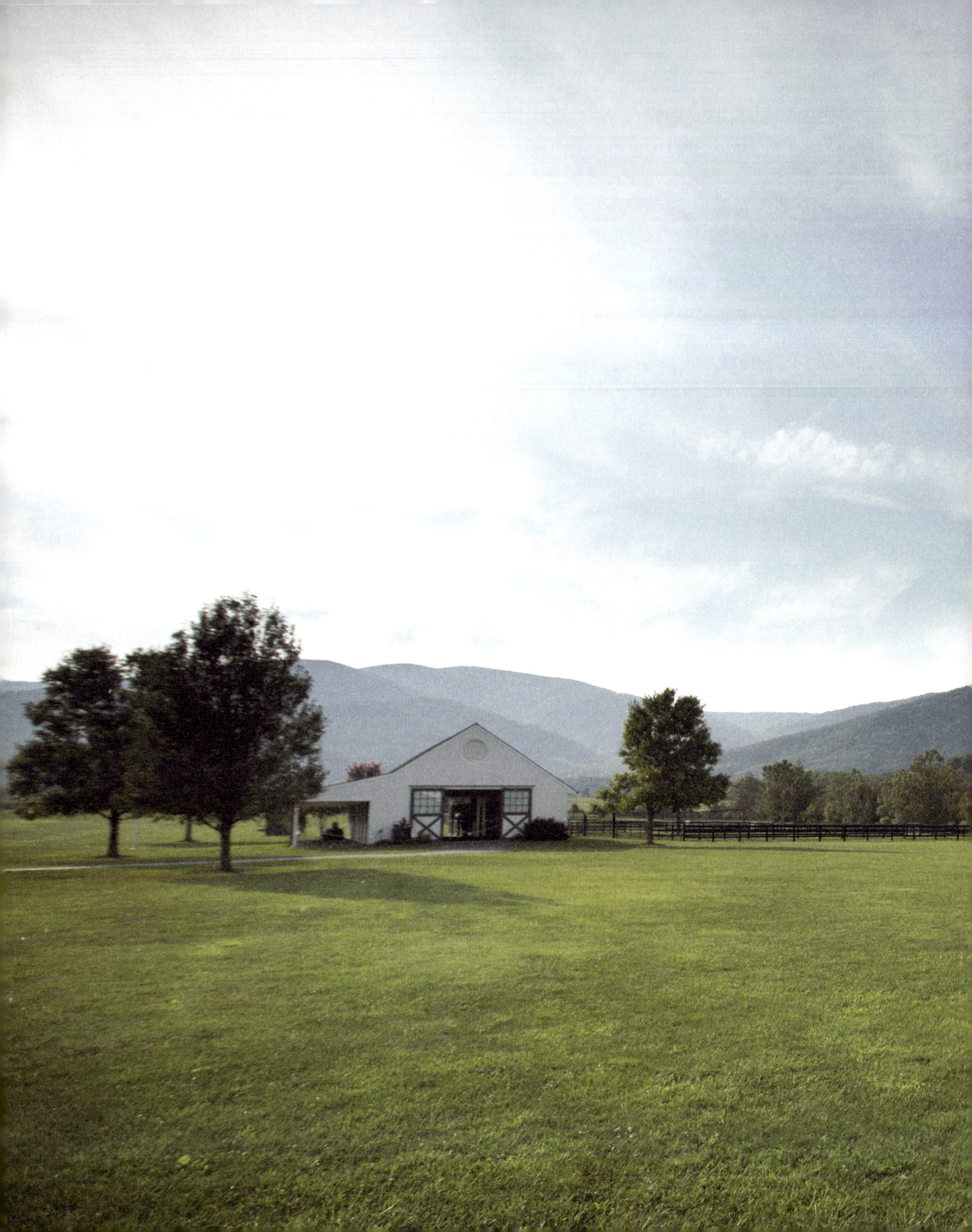

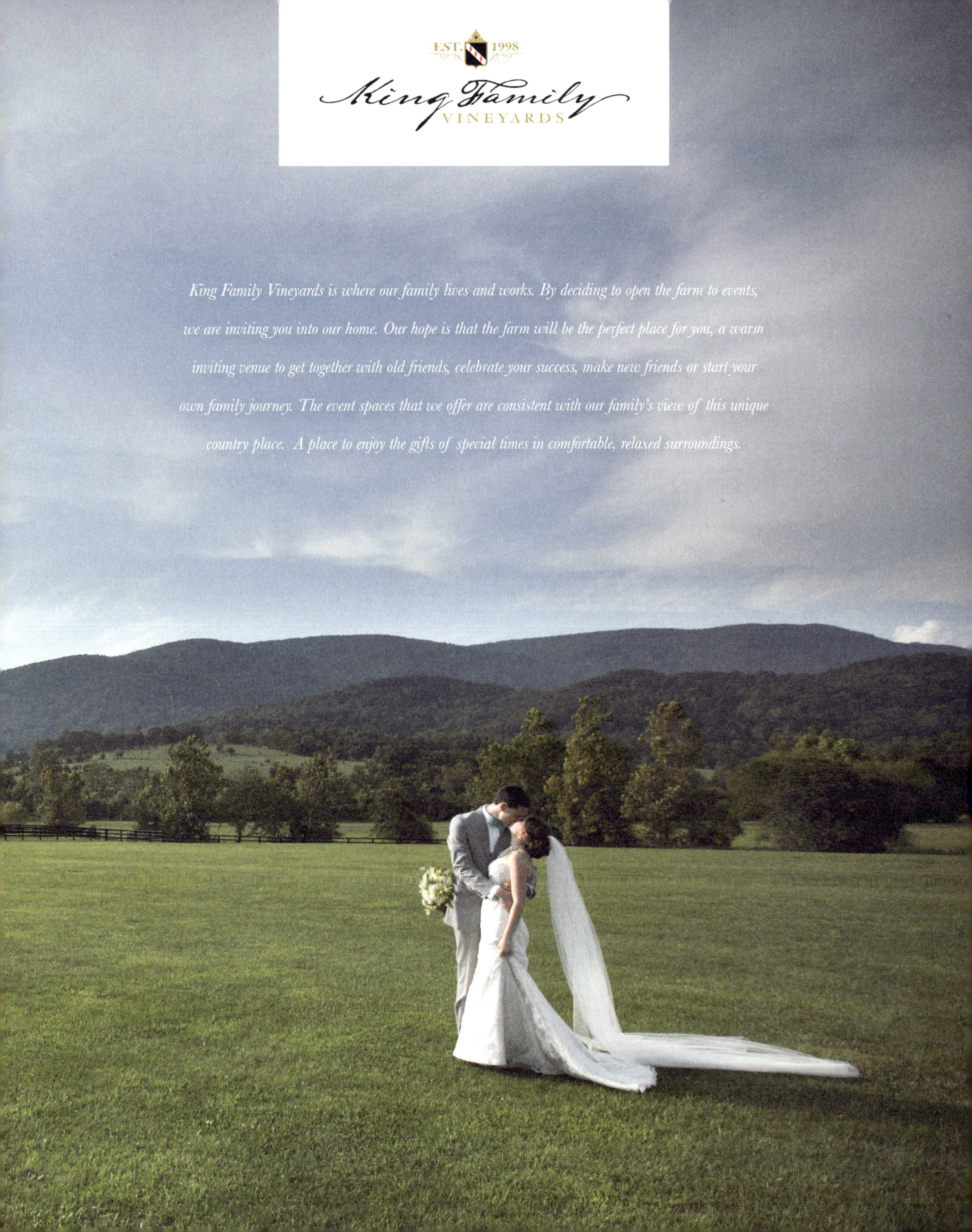
EST. 1998
King Family
VINEYARDS
King Family Vineyards is where our family lives and works. By deciding to open the farm to events, we are inviting you into our home. Our hope is that the farm will be the perfect place for you, a warm inviting venue to get together with old friends, celebrate your success, make new friends or start your own family journey. The event spaces that we offer are consistent with our family's view of this unique country place. A place to enjoy the gifts of special times in comfortable, relaxed surroundings.

Eve Watters

Music has been my North Star since childhood.

I am self-taught and perform on several instruments, but I know harp brings special enchantment. Its rich versatility shines in every genre, gracing each occasion, speaking directly to the heart, to spark the senses and soothe the spirit.

A touring artist for two decades, I have shared this amazing alchemy with thousands of audiences, from the Australian Bush to hospital bedsides to the National Cathedral for over 750 weddings. I am still learning, and it is still a joy to see the magic unfold each time. Visit my website for more information at **evewatters.com**.

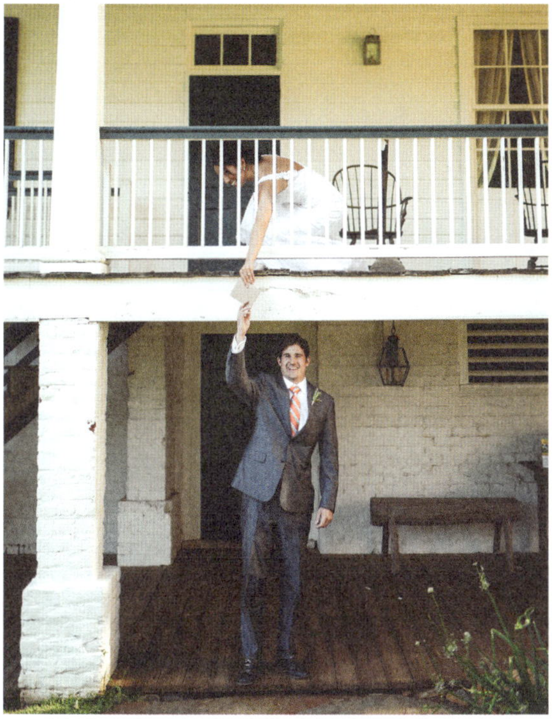

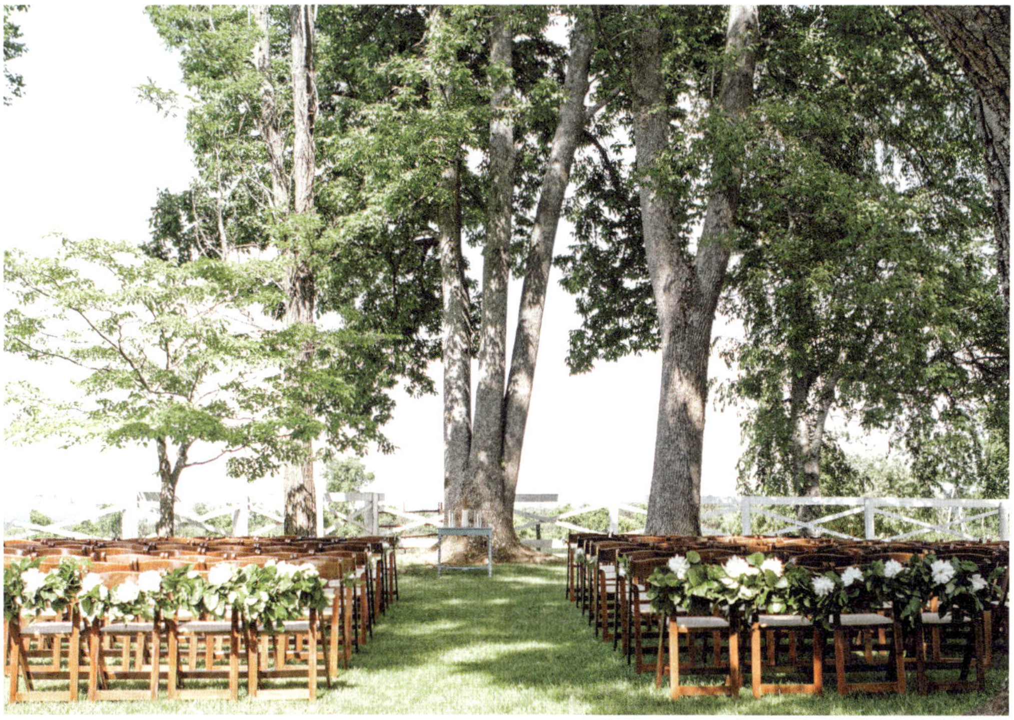

PICTURE YOUR WEDDING IN PRESIDENTIAL STYLE.

A HISTORIC HOUSE once home to James Monroe, America's fifth president and last founding father, Ash Lawn-Highland offers a breathtaking backdrop for weddings with blooming gardens, rolling pastures and mountain vistas. Nestled along Carter Mountain ridge just minutes from downtown Charlottesville, this historic site has both indoor and outdoor facilities that showcase the beauty of the Albemarle countryside. Select from the covered, open-air, hilltop pavilion or the heated and air-conditioned two-story event barn and any combination of the property's shaded lawns and manicured gardens.

ASHLAWNHIGHLAND.ORG

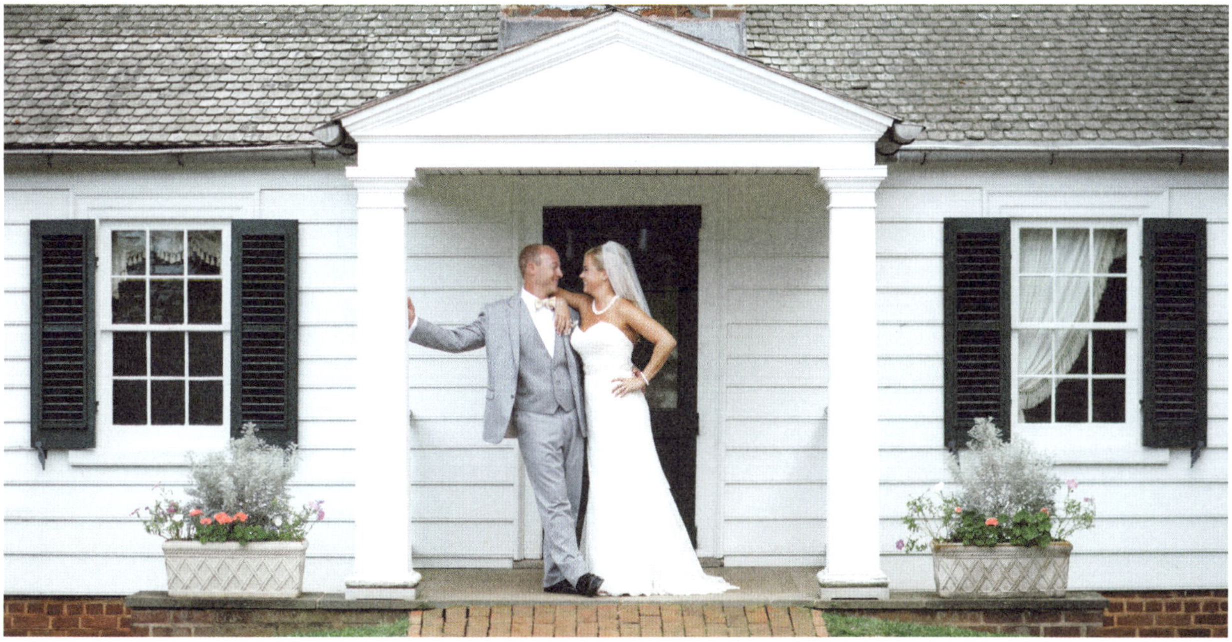

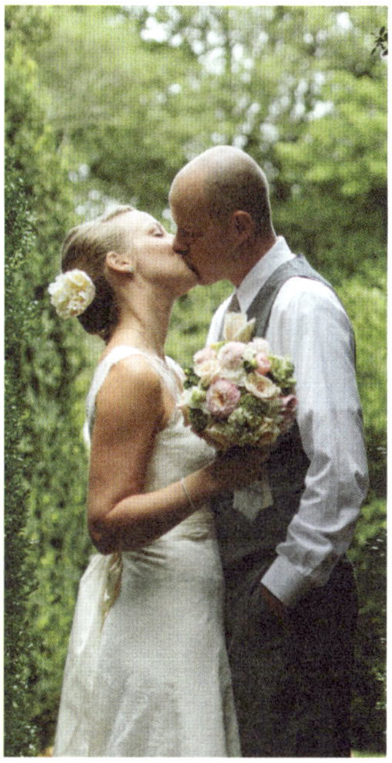

ASH LAWN-HIGHLAND

Home of James Monroe

THE VIRGINIA SHOP is a locally owned gift shop in Charlottesville, Virginia, at the Barracks Road Shopping Center with an exciting new **second** location on the Historic Downtown Mall. For nearly 25 years the shop has catered to the wedding industry with our **Virginia welcome bag service**; a longtime tradition in southern hospitality. We provide our Virginia Shop bag, tissue, ribbon, assembly, and local delivery to all the hotels and venues your guests are staying **complimentary** with purchase of our goods. Much time, effort, research, and old-fashioned legwork has gone into finding and selecting our products. We are always looking for unique goods that are from Virginia, or remind us of the Virginia lifestyle for our boutique.

We are also known for our gift baskets, local foods and wine, and one of a kind University of Virginia gifts. We look forward to serving you.

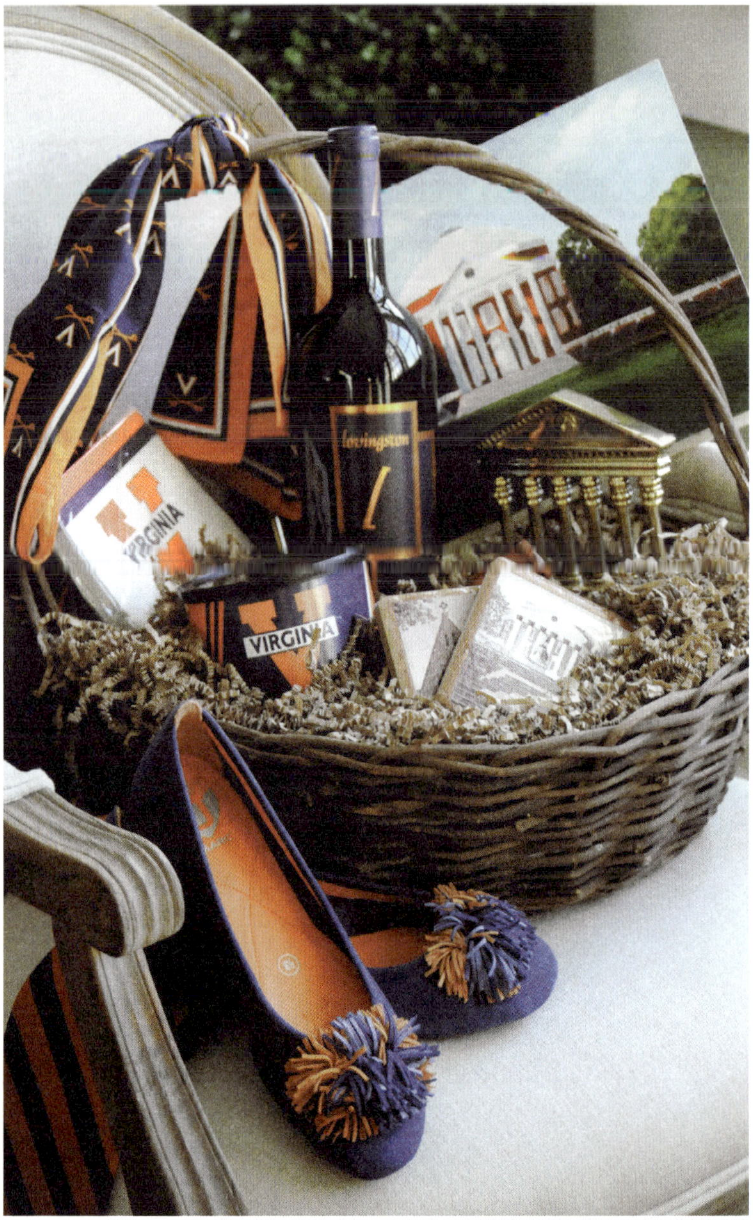

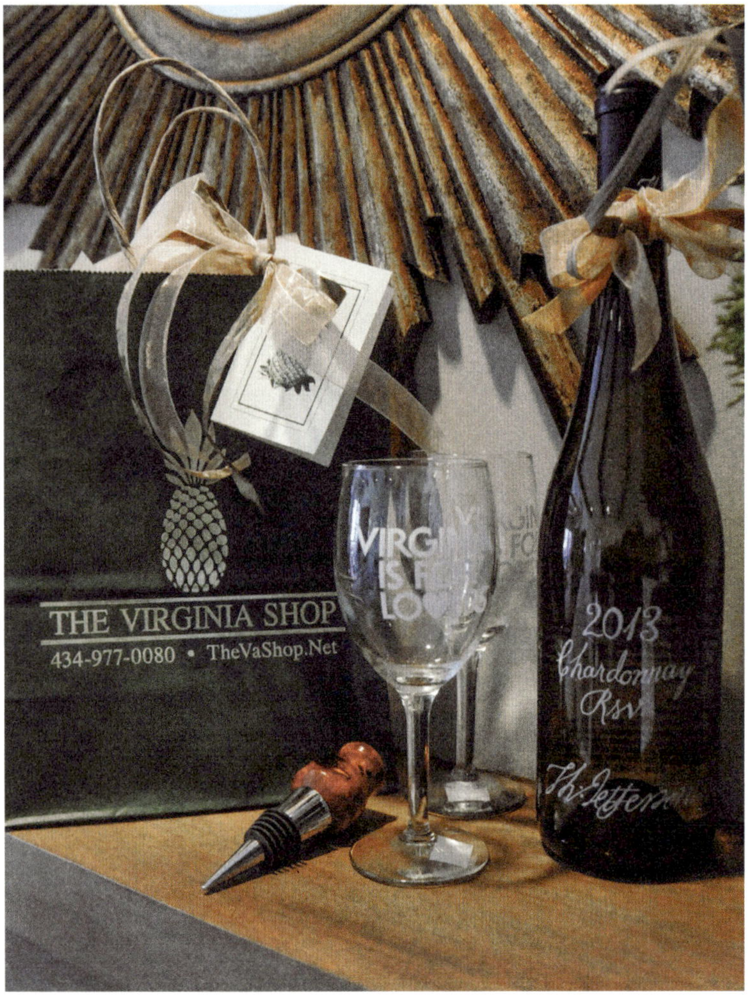

The Virginia Shop
Locally owned since 1990

434.977.0080 | TheVaShop.net

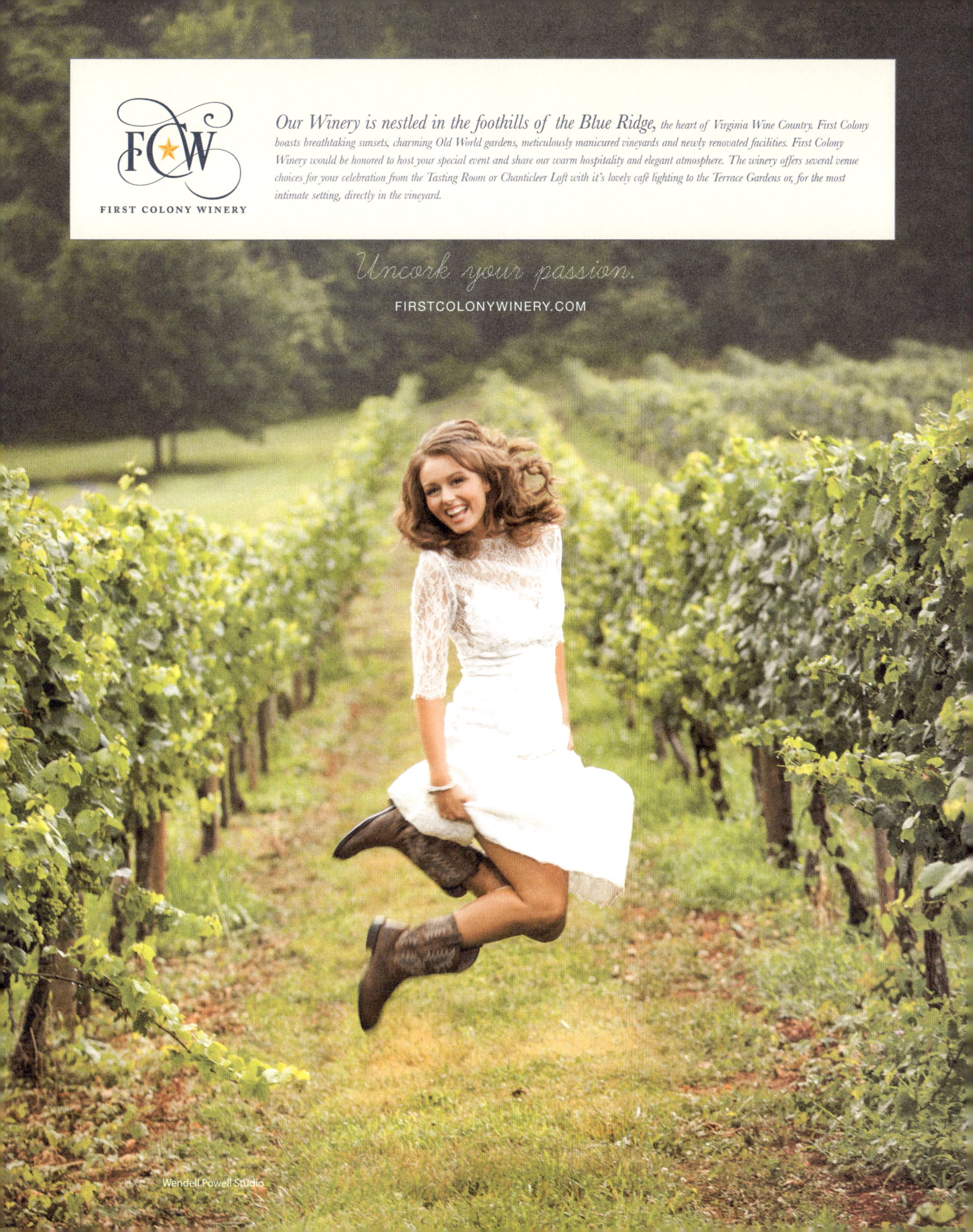
FCW
FIRST COLONY WINERY
Our Winery is nestled in the foothills of the Blue Ridge, the heart of Virginia Wine Country. First Colony boasts breathtaking sunsets, charming Old World gardens, meticulously manicured vineyards and newly renovated facilities. First Colony Winery would be honored to host your special event and share our warm hospitality and elegant atmosphere. The winery offers several venue choices for your celebration from the Tasting Room or Chanticleer Loft with it's lovely café lighting to the Terrace Gardens or, for the most intimate setting, directly in the vineyard.
Uncork your passion.
FIRSTCOLONYWINERY.COM
Wendell Powell Studio

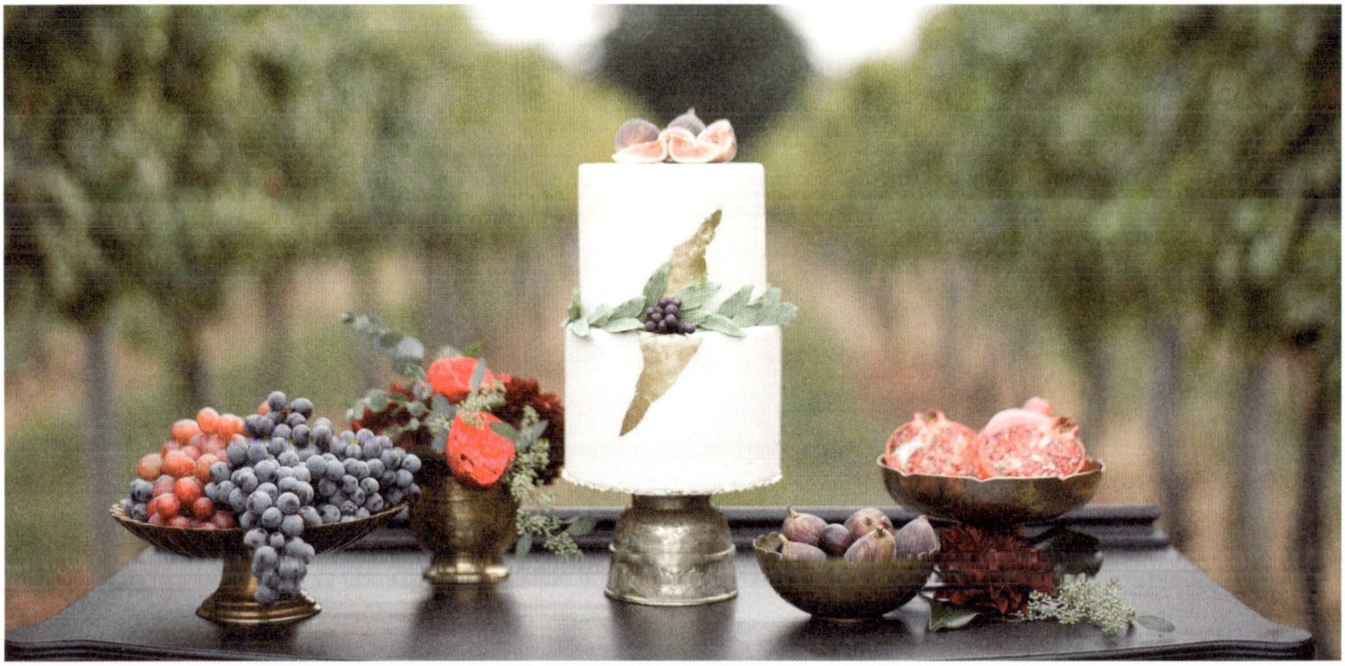

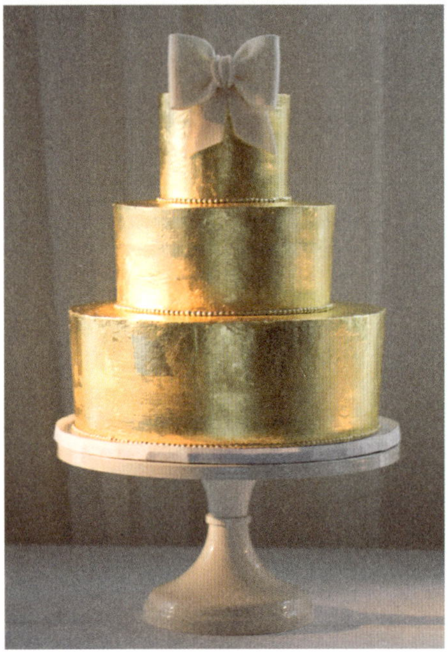

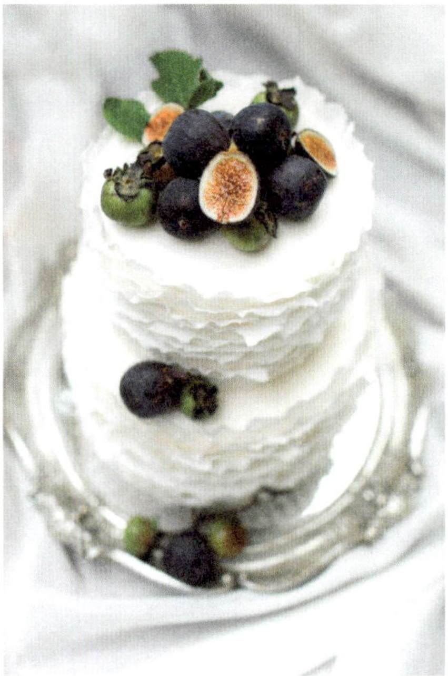

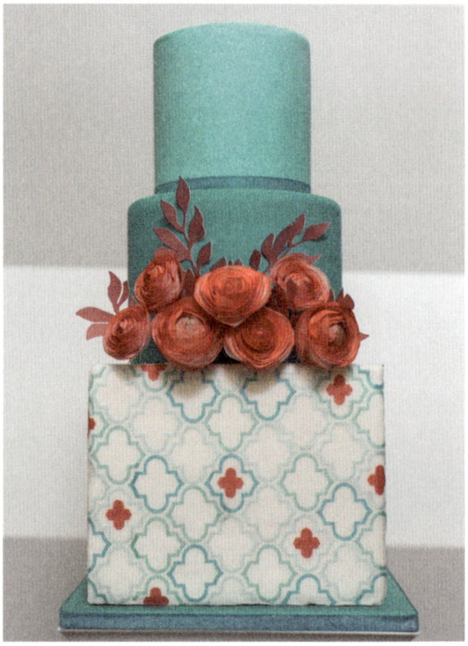

Maliha Creations is an award-winning boutique bakery helping clients celebrate momentous occasions since 2006. Serving Central Virginia, Maliha Creations is dedicated to crafting beautiful, delicious and truly exquisite confections for the most discerning clients. Our passion lies in developing long-term relationships with our couples. From the moment they contact us, through their tasting and planning sessions, all the way to their first anniversary, and sometimes beyond as their families begin to grow, we cultivate a warm and personalized experience.

Owned and operated by cake artist, Anita Gupta, Maliha Creations has been featured in top industry publications, including Town & Country Weddings, Southern Weddings, Martha Stewart Weddings, The Knot, Weddings Unveiled, Brides Magazine, among others.

Maliha Creations

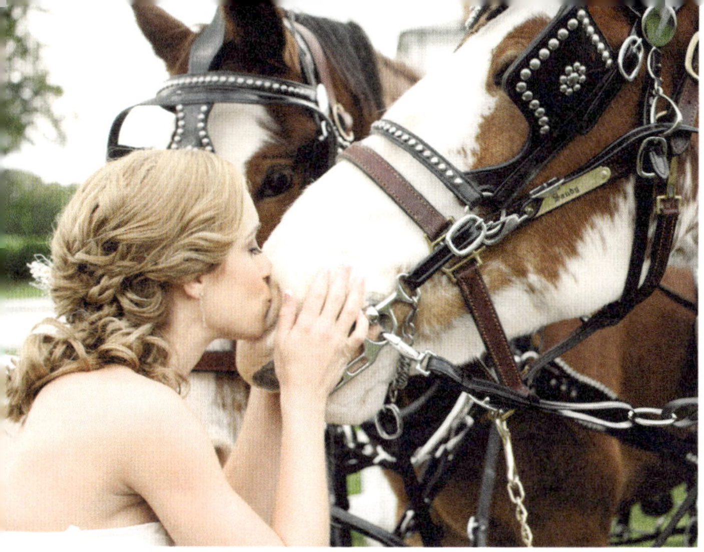

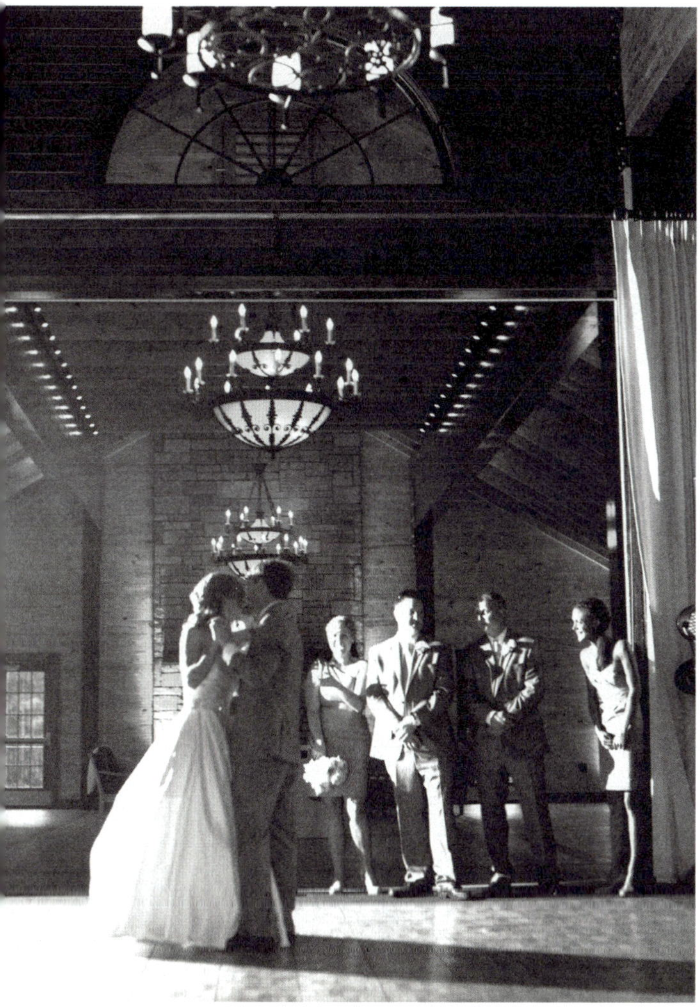

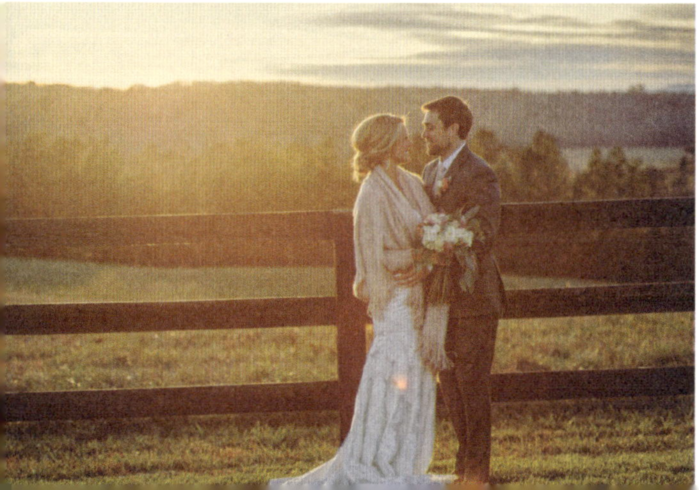

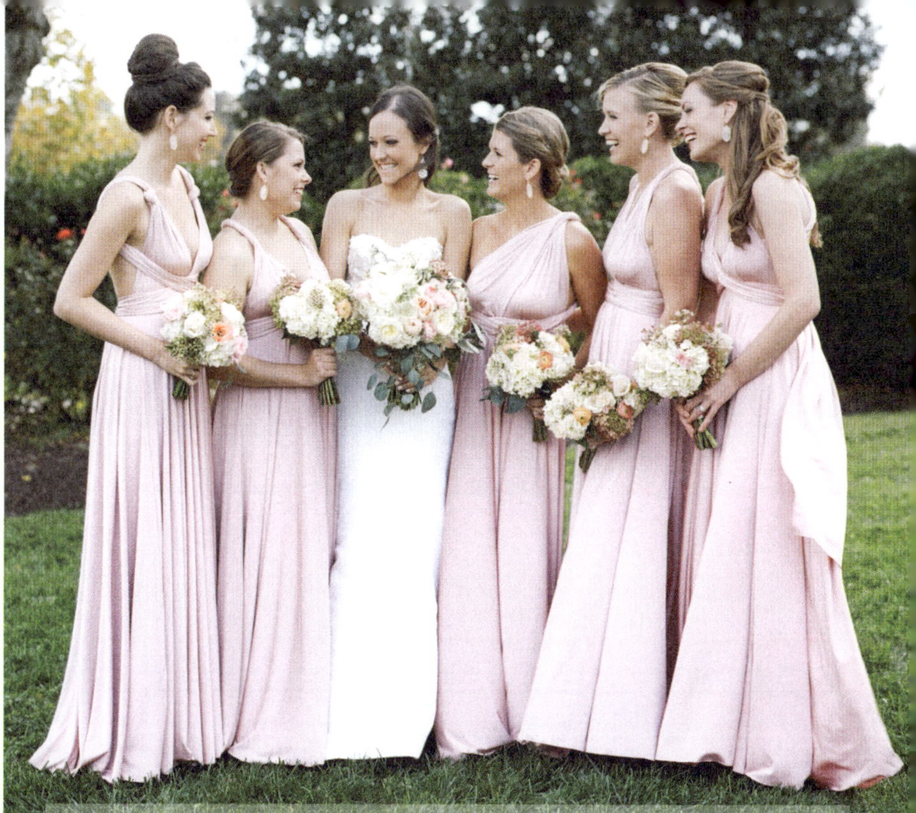

Mount Ida Farm

From destination wedding venues to private events in Charlottesville, Virginia, Mount Ida Farm has it all. Mount Ida Farm is a unique wedding venue located south of Charlottesville on a secluded 6000-acre sanctuary. Spectacular scenic vistas, historic homes, horse-drawn carriages, tree-lined drives, historic plantation accommodations and cocktail parties lake or stable-side all combine to create the venue of your dreams. Coming this spring for fall bookings is our Mountain View Lodge, boasting lofts, a bridal suite, indoor/outdoor cocktailspace and the gorgeous Grove overlooking the Jefferson Sea view. All Fall 2015 dates are available for The Event Lodge!

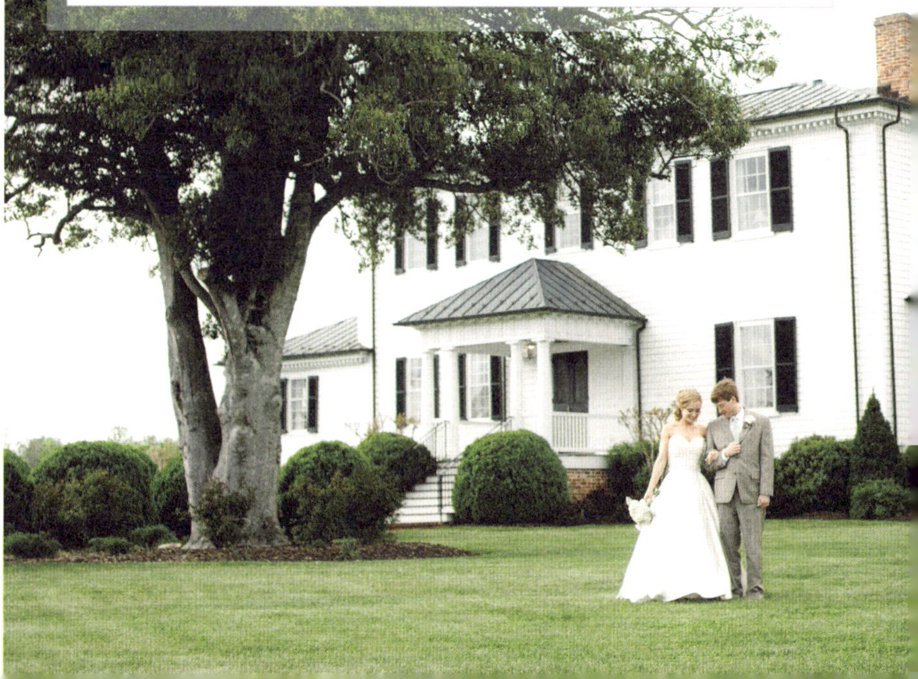

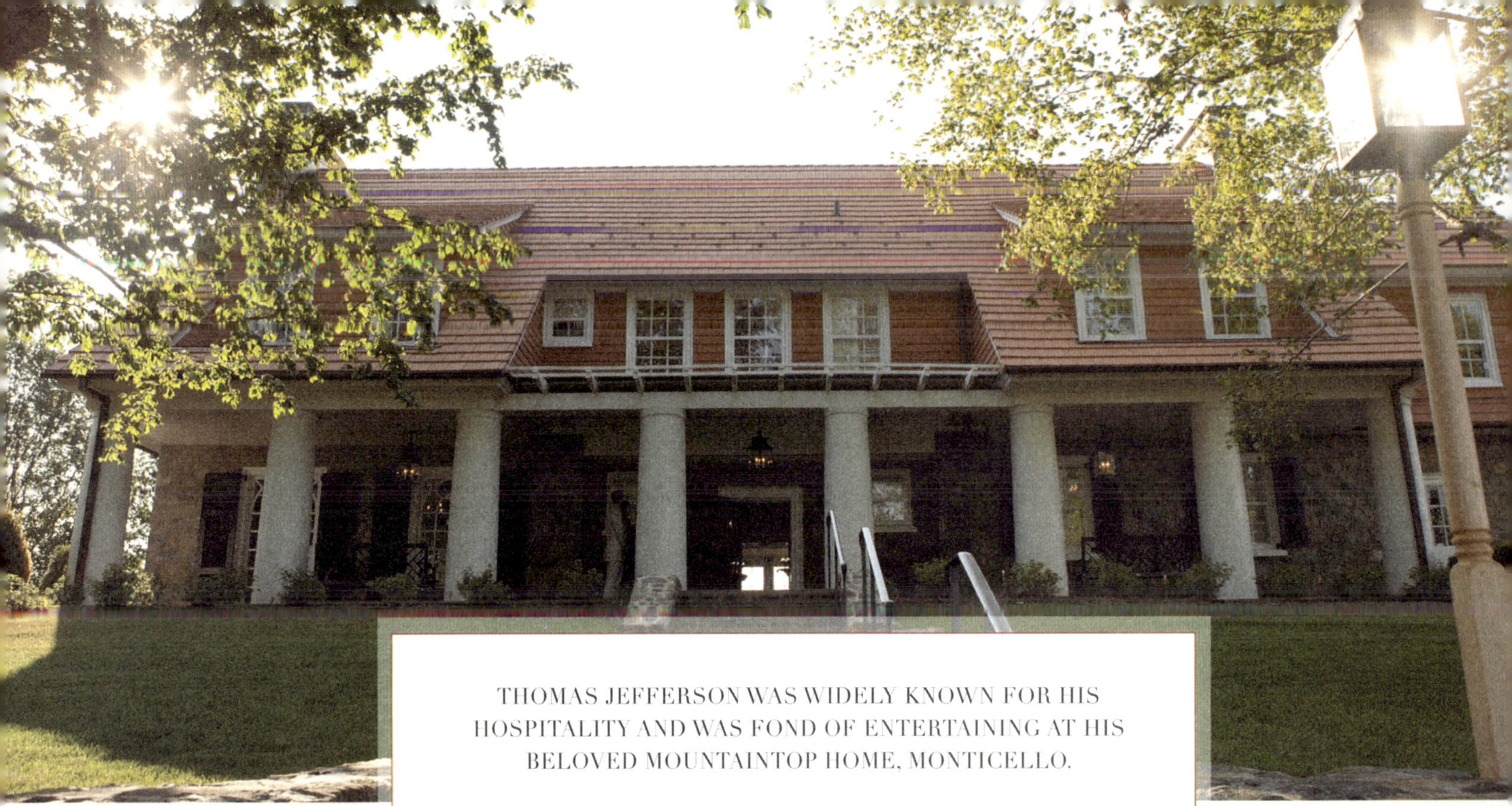

THOMAS JEFFERSON WAS WIDELY KNOWN FOR HIS HOSPITALITY AND WAS FOND OF ENTERTAINING AT HIS BELOVED MOUNTAINTOP HOME, MONTICELLO.

Our third President's historic grounds, owned and operated by the Thomas Jefferson Foundation since 1923 with a mission of education and preservation, offer a variety of inspired settings that provide an unparalleled opportunity to experience Jefferson's Virginia.

At Montalto, overlooking Monticello, 360-degree panoramic vistas of Charlottesville and the Blue Ridge change with the sunlight and the seasons. Repose, the gracious 11,000-square-foot country home perched atop Jefferson's "high mountain," offers a variety of possibilities for events of every kind and is one of the most distinctive, elegant spaces in Virginia.

From our timeless venues to our gracious sense of true Virginia hospitality, here, we will surpass your visions for your celebration and help you create memories that will last forever.

MONTICELLO.ORG

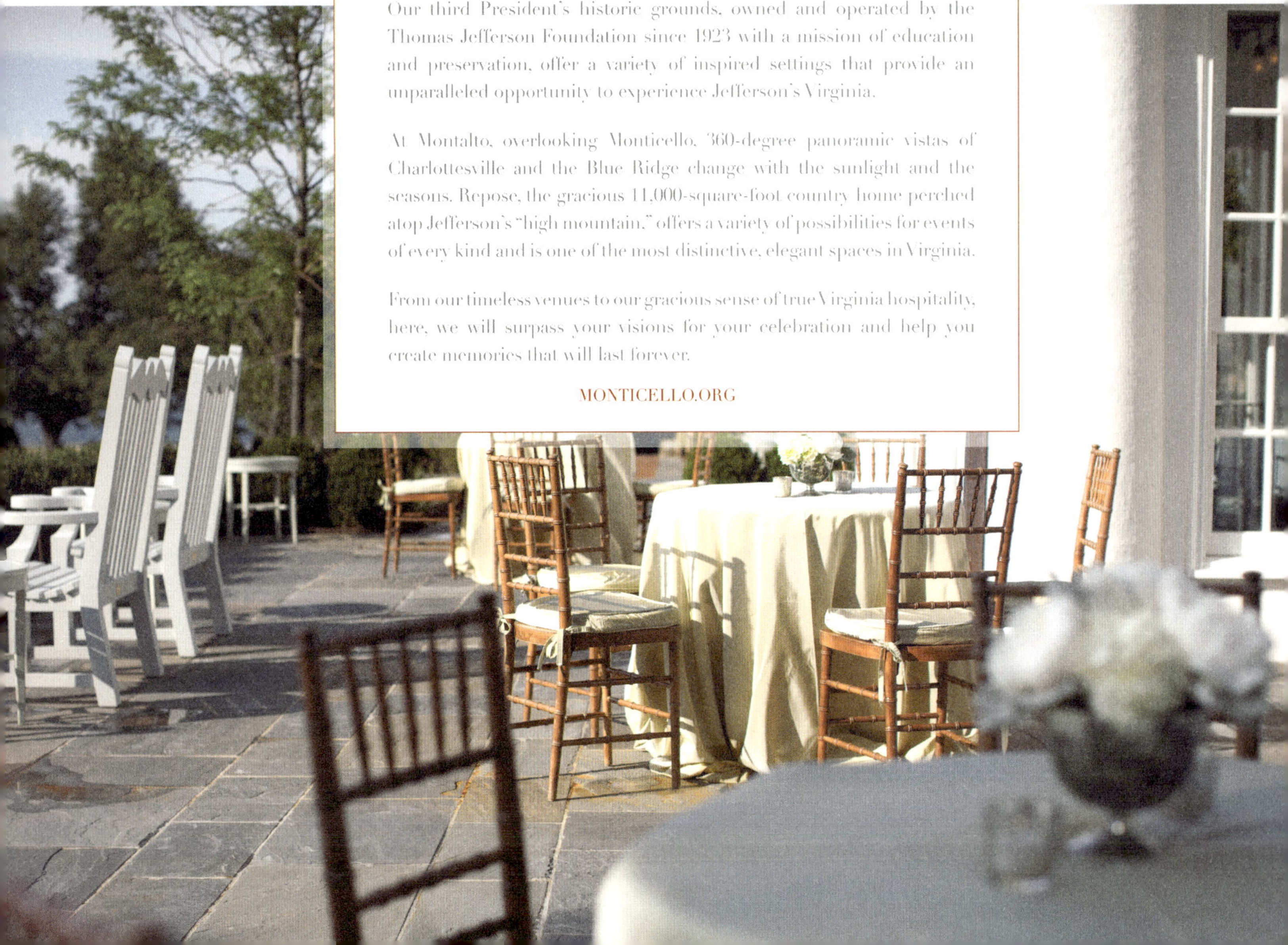

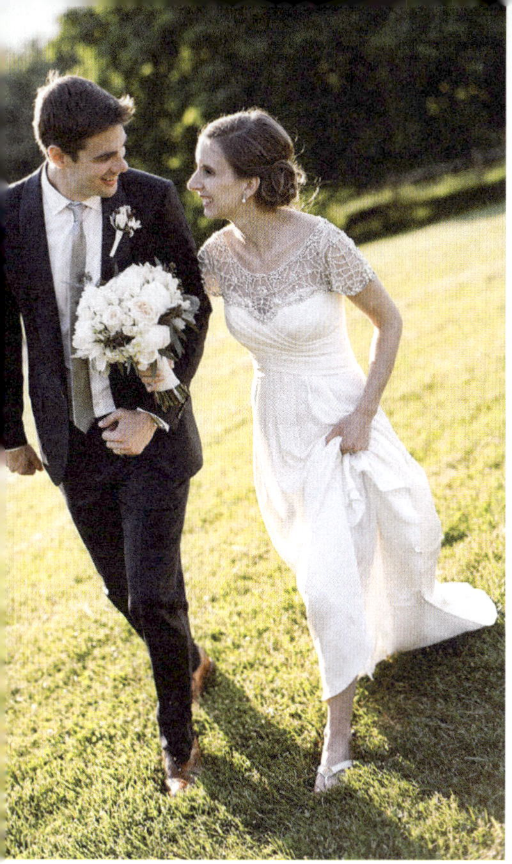

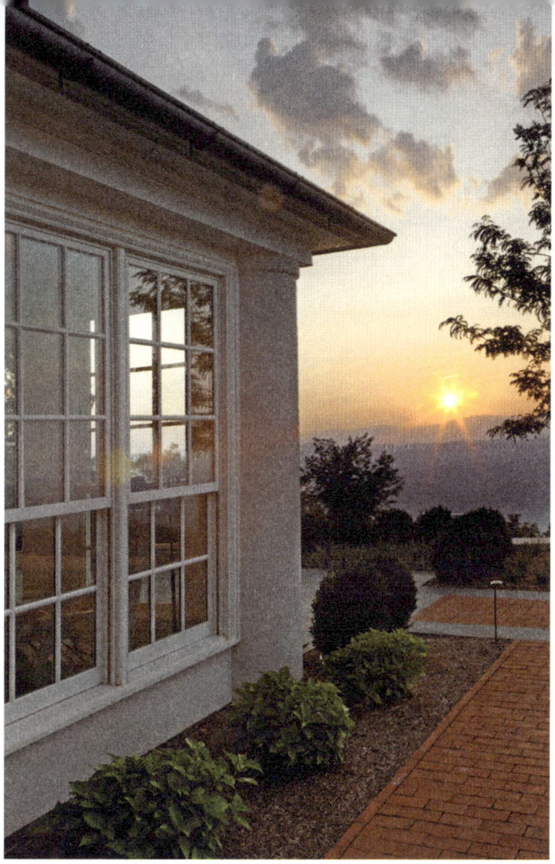

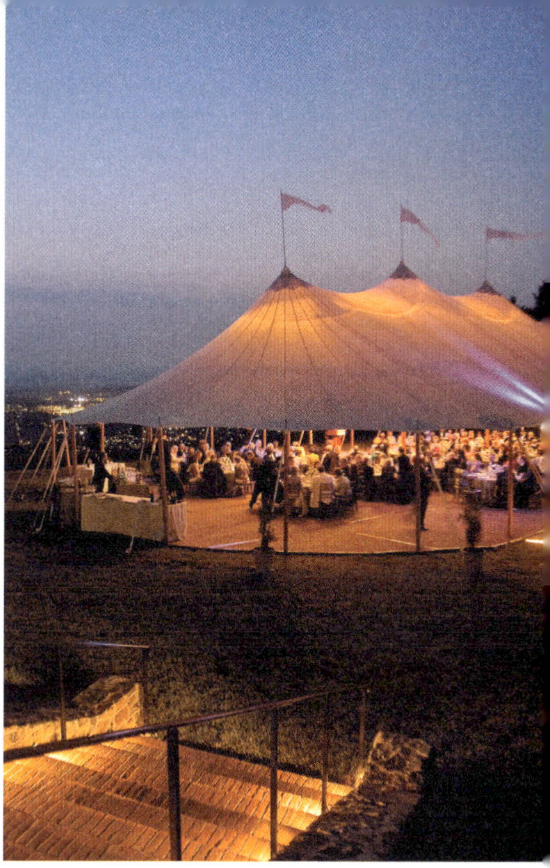

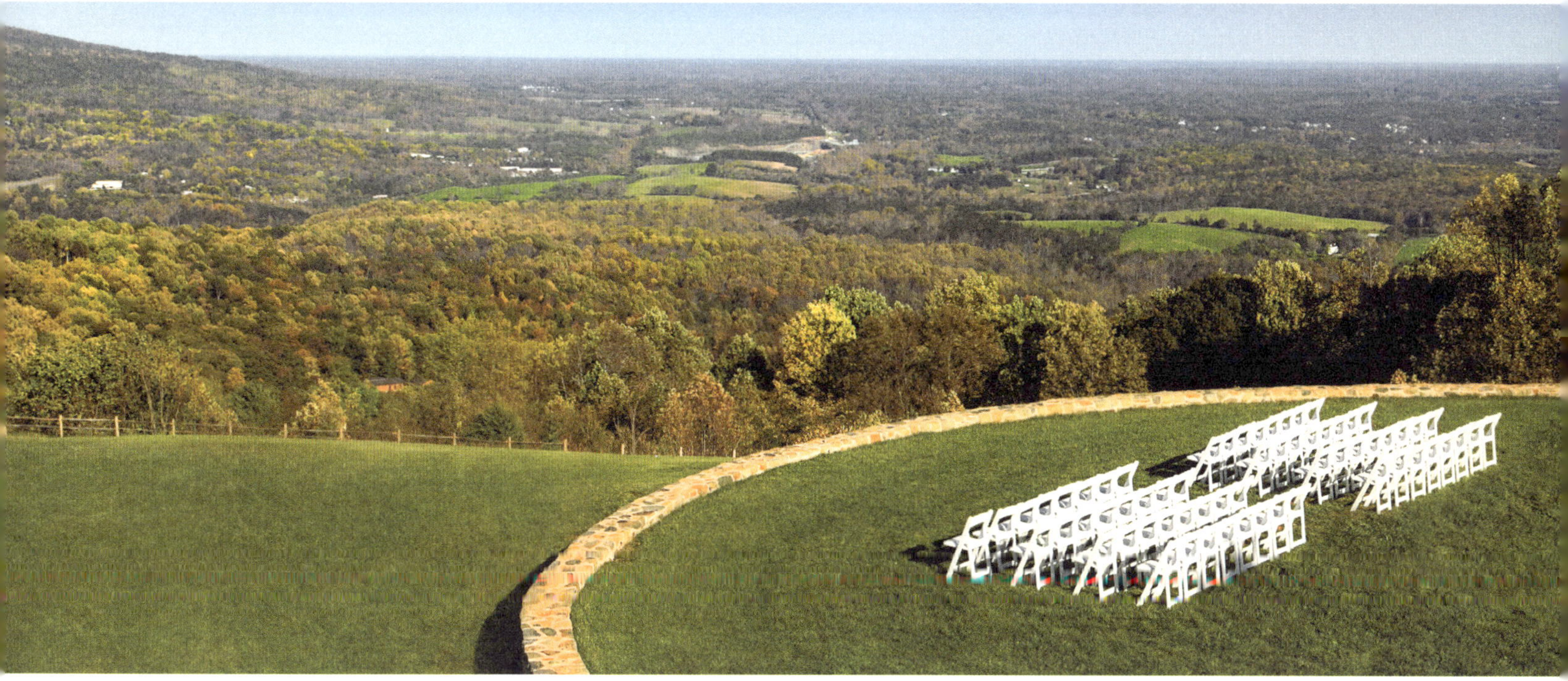

"And our own dear Monticello, where has nature spread so rich a mantle under the eye? Mountains, forests, rocks, rivers. With what majesty do we there ride above the storms! How sublime to look down into the workhouse of nature, to see her clouds, hail, snow, rain, thunder, all fabricated at our feet! And the glorious Sun, when rising as if out of a distant water, just gilding the tops of the mountains, and giving life to all nature!"

–Thomas Jefferson, 1786

Th: Jefferson

MONTICELLO

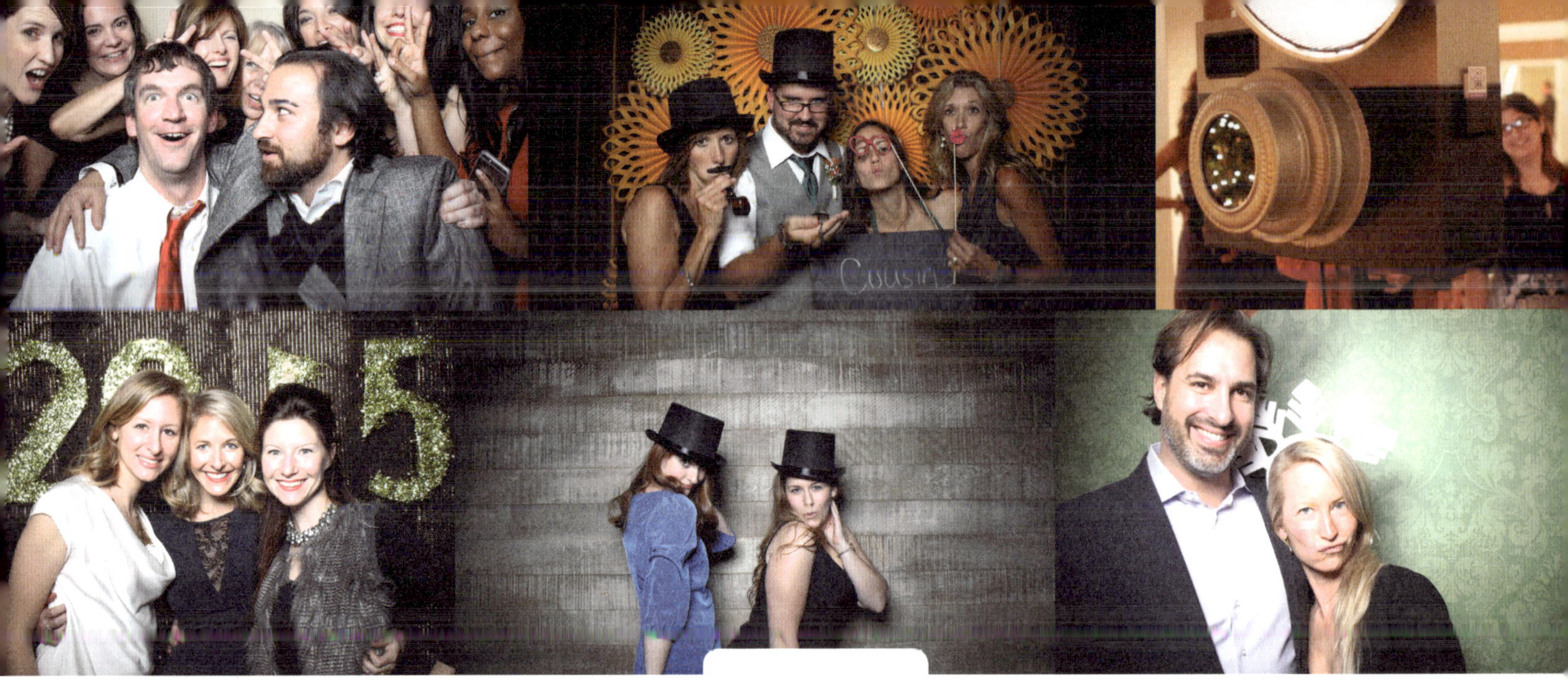

MOX
BOX

A Social Photo Booth Experience

INSTANTLY SHARE THE BEST MOMENTS OF YOUR LIVES.

"MoxBox gives you the tools and freedom to create your own story, your own memories. It is incredibly heartwarming to watch people come alive in front of the camera or see generations of family members gather in one picture. Moxbox's greatest feature is that it gets the photo booth out of the way and allows guests to explore their creative side. As there are no restrictions on group size or number of pictures taken, the combinations of people and funny faces are endless. For those unable to attend an event, watching it unfold online and adding their comments to pictures helps bring the event a little closer to them."

— Jeff Shafer, MoxBox Inventor

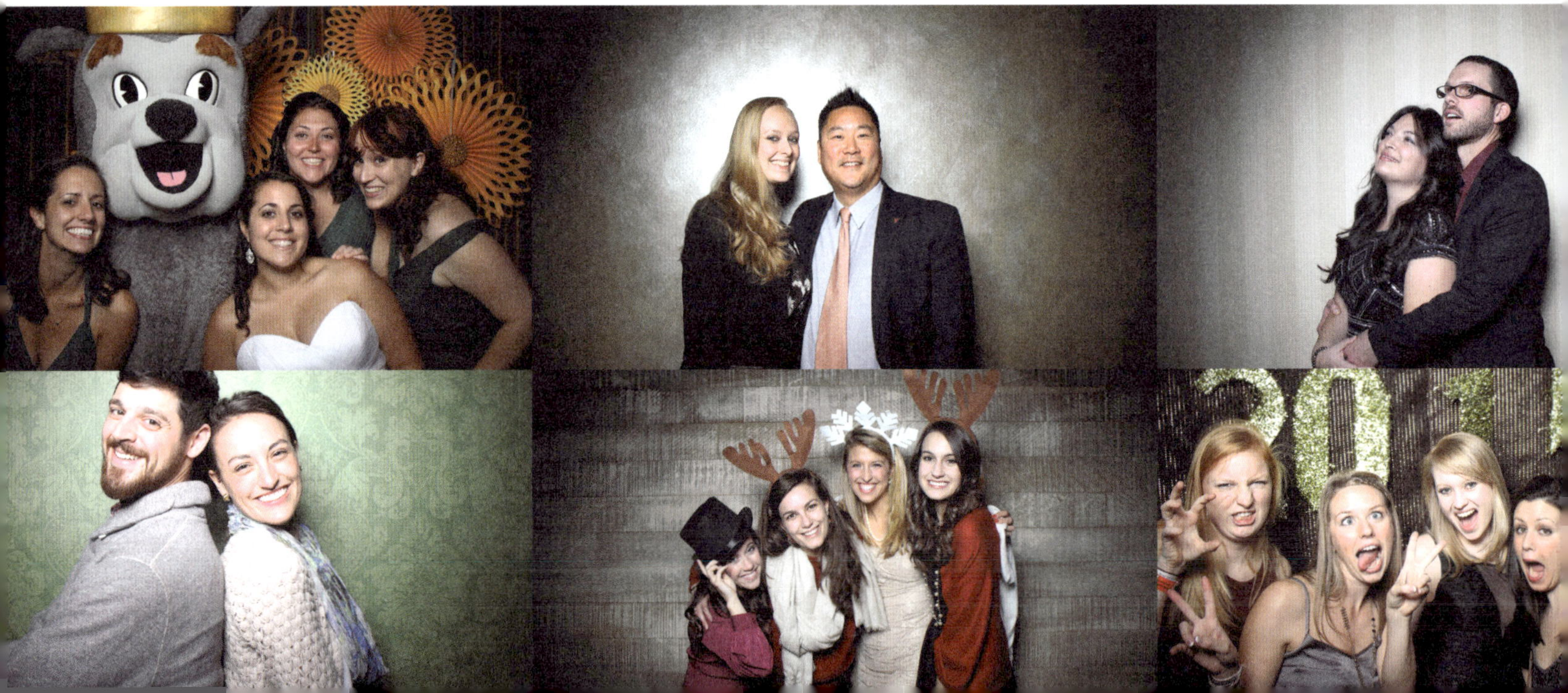

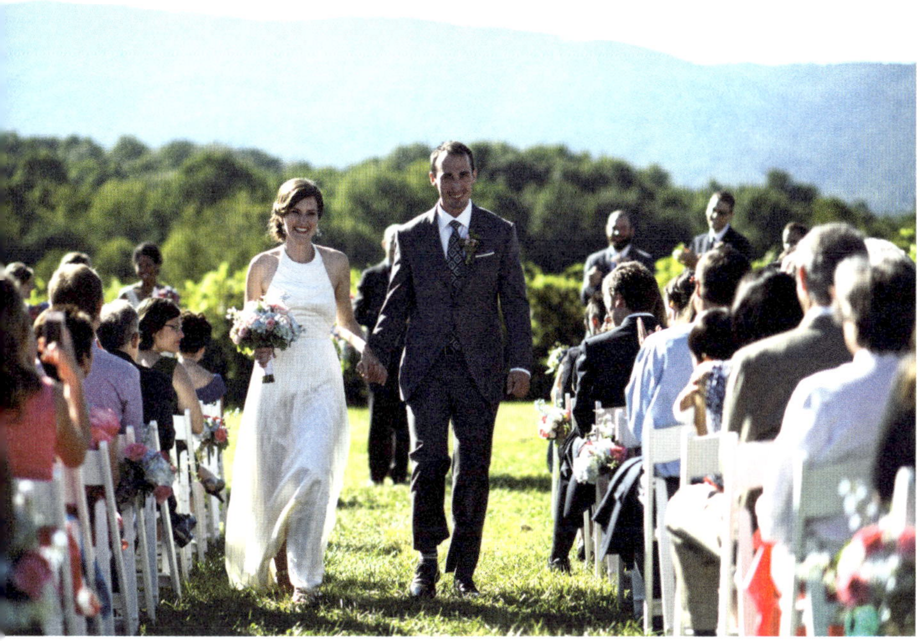

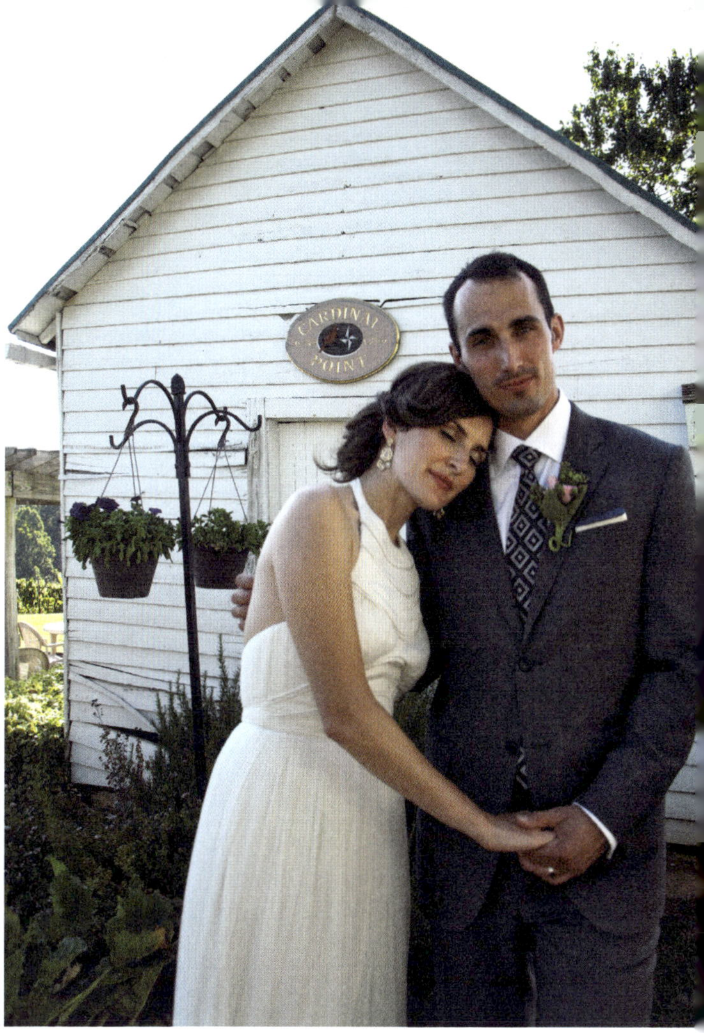

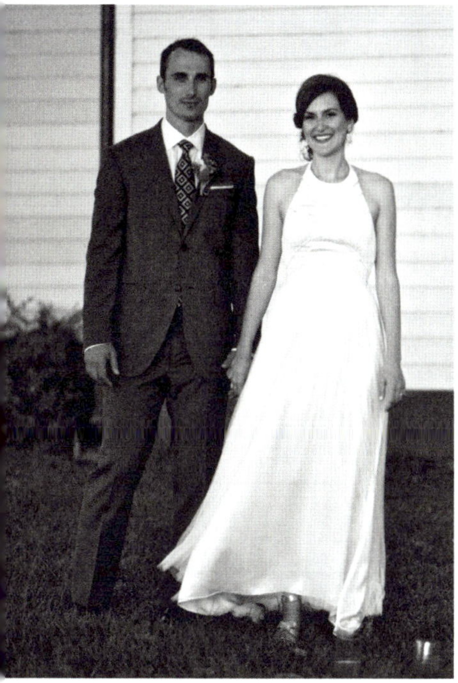

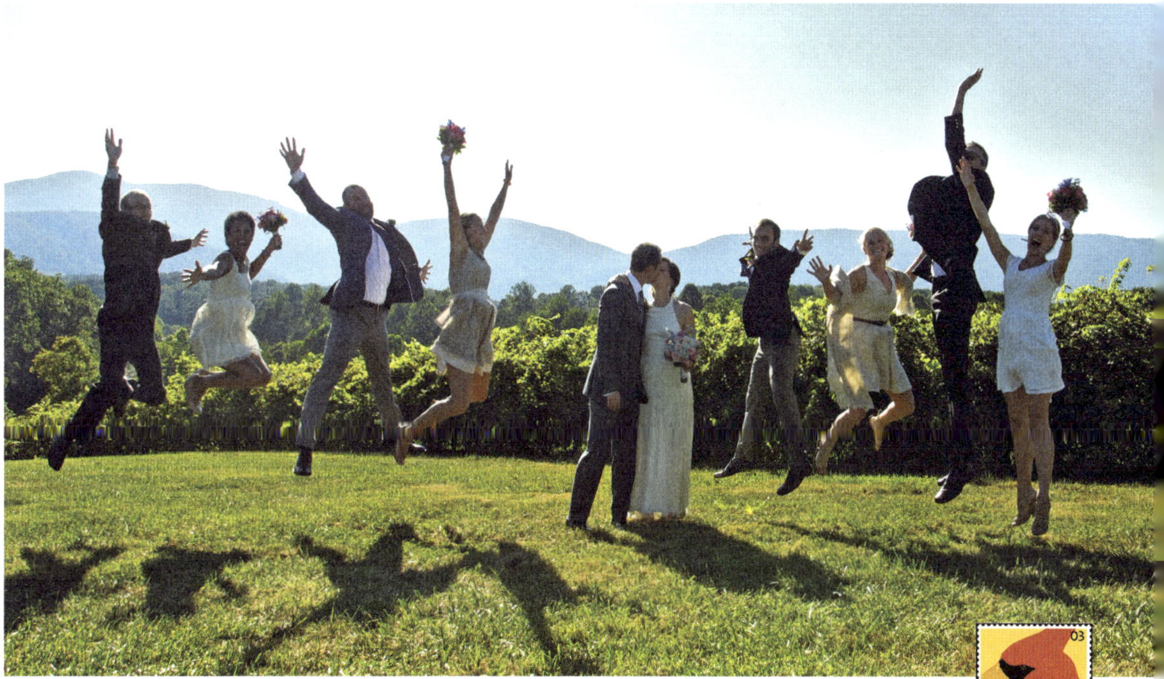

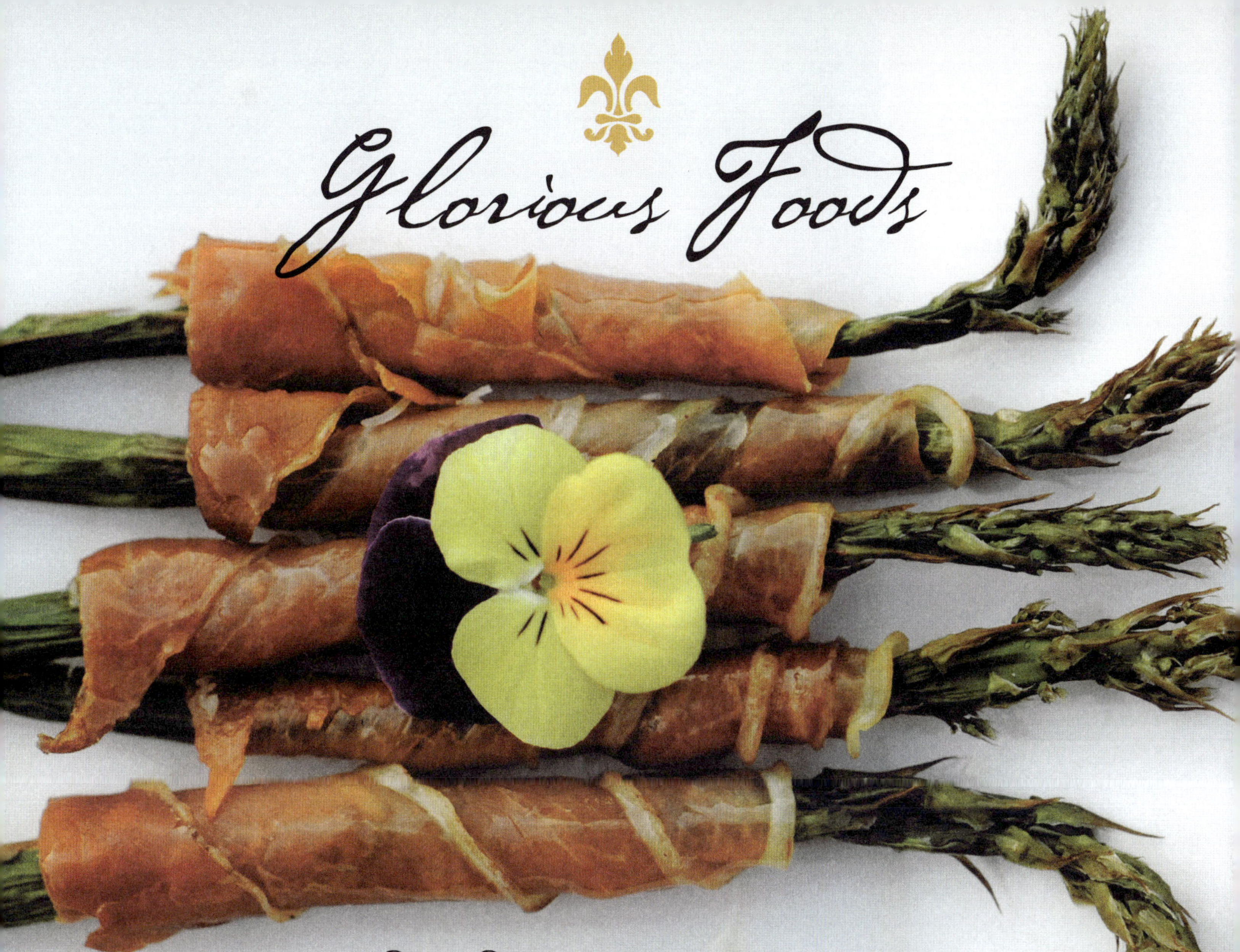

Glorious Foods

Owner Chef Maria Mayo, though her family originated in Italy, was raised in La Lorraine France. She has vast cooking experience that started with her formal training in a two-year apprenticeship at Boulangerie Patisserie in France. Later, Maria trained with an expert French Chocolatier as well. Maria relocated to Charlottesville, Virginia in 1983 where she has acquired many years experience in all aspects of catering.

Maria can be reached at GloriousFoodsCatering.com.

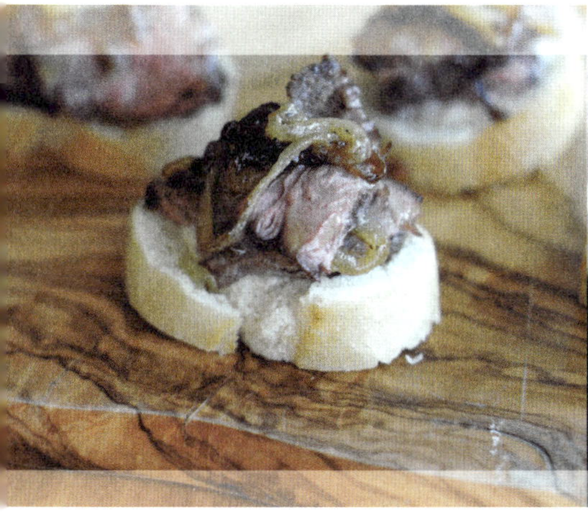

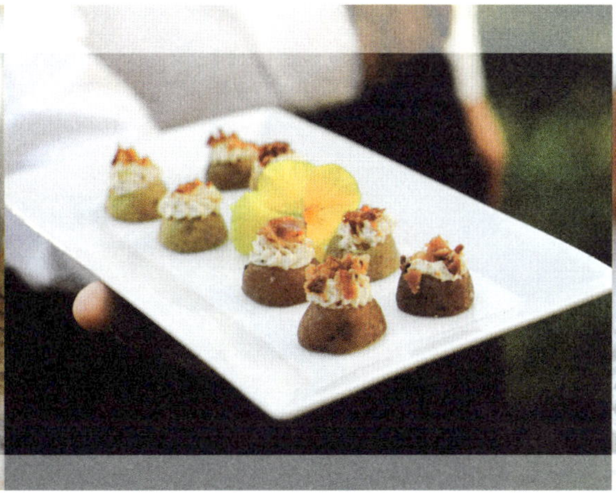

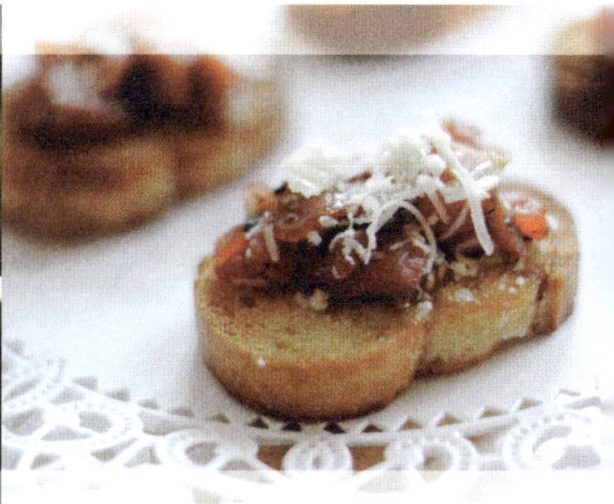

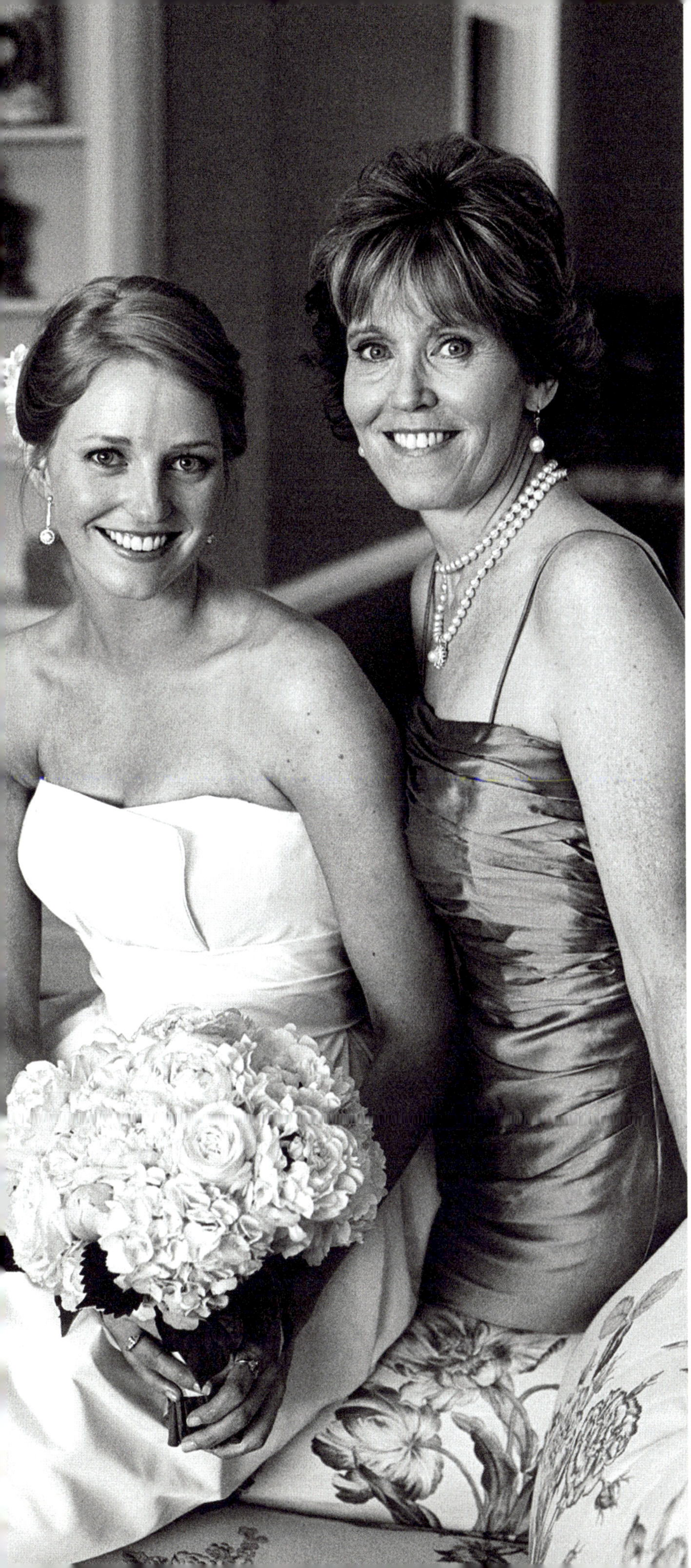

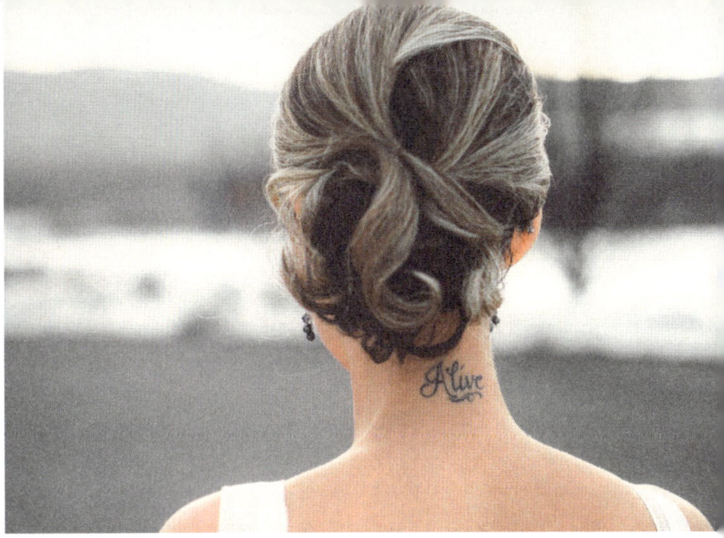
Alive

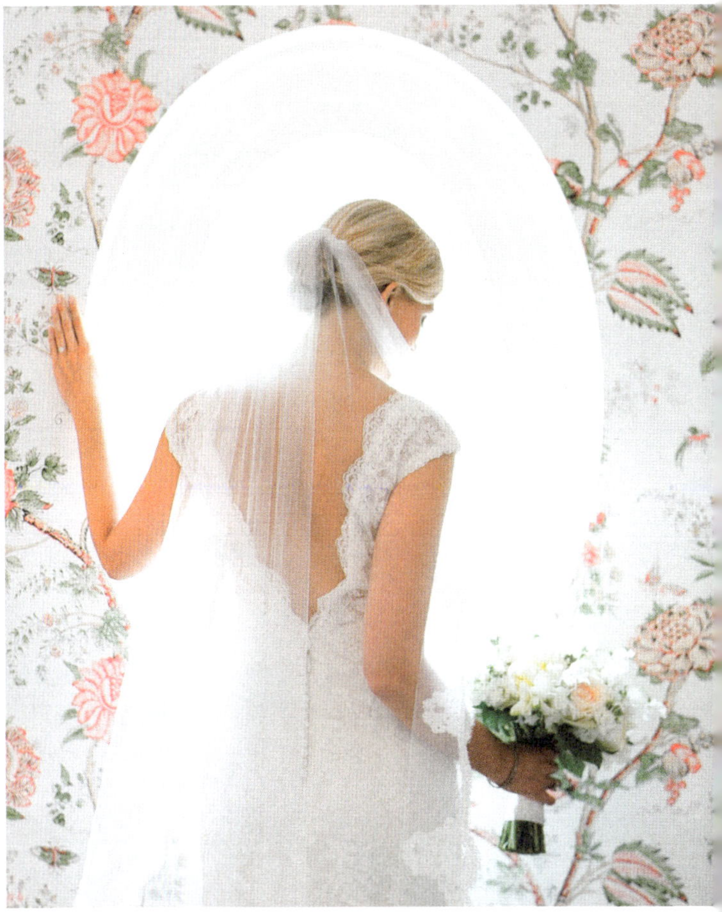

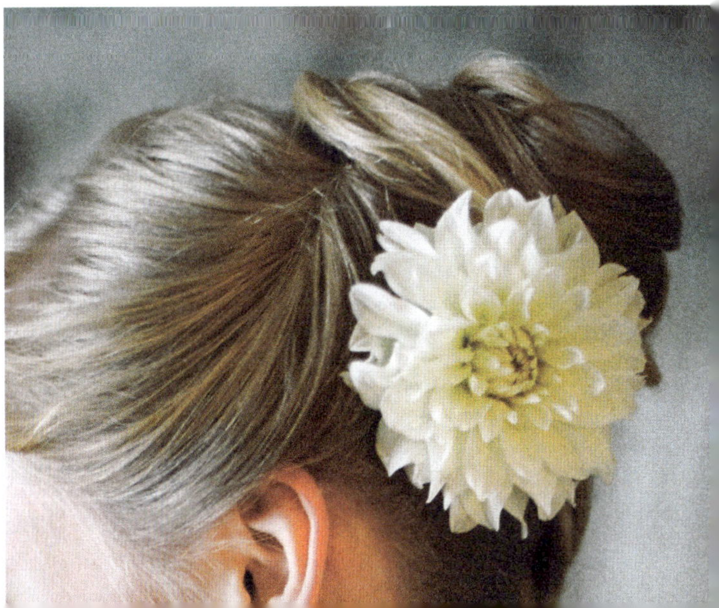

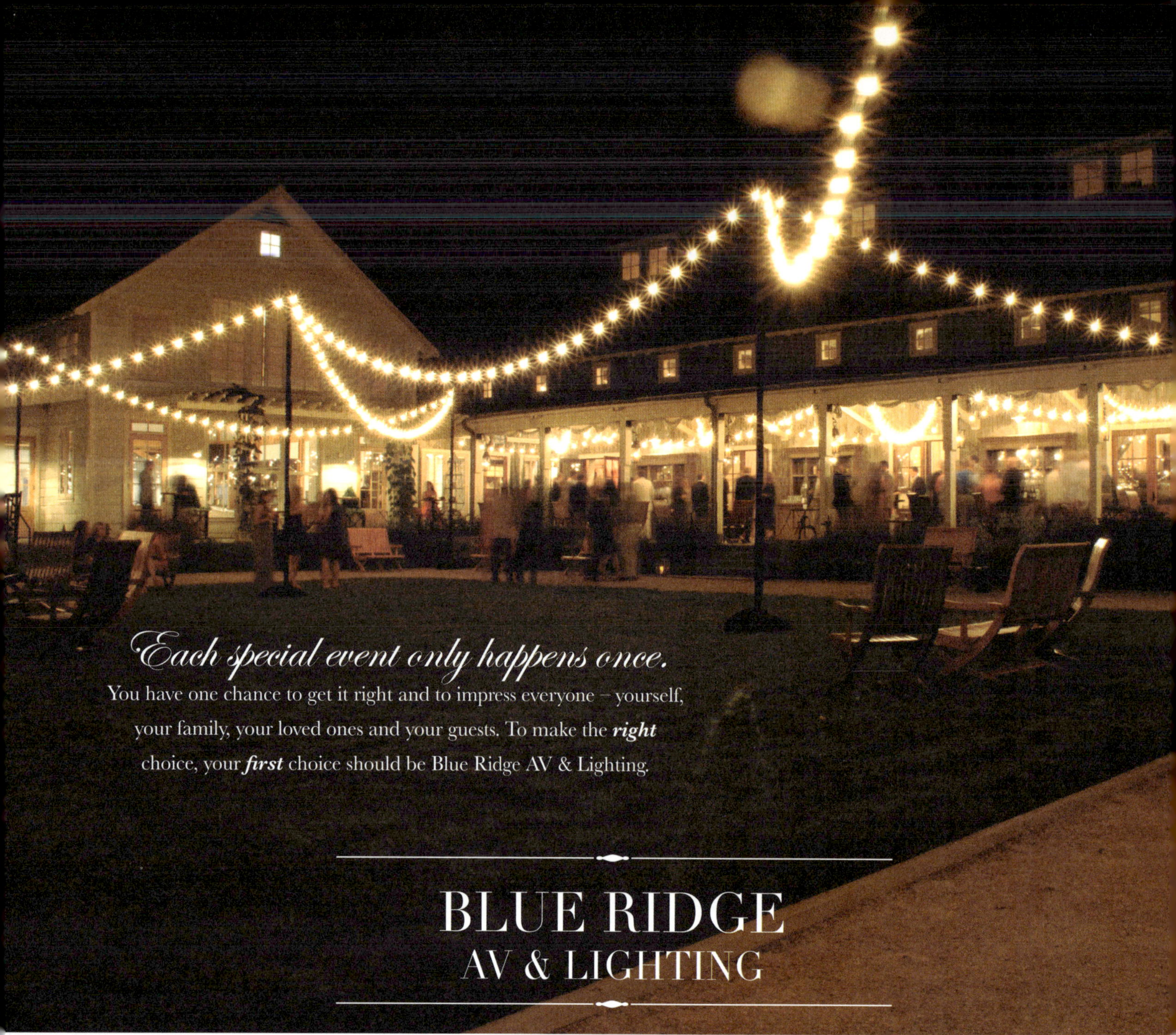

Each special event only happens once.
You have one chance to get it right and to impress everyone – yourself, your family, your loved ones and your guests. To make the right choice, your first choice should be Blue Ridge AV & Lighting.
BLUE RIDGE
AV & LIGHTING

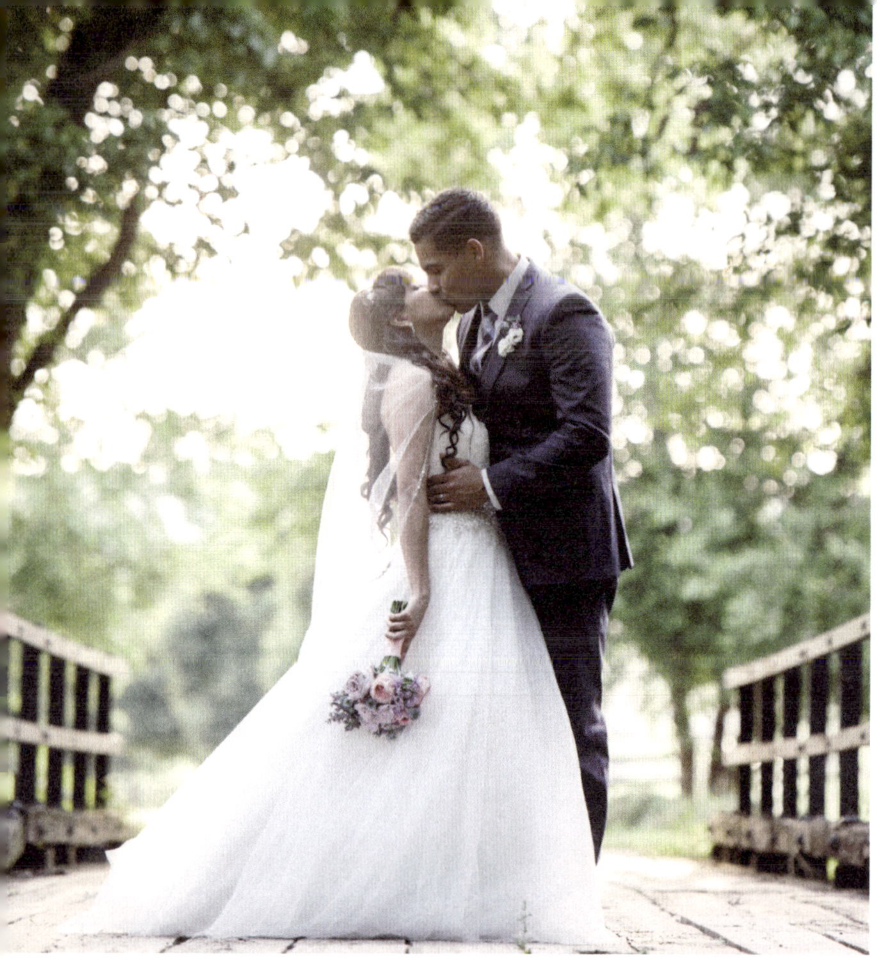
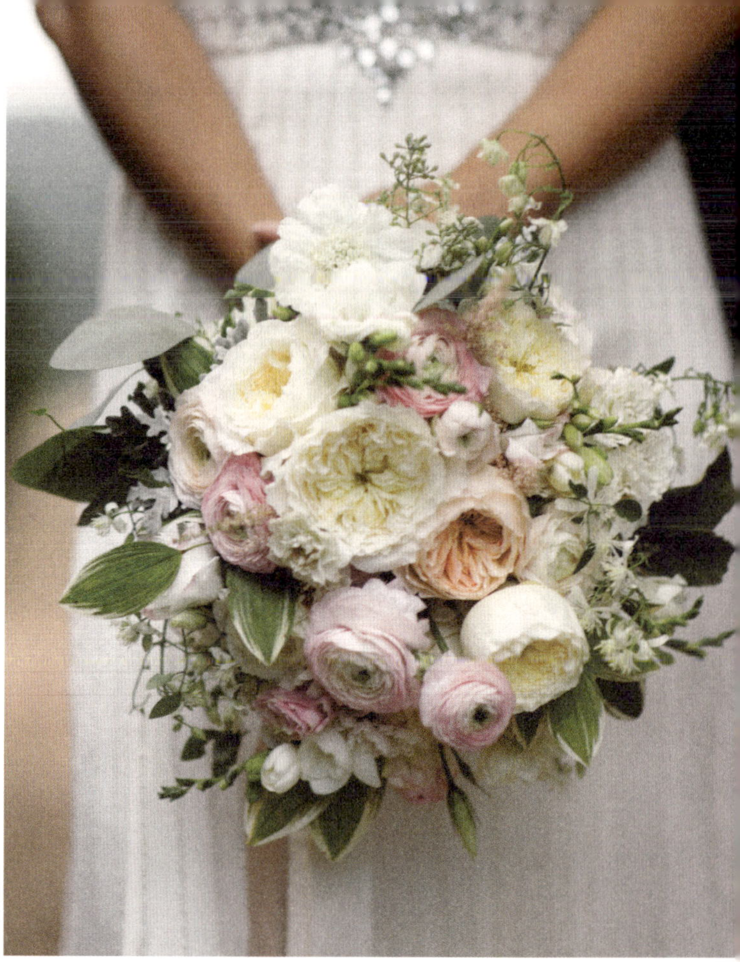
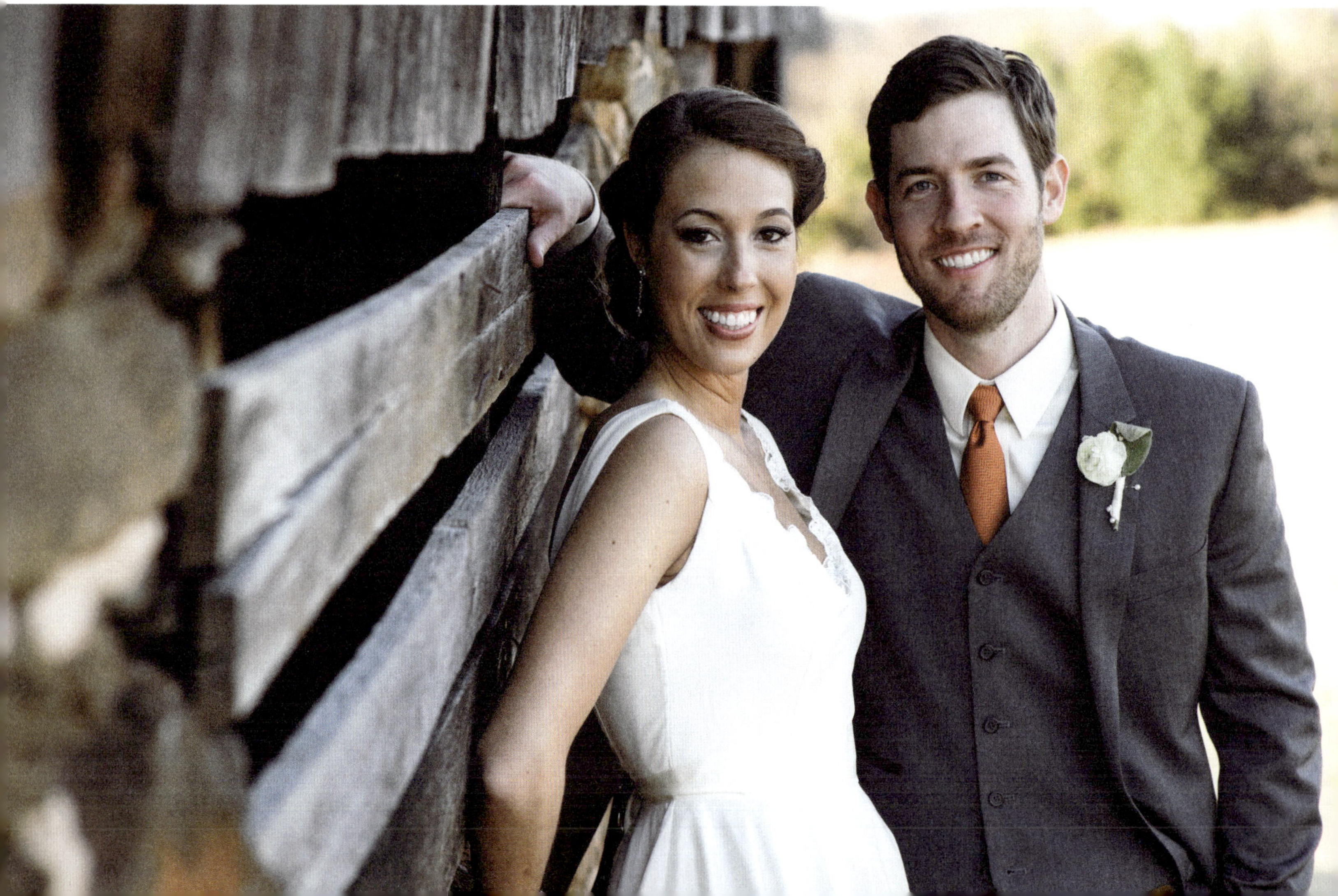

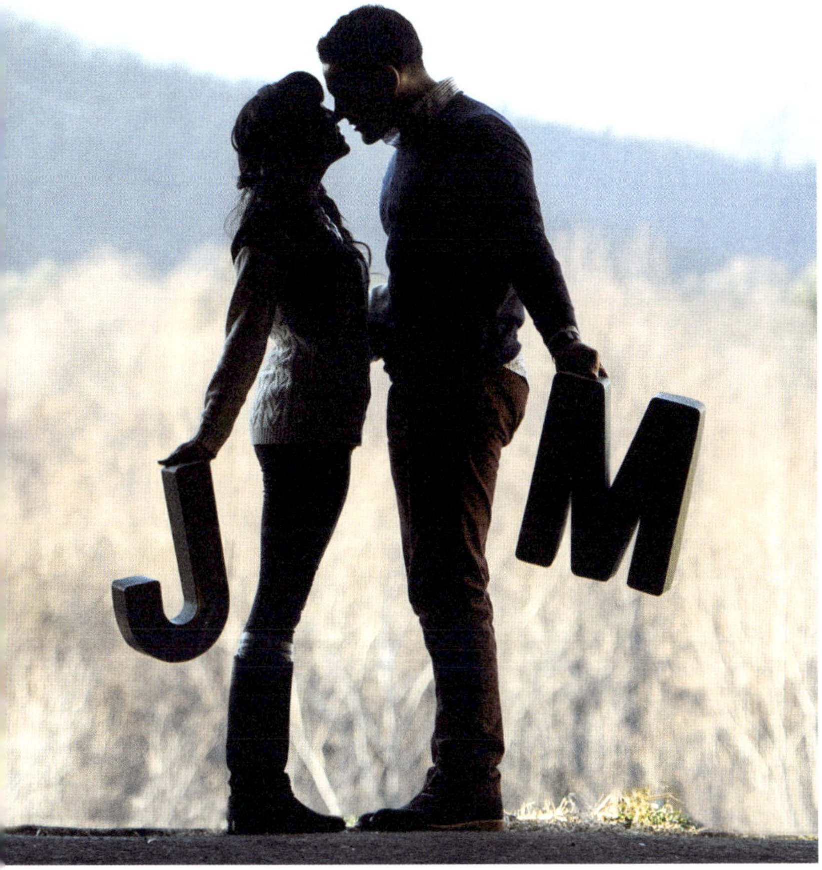

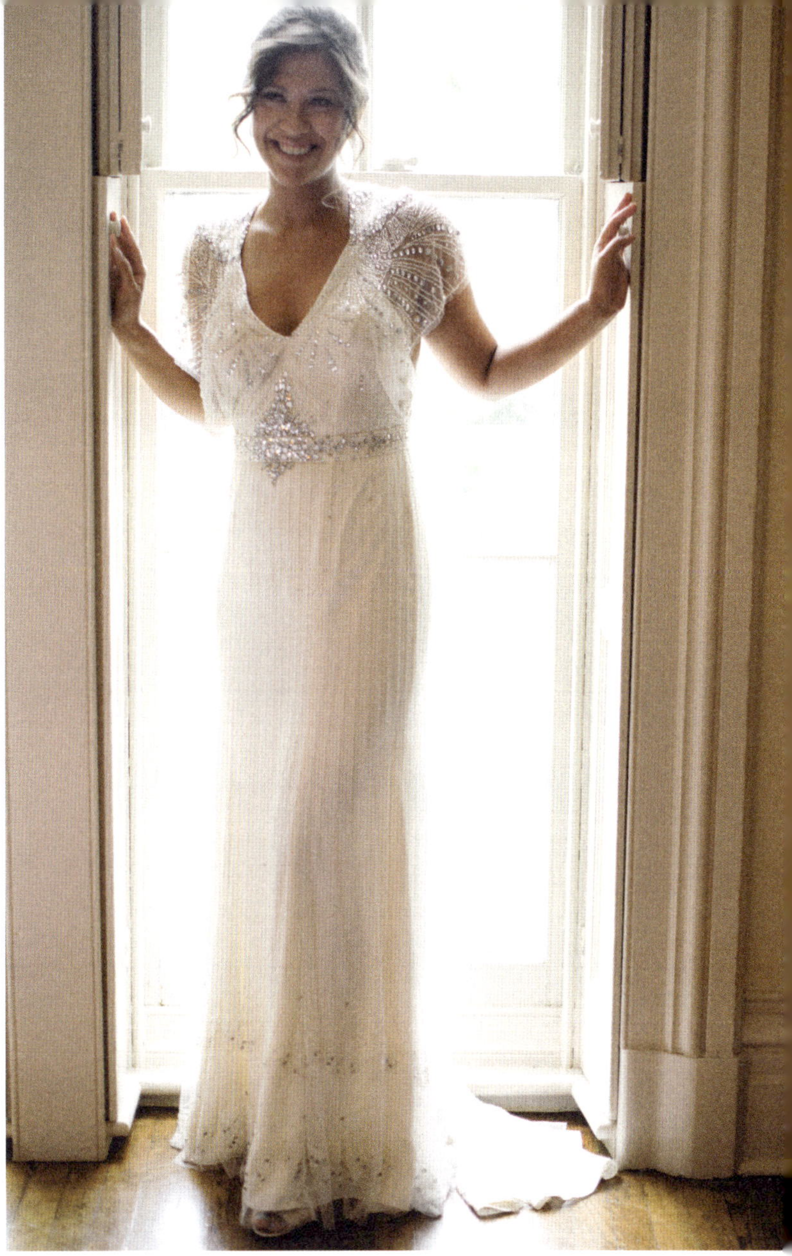

PART OF LIFE'S BEAUTY IS THAT IT IS FULL OF UNFORESEEN TWISTS AND TURNS.

Just when we think we are set to go one way, the journey often directs us someplace completely unexpected. As an Economics major, I spent a year abroad in Paris where I took a photography class and realized I had a passion for being behind the lens. I have never looked back and am grateful that I have been able to develop this passion into a career.

Over 20 years later, I still find joy in every close of the shutter. It is my honor to capture the purest and most sincere moments in peoples' lives. Not only do I take pride in providing my clients with stunning images, I do so in a way that is always professional and engaging. Weddings don't always go exactly as planned. Sometimes there is bad weather, poor lighting, or the timeline just gets derailed. It happens! My clients know that they never need to worry. Dealing with surprises is second nature to me, and my career as a seasoned photographer allows me to never skip a beat. Your precious memories will always be captured beautifully.

My photography style is timeless and classic. My clients tell me that my laid-back personality helps to put everyone at ease and allows the story of the day to unfold naturally and with joy. It is an honor and a privilege that I don't take lightly.

robert radifera
PHOTOGRAPHY

RADIFERA.COM

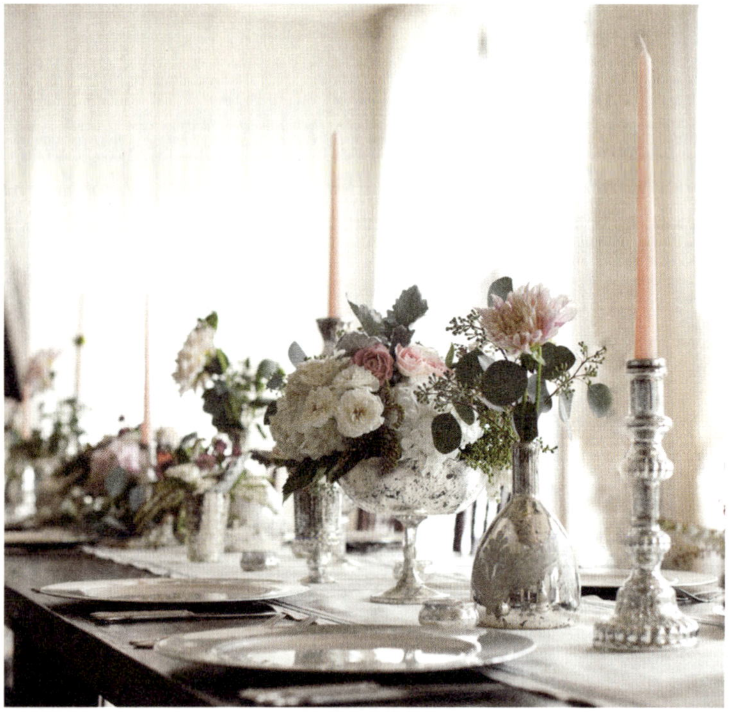

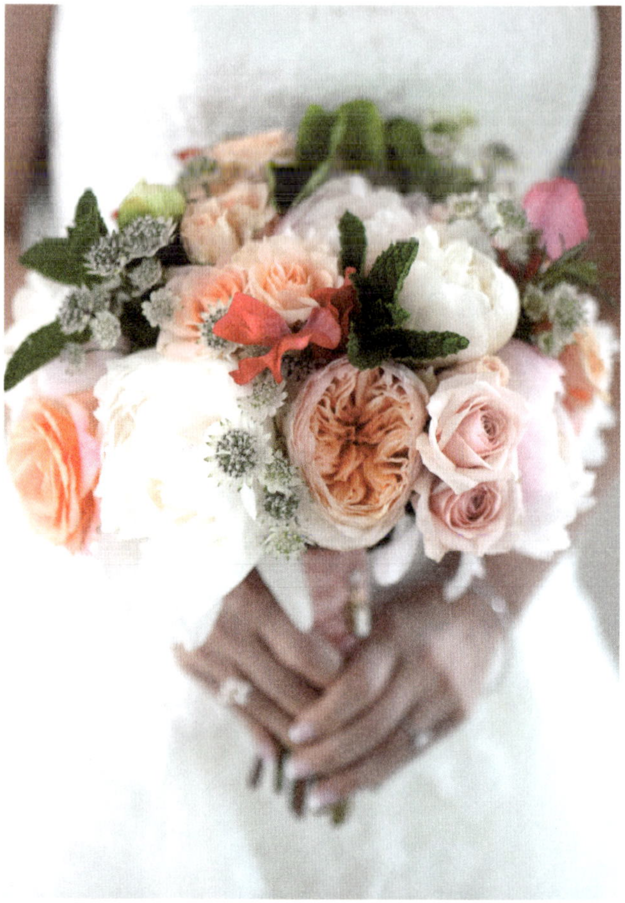

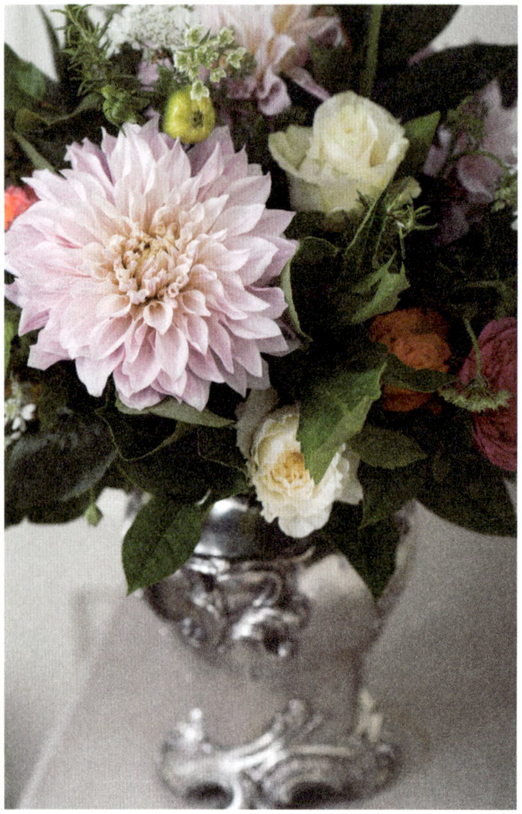

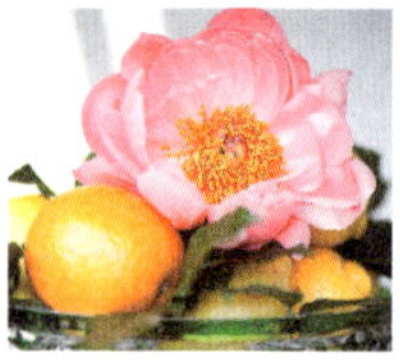

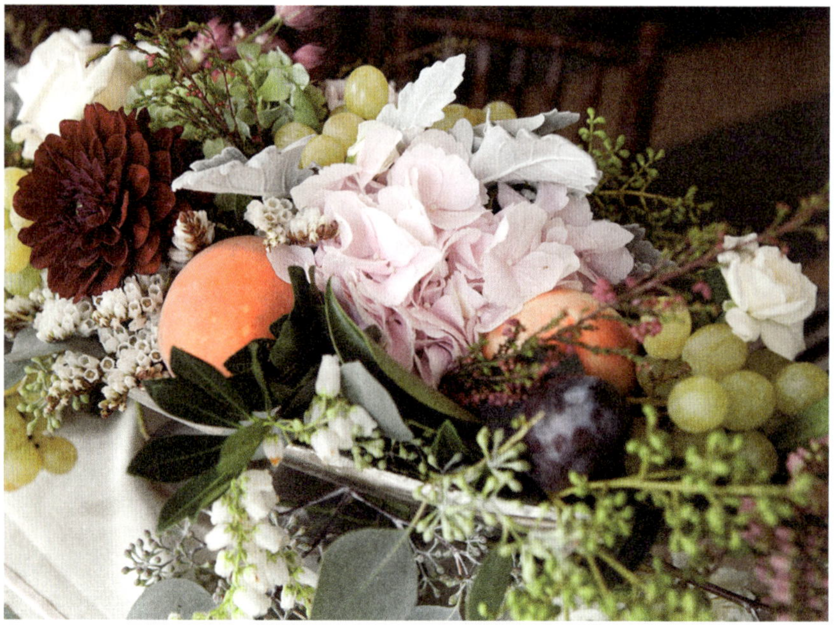

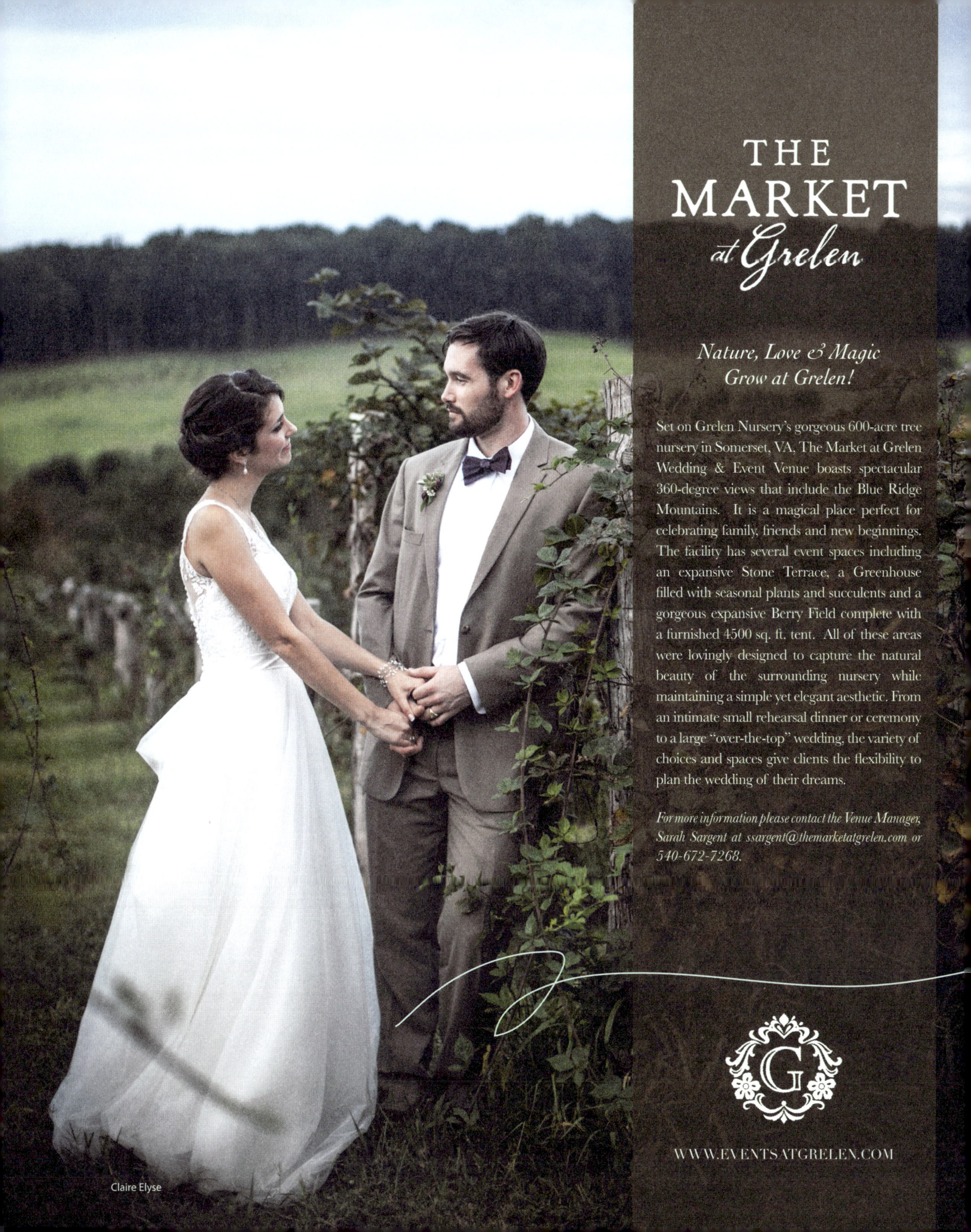

Claire Elyse

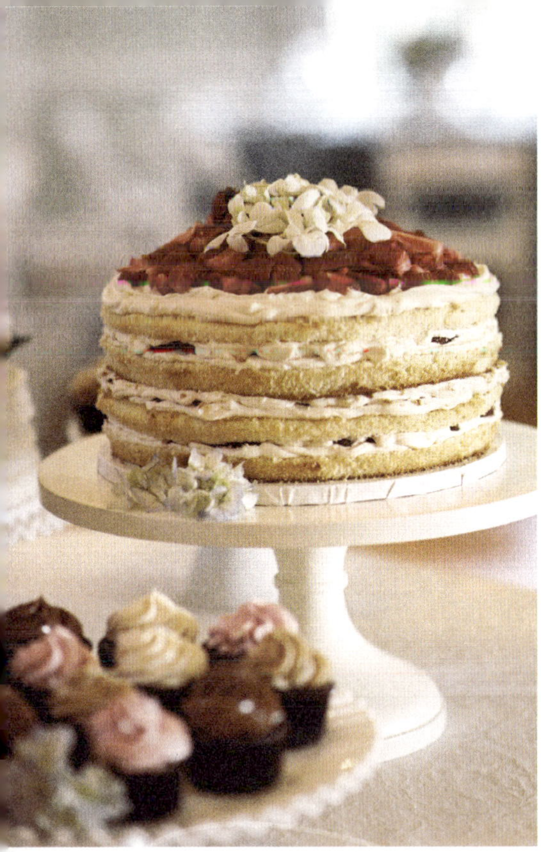

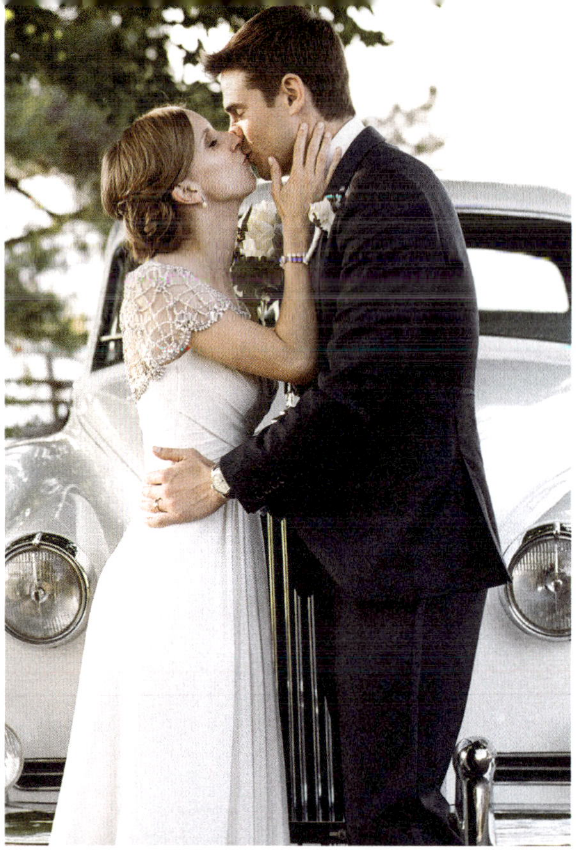

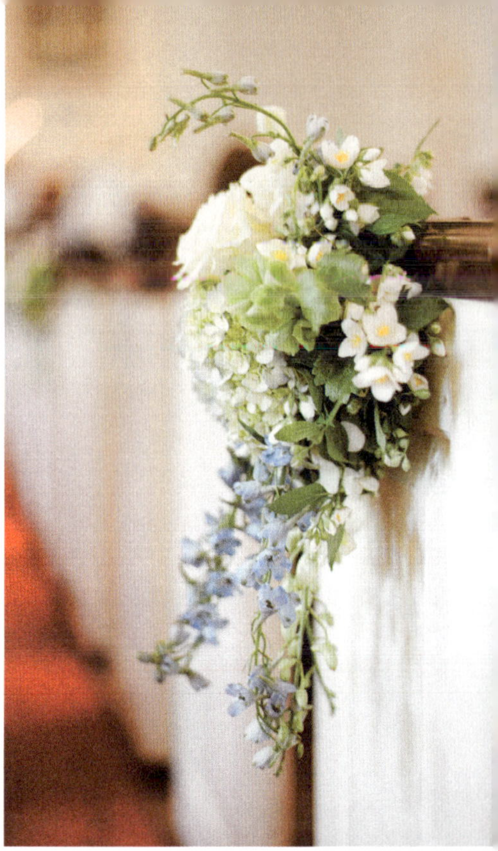

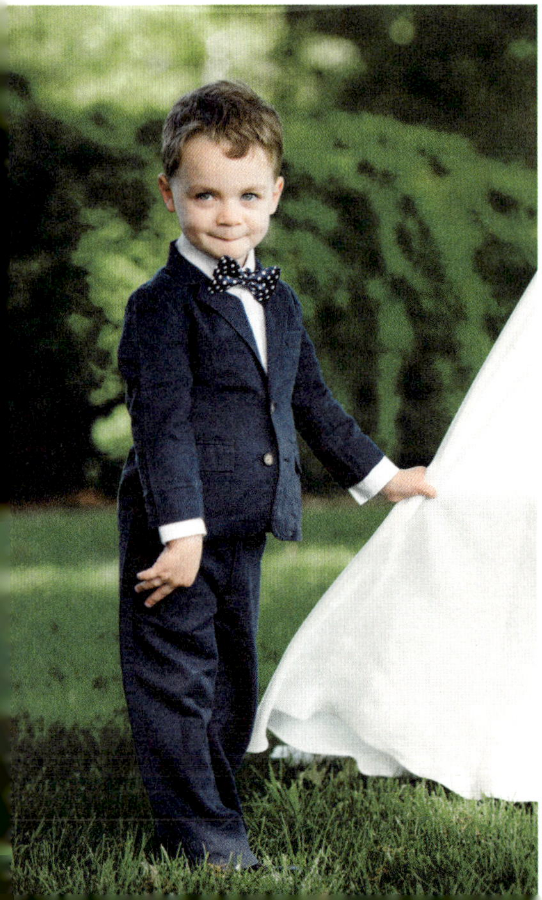

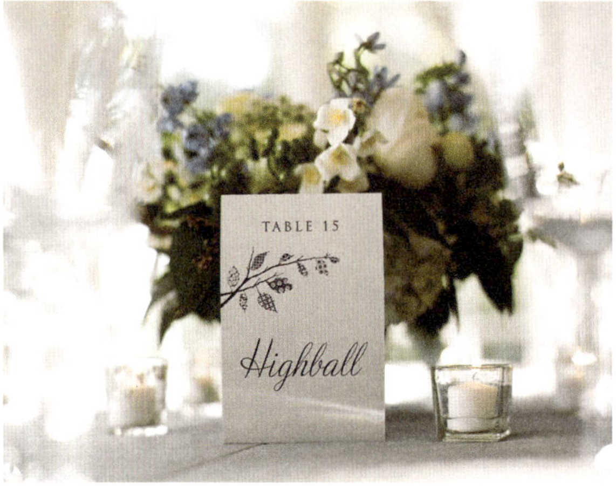
TABLE 15
Highball

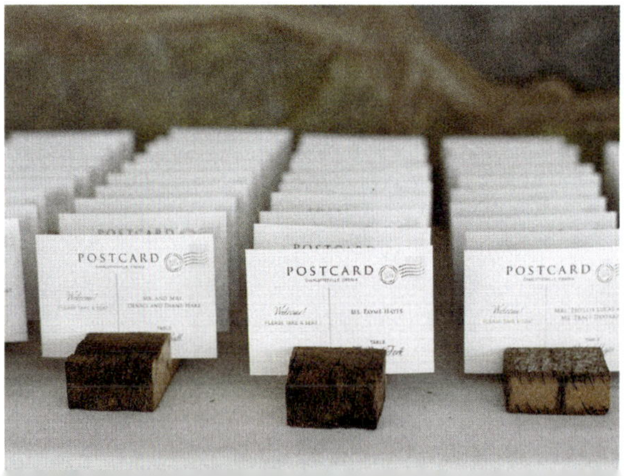
POSTCARD
POSTCARD
POSTCARD

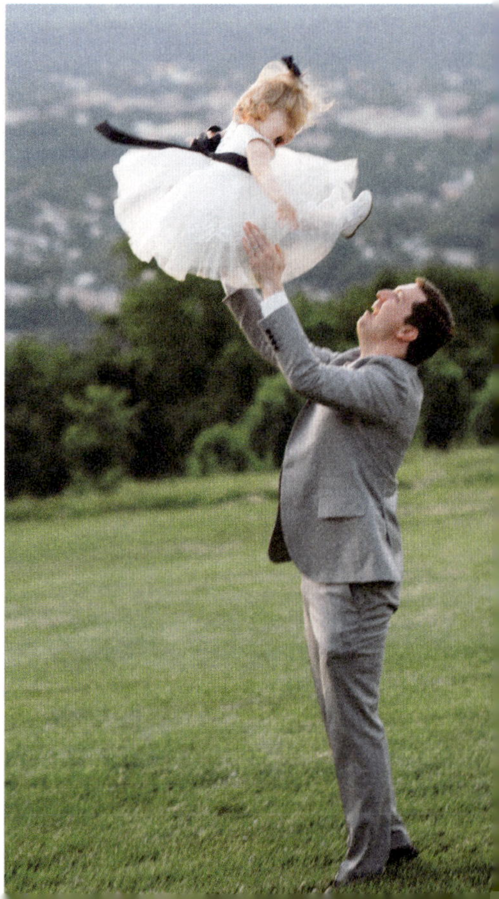

WHITE BIRCH *events*

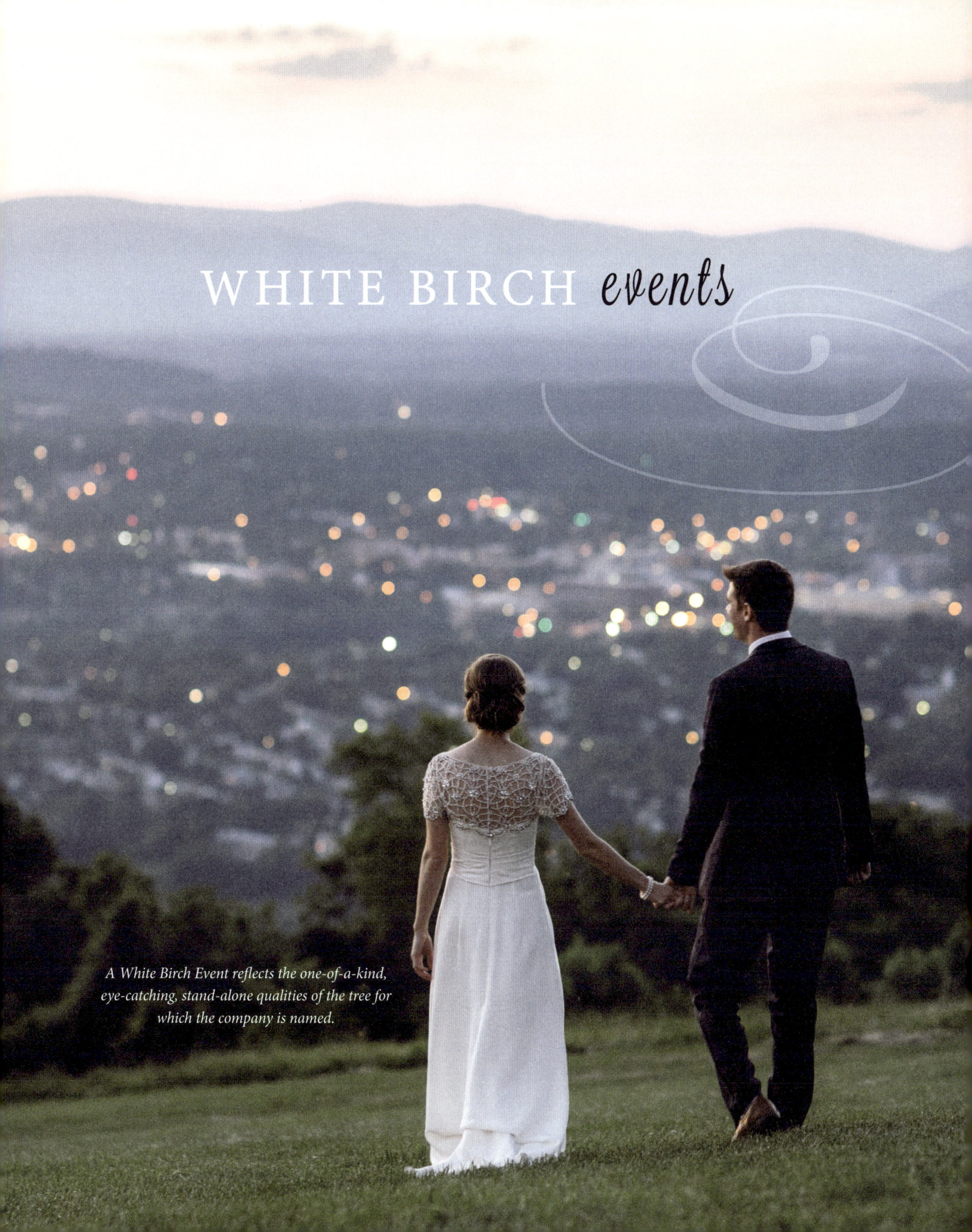

A White Birch Event reflects the one-of-a-kind, eye-catching, stand-alone qualities of the tree for which the company is named.

DONOVAN-GROVES EVENTS

"It couldn't have been a more perfect wedding weekend. You were with us all three days of events, ensuring everything was going as planned. It was better than we could have ever imagined!"

Cara, Bride

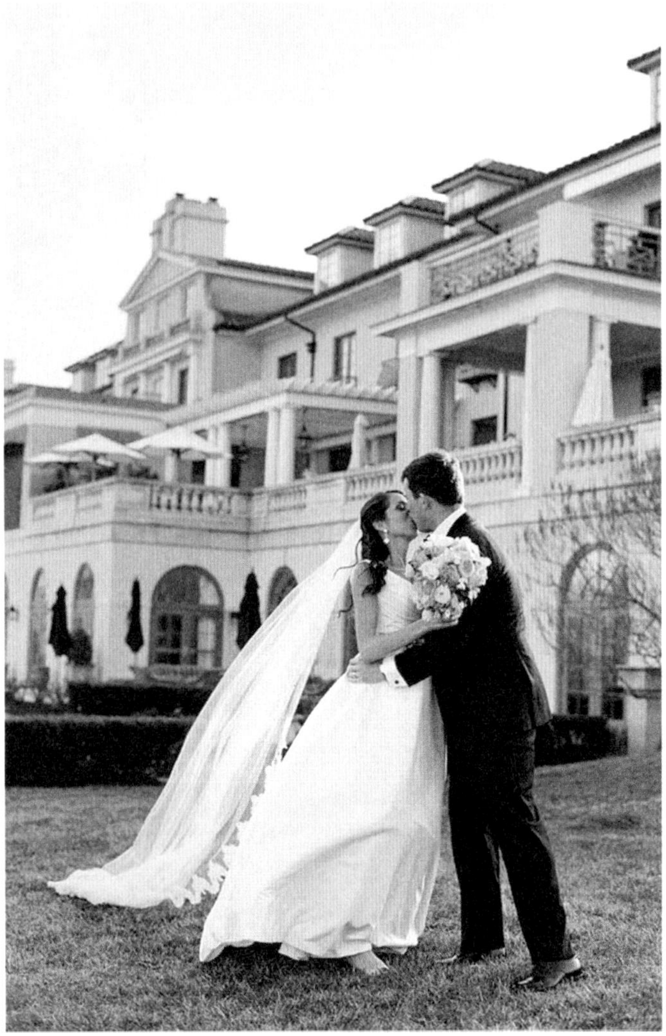

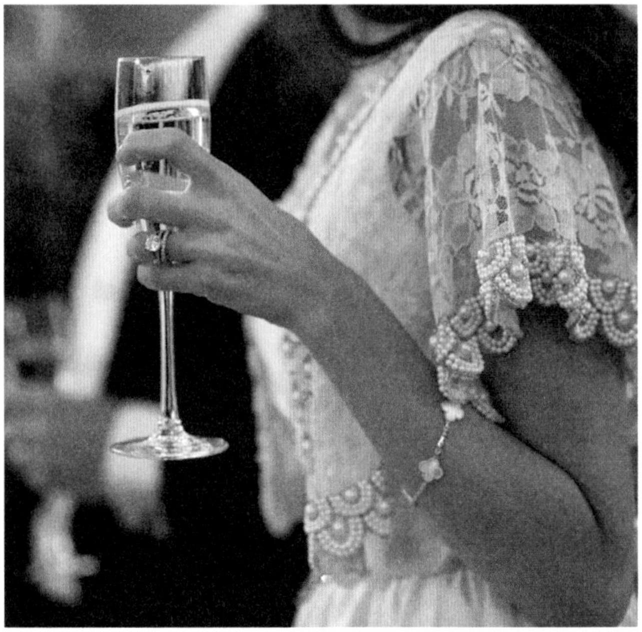

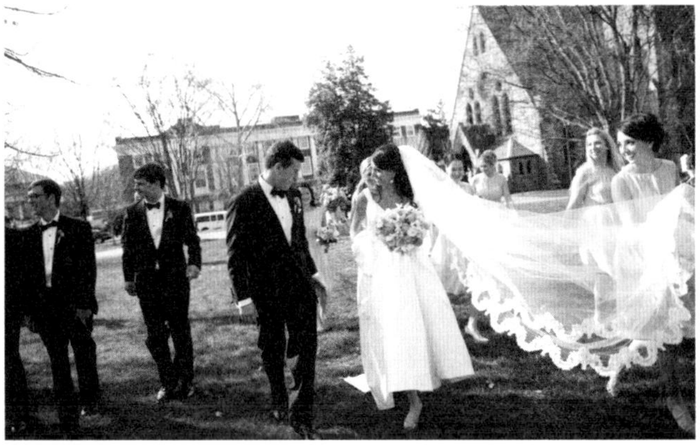

DONOVANGROVESEVENTS.COM | 434.249.2424

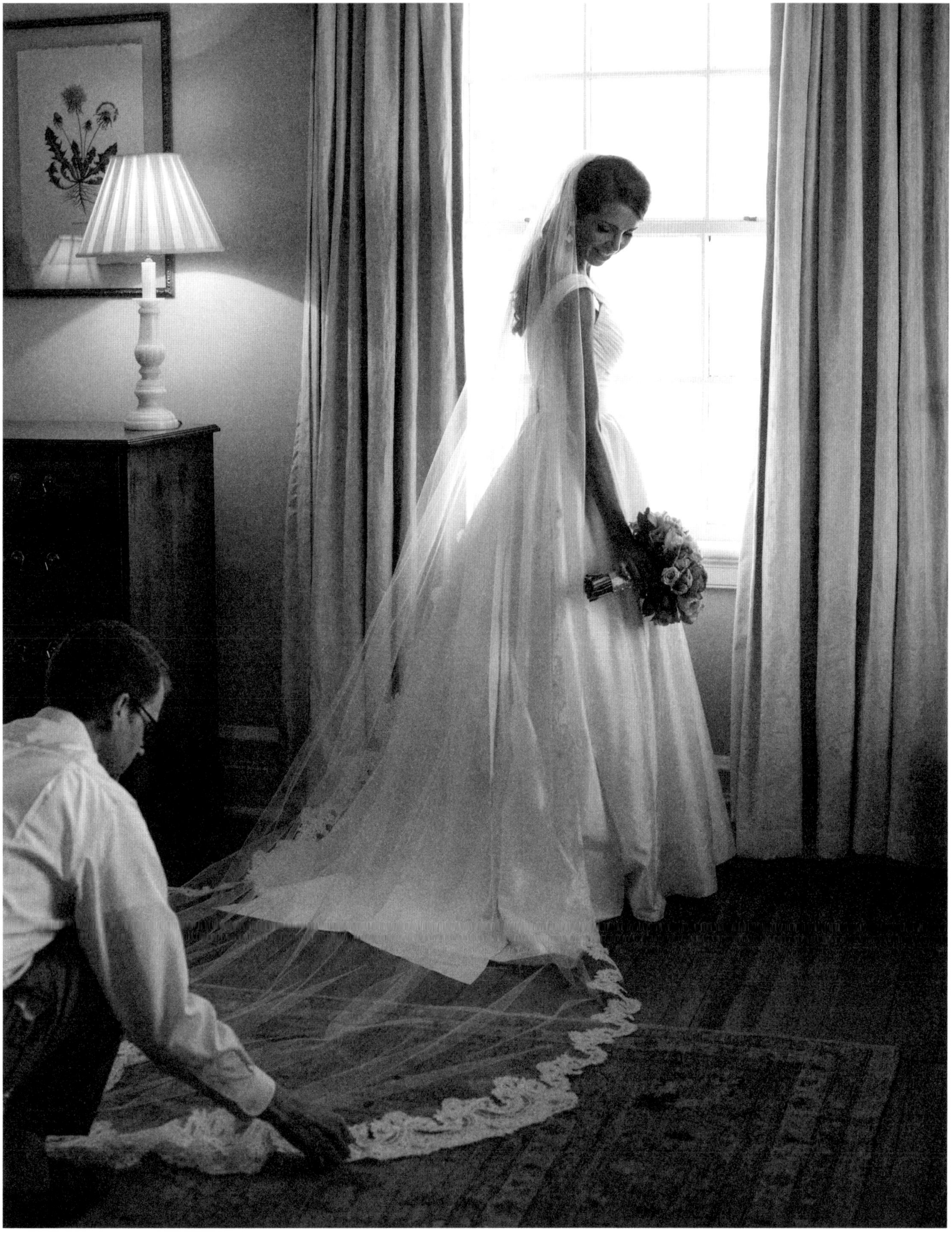

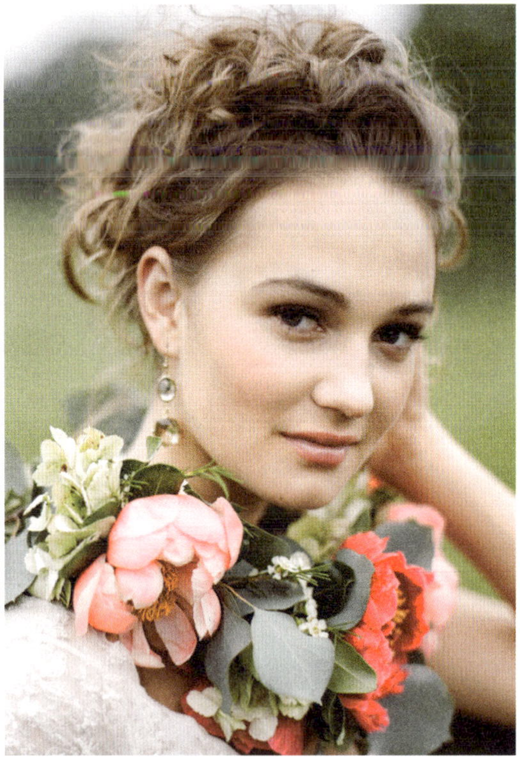
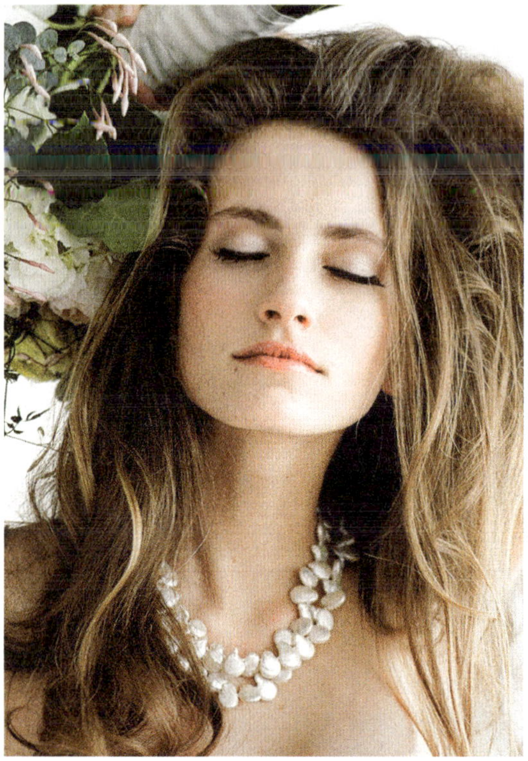

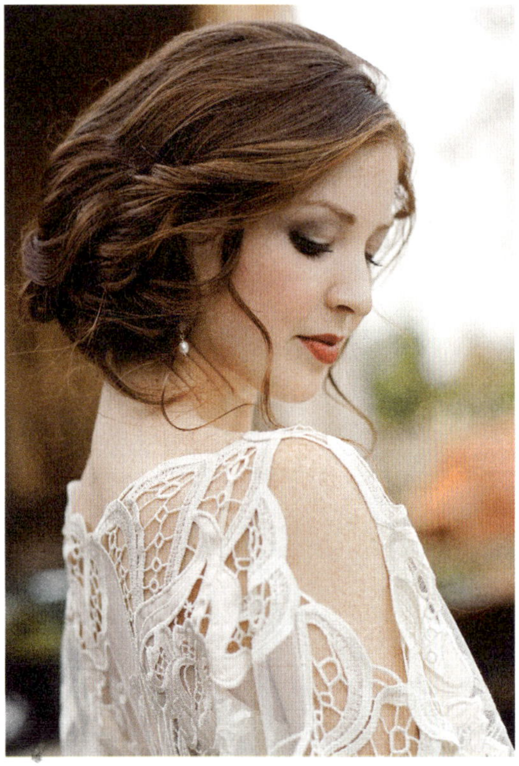
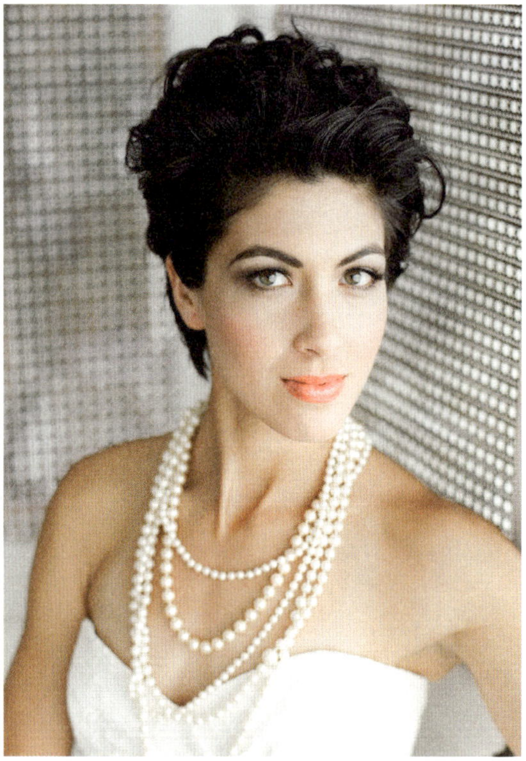

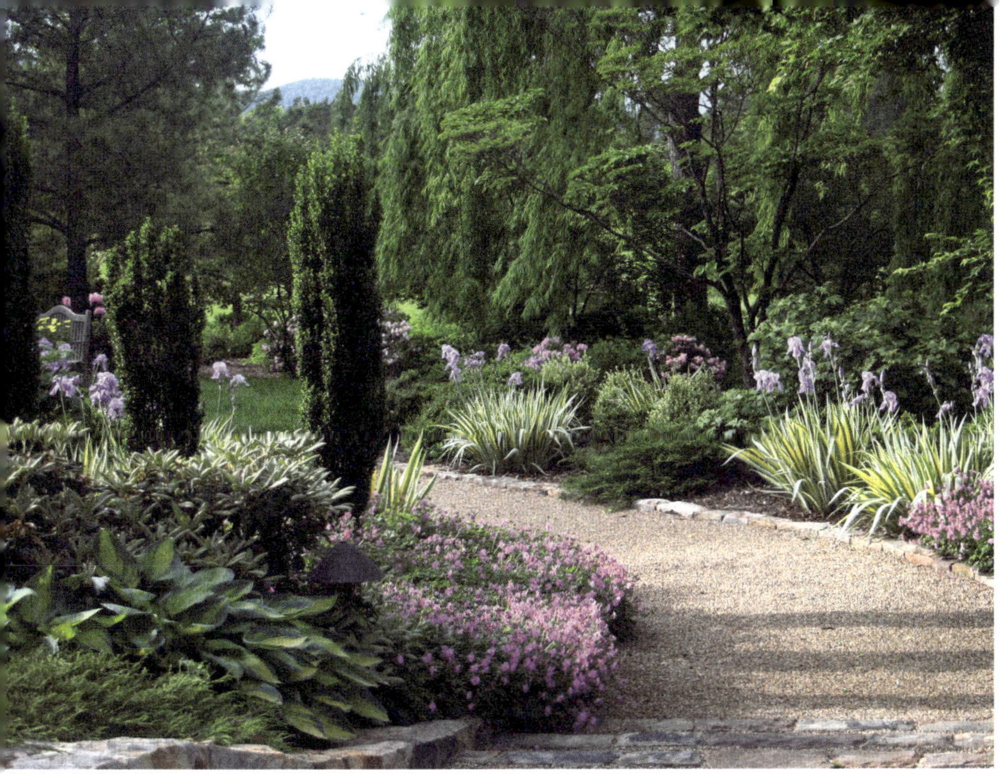

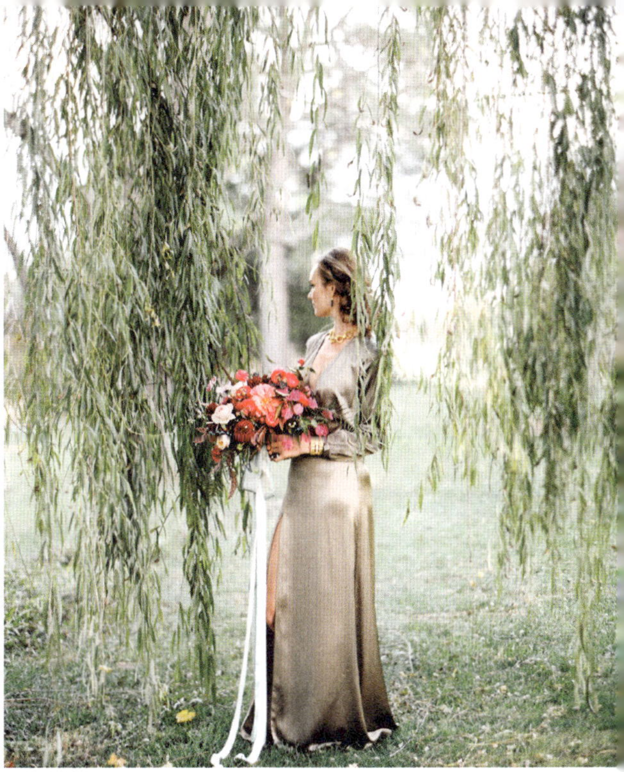

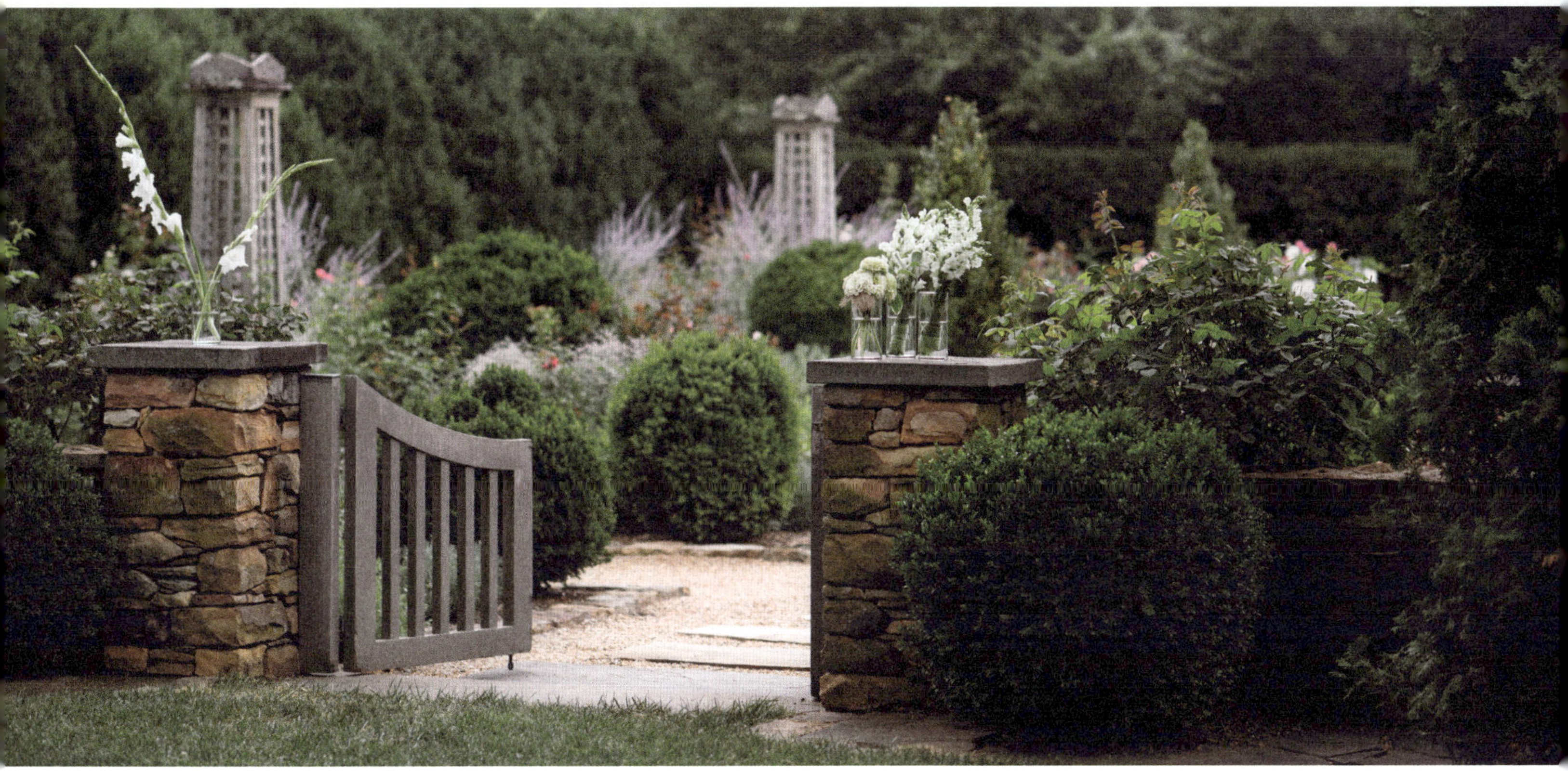

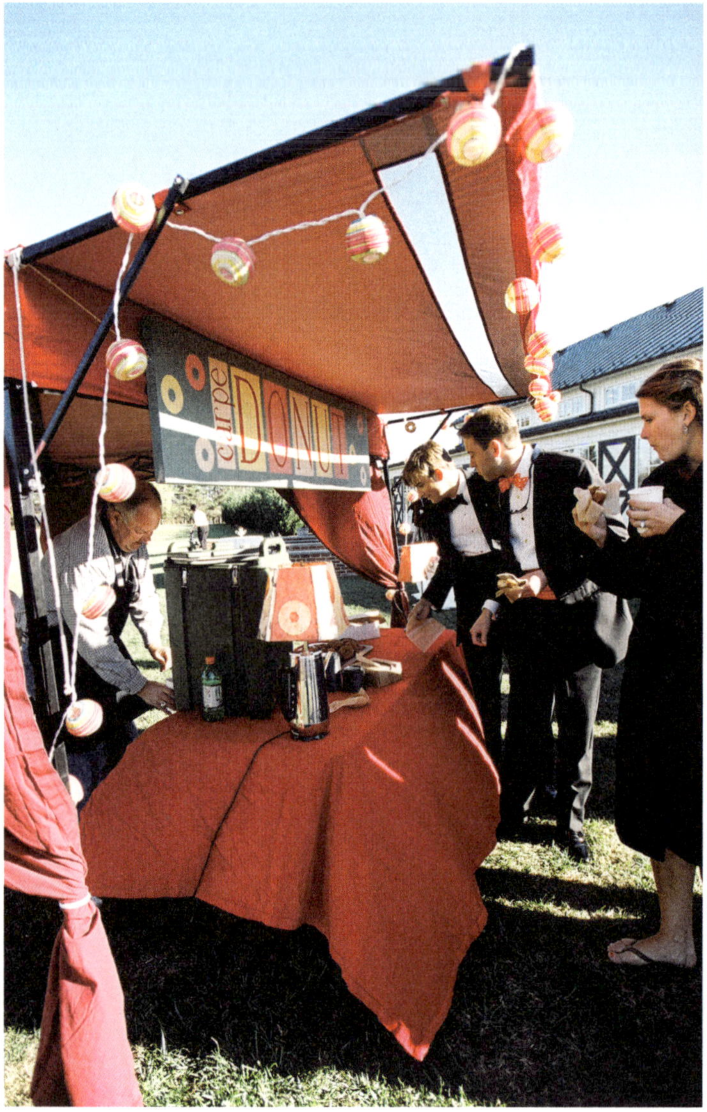

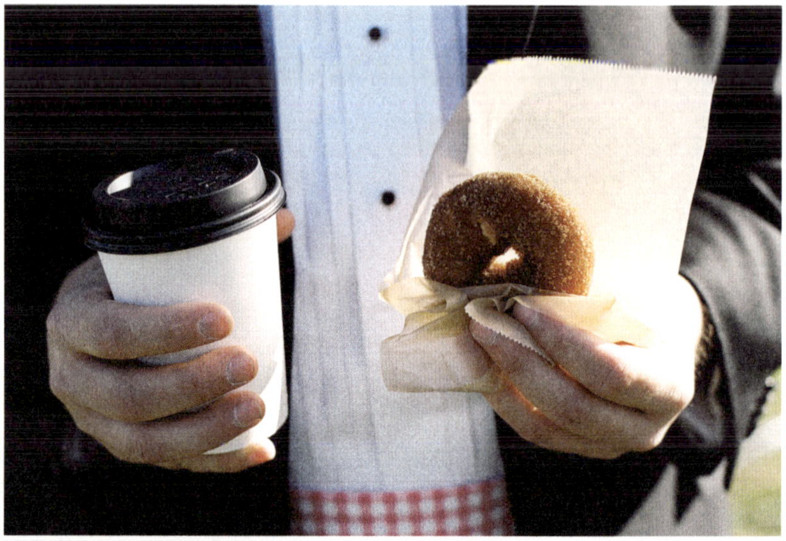

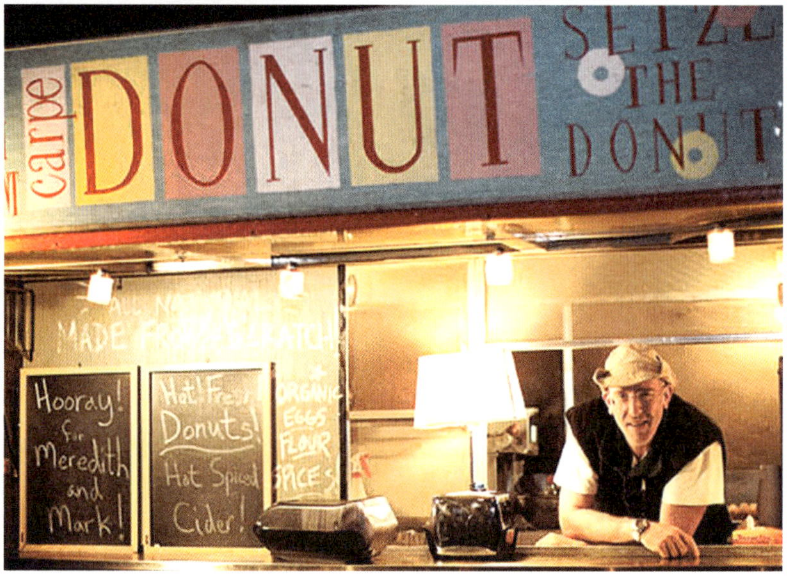

We can provide a truly memorable, festive, and delicious experience for your guests to help mark your special day.

Our yummy donuts are homemade, handmade, and custom to your event. Our cart provides a unique and celebratory look, our apple cider donuts are made hot and fresh on-site, and our company is local, employee-owned, and one-of-a-kind.

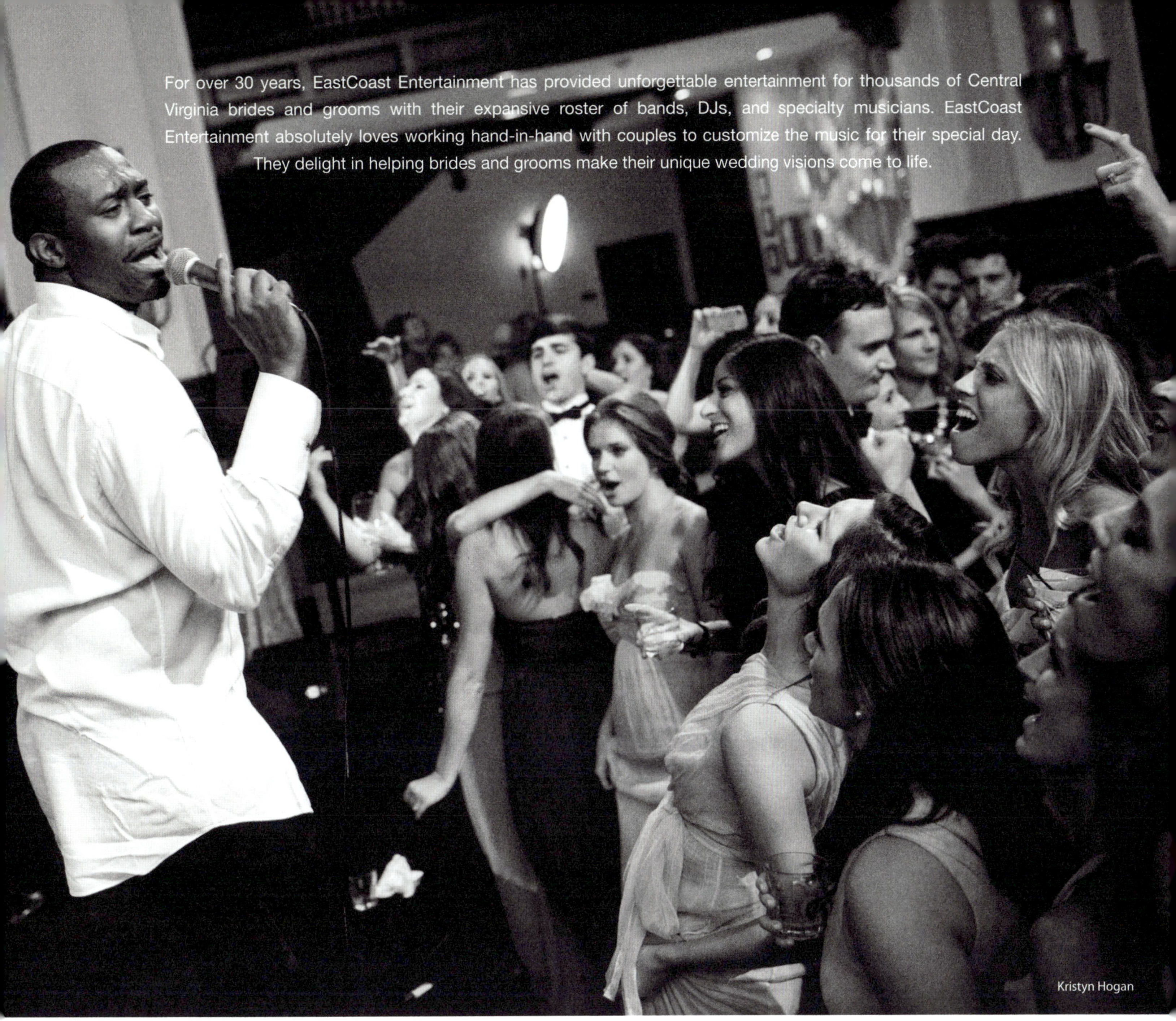

For over 30 years, EastCoast Entertainment has provided unforgettable entertainment for thousands of Central Virginia brides and grooms with their expansive roster of bands, DJs, and specialty musicians. EastCoast Entertainment absolutely loves working hand-in-hand with couples to customize the music for their special day. They delight in helping brides and grooms make their unique wedding visions come to life.

Kristyn Hogan

EastCoast ENTERTAINMENT

www.eastcoastentertainment.com | 800.277.6874

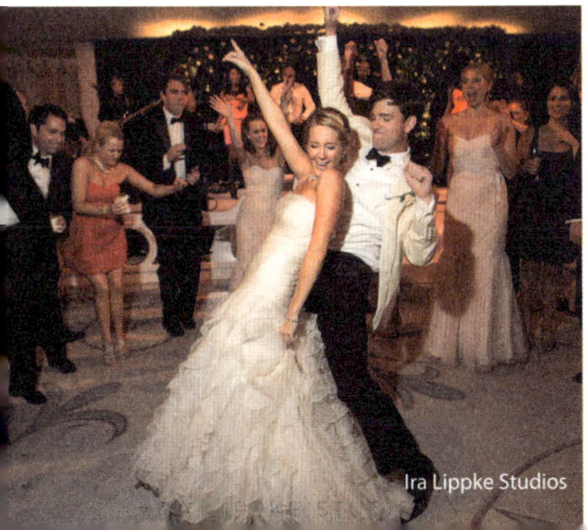

Ira Lippke Studios

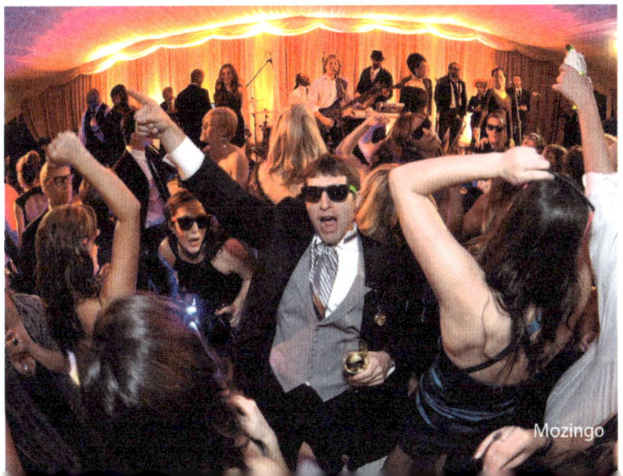

Mozingo

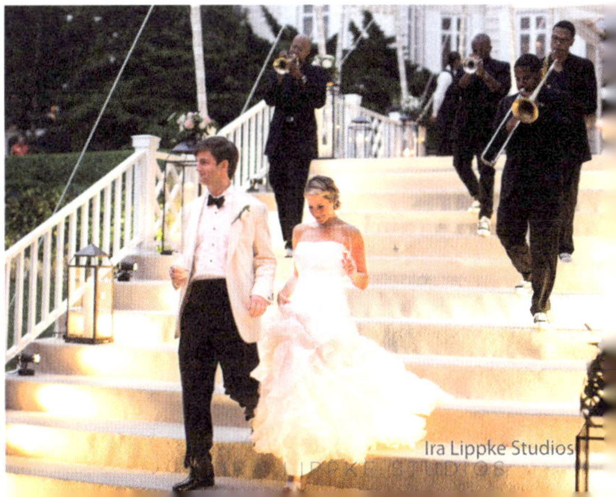

Ira Lippke Studios

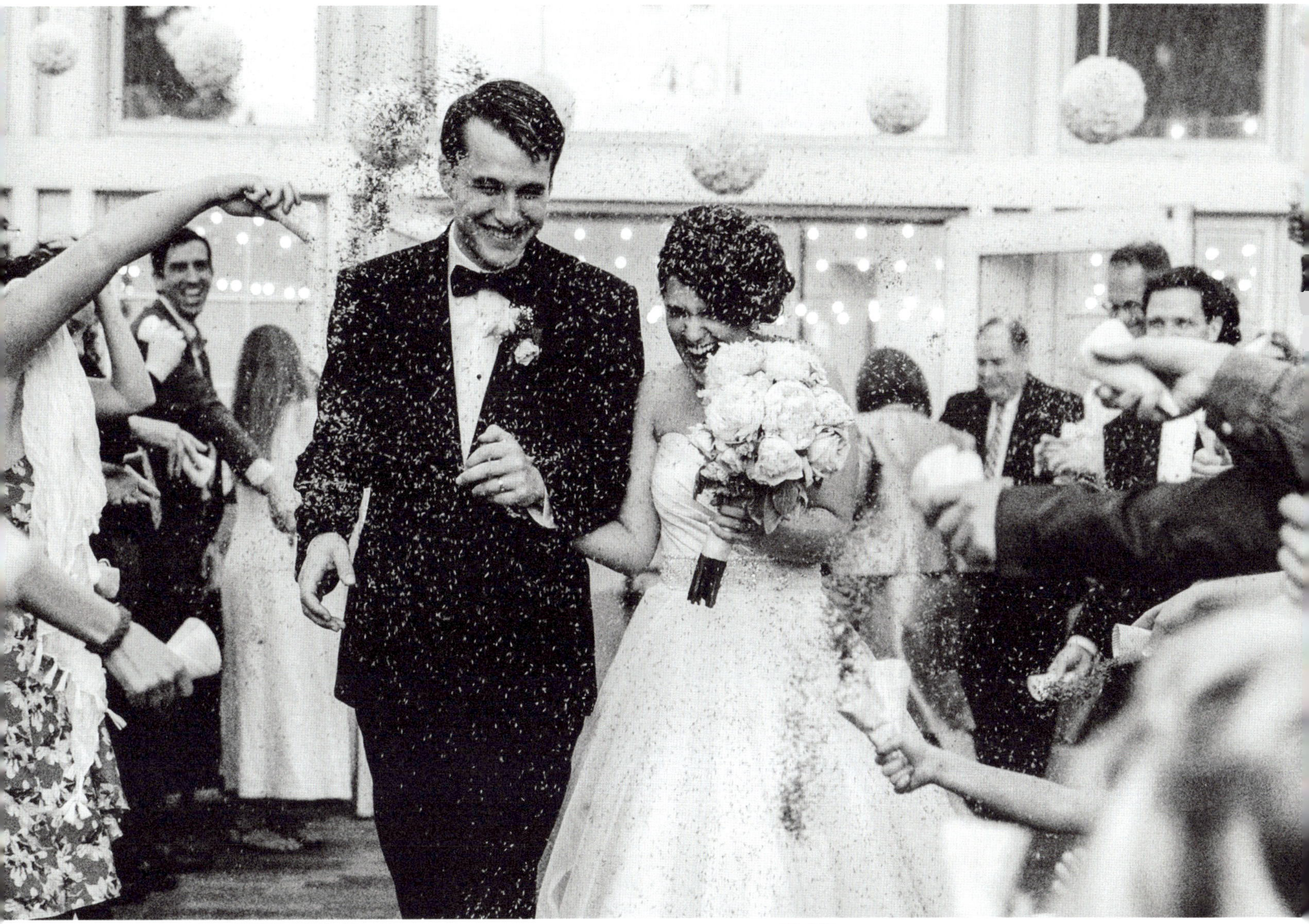

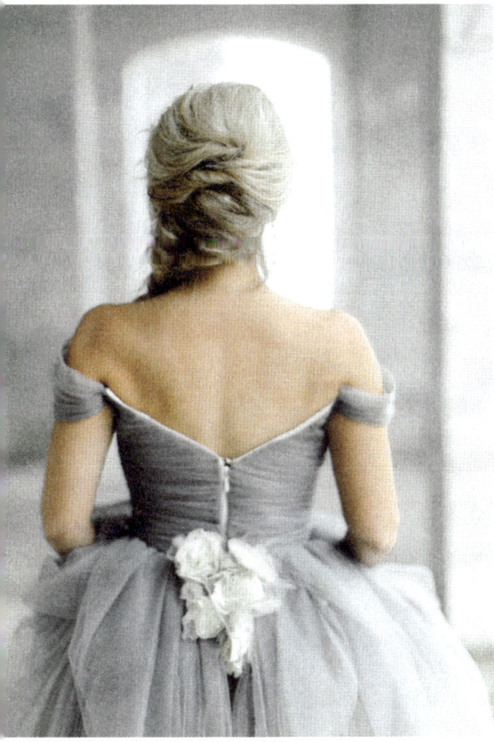

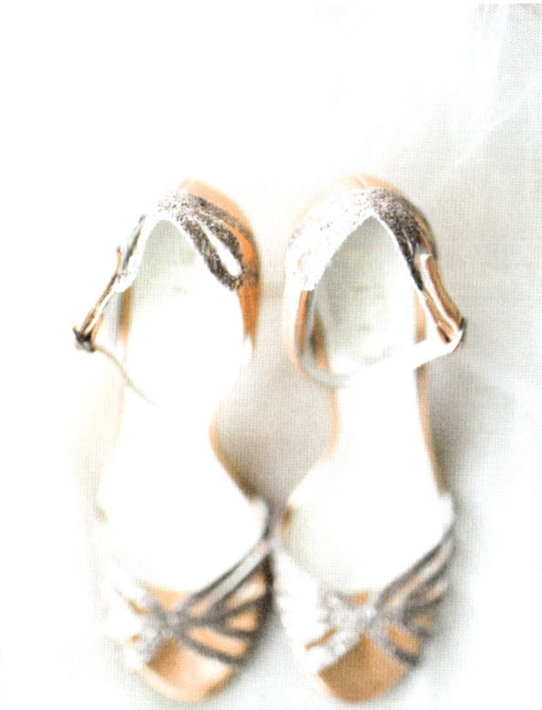

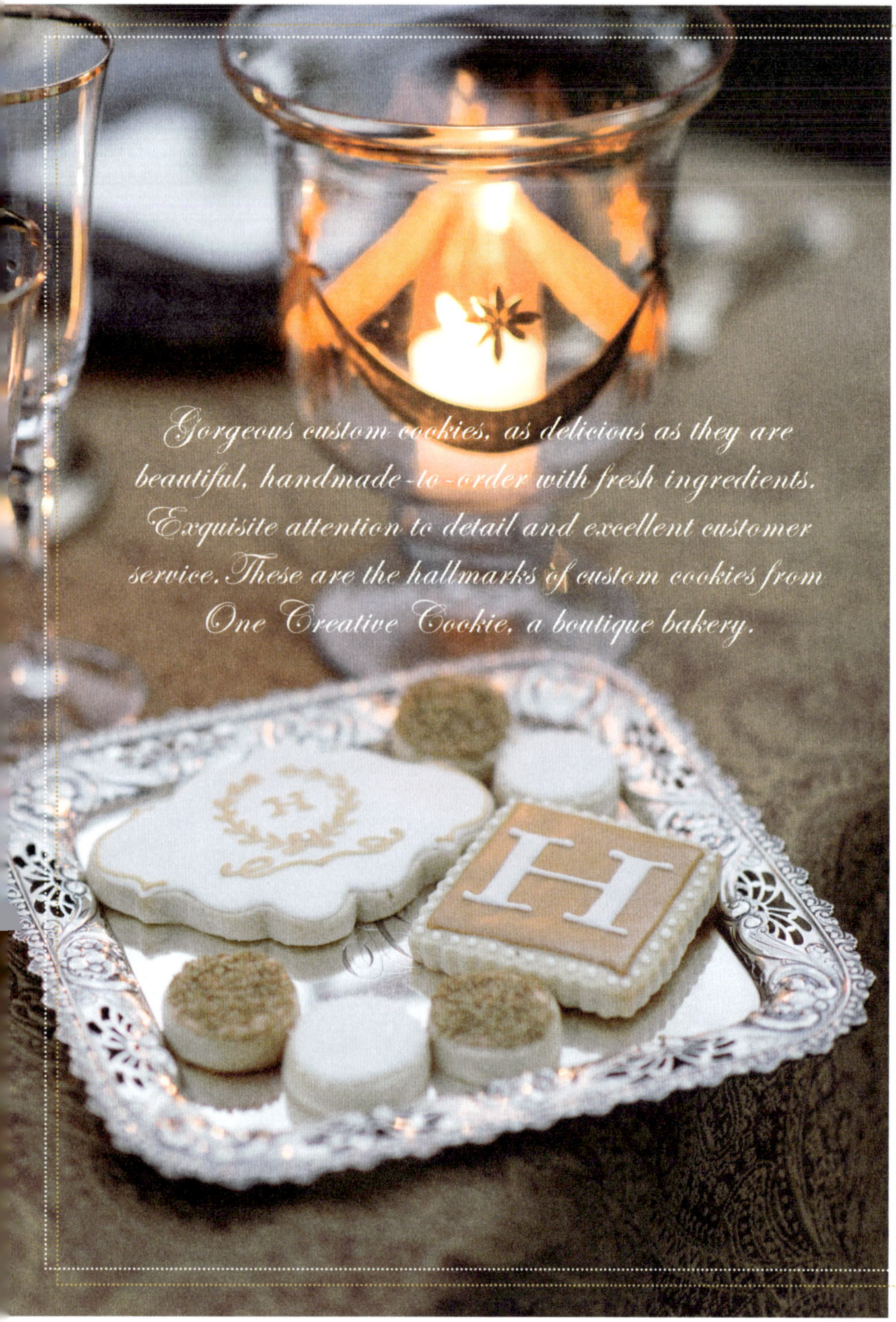
Gorgeous custom cookies, as delicious as they are beautiful, handmade-to-order with fresh ingredients.
Exquisite attention to detail and excellent customer service. These are the hallmarks of custom cookies from One Creative Cookie, a boutique bakery.

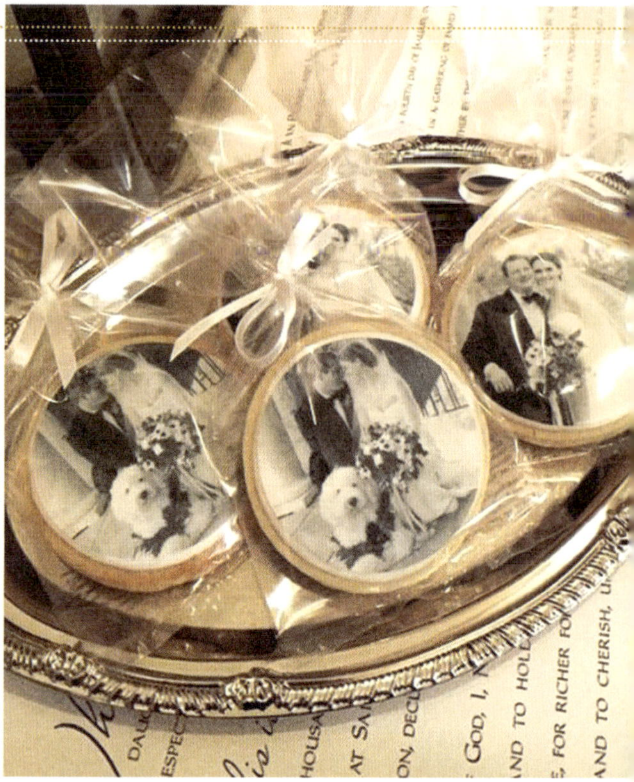

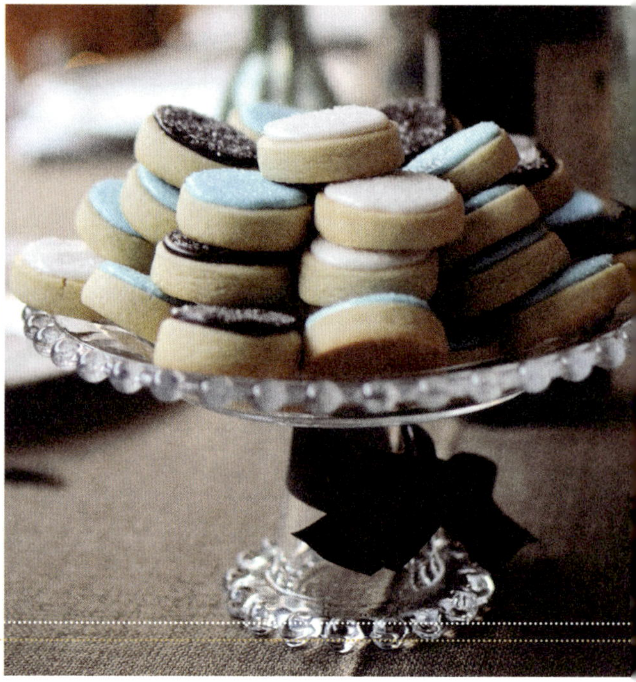

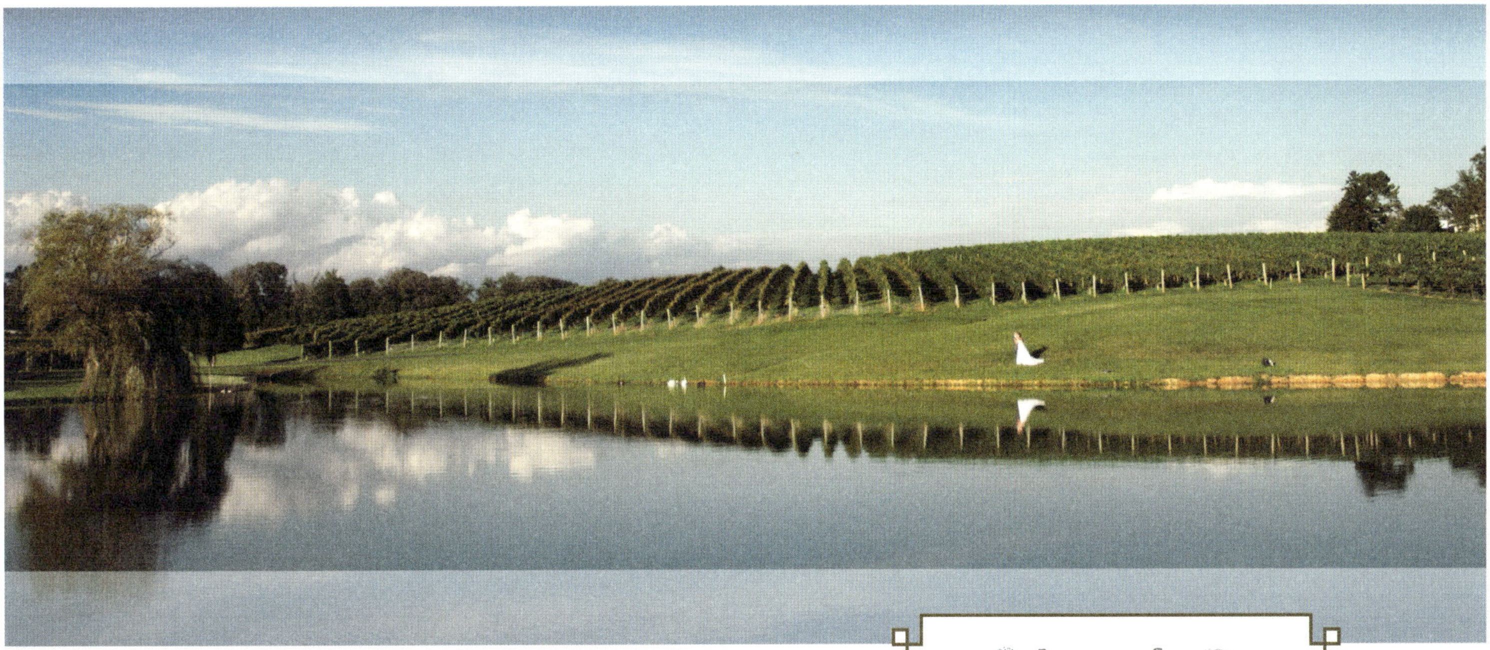

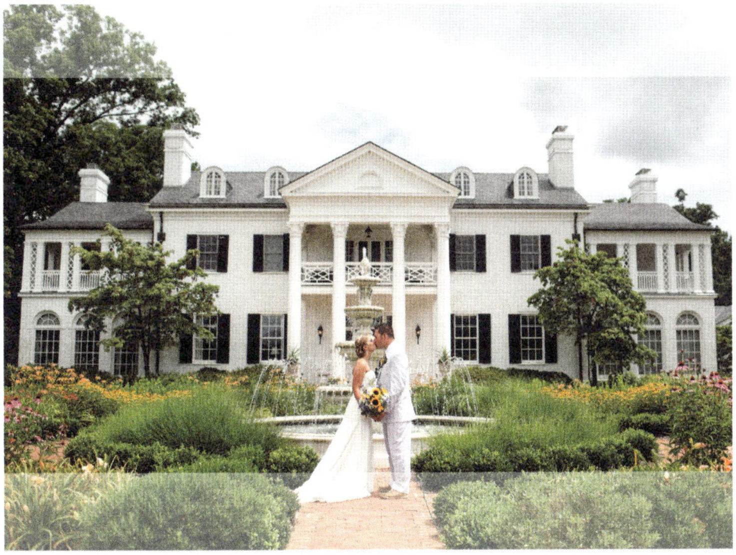

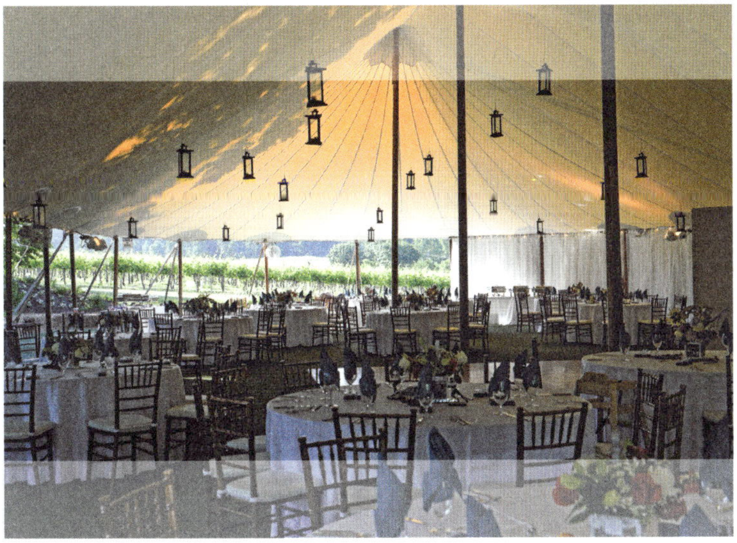

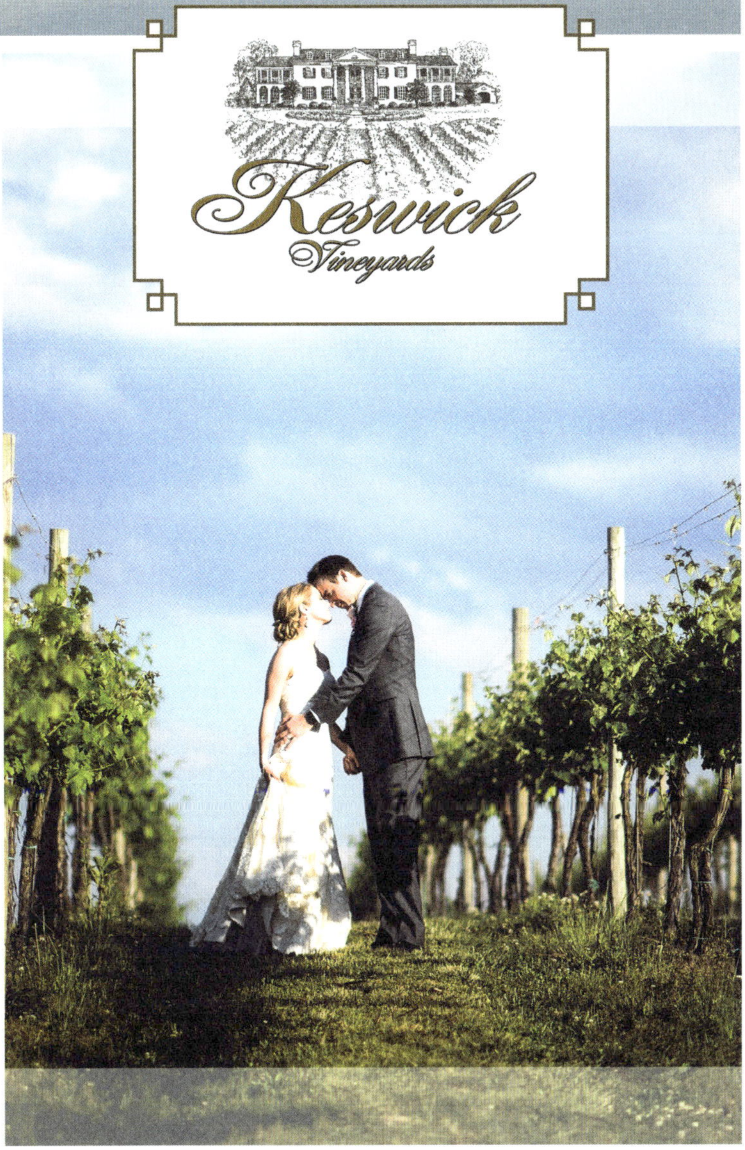

Keswick Vineyards is an award-winning winery featuring some of Virginia's best wines. We offer you a unique estate setting like no other. Rich in history dating back to the Revolutionary War and nestled in a valley of rolling farmland surrounded by the Blue Ridge Mountains, Keswick Vineyard lends itself as the perfect backdrop for your ceremony, cocktail hour and reception.

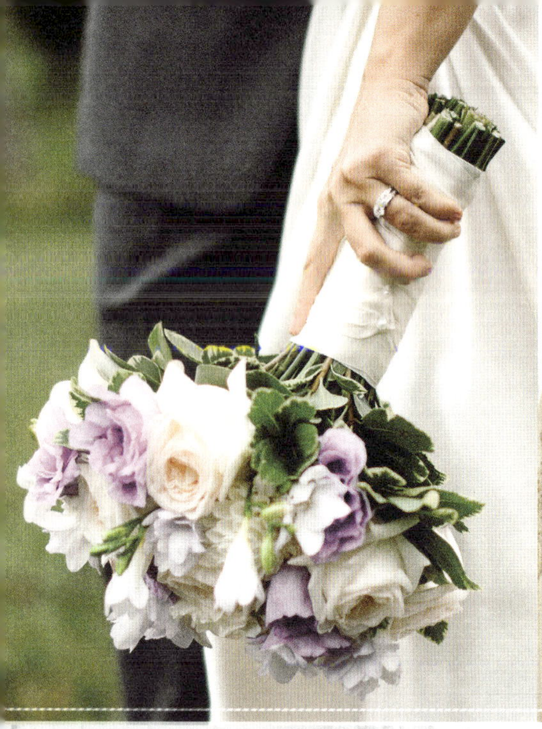

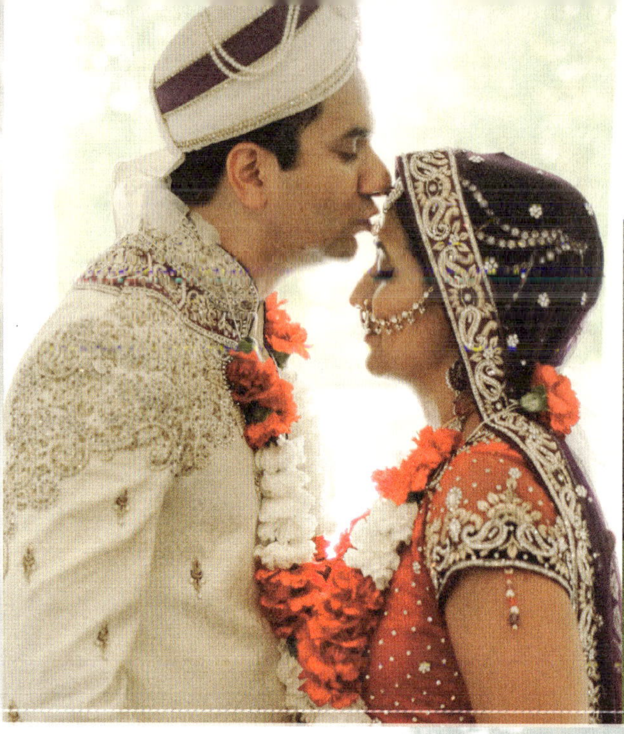

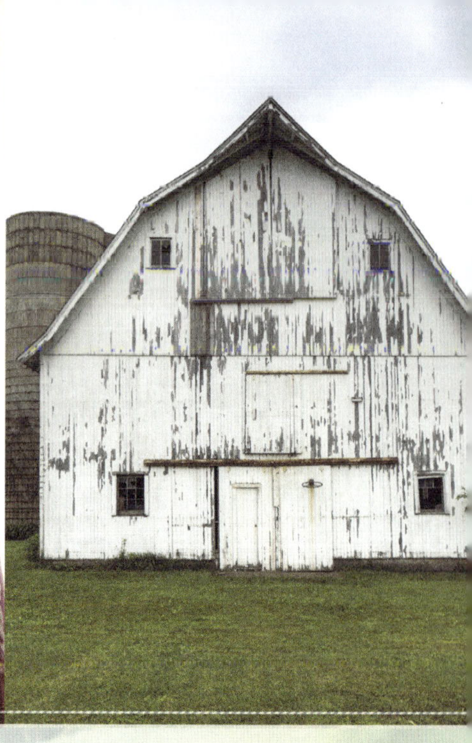

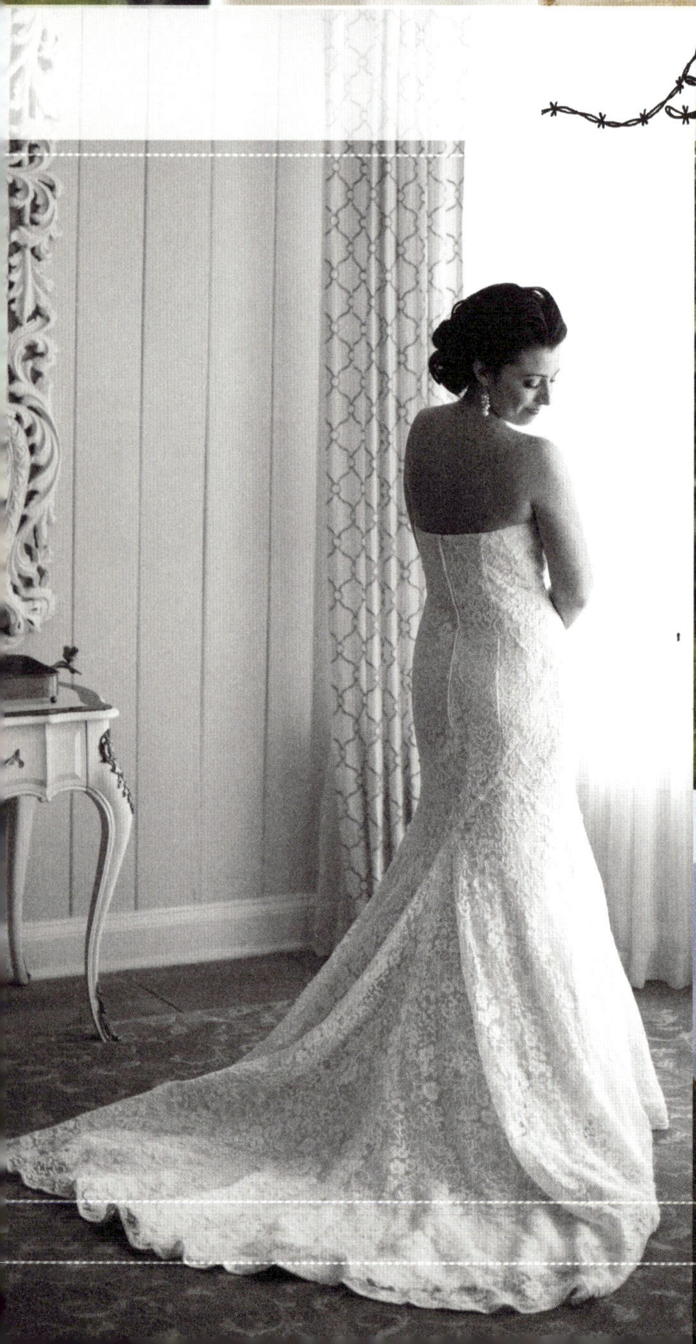

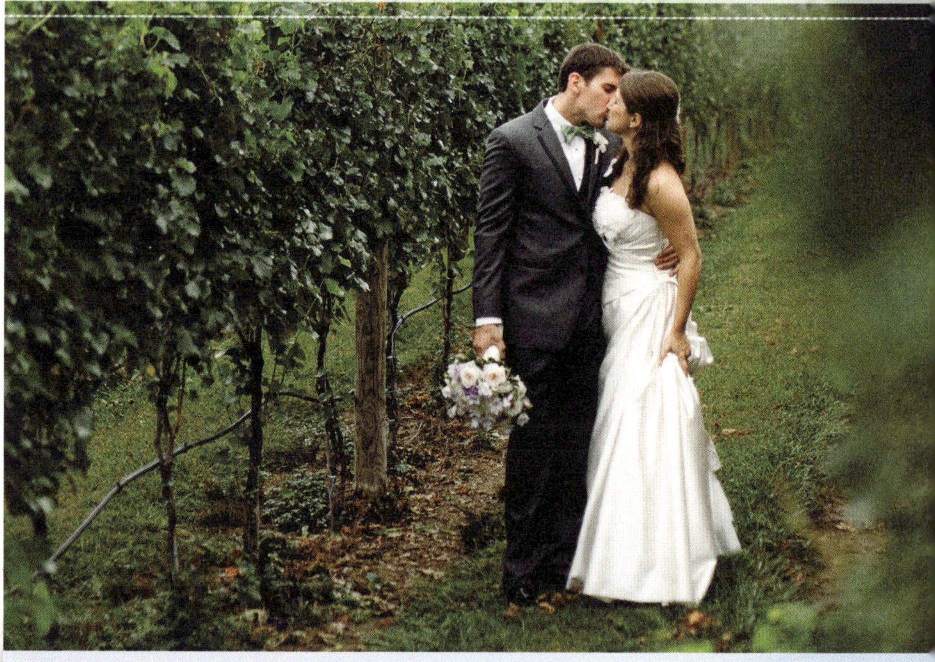

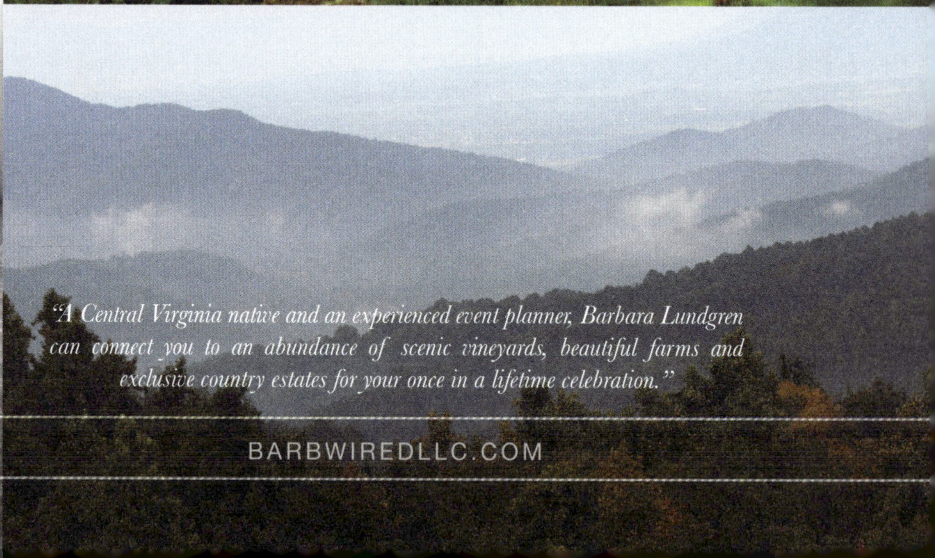

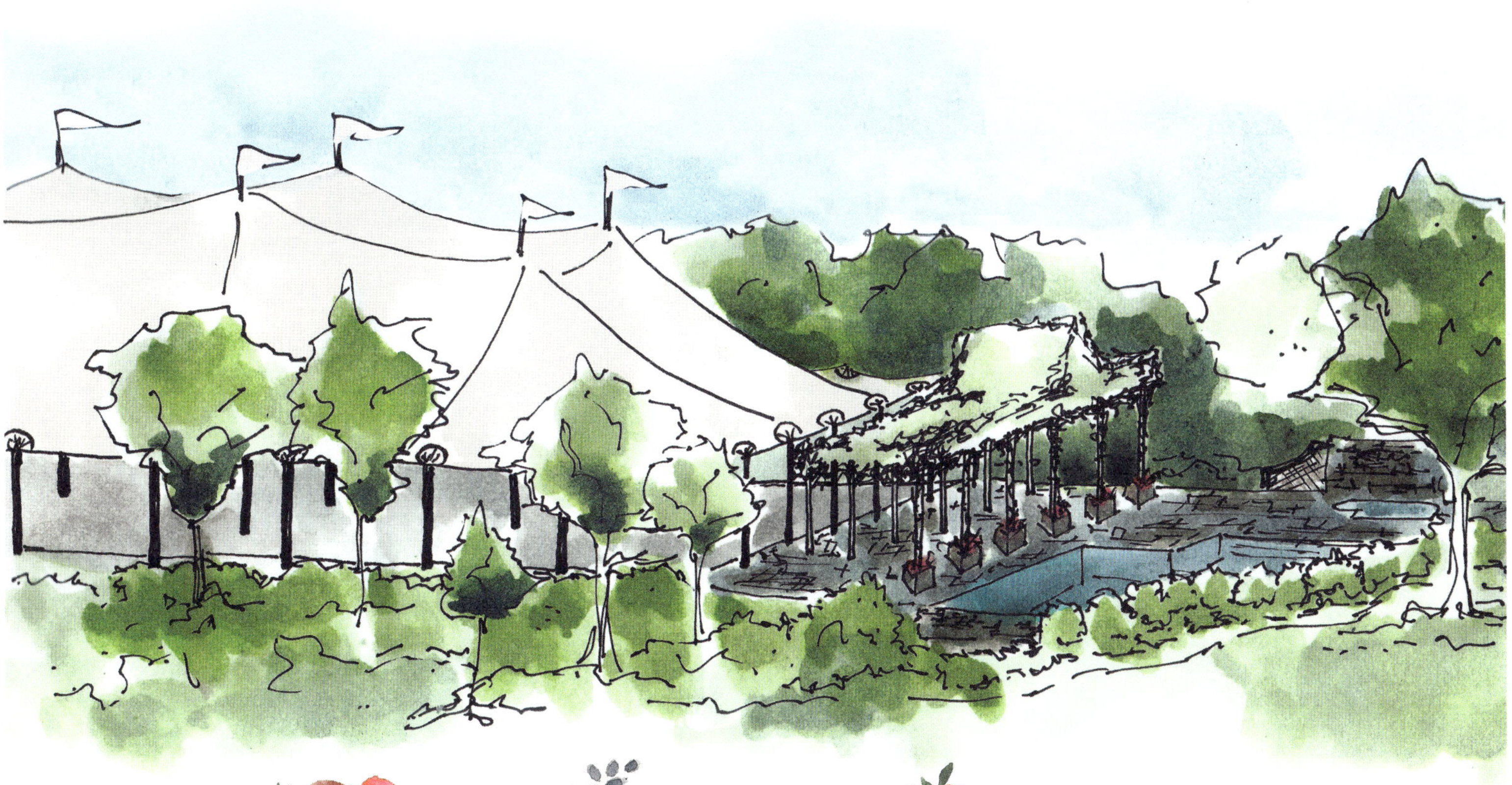

THE CLIFTON INN
THE COURT

Watercolour by Amanda Powers

SITUATED AMONG THE SPRAWLING HILLS OF CHARLOTTESVILLE, ON 100 ACRES OF PRISTINE GARDENS WITH A PRIVATE LAKE AND MAJESTIC VIEWS, THE HISTORIC CLIFTON INN, A RELAIS & CHATEAUX PROPERTY, CREATES AN IDYLLIC SCENE FOR THE FAIRY TALE WEDDING OF YOUR DREAMS.

WALK UP THE LAVENDER PATHWAY AND THROUGH THE WISTERIA ARBOR TO THE COURT, THE CLIFTON INN'S NEW PREMIER EVENT SPACE. CELEBRATE YOUR EXCLUSIVE WEEKEND AT CLIFTON WITH FAMILY AND FRIENDS. OUR ELEGANT SPERRY TENT WITH HARDWOOD FLOORS PROVIDE THE PERFECT BACKDROP WHILE DINING AND DANCING BENEATH THE STAR-FILLED VIRGINIA SKY.

The Court at Clifton is available for all special events with between 75 and 250 guests. For more information on this exciting new space please contact Chelsea Allen Osborn at cosborn@clifton-inn.com

HEDGE
fine blooms

At Hedge Fine Blooms we listen very carefully to our client's thoughts, hints, and inspirations. Every event, regardless of size, is custom matched to their inclination and direction. We then translate these dreams into unique and captivating floral designs, wowing clients and guests alike.

WE ARE NOT FLORISTS, WE ARE ARTISTS.

Hedge has been designing gorgeous weddings since 2007. Founding floral artist **Karen Walker** explains, *"It's all about realizing aspirations. Anybody can put together a pleasing arrangement, but matching design to a bride's vision is what really makes exciting floral surroundings. Exceeding our client's expectations is what fuels my passion for this business."*

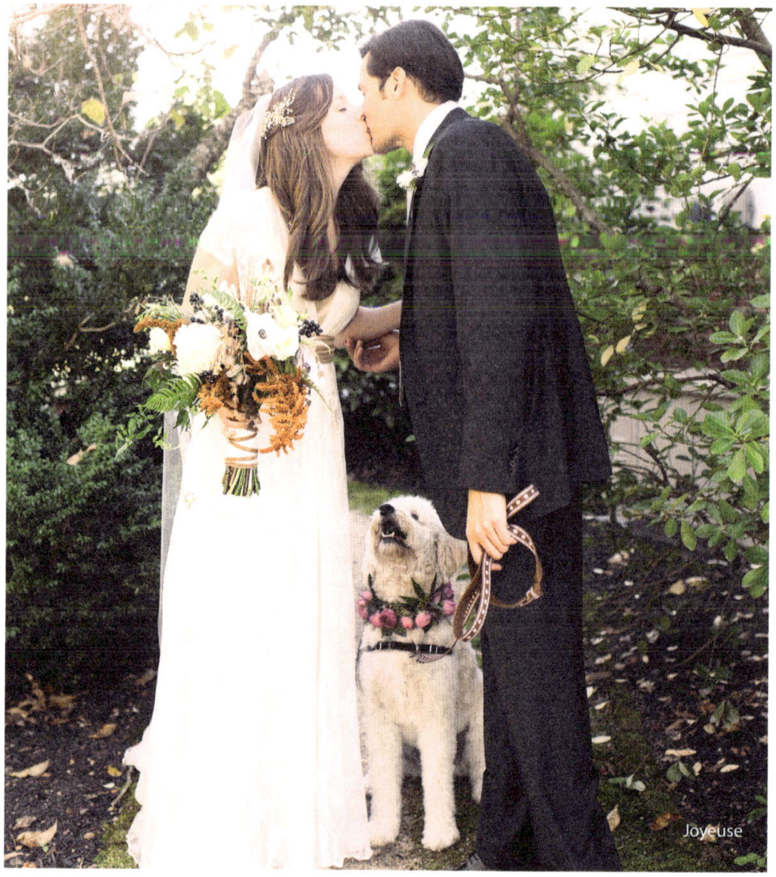

Joyeuse

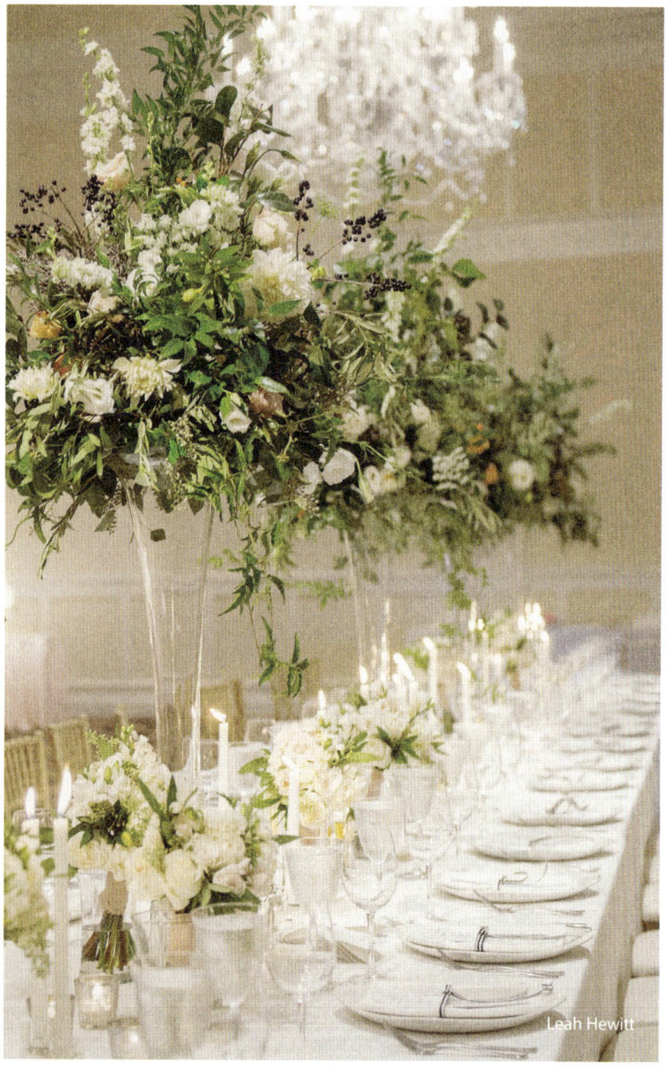

Leah Hewitt

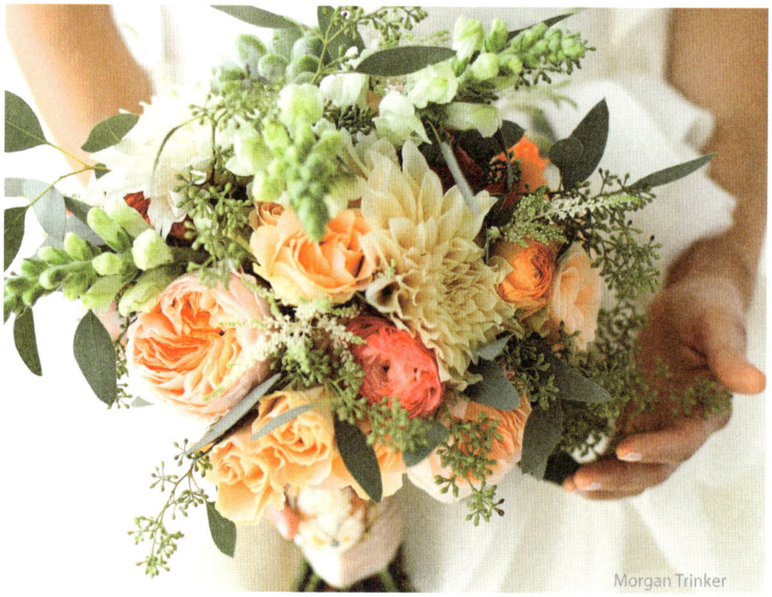

Morgan Trinker

HEDGEFINEBLOOMS.COM

Creative Director **Tasha Tobin** has been practicing the art of floristry for 20 years with artists from around the globe. Tasha has demonstrated her creative talent on television and travels the country to present on stage to large audiences. She has chosen Charlottesville because of the unique venue opportunities. *"I want everything we create equal in beauty to the surrounding countryside."*

"This is a tricky business," Tasha declares. *"Flowers are fragile. We understand what holds up best in different seasons and environments. Problems can occur if you don't know your way around. With our hand chosen list of suppliers we are able to procure only the finest, freshest flowers from anywhere in the world."*

"We are fun to work with," Karen adds. *"Our team has a blast together. Often clients stop by just to join in the camaraderie." Come have fun with us at Hedge Fine Blooms!*

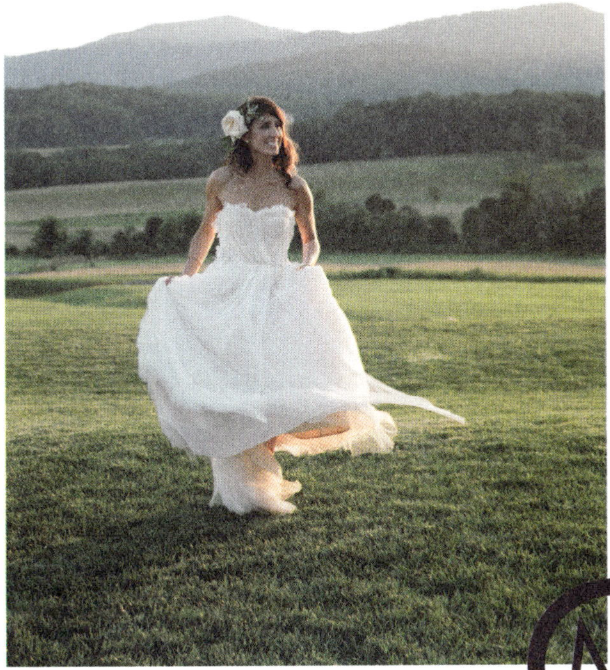
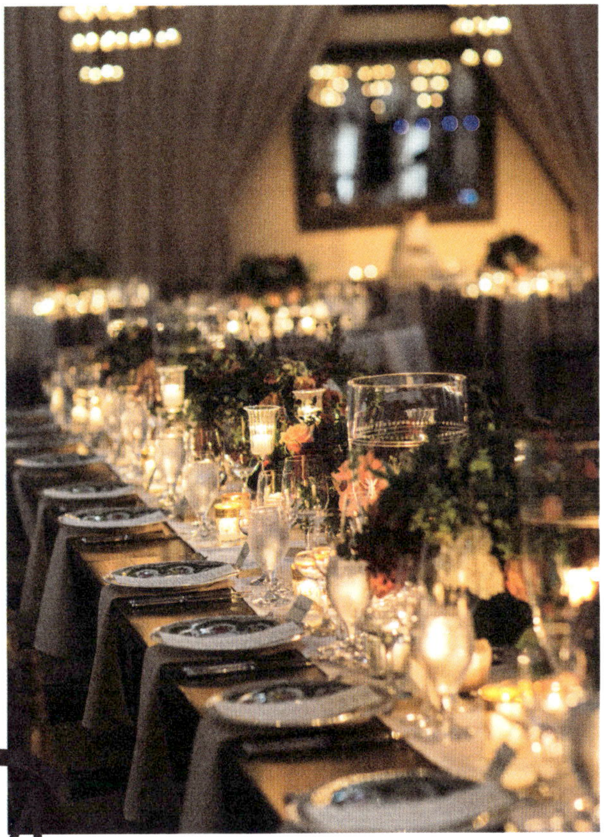
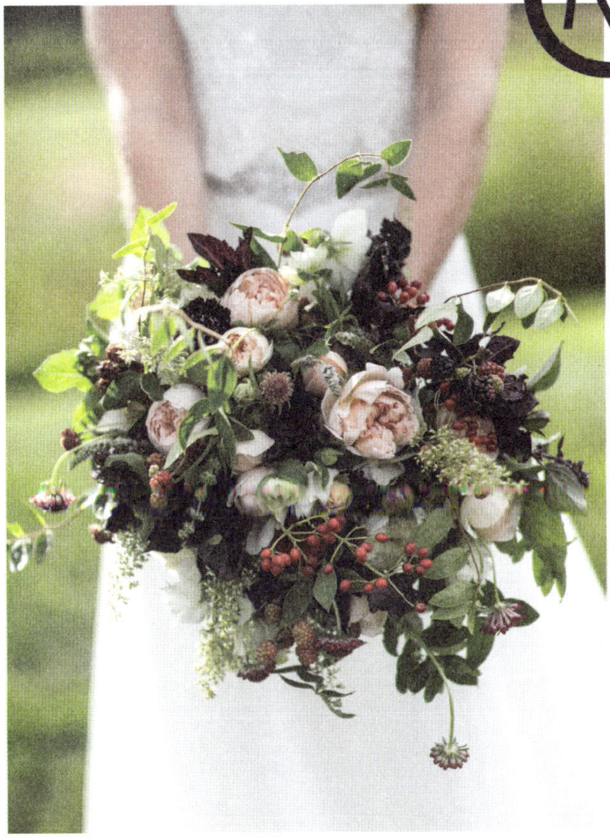
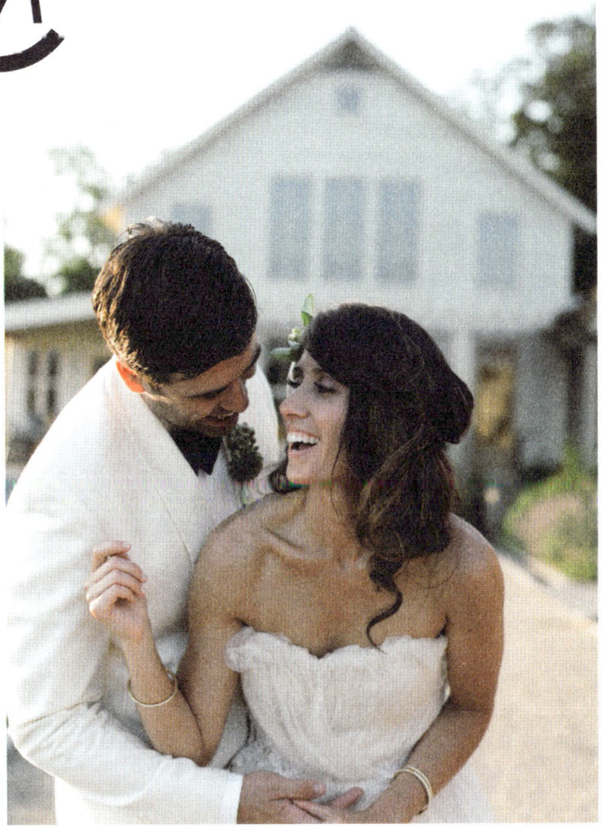

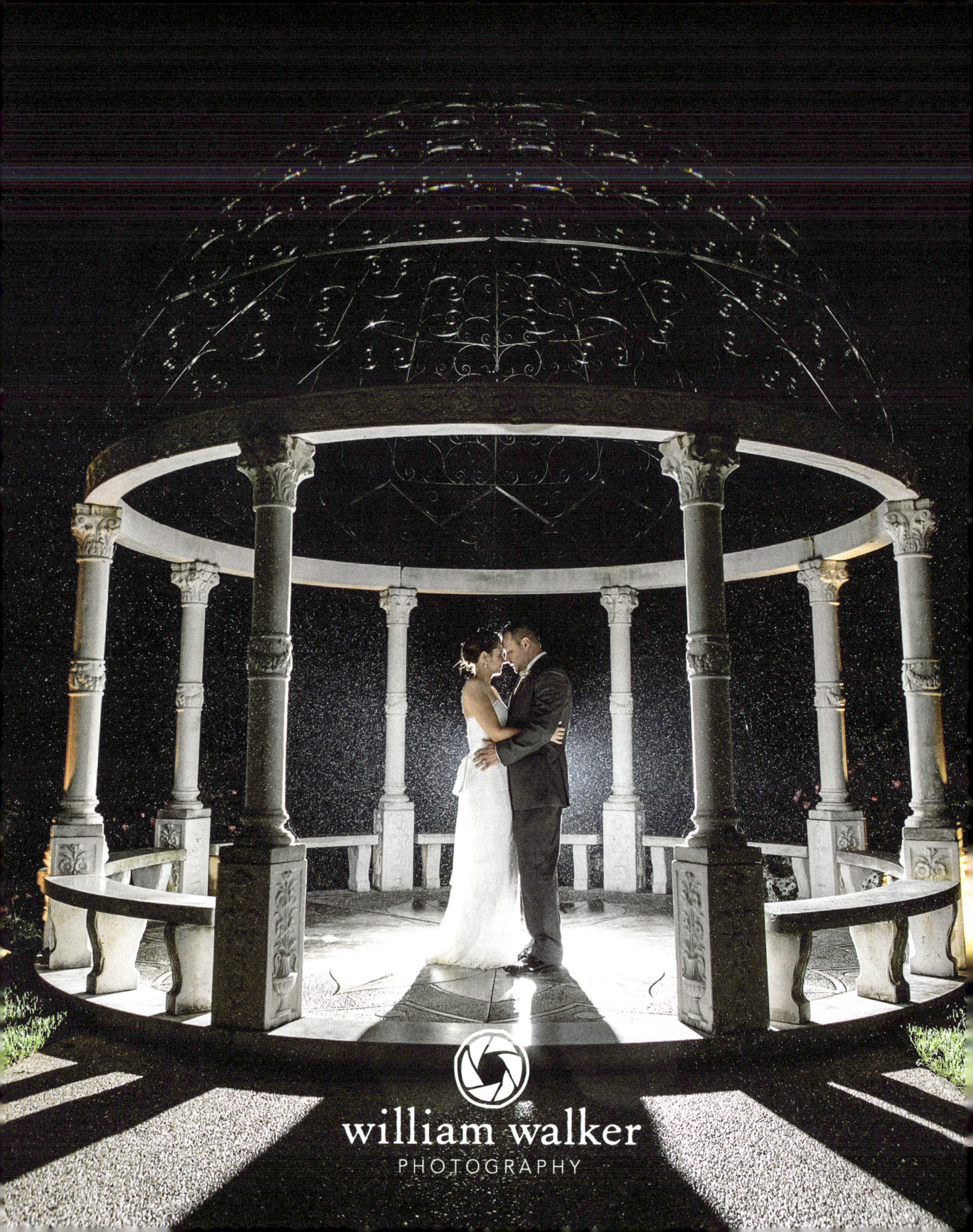
william walker
PHOTOGRAPHY

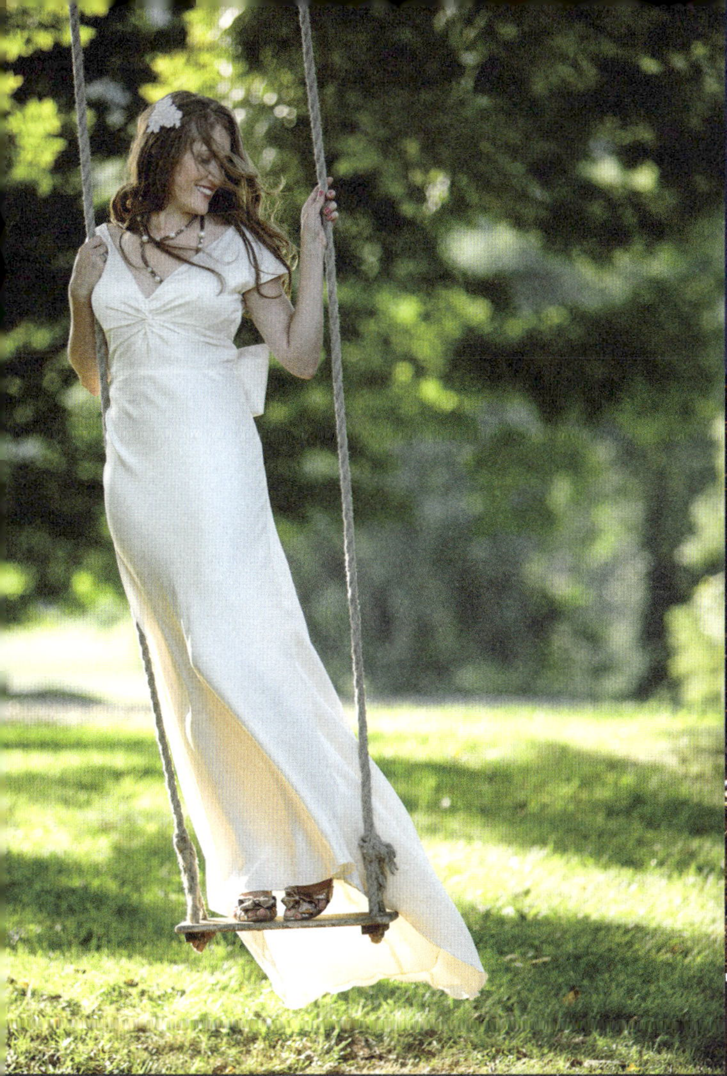

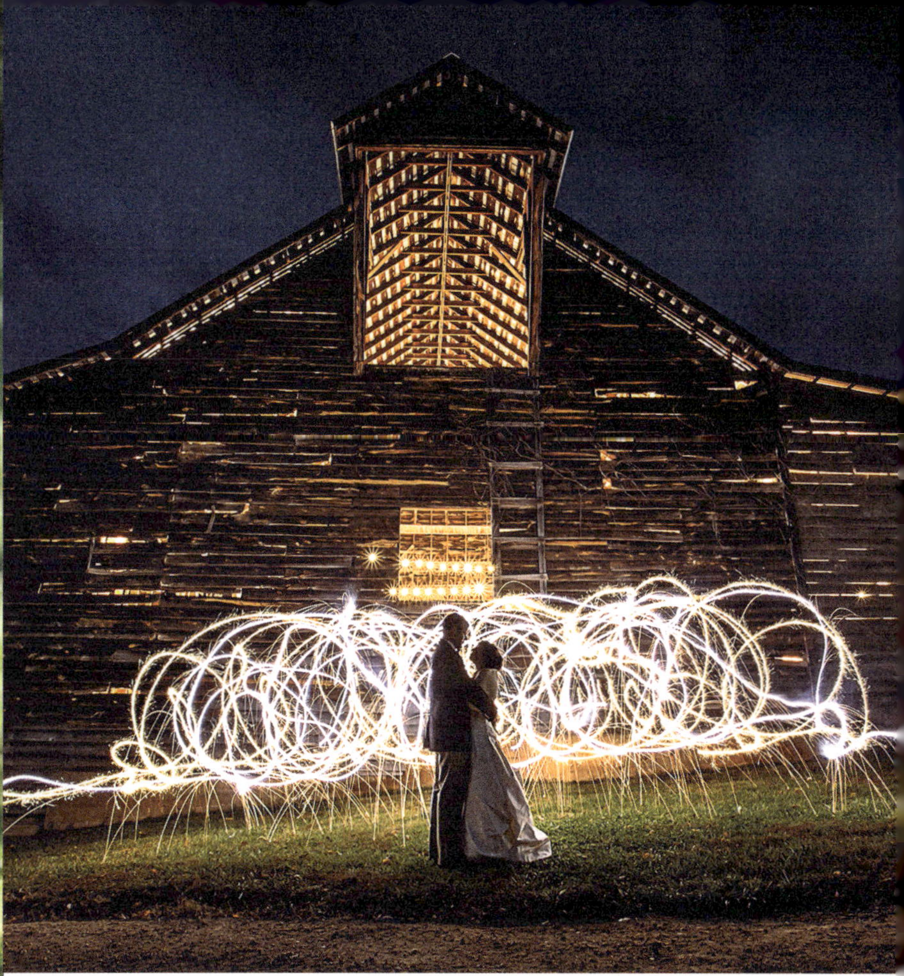

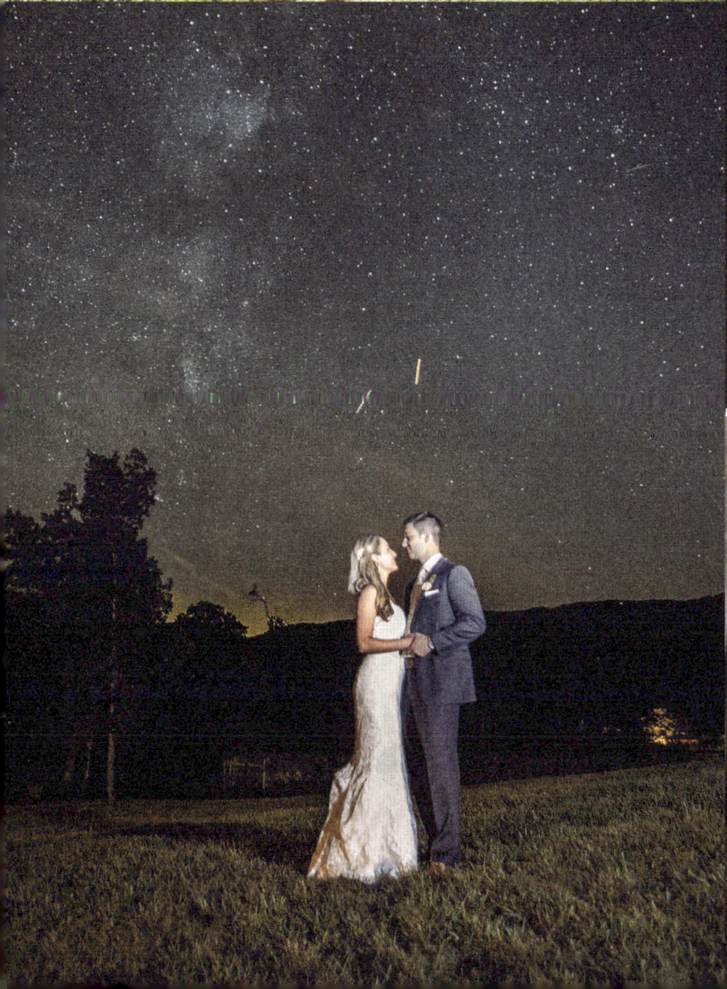

Husband and wife team, Will and Jess, love awesome, sweet, funny couples that like to have fun just like us. We adore thoughtful, creative, nerdy, goofy people in love. Your wedding day is about coming together with family and friends, seeing your vision come to life, embracing all the hard work invested in planning. We are there to capture the day in a photo-journalistic fashion, creating unique and dramatic portraits that reflect the day, be it sunny, cloudy, rainy, or star-filled. Champagne toasts for the girls, and Bourbon cheers for the guys!

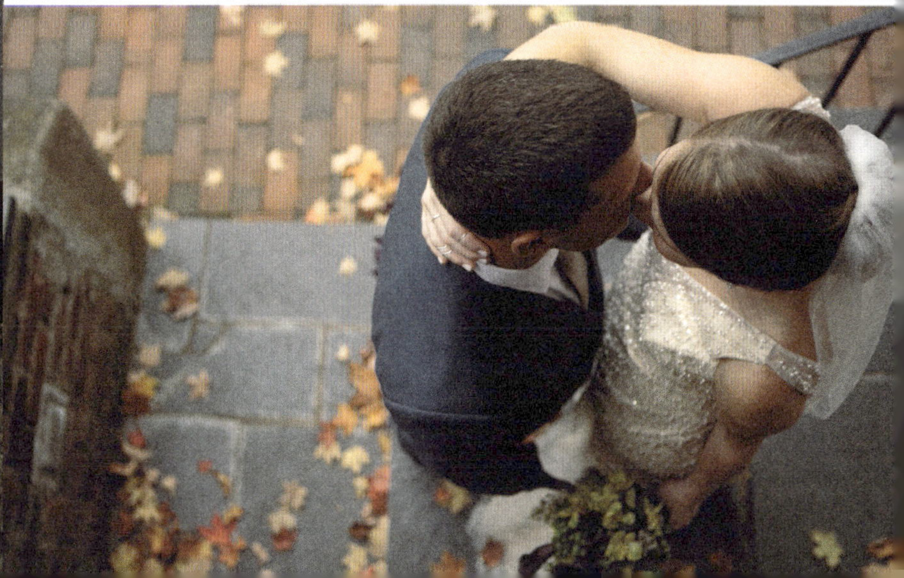

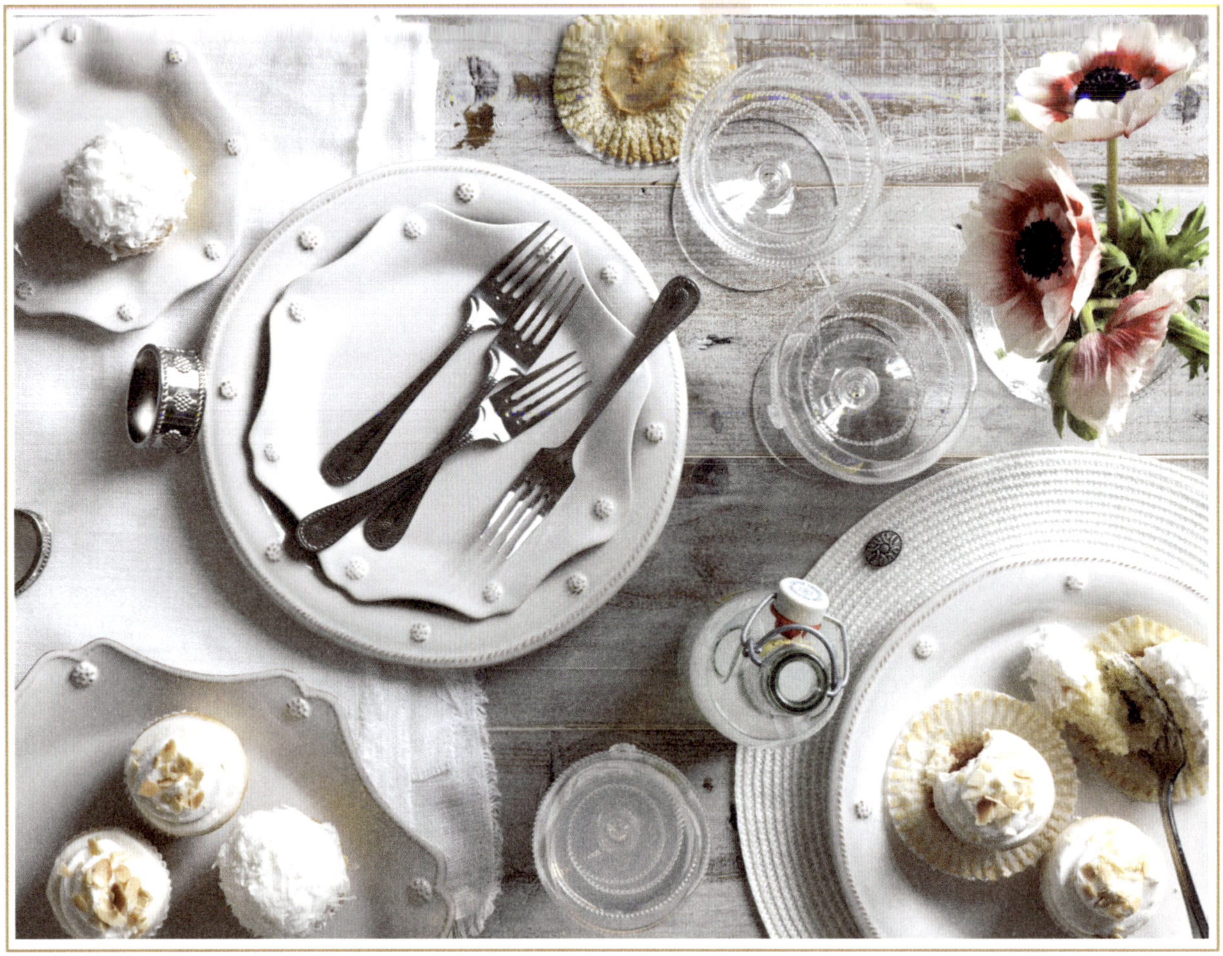

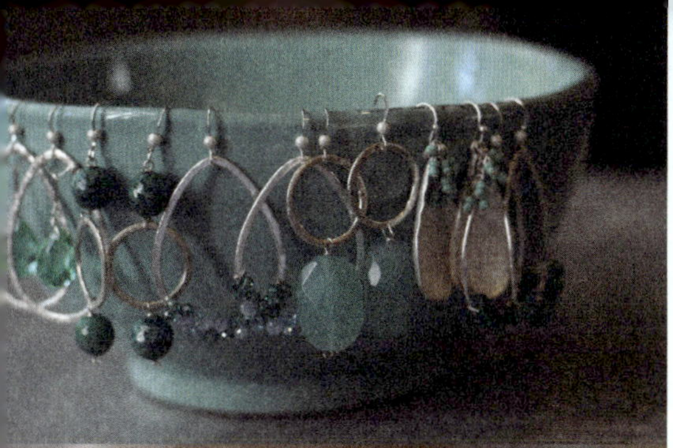

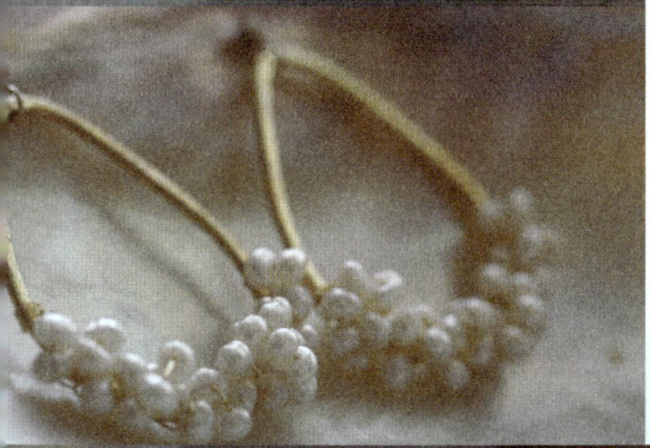

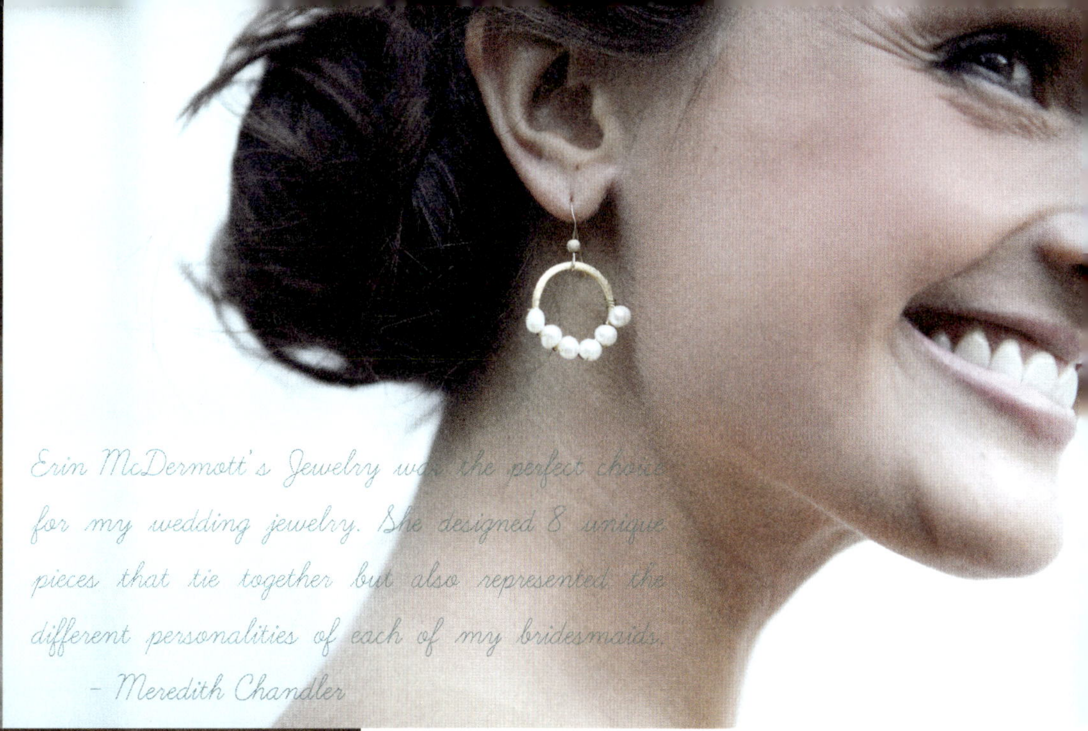

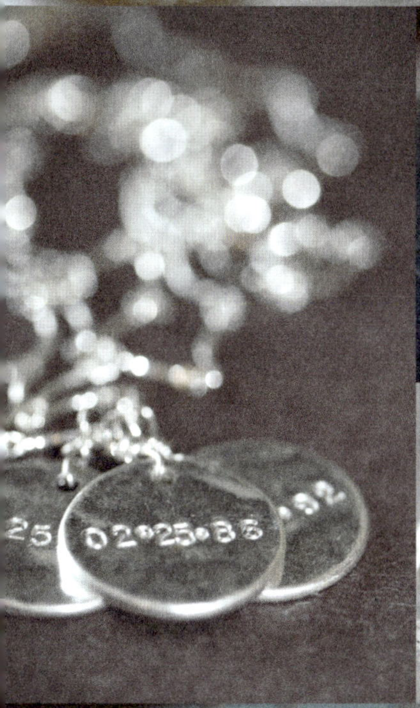

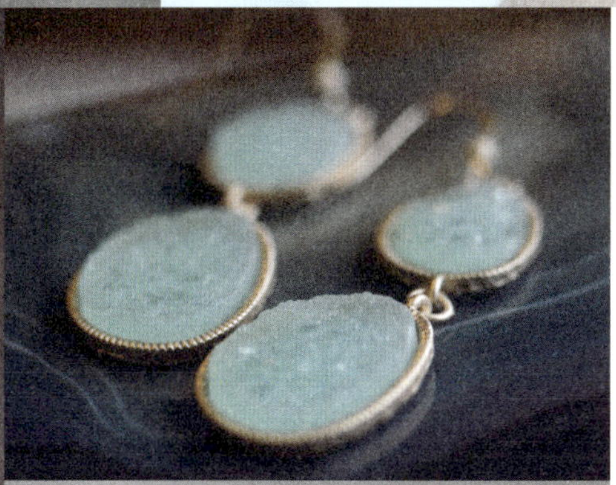

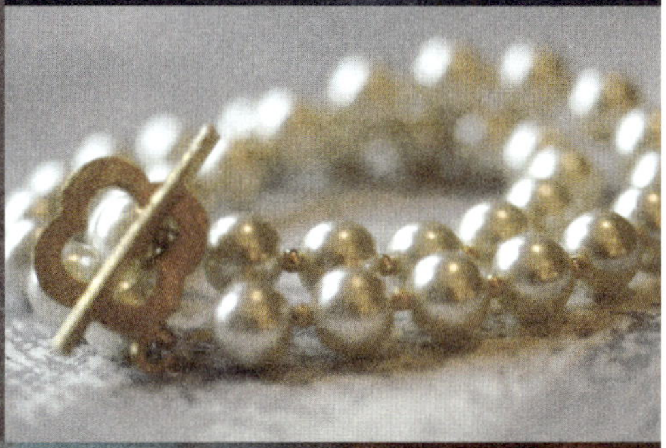

Eight years ago, after graduating from the University of Virginia, I began *Erin McDermott Jewelry* with the intent of creating fresh and timeless pieces. When planning my own wedding, I realized how difficult it is to find bridesmaid's gifts that represent how important each girl is to me and easily transition to life after the wedding. I decided to create a piece of jewelry for each of my bridesmaids. Fast forward to 2015, I now design bridal jewelry for over 200 weddings a year. I love to work with each bride to create the perfect pieces to match their vision at any budget.

ERIN MCDERMOTT JEWELRY

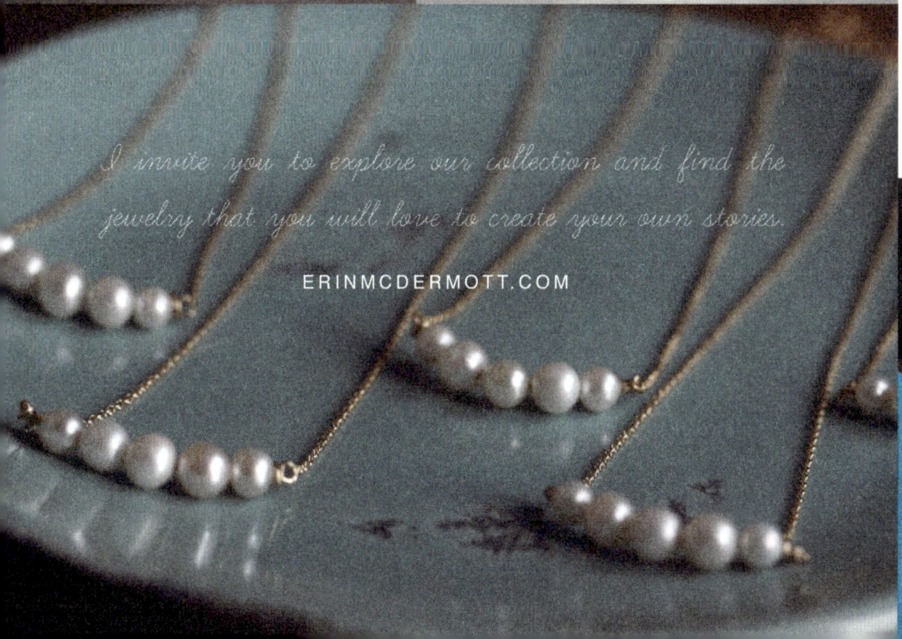

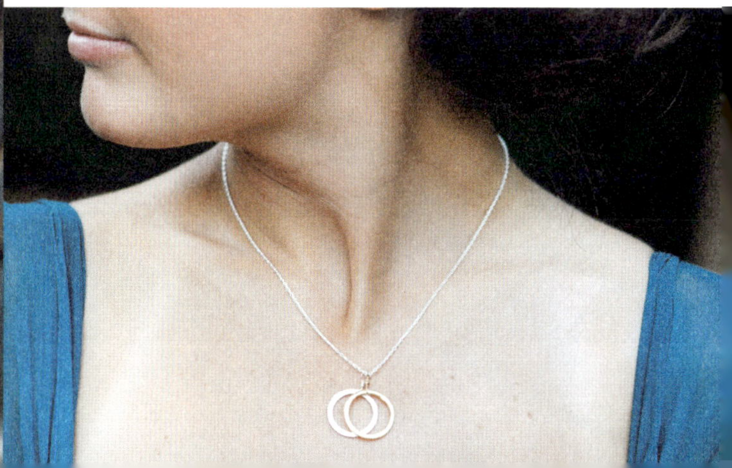

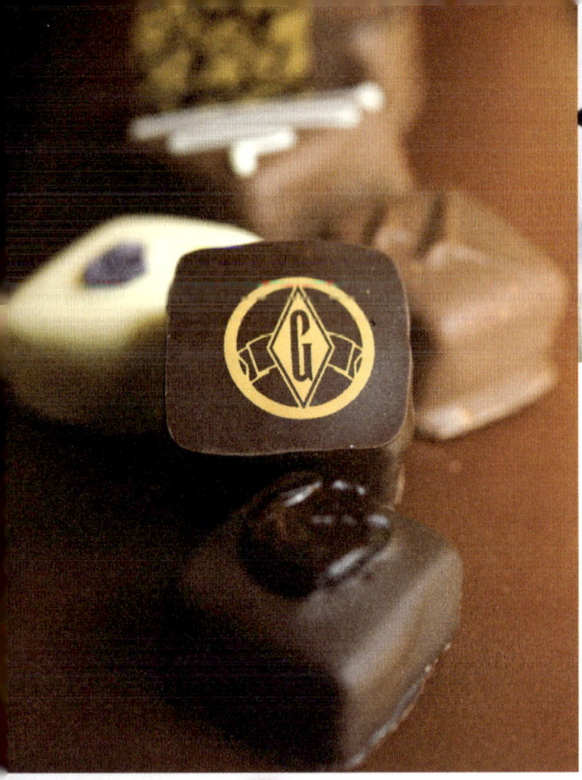

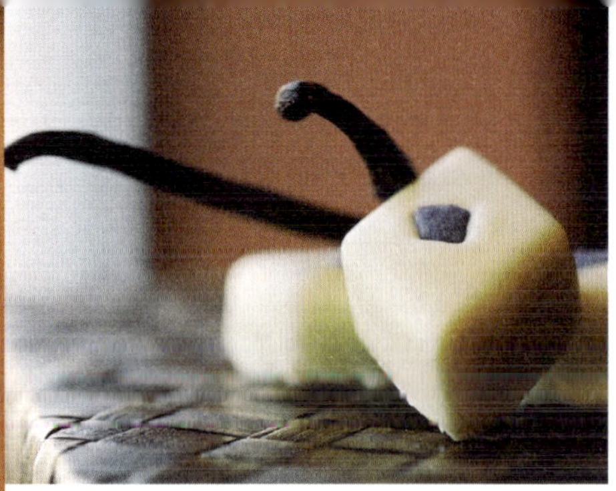

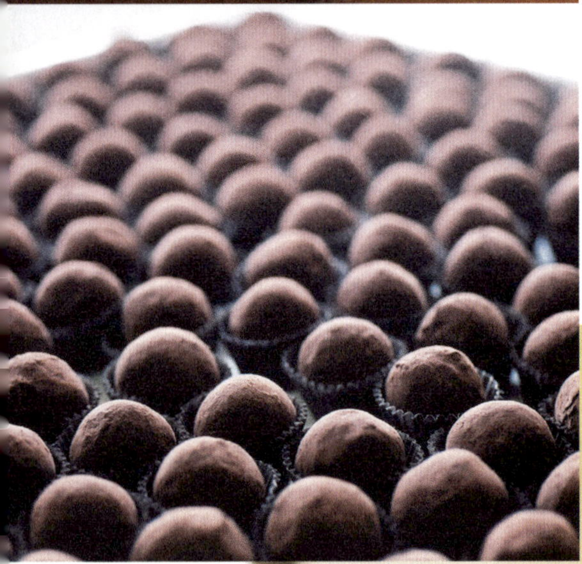

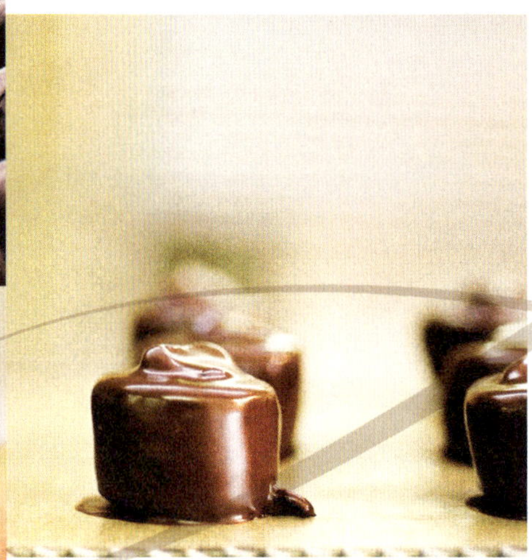

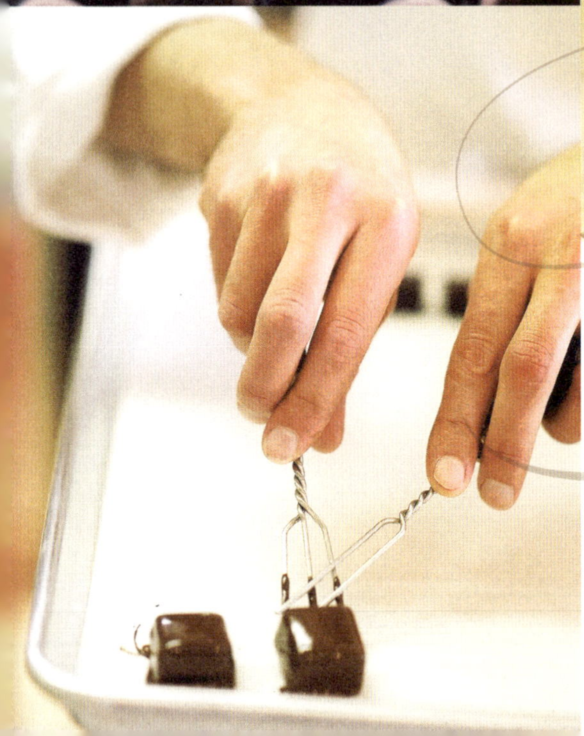

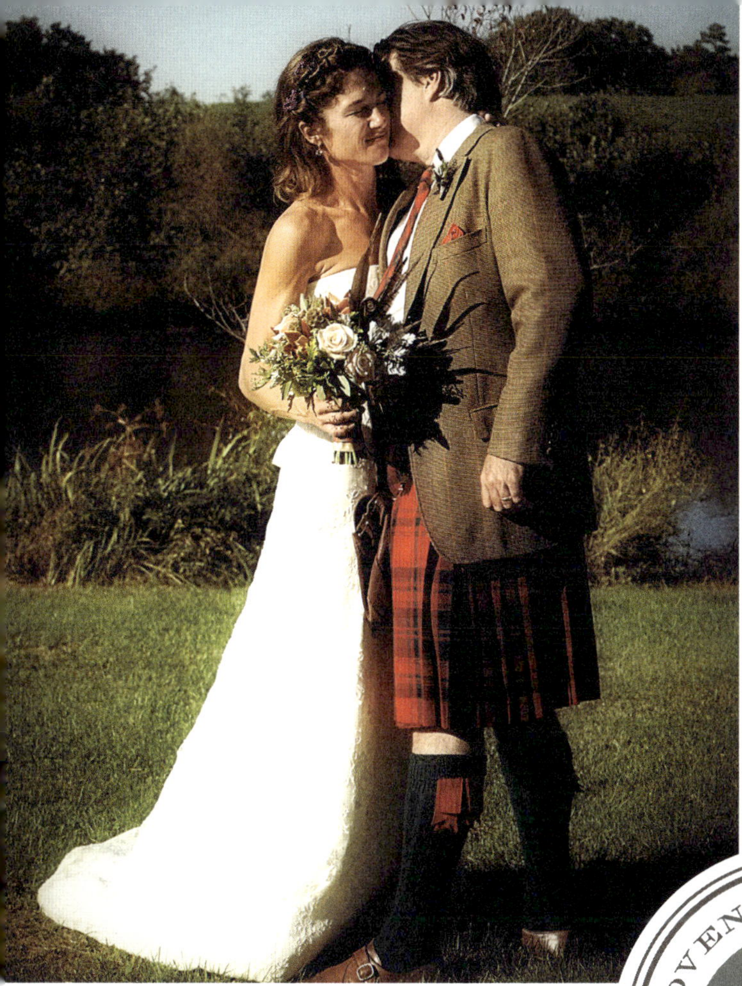

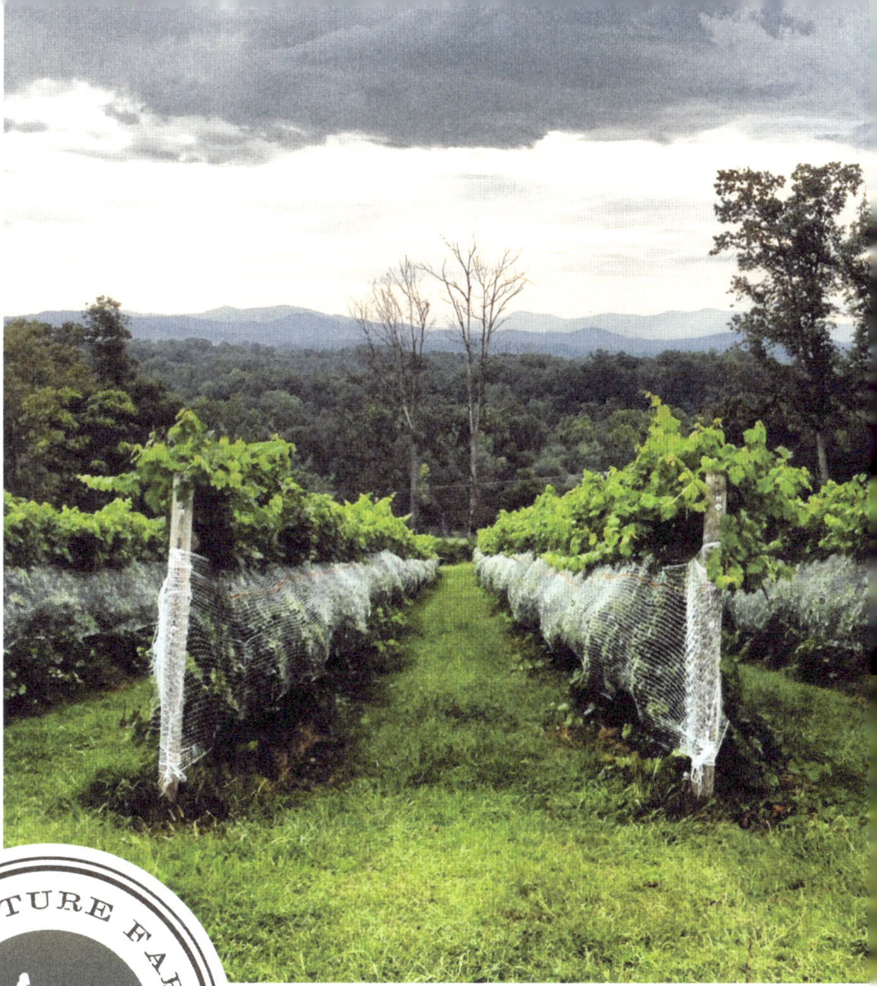

A FAMILY TRADITION SINCE 1950

434.971.8790 | adventurefarm.net | Earlysville, Virginia

A vintage, family-owned farm providing a range of idyllic settings for your wedding. Adventure Farm offers spectacular views of the Blue Ridge Mountains, rolling pastures, lakes, woods and rows of grape vines marching up and over the hills. Your guests will be captivated by the ambiance of a traditional working farm and the charming tasting room, meadow and pond sites. To make it a real farm-to-table event, Adventure Farm can work with your caterer to use their produce, pasture raised beef and small lot wines made with 100% estate grown grapes.

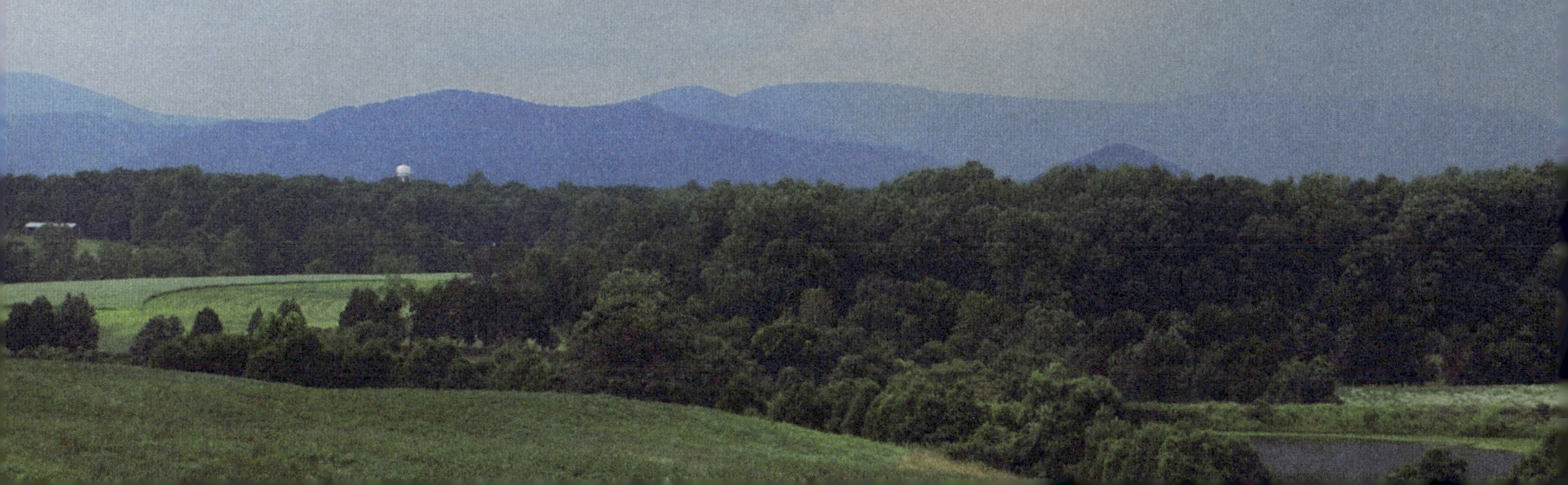

FESTIVE FARE®

A Classic Party Rentals Company

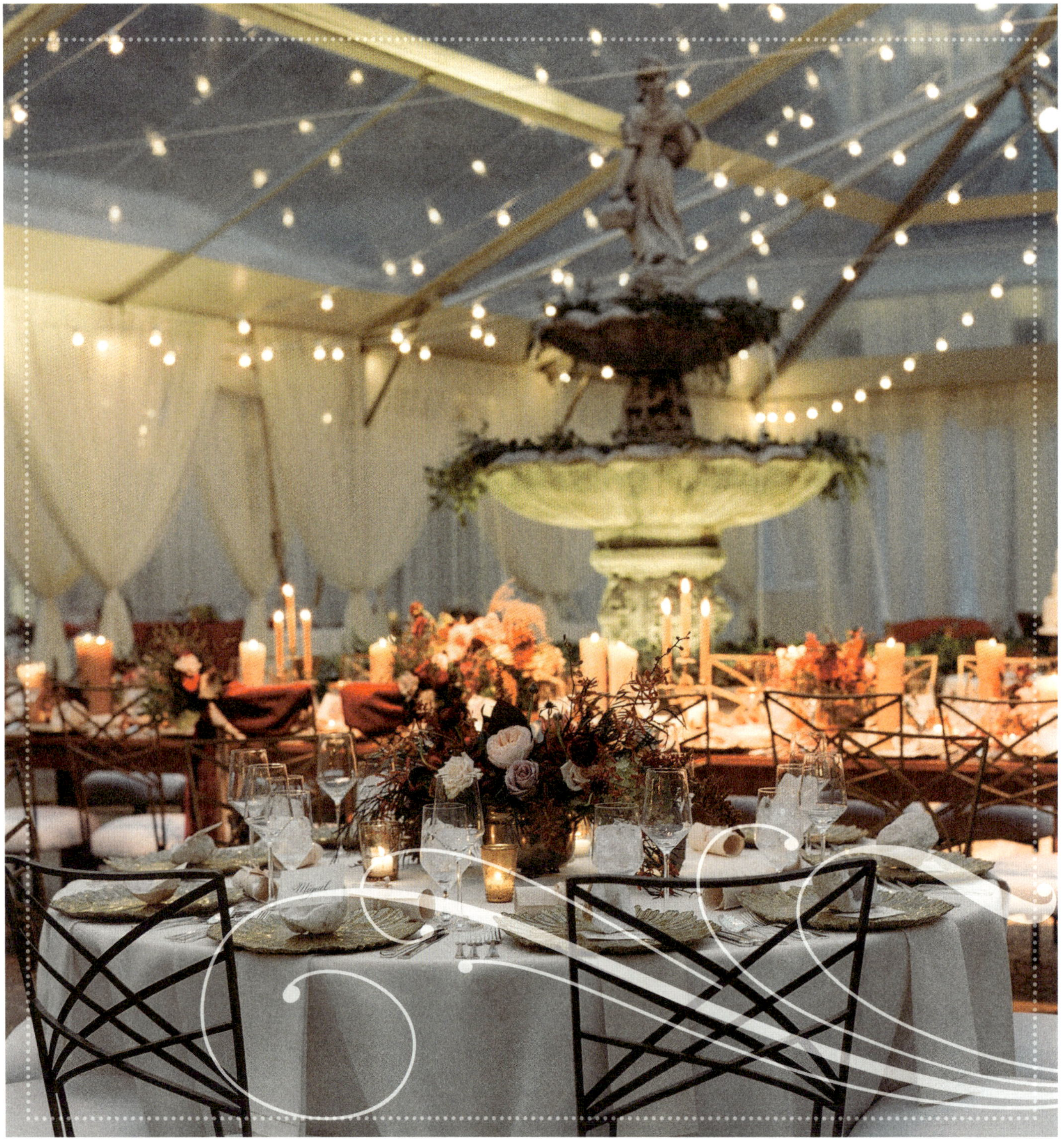

OUR EXTENSIVE COLLECTION OF RENTAL ITEMS WILL MAGICALLY TRANSFORM ANY ROOM, BARN, OR TENT AND CREATE A MEMORABLE AMBIENCE YOU AND YOUR GUESTS WILL TREASURE. FROM DELICATE GLASSWARE AND LINENS TO CHIAVARI CHAIRS, CUSHIONS AND FARM TABLES, YOU ARE SURE TO FIND THE PERFECT ITEMS.

festivefarerentals.com 434.296.5496

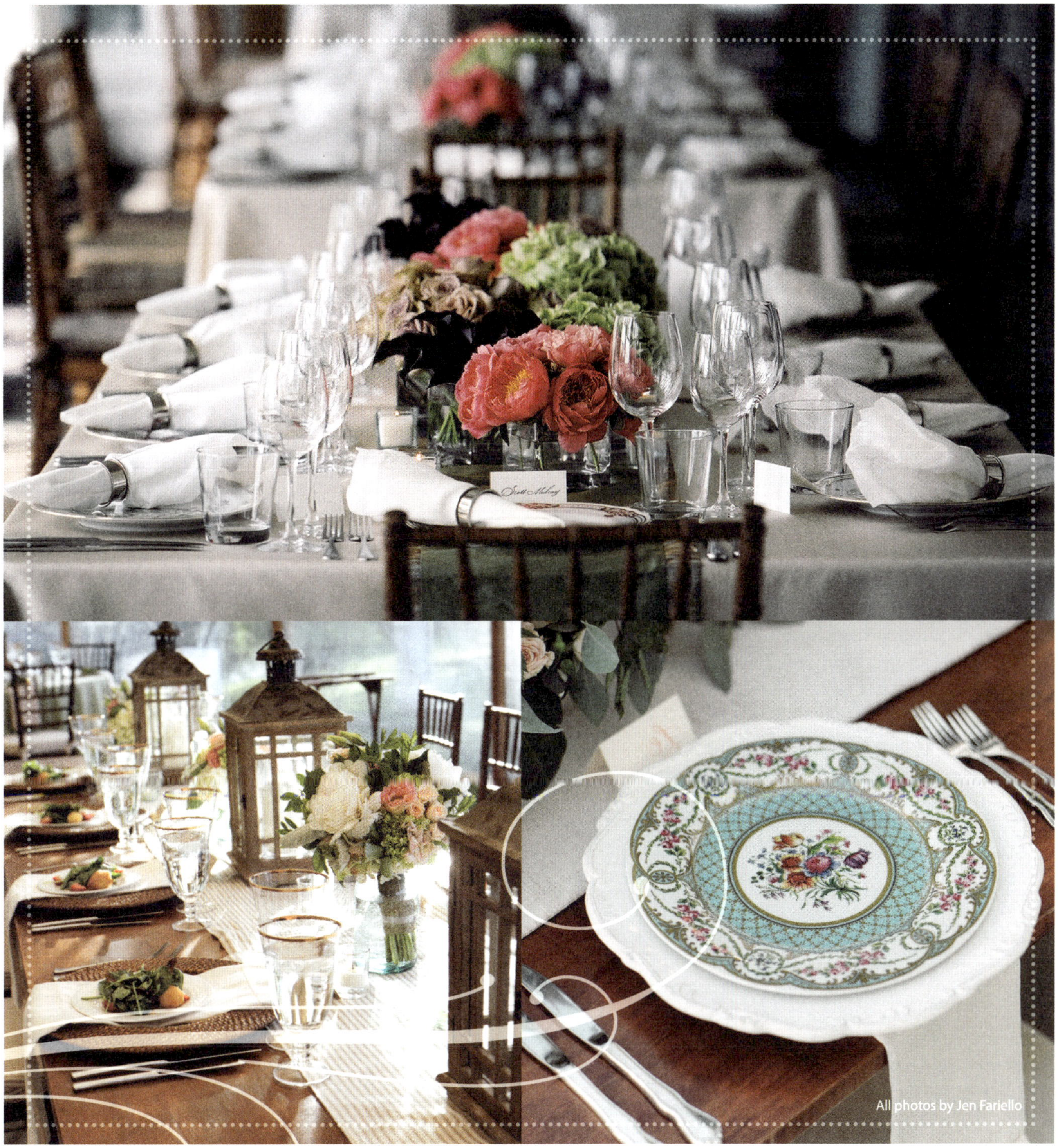

All photos by Jen Fariello

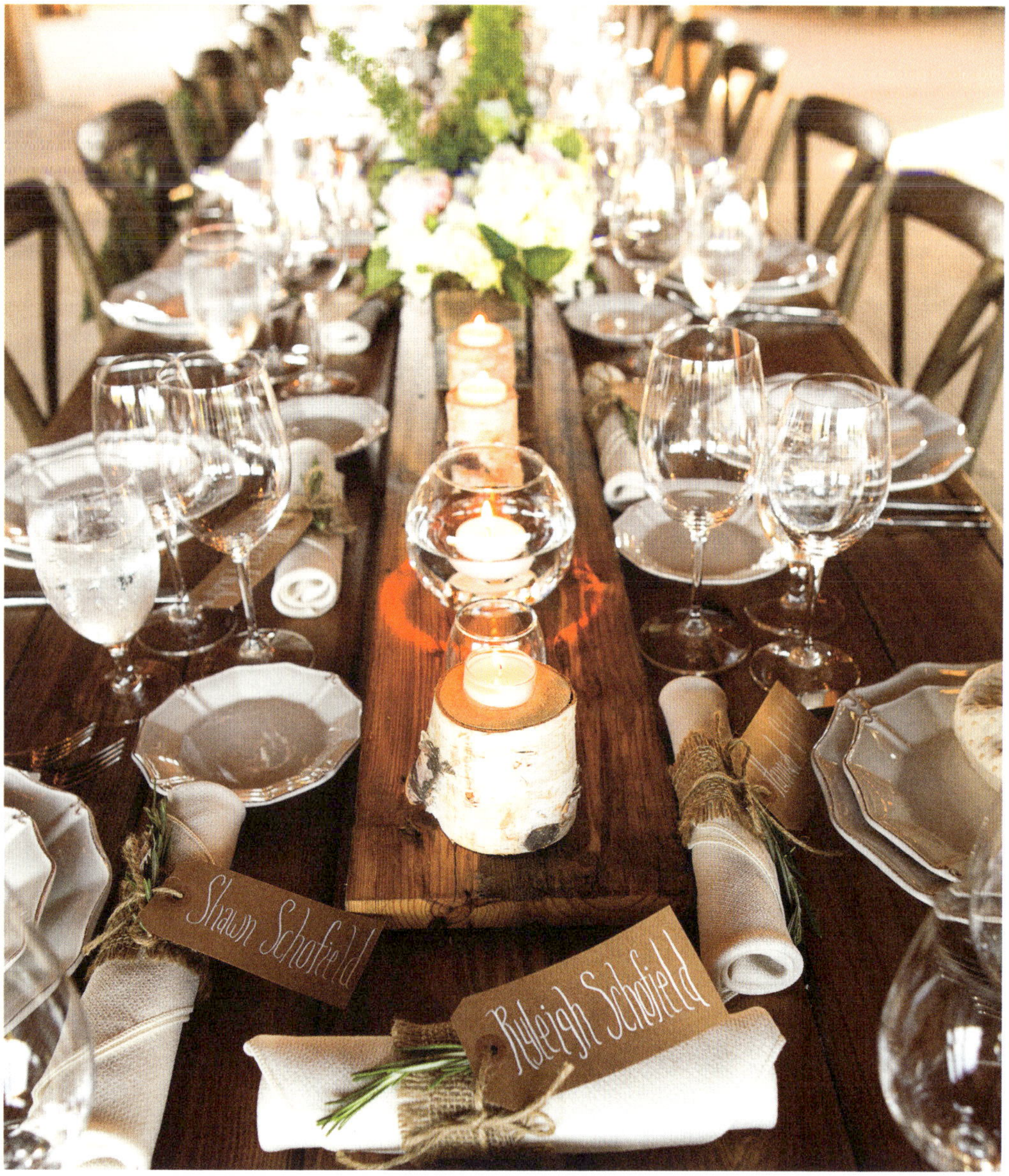
Shawn Schofield
Ryleigh Schofield

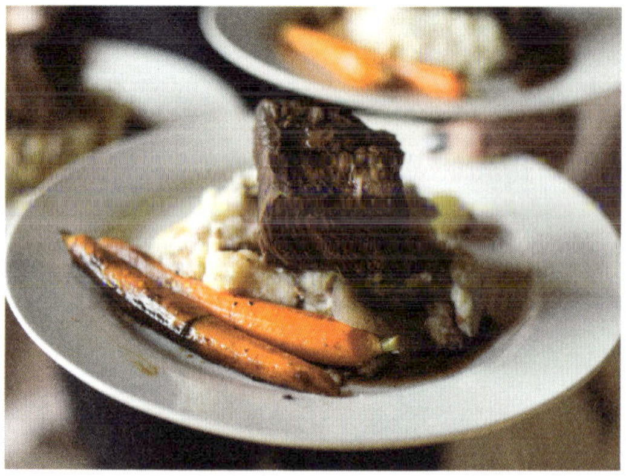

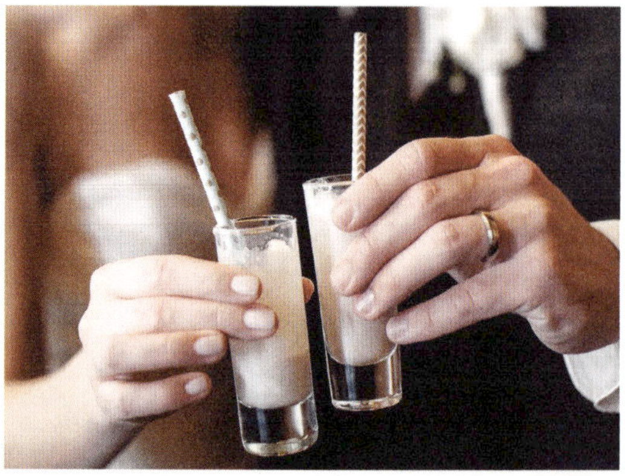

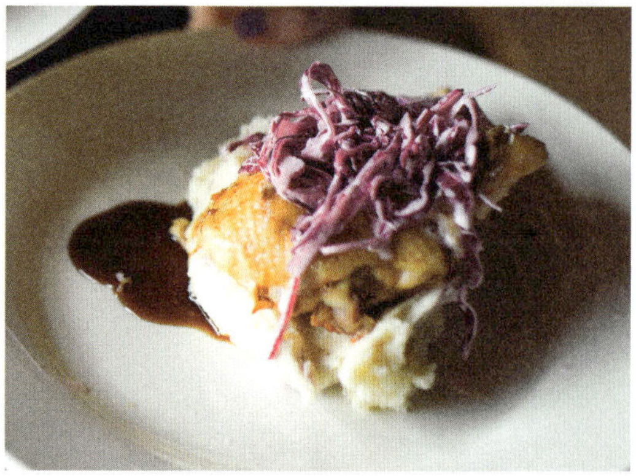

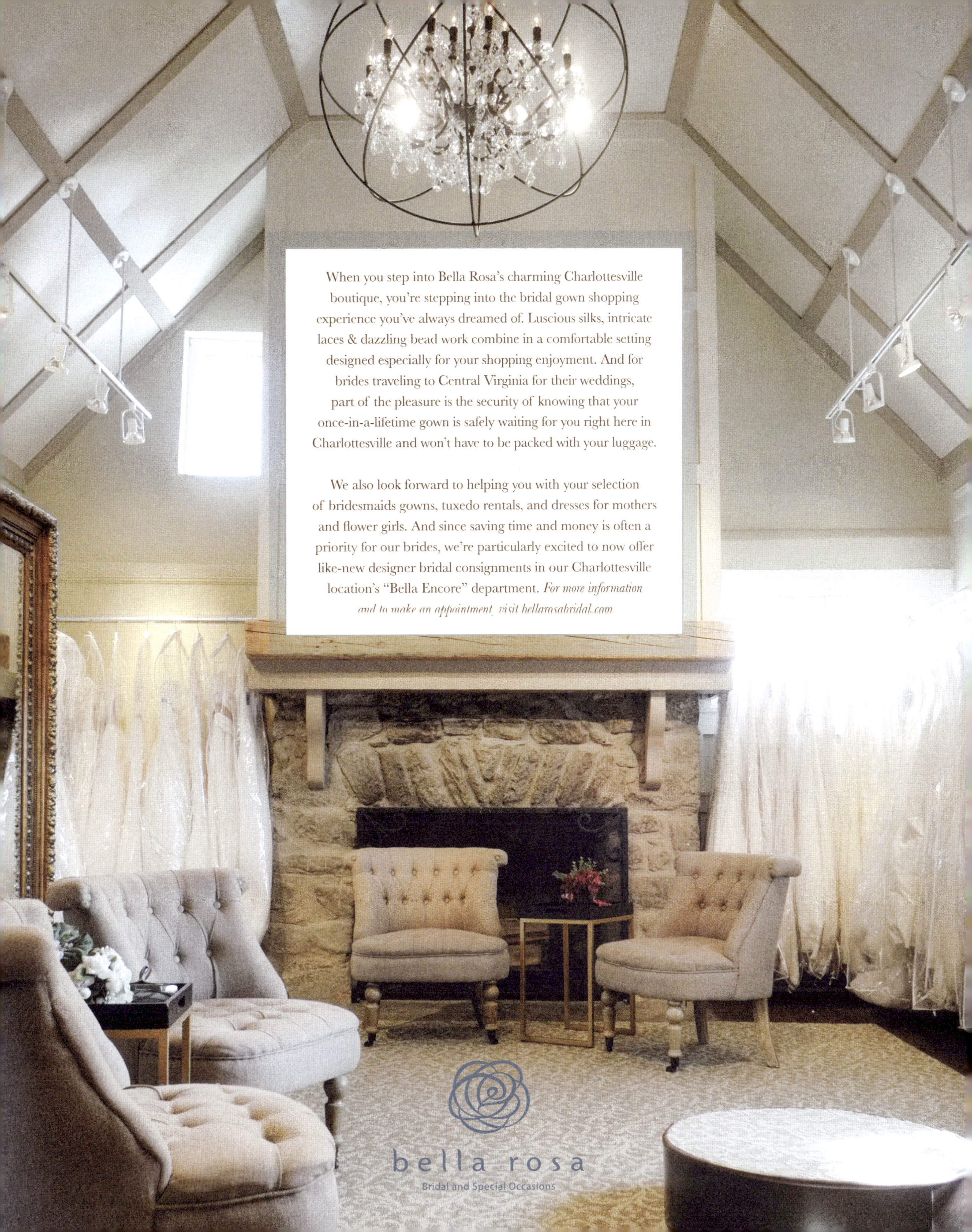
When you step into Bella Rosa's charming Charlottesville boutique, you're stepping into the bridal gown shopping experience you've always dreamed of. Luscious silks, intricate laces & dazzling bead work combine in a comfortable setting designed especially for your shopping enjoyment. And for brides traveling to Central Virginia for their weddings, part of the pleasure is the security of knowing that your once-in-a-lifetime gown is safely waiting for you right here in Charlottesville and won't have to be packed with your luggage.
We also look forward to helping you with your selection of bridesmaids gowns, tuxedo rentals, and dresses for mothers and flower girls. And since saving time and money is often a priority for our brides, we're particularly excited to now offer like-new designer bridal consignments in our Charlottesville location's "Bella Encore" department. For more information and to make an appointment, visit bellarosabridal.com
bella rosa
Bridal and Special Occasions

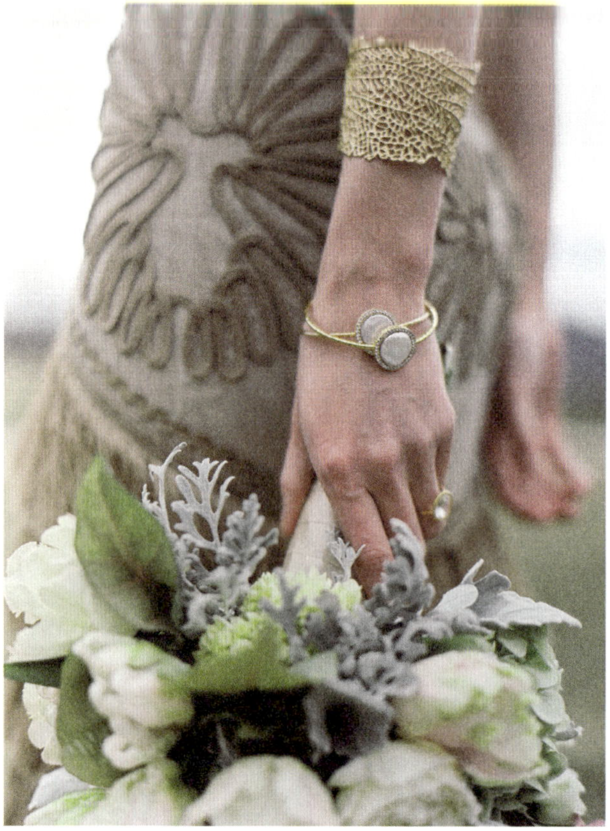

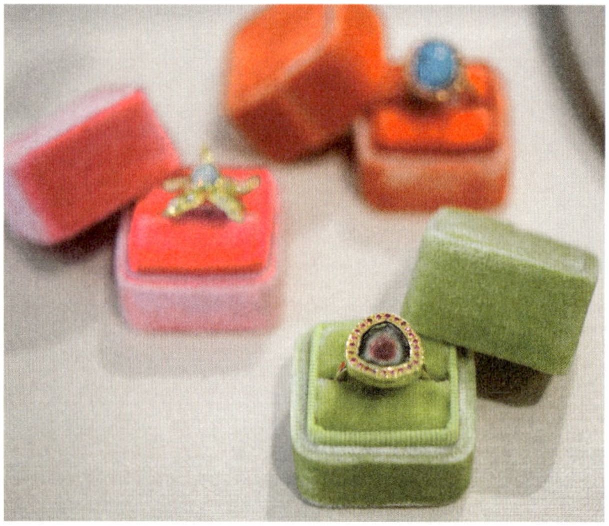

SUZ SOMERSALL

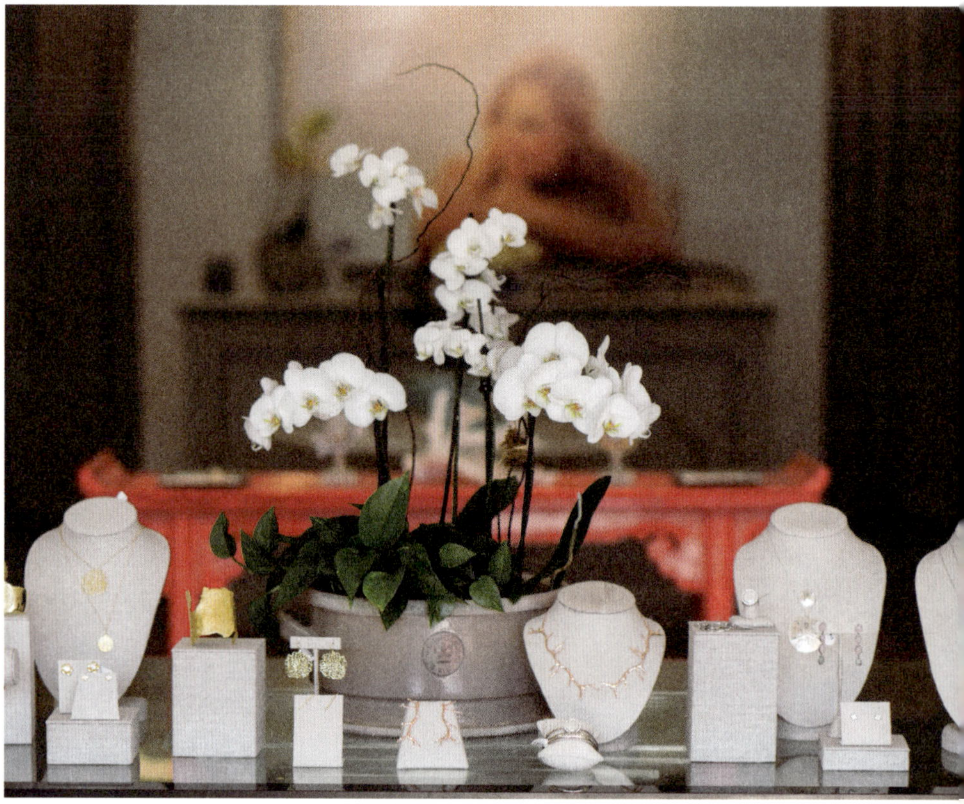

Suz Somersall, a travel inspired jewelry brand based in Charlottesville, Virginia, specializes in both custom engagement rings and jewelry for wedding parties and brides. Explore their antique, organic, and wanderlust designs at the Suz Somersall boutique located in The Shops at Stonefield.

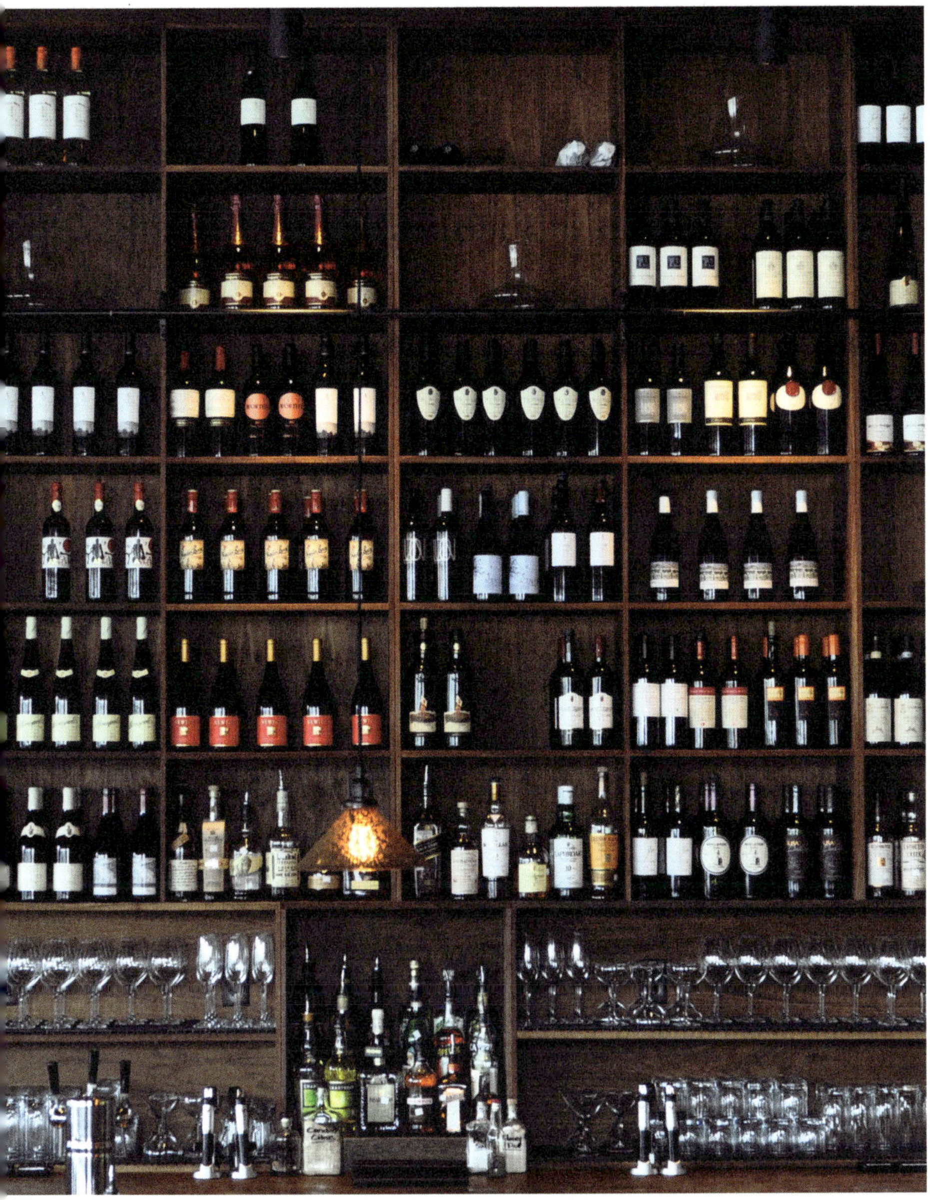

PARALLEL 38

"This style of cooking would be very much at home in a three-star restaurant in Washington, San Francisco or New York."

–Tom Seitsema, Food Critic Washington Post

Parallel 38's story is ultimately a love story. Owner Justin Ross met his significant other while they worked together in D.C. After she moved to Charlottesville, the two reconnected, fell in love and dove headfirst into the dreaded long-distance relationship. They found themselves driving back and forth between Charlottesville and D.C. 3 or 4 times a week. "It was rough!" laughs Justin. And that's when fate worked its magic. "An incredible opportunity presented itself to open a restaurant in Charlottesville, and the rest is history."

Parallel 38 offers a small plate dining experience inspired by iconic food and wine regions along the 38th parallel – The Mediterranean, Napa Valley and Charlottesville (to name a few). Their food, wine and cocktail programs have received abundant praise – "Best New Restaurant" (Cville Weekly), an invitation to cook at the prestigious James Beard House, recognition as an original member of Charlottesville's 29 Best Restaurants in "Charlottesville 29," etc.

P38 offers ample space for wedding parties, rehearsal dinners and more in a modern, romantic setting. Conveniently located near the Hyatt Place in the Shops at Stonefield.

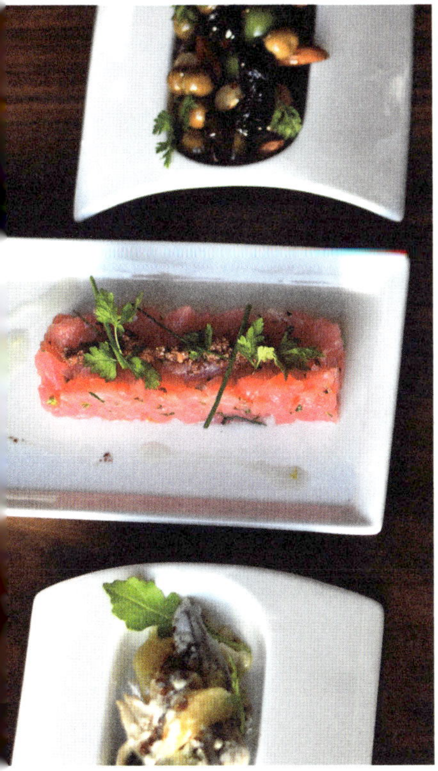

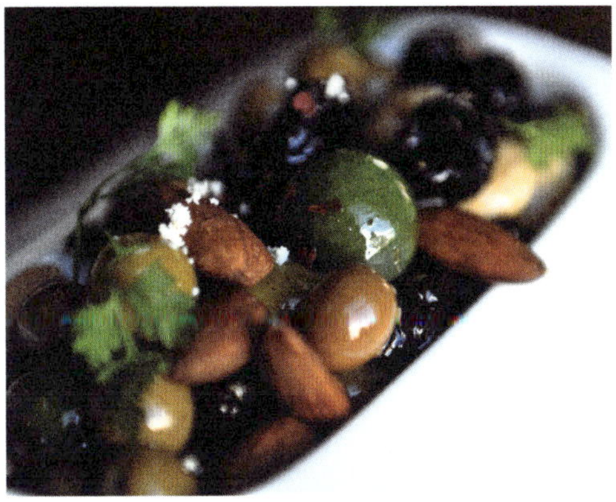

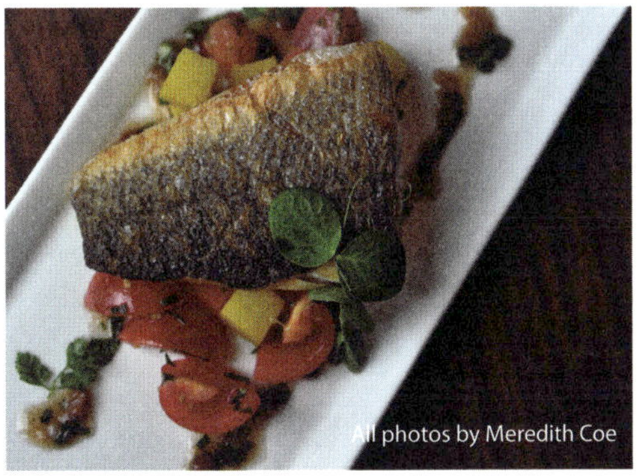

All photos by Meredith Coe

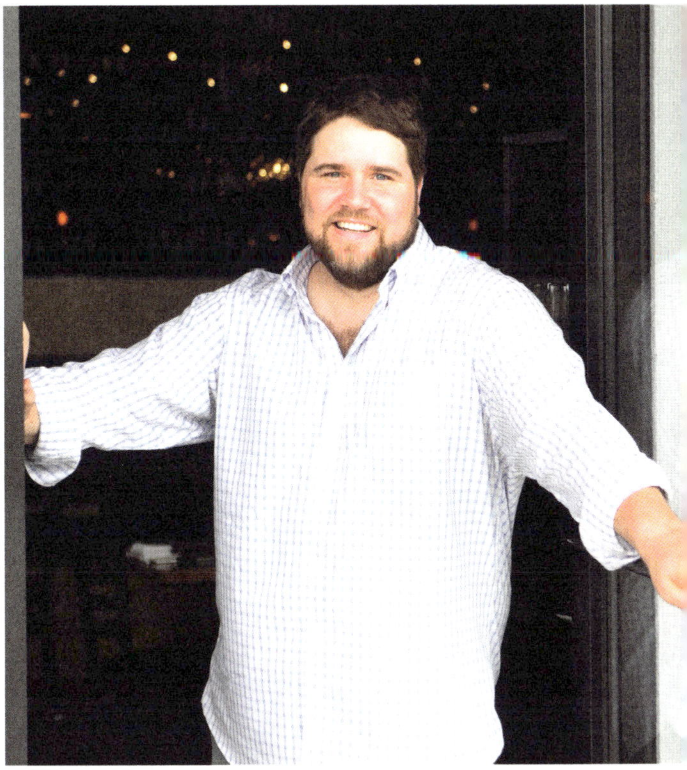

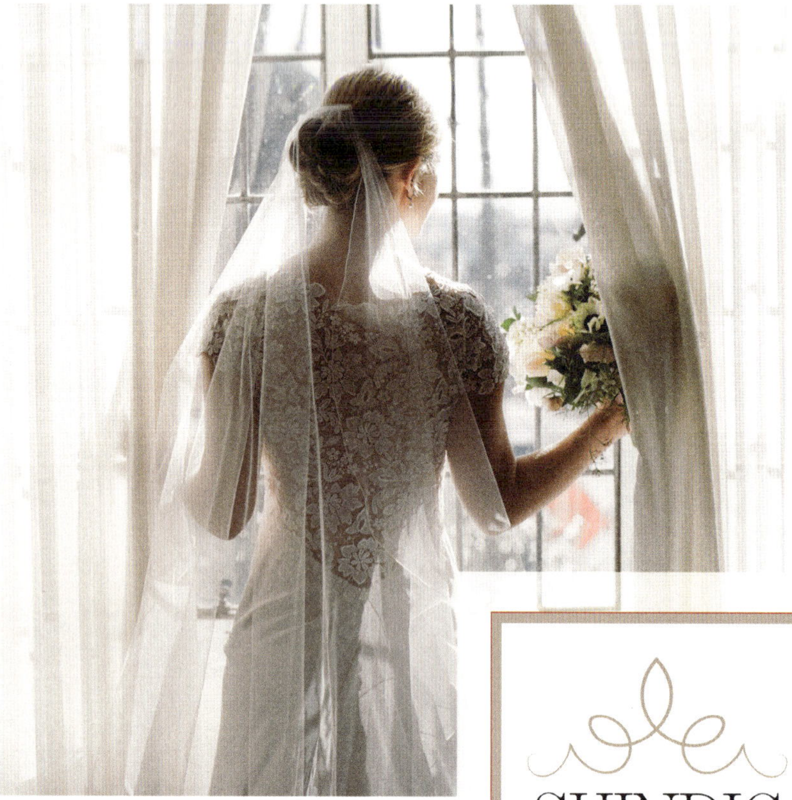

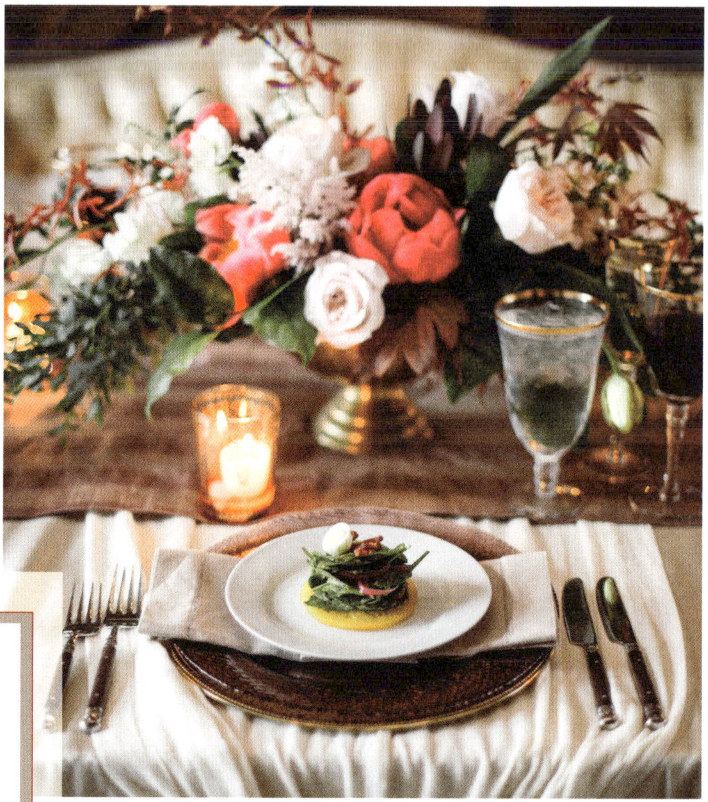

SHINDIG

weddings • events

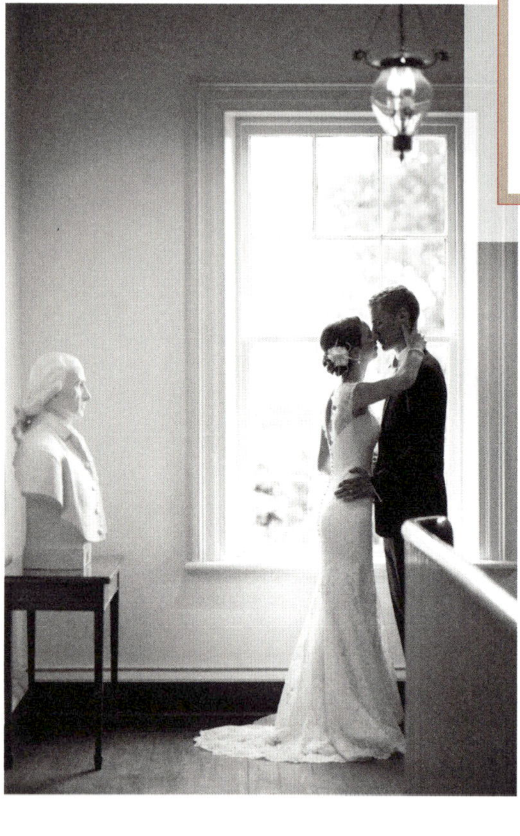

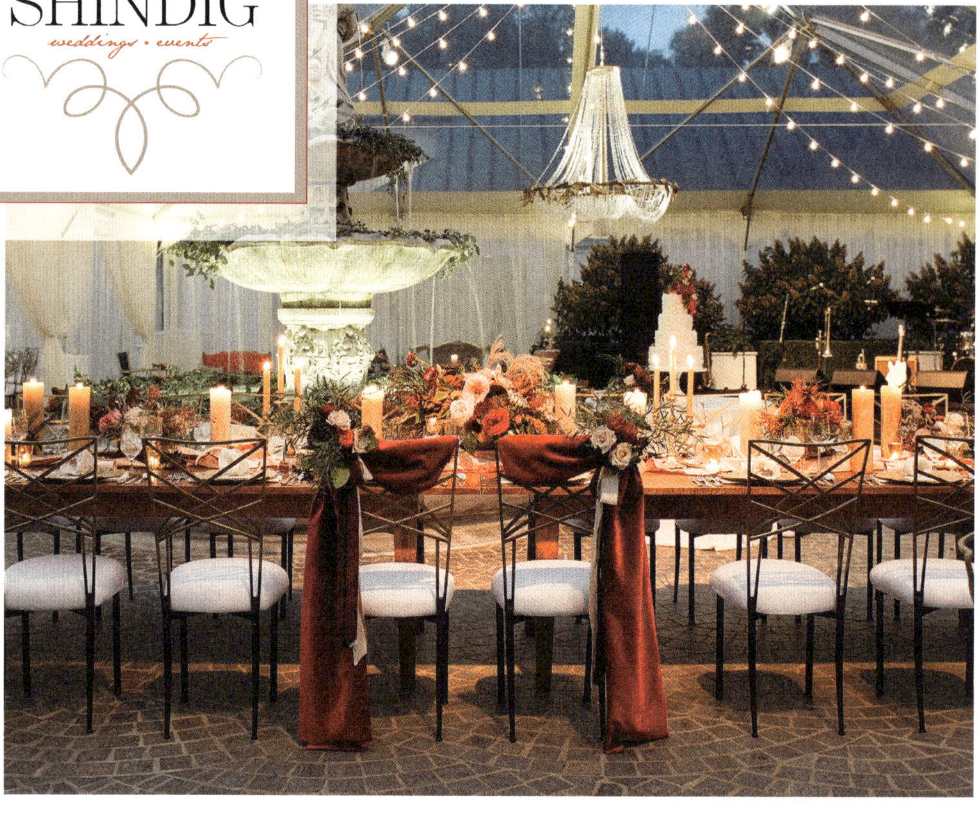

THE VERY NATURE OF OUR NAME IMPLIES A DIFFERENT APPROACH TO WEDDINGS, and the philosophy of Shindig is to infuse each wedding with a distinctive design and structure, well suited to the couple. We rejoice in handmade details. We delight in instilling surprise in every event, be it as large as fireworks or as intimate as a hidden note from the groom to the bride. We celebrate good papers, we applaud great music, and we revel in the tiniest of details, from the exact angle of an escort card to the precise placement of a menu.

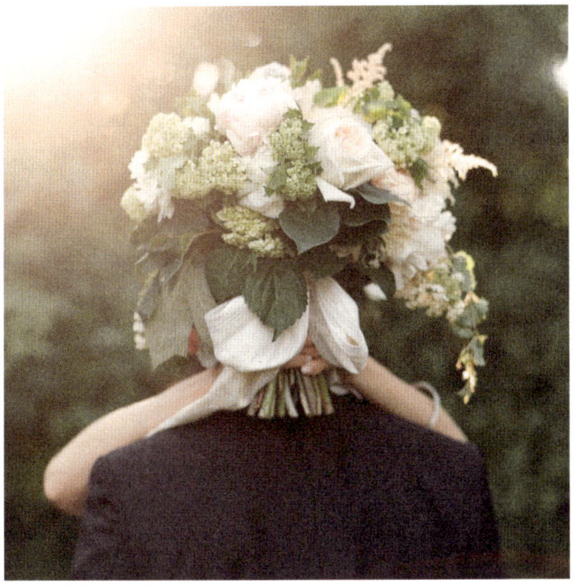

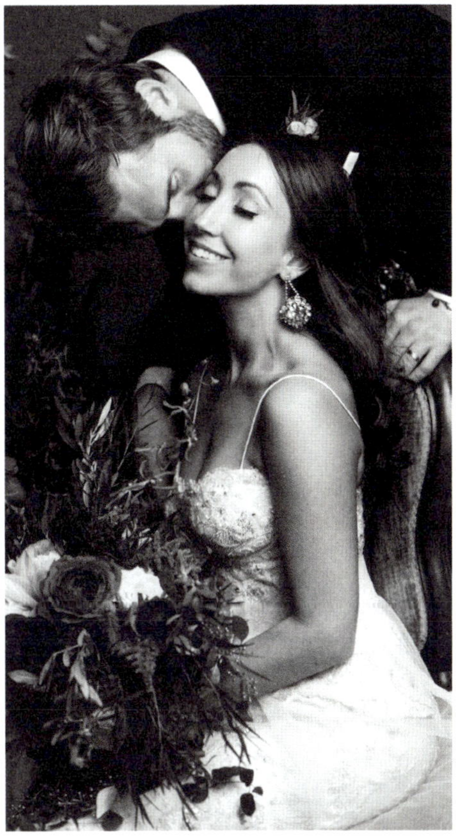

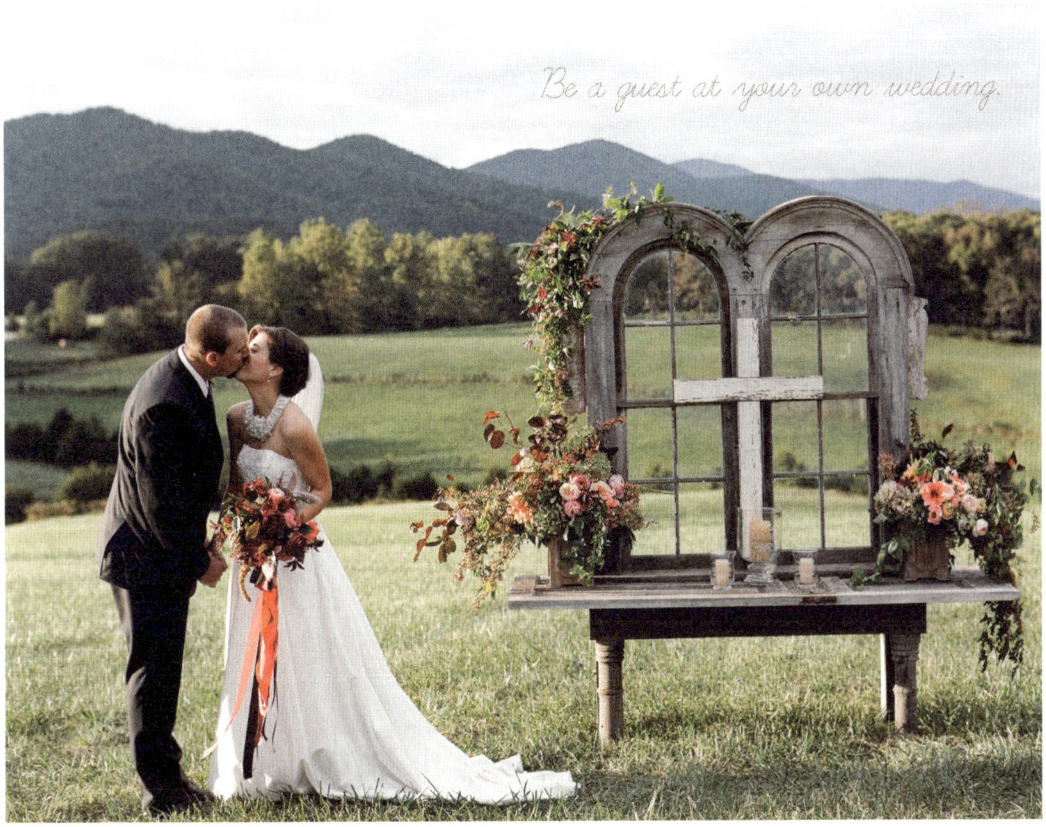

The underlying thread of the Shindig team is that we all love what we do, and because of that, we painstakingly prepare for not only the details of your actual wedding day, but also for all of the emails, phone calls, and meetings leading up to it. Because of our relentless attention to detail management, from the first day of consulting to the last sparkler's light, our clients have the luxury of peace in the midst of planning, of knowing their details are being competently and professionally managed, and ultimately, of being able to be guests at their own wedding.

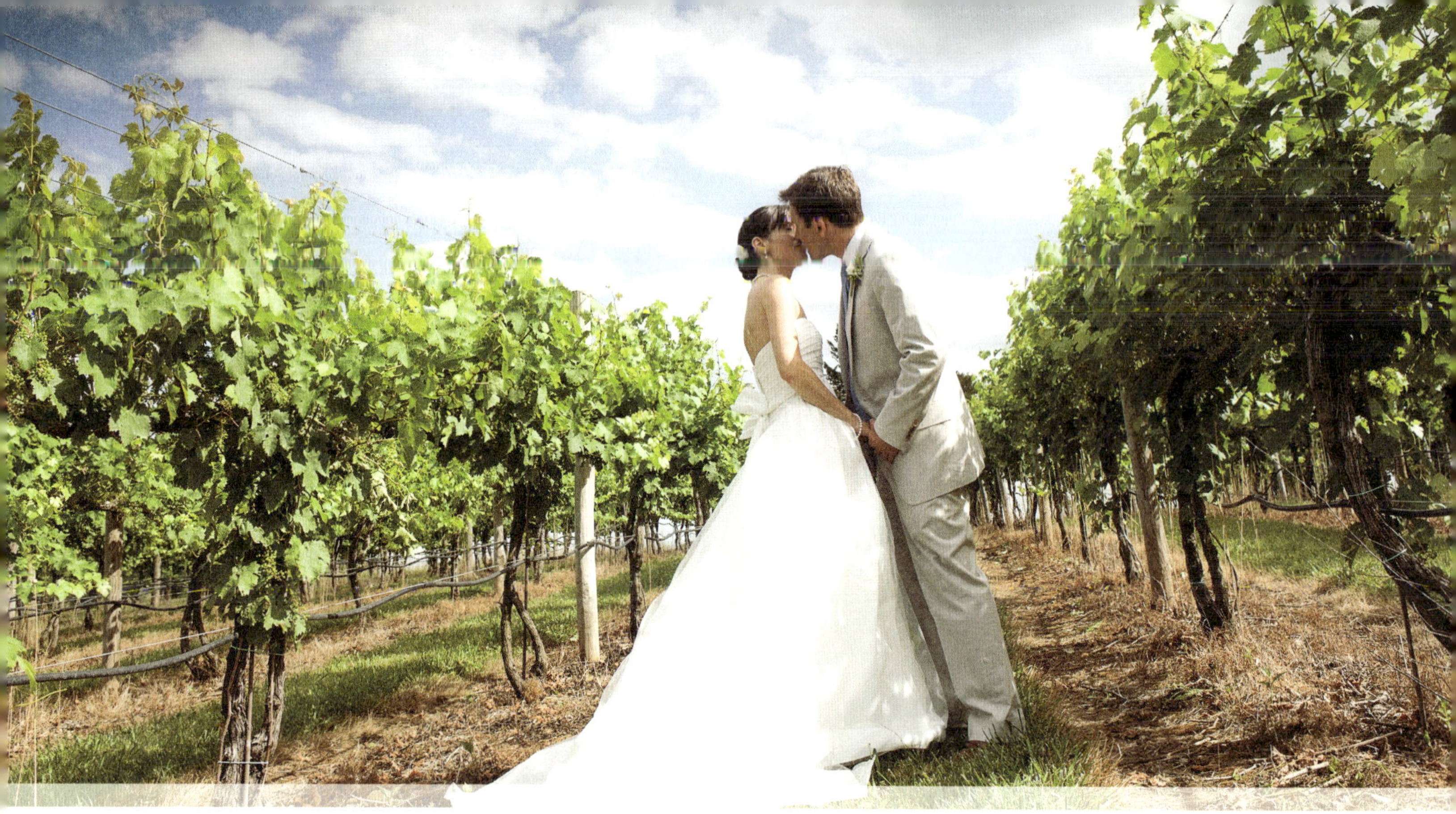

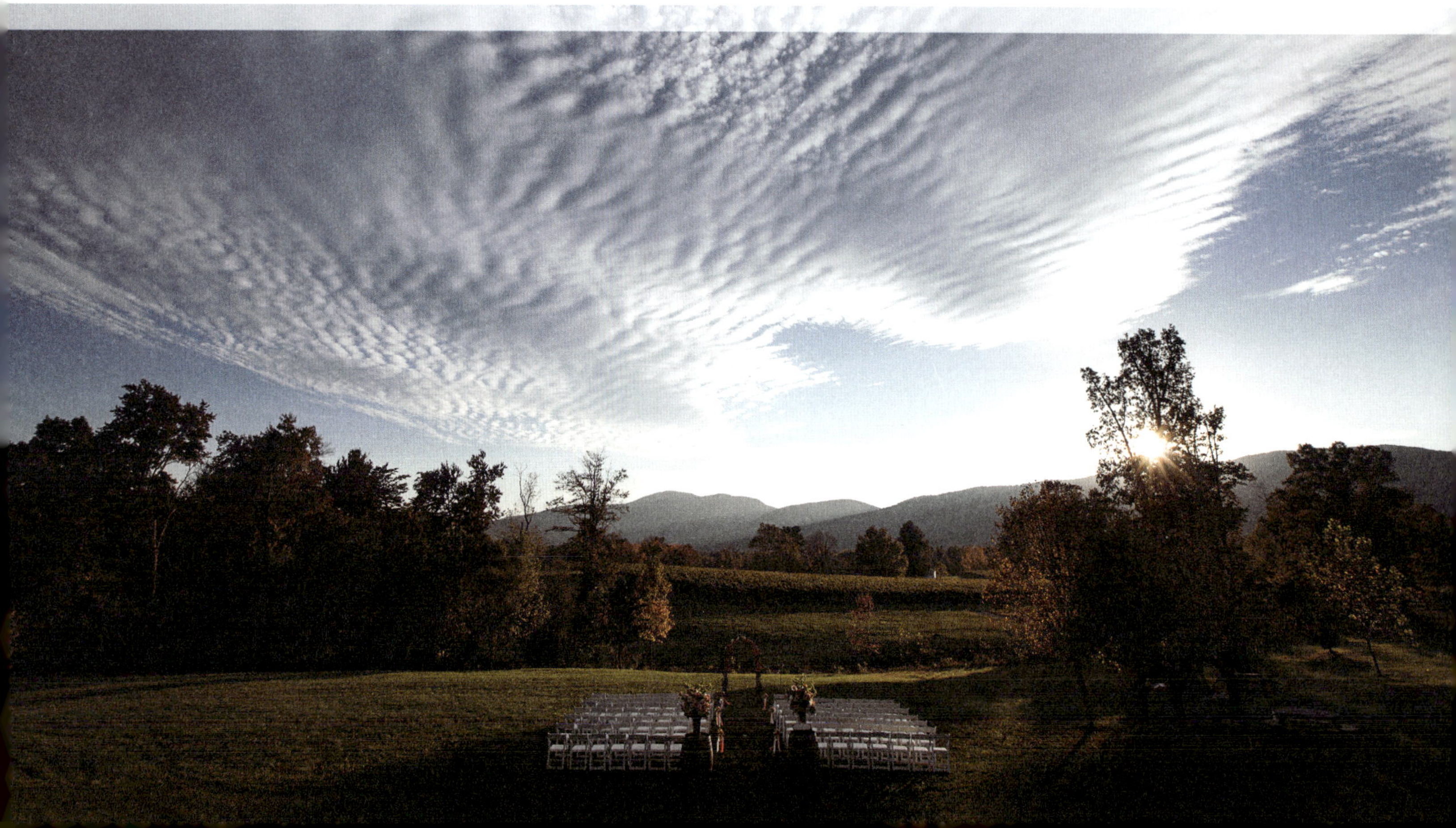

As one of the leaders in the Virginia Wine Industry, Veritas has contributed significantly to fulfilling Thomas Jefferson's dream of establishing Central Virginia as a distinguished and burgeoning producer of nationally and internationally acclaimed wine.

But there is more to Veritas than meets the eye. Beyond consistently producing a range of complex and elegant wines, Veritas features a variety of inviting indoor and outdoor event spaces and has garnered praise as one of Virginia's most sought-after venues.

Whether you prefer an intimate sit-down dinner at the Farmhouse or an all-out celebration in Saddleback Hall, the accommodating and professional event staff at Veritas stands ready to make your dream event a reality. Each event is carefully crafted from the initial consultation through to the final good-bye, with a level of attention to detail that is unsurpassed. This idyllic setting awaits only your personal touch for a truly unique and memorable event.

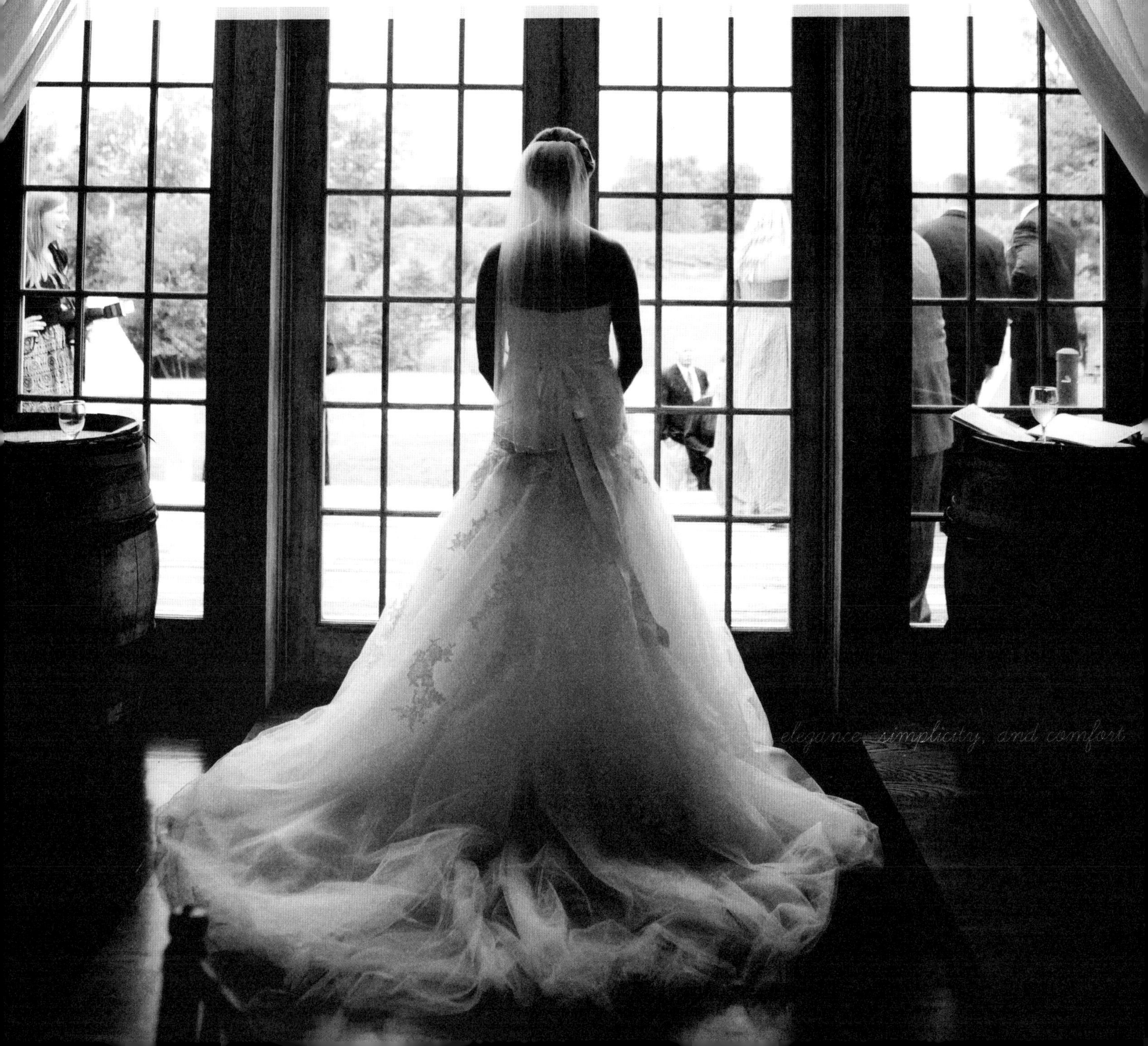

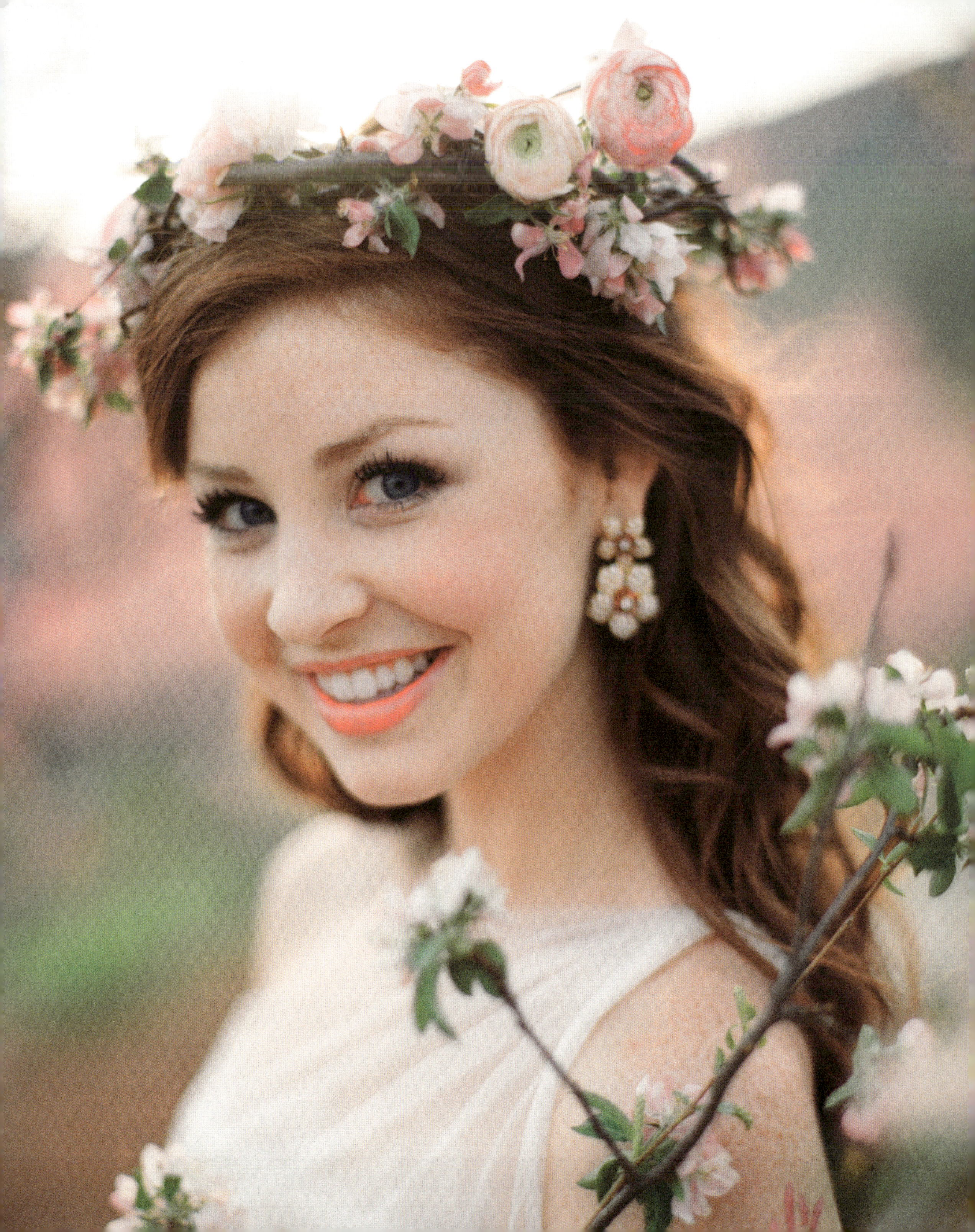

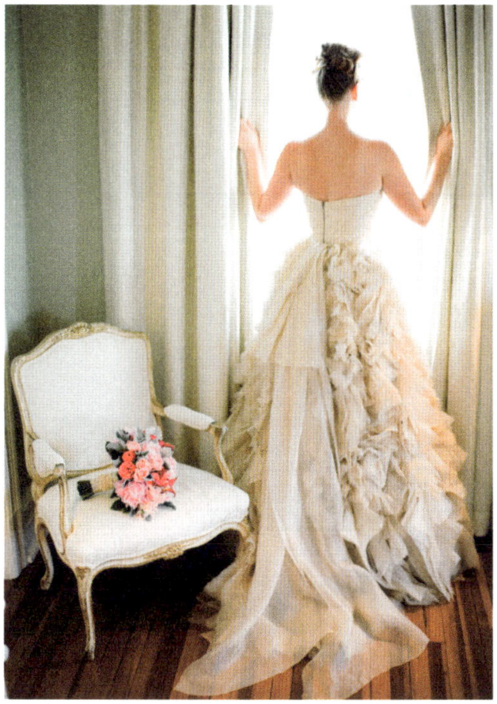

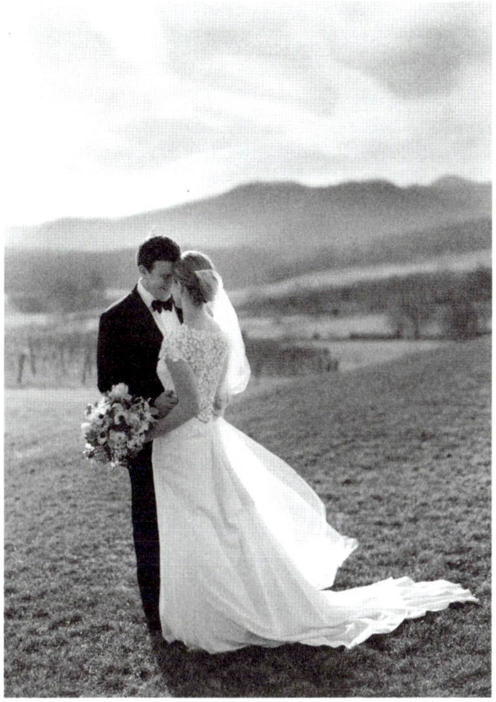

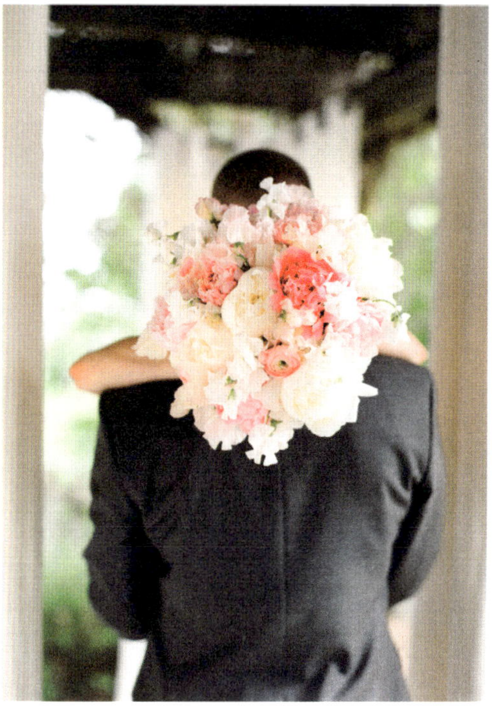

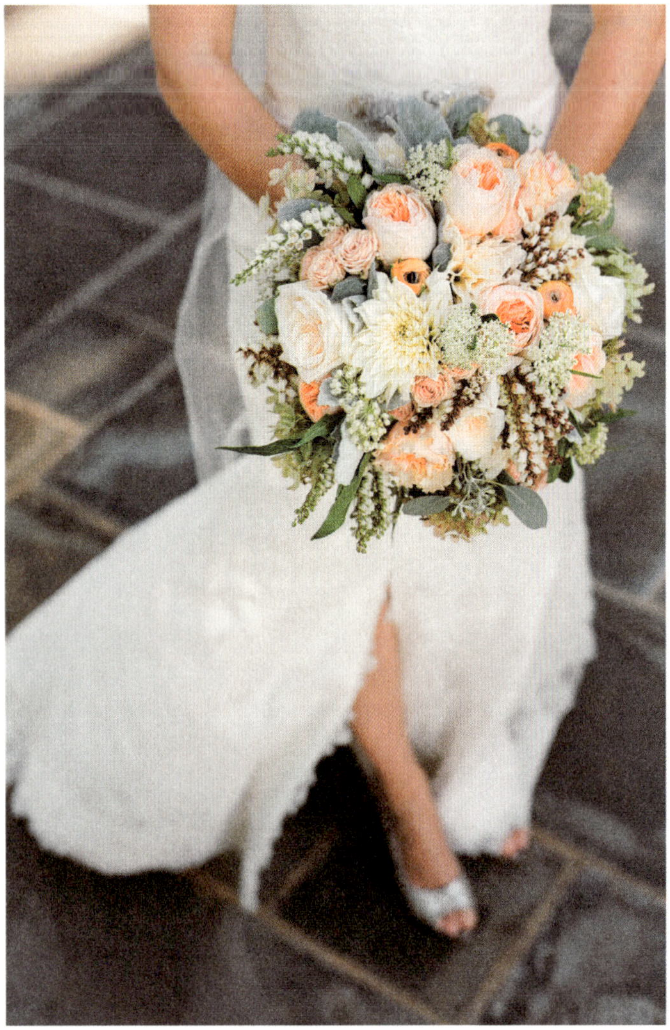

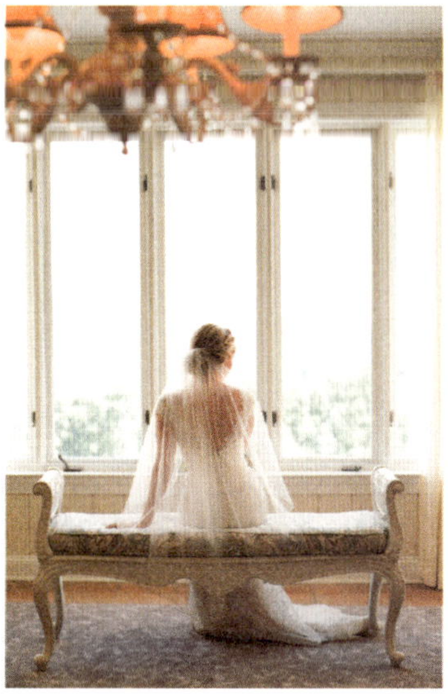

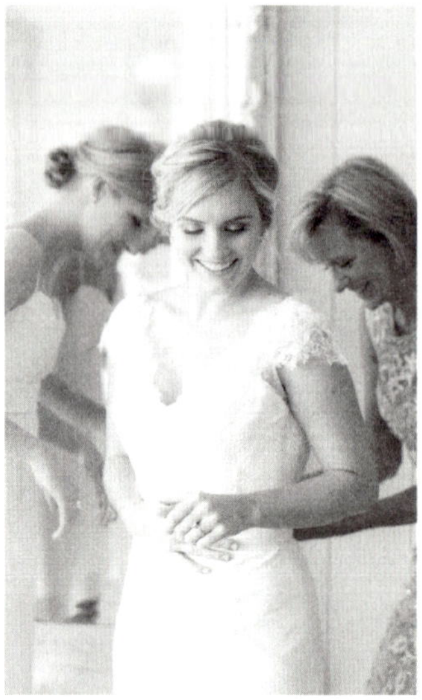

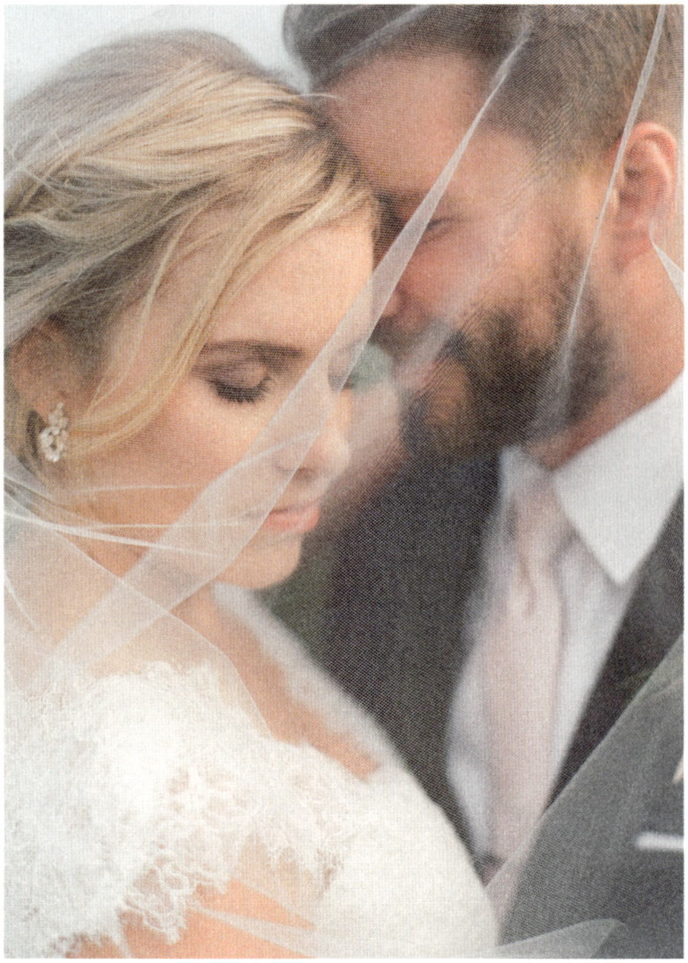

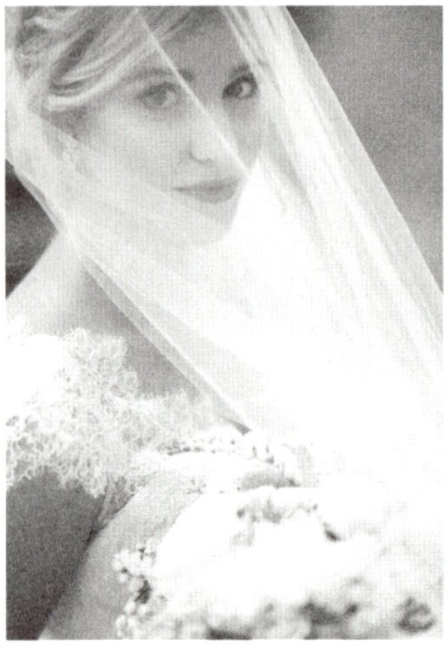

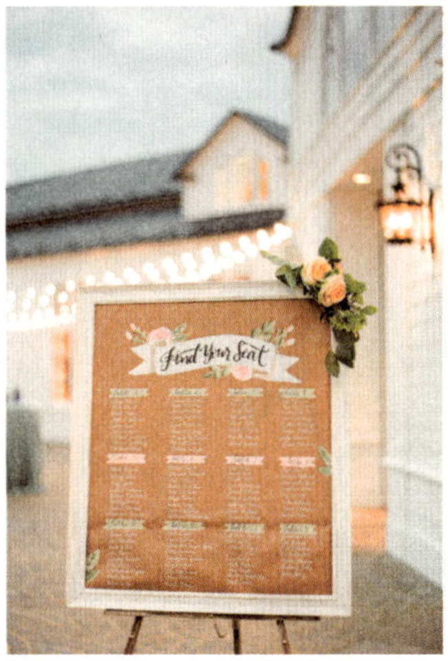

jenfariello.com | 434.963.7976

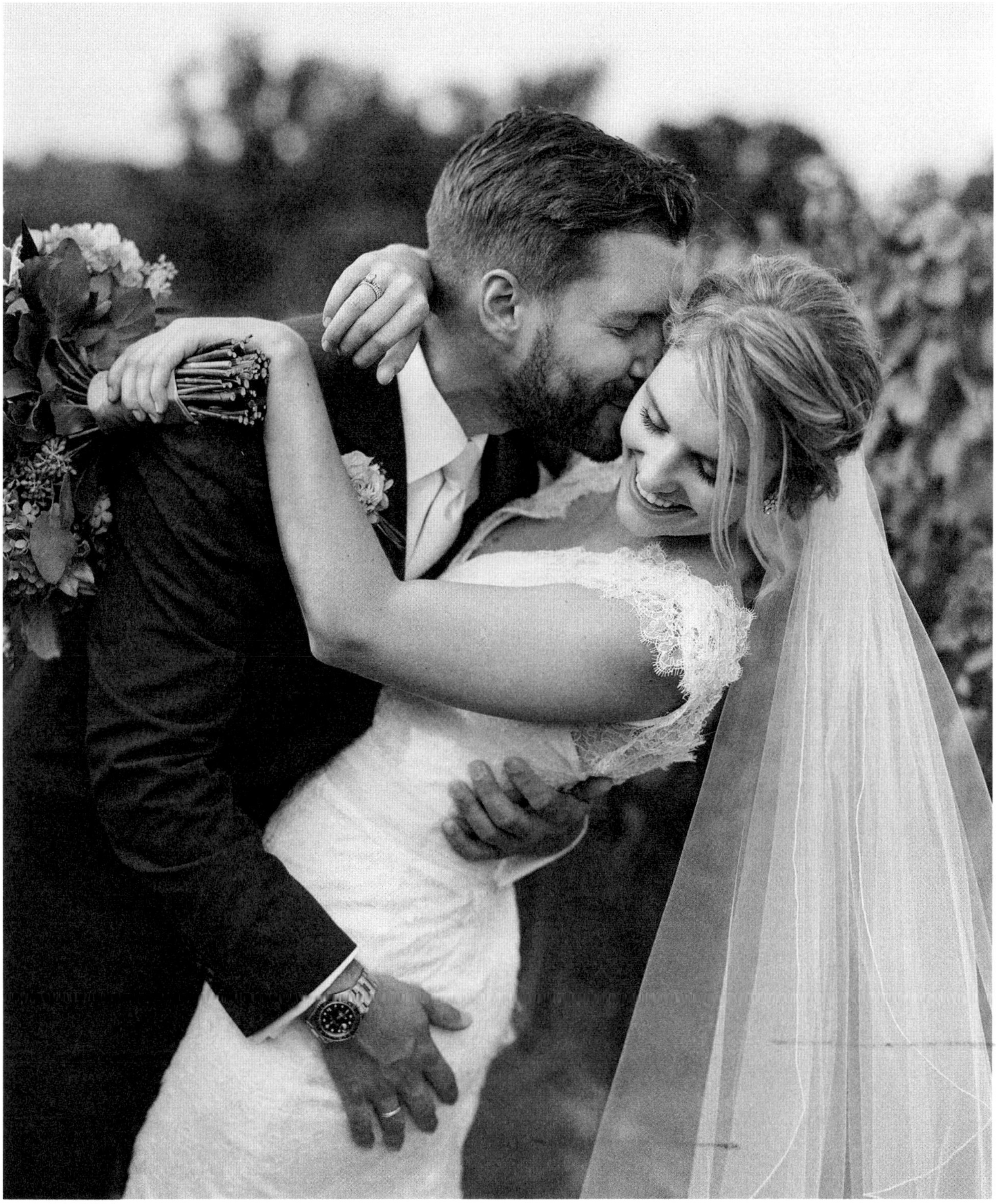

jenfariello
PHOTOGRAPHY

Index & CREDITS

Adventure Farm
adventurefarm.net
434.971.8796
Photos: #1 by Elizabeth Bogh, #3 by Cass Chisholm

Ash Lawn-Highland
ashlawnhighland.org
434.293.8000
Photos: #1 by Jason Collins, #2 by Rob Garland, #3 by JMK Photos, #4 by Redkite

Barb Wired
barbwiredllc.com
434.531.3247
Photos: #2 by Jason Keefer, #1 & 4 by Dominique Attaway, #4 by William Mahone, #6 by Lindsay Fauver

Bella Rosa Bridal
bellarosabridal.com
434.284.9500
Photo: by Jason Keefer

Belle Haven
bellehavenonthejames.com
434.989.8482

Blue Ridge AV and Lighting
blueridgeavandlighting.com
434.975.3540

Cardinal Point Vineyard & Winery
cardinalpointwinery.com
540.456.8400
Photos: by Will Kerner

Carpe Donut
carpedonut.org
434.806.6202

Castle Hill Cider
castlehillcider.com
434.296.0047
Photos: #1 by Eric Kelley, #2 by William Mahone

The Catering Outfit
cateringoutfit.com
434.951.4699
Photos: #3,4,7,8,9,10,12 & 13 by Jen Fariello, #2 & 5 by Robert Radifera, #1,6 & 11 by Kristen Moore

Clifton Inn
cliftoninn.net
434.971.1800

Colleen Miller Events
colleenmillerevents.com
540.471.6567
Photos: #1 & 3 by Meg Runion Studios, #2 & 4 by Josephine Sittenfeld

Donovan-Groves Events
donovangrovesevents.com
434.249.2424
Photos: by Jen Fariello

EastCoast Entertainment
eastcoastentertainment.com
804.355.2178

Elizabeth Woodson Gift Baskets
elizabethwoodson.com
434.589.2484

Erin McDermott Jewelry
erinmcdermott.com
704.724.6145
Photos: #3 & 8 by Amy Free, all others by Erin McDermott

Eve Watters, Harpist
evewatters.com
434.823.8600

Face Value Salon-Aveda
facevaluestudio.com
Old Trail 434.823.2009
Stonefield 434.984.1254
Photos: #2 by Jennifer Carroll, #1, 3, & 4 by Jen Fariello

Favorite Cakes by Kathy Watkins
favoritecakes.com
434.974.9229
Photos: #1 & 2 by Jen Fariello, #3 by Jose Villa

Festive Fare
charlottesville.classicpartyrentals.com
434.296.5496

First Colony Winery
firstcolonywinery.com
434.979.7105

Foxtail Cottage Floral
foxtailcottage.com
434.823.7272
Photos: #1 & 4 by Hannah Chen, #2 by Sam Stroud, #3 by 3 Cats Photo

Gearharts Fine Chocolates
gearhartschocolates.com
434.972.9100
Photos: by Jen Fariello

Glorious Foods Gourmet To Go & Catering
gloriousfoodscatering.com
434.817.7278

The Happy Cook
thehappycook.com
434.977.2665

Hedge Fine Blooms
hedgefineblooms.com
434.293.8825

Jen Fariello Photography
jenfariello.com
434.963.7976

Keswick Vineyards
keswickvineyards.com
434.295.1102
Photos: #2 by Katelyn Jones, all others by Keswick Vineyards

King Family Vineyards
kingfamilyvineyards.com
434.823.7800
Photo: by Aaron Watson

The Local Restaurant & Catering
thelocal-cville.com
434.984.9749
Photos: #1 by Jack Looney, #2 & 4 by Ksant, #3 by Sera Petras

Maliha Creations
malihacreations.com
434.973.3183
Photos: #1 by Kristen Lynne, #2 by Aaron Watson, #3 by Rachel May, #4 by Andrea Hubbell

The Market at Grelen
themarketatgrelen.com
eventsatgrelen.com
540.672.7268

Events at Monticello
monticello.org/private-events
434.984.7578

Mount Ida Farm
mountidafarm.com
434.566.5562
Photos: #1 & 2 by Ron Dressel, #3 by Sera Petras, #4 by Tim Rothwell, #5 by Ron Dressel

MoxBox
getmoxbox.com
540.583.6626

Nature Composed
naturecomposed.com
540.672.0100
Photo: by Katie Stoops

One Creative Cookie
onecreativecookie.com
434.466.2151
Photos: #1& 2 by Jen Fariello, #3 by Jennifer Carroll

Parallel 38
p38cville.com
434.923.3838

Pippin Hill Farm & Vineyards
pippinhillfarm.com
434.202.8063

Rachel May Photography
rachel-may.com

Robert Radifera Photography
radifera.com
434.245.8547

Rock Paper Scissors
thinkrockpaperscissors.com
434.979.6366

Rouge 9 Make Up Studio
434.939.7870
Photos: by Jen Fariello

Sacred Ground Ceremonies
sacredgroundceremonies.com
434.296.9885
Photo: by Dominique Attaway

Shindig Weddings & Events
shindigweddings.com
434.987.9581
Photos: by Jen Fariello

Southern Blooms
patsfloraldesigns.com
540.948.5611
Photos: by Jose Villa

Suz Somersall
suzsomersall.com
646.543.9181
Photos: #1 by Eric Kelley, #2 & 3 by Jen Fariello

Veritas Vineyard & Winery
veritaswines.com
540.456.8000
Photos: #1 by Dominique Attaway, #2 by Jack Looney, #3 by Katie Wilson

The Virginia Shop
thevashop.net
434.977.0080

Waterperry Farm
waterperryfarm.com
434.973.0385
Photos: #2 by Katie Stoops, #3 by Jen Fariello

White Birch Events
whitebirchevents.com
434.409.8483
Photos: by Jen Fariello

William Walker Photography
williamwalkerphoto.com
434.960.2297

Photo credits required by the portfolio clients are either noted directly on the portfolio photos or listed above as requested. Credits are noted by number in order of appearance from top left and going clockwise on the portfolio page.

InterActive Nonfiction Reader

McDougal Littell

BRIDGES TO LITERATURE

LEVEL 3

McDougal Littell
A DIVISION OF HOUGHTON MIFFLIN COMPANY

Cover Art Credits

Basketball © Getty Images; *microbes* © Getty Images; *mountains* © Getty Images; *running* © Getty Images; *dock* © Getty Images; *eyes* © Getty Images; *wheat* © Sunset Avenue Productions/Artville/PictureQuest; *baseball* © Getty Images; *covered wagon* National Archives; *lightning* © Storm Pirate Productions/Artville/PictureQuest; *karate* © Getty Images; *clouds* © Getty Images; *book background* photo by Sharon Hoogstraten.

ISBN-13: 978-0-618-97758-1 ISBN-10: 0-618-97758-9

Printed in the United States of America.

2 3 4 5 6 7 8 9 – 1409 – 11 10 09

Note to the Student

This Workbook will introduce you to strategies you'll need to read all types of informational nonfiction. The examples here range from magazines you read for fun, to textbooks and bus schedules. Use the simple and effective techniques presented on these pages to become a successful reader of the many texts you encounter each day.

Table of Contents

Reading a Magazine Article

A magazine article is designed to catch and hold your interest. Learning how to recognize the items on a magazine page will help you read even the most complicated articles. Look at the sample magazine article as you read each strategy below.

A Read the **title** and other **headings** to get an idea of what the article is about. Frequently, the title presents the article's main topic. The smaller headings introduce subtopics related to the main topic.

B Note text that is set off in some way, such as an **indented paragraph** or a passage in a **different typeface.** This text often summarizes the article.

C Study **visuals**—photos, pictures, maps. Visuals help bring the topic to life and enrich the text.

D Look for **special features,** such as charts, tables, or graphs, that provide more detailed information on the topic or on a subtopic.

E Pay attention to terms in **italics** or **boldface.** Look for definitions or explanations before or after these terms.

MARK IT UP Use the sample magazine page and the tips above to help you answer the following questions.

1. What is the article's main topic? ______________________

   What two subtopics does the article cover? ______________________

2. Draw a star next to the paragraph that summarizes the article.

3. Circle the photo that shows cowboys at work. Put a checkmark beside the one that shows cowboys at play.

4. What is the subject of the chart?

   ____

5. How many boldfaced terms are explained in the chart? ______________________

6. Underline the sentence that explains what steer wrestling is.

A

Modern Cowboys

B *If you think cowboys rode off into the sunset in the 1890s, think again. American cowboys are alive and well and living in the western United States and Canada. Although life has changed greatly for cowboys—long cattle drives are a thing of the past, for instance—roping and riding still go with the territory.*

C

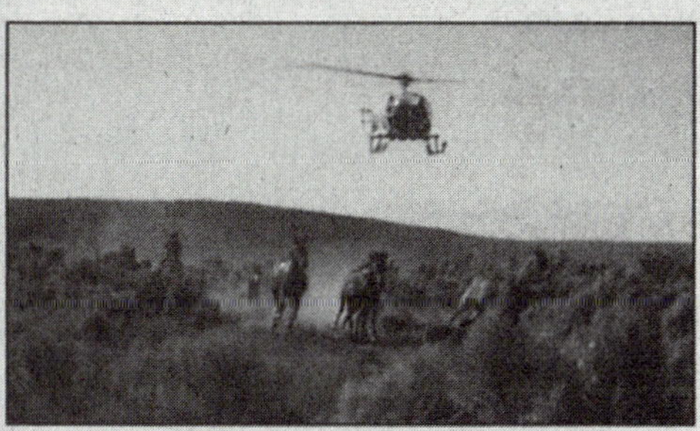

A **At Work** Many cowboys today work on cattle ranches. Like the cowboys of the Wild West, modern cowhands work long hours in all kinds of weather. However, unlike old-time cowboys, today's ranchers use machines for many of their jobs. Cowboys still use their horses to rope calves and do other work. But the livestock are often carried in trucks across the large, fenced-in ranches. And when a cow wanders far from the herd, cowboys sometimes use a helicopter to round up the stray.

A **At Play** Rodeos are rooted in the Old West. After working on a cattle drive, cowboys competed and showed off their skills in roping and riding. Today, the rodeo recalls the spirit of these cowboys. The events at a rodeo are divided into two main groups: rough stock events and timed events. Rough stock events include riding bucking horses or bulls. Timed events include calf roping and steer wrestling.

C

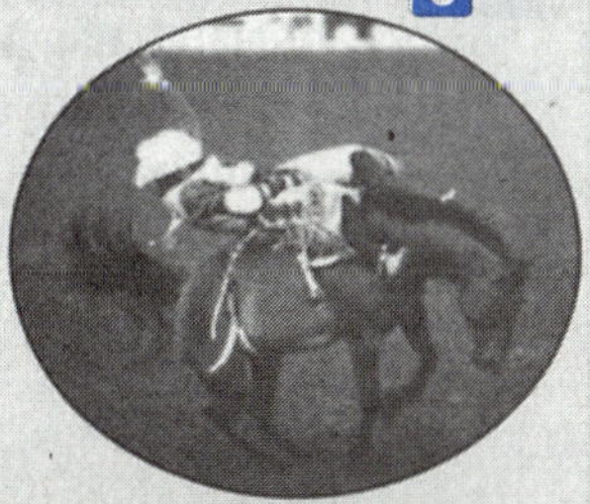

D

TYPICAL RODEO EVENTS

Bareback Bronc Riding For 8 seconds, the rider spurs the horse as it bucks.

Saddle Bronc Riding The rider uses a saddle and must stay on the horse for 8 or 10 seconds.

Bull Riding The rider tries to stay on the bull for 8 seconds (no spurring needed).

Calf Roping The rider chases the calf on horseback, ropes it, and then gets off the horse to tie up the calf.

Steer Wrestling The cowboy grabs the steer's horns and wrestles the animal to the ground.

E **Team Roping** A team of two rope and tie a steer.

Reading a Textbook

The first page of a textbook lesson introduces you to a particular topic. The page also provides important information that will guide you through the rest of the lesson. Look at the sample textbook page as you read each strategy below.

A Preview the **title** and other **headings** to find out the lesson's main topic and related subtopics.

B Look for a list of **vocabulary terms.** These words will be identified and defined throughout the lesson.

C Read the **main idea** or **objectives.** These items summarize the lesson and establish a purpose for your reading.

D Notice text on the page that is set off in some way. For example, text placed in a tinted, or colored, box may be from a **primary source** that gives firsthand knowledge about the topic.

E Examine **visuals,** such as photos and drawings, and their **captions.** Visuals can help the topic come alive.

F Find words set in special type, such as **italics** or **boldface.** Also look for material in **parentheses.** Boldface is often used to identify the vocabulary terms in the lesson. Material in parentheses may refer you to another page or visual in the lesson.

MARK IT UP Use the sample textbook page and the tips above to help you answer the following questions.

1. What part of the country does the lesson focus on? ____________________

2. Circle the vocabulary terms that will be defined in the lesson.

3. Underline the main idea that is developed in the lesson.

4. Put a checkmark beside the excerpt from the primary source. Who wrote the excerpt?

____

5. Who was Nat Love? ____________________

6. Circle the vocabulary term that refers to the area from the Missouri River to the Rocky Mountains. Underline the sentence that directs readers to a map on another page.

A

1 Miners, Ranchers, and Cowhands

B **TERMS & NAMES**
frontier
Great Plains
boomtown
long drive
vaquero
vigilante

C **MAIN IDEA**
Miners, ranchers, and cowhands settled in the West seeking economic opportunities.

WHY IT MATTERS NOW
The mining and cattle industries that developed then still contribute to American economic growth.

A **ONE AMERICAN'S STORY**

D Nat Love was born a slave in Tennessee in 1854. After the Civil War, he was one of thousands of African Americans who left the South and went west. In 1869, Love headed for Dodge City, Kansas. He was 15 and now free.

Love's horse taming skills landed him a job as a cowhand. For 20 years, he took part in the cattle drives that brought Texas cattle to Kansas stockyards. He became well known for his expert horsemanship and his rodeo riding and roping. In his 1907 autobiography, Love offered a lively but exaggerated account of his life. He told how he braved hailstorms, fought wild animals, and held off human attackers.

A VOICE FROM THE PAST

D I carry the marks of fourteen bullet wounds on different parts of my body, most any one of which would be sufficient to kill an ordinary man. . . . Horses were shot from under me, men killed around me, but always I escaped with a trifling wound at the worst.

Nat Love, *The Life and Adventures of Nat Love*

As you will read in this section, few cowhands led lives as exciting as that described by Nat Love, but they all helped to open a new chapter in the history of the American West.

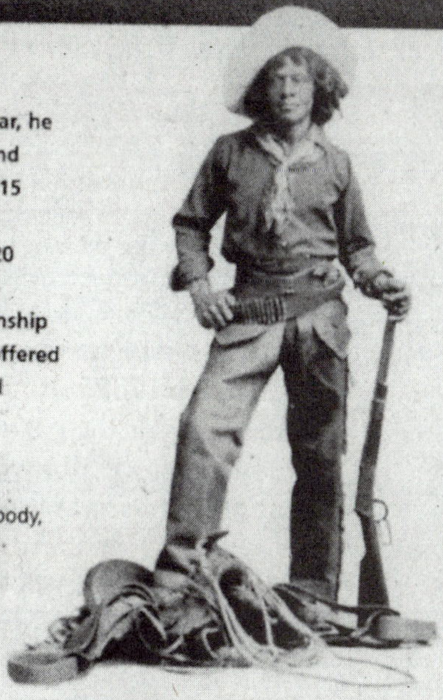

Nat Love was an African-American cowhand who became a rodeo star.

E

A Geography and Population of the West

F In the mid-1800s, towns such as St. Joseph and Independence, Missouri, were jumping-off places for settlers going west. They were the last cities and towns before the frontier. The **frontier** was the unsettled or sparsely settled area of the country occupied largely by Native Americans.

Many white settlers thought of the **Great Plains**—the area from the Missouri River to the Rocky Mountains—as empty. (See map on page 558.) Few had been attracted to its rolling plains, dry plateaus, and deserts. However, west of the Rockies, on the Pacific Coast, settlers had followed miners streaming into California after the 1849 gold rush. By 1850, California had gained statehood. Oregon followed in 1859.

Reading Graphs

Graphs are used to present facts and statistics. Bar graphs and circle graphs are useful for making comparisons. Use the following strategies along with the examples below to help you read graphs.

A Read the **title** to help you understand what the graph is about.

B In bar graphs, look at the data on the horizontal line and the data on the vertical line to find a value or estimate.

C In circle graphs, read the **headings** to learn what each percent number stands for.

D Compare the information from circle graphs and bar graphs to see how they relate. Sometimes they will give the same information. Other times one will give additional information.

E Check the credit to see if the information is up to date and from a respected source.

The following graphs show the results of a survey conducted by *Zillions*, the consumer magazine for children. More than half the participants ages 8 to 14 said they do not get an allowance although some do get spending money. What other observations can you make?

A **Allowance: Who gets one and how much?**

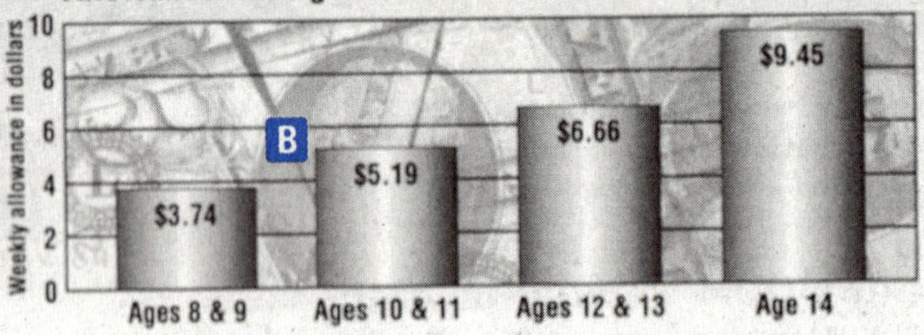

Percent of Kids Who Get:

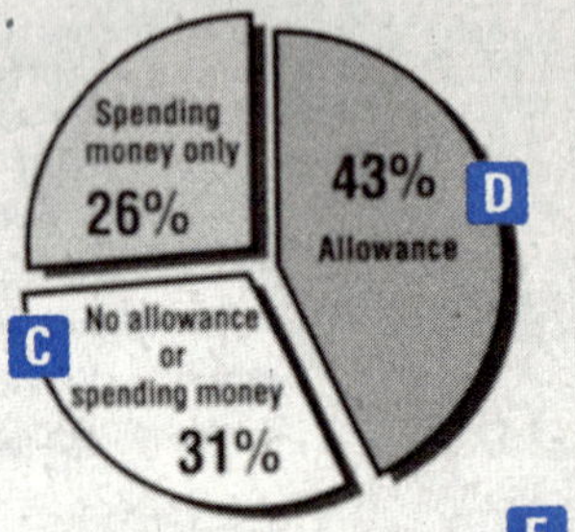

E

Source: *Zillions* Jan/Feb, 1999

MARK IT UP Answer the following questions using the graphs and tips.

1. Draw a box around the graph that shows data on the amount of allowance kids get.
2. How many kids do not get an allowance? Circle your answer.
3. According to the bar graph, how much more allowance does a 13 year-old get than a 10 year-old? ______________________________

Reading a Transit Map

It's important to know how to read a map so you can find your way around without becoming lost. Look at the example below as you read each strategy in this list.

A Scan the **title** to know the main idea of the map.

B Interpret the **key,** or **legend,** to find out what the symbols on the map stand for.

C Study **geographic labels** to understand specific places on the map.

D Notice the **scale and pointer,** or **compass rose,** to determine distance and direction.

A

B

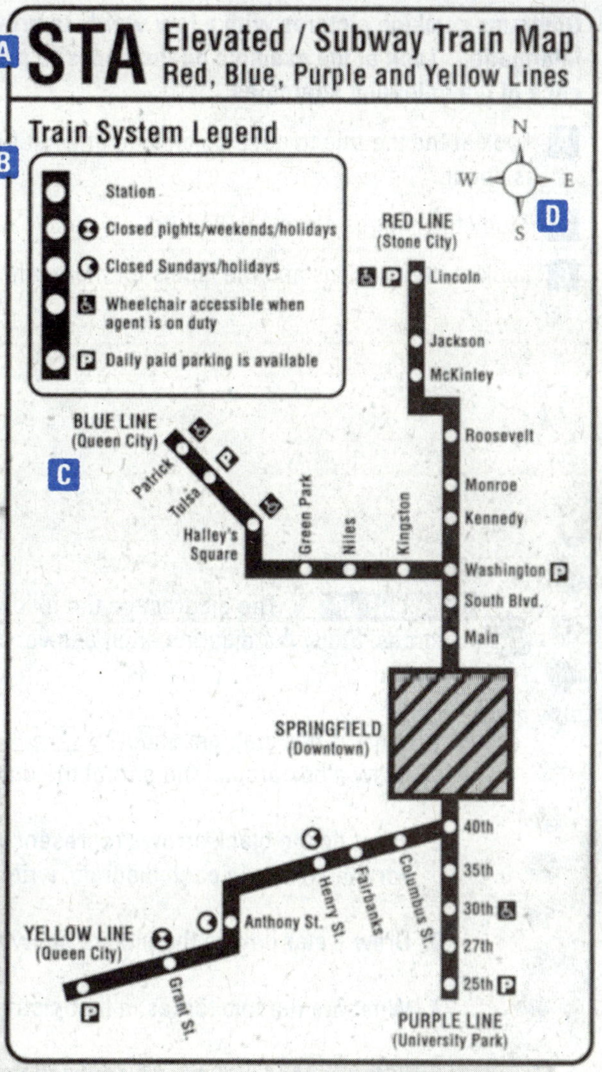

MARK IT UP Use the map to answer the following questions.

1. What is the purpose of this map?

____

2. What do the symbols mean together?

____

3. Circle the three stations between 40th and 25th on the Purple Line.

4. Are any of these three stations accessible to commuters who use wheelchairs? ________ If so, underline the station(s) on the map.

5. Does the Red Line run north and south or east and west? ________ Put an "X" by the label of another train line that runs in the same direction as the Red Line.

Reading a Diagram

Diagrams combine pictures with a few words to provide a lot of information. Look at the example on the opposite page as you read each of the following strategies.

A Look at the the title to get a quick idea of what the diagram is about.

B Study the images closely to understand each part of the diagram.

C Look at the captions and the labels for more information.

MARK IT UP The diagram on the following page shows balanced and unbalanced forces. Study the diagram, then answer the following questions using the strategies above.

1. What is this diagram about? ______________________________
Draw a box around the part of the diagram where you found this information.

2. What do the black arrows represent in these pictures? ______________________________
For the arrows in each diagram, write labels that explain what the arrows mean.

3. Draw a star next to the picture showing unbalanced forces.

4. What are the two forces in that picture? ______________________________

5. In the second picture, why does the car rise up from the ground?

____

6. In the second picture, circle the arrow that represents the greater of the two forces.

7. Which two pictures show the same set of forces? Draw an "X" next to each of the two pictures.

A Balanced and Unbalanced Forces

***Newton's First Law of Motion:* As long as the forces on an object balance each other, the object's motion will not change.**

The force of gravity pulling down on the car is balanced by the force of the ground pushing up on the car. The car remains at rest.

C ***Newton's Second Law of Motion:* When an unbalanced force acts on an object, the object will accelerate in the direction that the unbalanced force points.**

The force of the crane pulling up on the car is greater than the force of gravity pulling down on it. The car begins to rise.

Once again, the force of gravity pulling down on the car is balanced by the force of the ground pushing up on it. The car is again at rest.

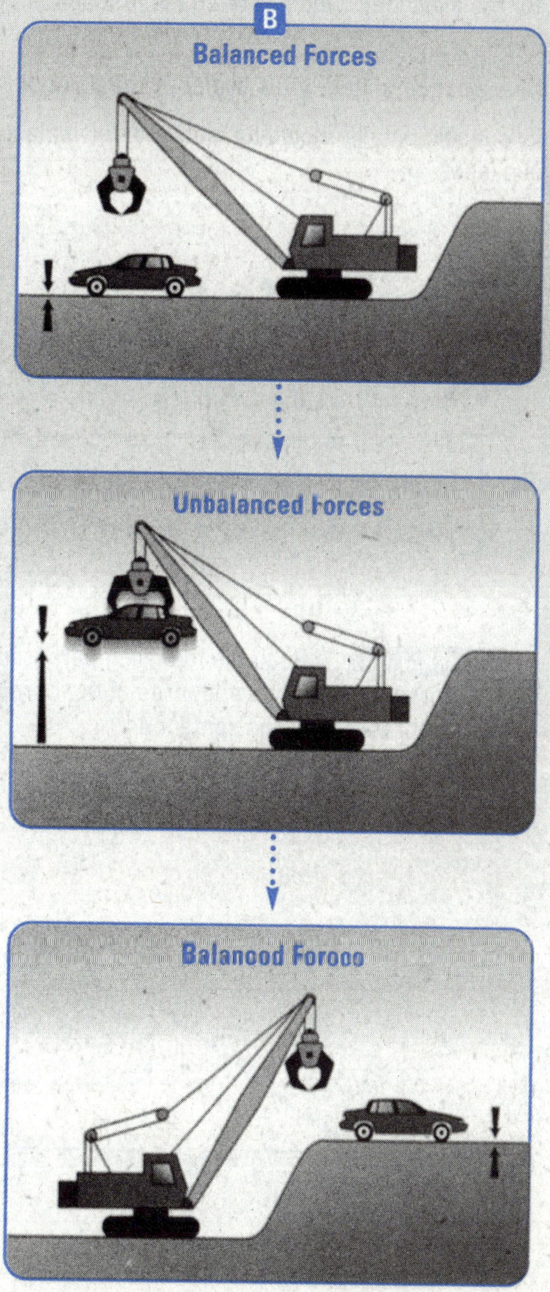

Main Idea and Supporting Details

The main idea in a paragraph is its most important point. Details in the paragraph support the main idea. Identifying the main idea will help you focus on the main message the writer wants to communicate. Use the following strategies to help you identify a paragraph's main idea and supporting details.

- Look for the main idea, which is often the first sentence in a paragraph.
- Use the main idea to help you summarize the point of the paragraph.
- Identify specific details, including facts and examples, that support the main idea.

Searching for E.T.

Main idea — Scientists on Project Phoenix search for extraterrestrials—beings from another planet.

Details — The scientists use radio telescopes to track radio signals from outer space. The telescopes are pointed at nearby, sun-like stars that are thought to be orbited by planets. So far, no clear signals have been received. However, scientists hope that the telescopes will finally help answer the question: Is anyone out there?

MARK IT UP Read the following paragraph. Circle its main idea and write it in the diagram below. Then add three of the paragraph's supporting details to the diagram, using key phrases from the sentences.

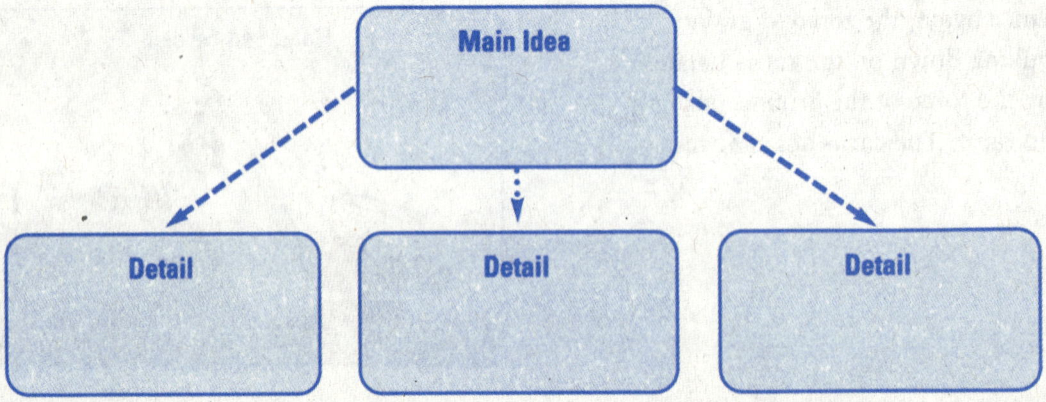

Problem and Solution

Does the proposed solution to a problem make sense? In order to decide, you need to look at each part of the text. Use the following strategies to read the text below.

- Look at the beginning or middle of a paragraph to find the problem.
- Find out why the problem is important.
- Look for the proposed solution.
- Identify the details that support the proposed solution.
- Think about whether the solution is a good one.

A Garden for Market Street?

Statement of problem — Explanation of problem

Anyone who has walked along Market Street has seen the big empty lot next to the public library. This lot has been empty for two years now, and it is ugly and dangerous. Paper trash and broken bottles cover the ground, and nothing grows there but tough nasty weeds. And who knows what kind of rodents might be crawling around in the dirt?

According to the mayor, the owner has long since deserted the property, and no one has any plans to build on it. This is valuable land, and it's right in the middle of town! The citizens should do something with it.

A community nature garden would be a great thing for the city. Teachers and students could share what they've learned about local plant wildlife. Other residents could volunteer to help plant the trees, grasses, and wildflowers. When finished, the garden would be both educational and lovely—a great improvement over the weedy lot!

MARK IT UP Read the text above and answer the questions.

1. In the third paragraph, underline the proposed solution.
2. Circle at least one detail that supports the solution.
3. Do you agree with the solution? Explain why or why not. ______________________

____

Sequence

It's important to understand the *sequence*, or order of events, in what you read. It helps you know what happens and why. Read the tips below to make sure a sequence is clear to you. Then look at the example on the opposite page.

- Read through the passage and think about what its main steps, or stages, are.
- Look for words and phrases that signal time: *today, Saturday, later,* or *9:30.*
- Look for words and phrases that signal order: *first, next, then, before, at last, after,* or *finally.*

The article on the next page describes how a sixteen-year-old spent her day as a movie extra. Use the information from the passage and the tips above to answer the questions.

MARK IT UP

1. Circle words and phrases that signal time.
2. Underline the phrases in the article that signal order.
3. Use the information from the article to complete this time line. Make sure to include signal words in your sentences.

6:45 A.M.	7:45 A.M.	9:30 A.M.	9:50 A.M.–1:30 P.M.	1:30 P.M.
Report to set.				

I Was a Movie Extra

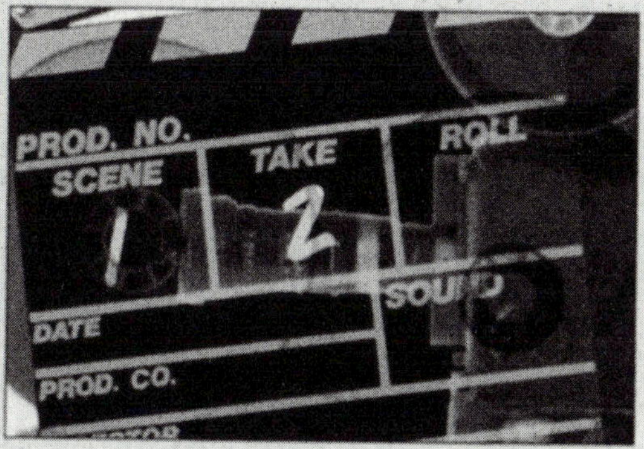

On a recent Saturday, Nicole M., 16, . . . spent the day as a movie extra. . . . She found out that life as an extra isn't exactly glamorous, but she did have fun. Here is her story . . .

I was one of nearly 600 extras who appeared in a fire-drill scene for the movie "Newport South.". . .

At 6:45 A.M. the day of filming, I reported to the set, an abandoned school building. . . . My day started off with registration and wardrobe check. . . . I was assigned to one of four sections: A, B, C or D (I landed in D, along with some of my friends). . . . After that, I was told to find my section and to sit there. My friends and I waited and waited. At 7:45 A.M., caterers arrived with doughnuts, lemonade, coffee, and hot chocolate. After munching down chocolate doughnuts, we waited again—till 9:30 A.M.

Finally, it was time for our big scene. A guy wearing a headset explained to us what we had to do, then directed us to one of four stairwells. We were smooshed: About 75 people stood shoulder to shoulder. It was 20 minutes before we got the signal to move, and we poured out of the school and headed for the football field. . . .

Before the scene was shot, it was stressed upon us not to look at the cameras. But it was stressed so much it was hard NOT to look. . . .

So, after that first take, we shot the scene two more times, then we got a snack. We had five minutes to use the washroom, eat, and do anything else we needed to. Then it was back to our stairwells. . . .

By 1:30 P.M., the shooting was done, and we all gathered in the gym. . . . I reported to wardrobe and returned my jacket. After standing in line to get paid, my friends and I left—feeling tired, cold, wet, hungry and a bit grouchy.

from *The Chicago Tribune*

Cause and Effect

A cause is an event that brings about another event. An effect is something that happens as a result of the first event. Identifying causes and effects helps you understand how the events are related. The strategies below can help you find causes and effects in any reading.

- Look for an action or event that answers the question "What happened?" This is the effect.
- Look for an action or event that answers the question "Why did it happen?" This is the cause.
- Identify words that signal causes and effects, such as *because, as a result, therefore, cause,* and *since.*

MARK IT UP Use the cause-and-effect passage on the next page to help you answer the following questions. Notice that the first cause and effect in the passage are labeled.

1. Underline the phrase that explains what happened because the *Sultana* was carrying so many people. Is this a cause or an effect? ____________________

2. Circle words in the passage that signal causes and effects. The first one is done for you.

3. Use the causes and effects in the last two paragraphs to complete the following diagram.

Cause: *The boat was carrying too many people.* → **Effect:** *The boilers leaked.*

Cause: → **Effect:**

Cause: → **Effect:**

The Sinking of the *Sultana*

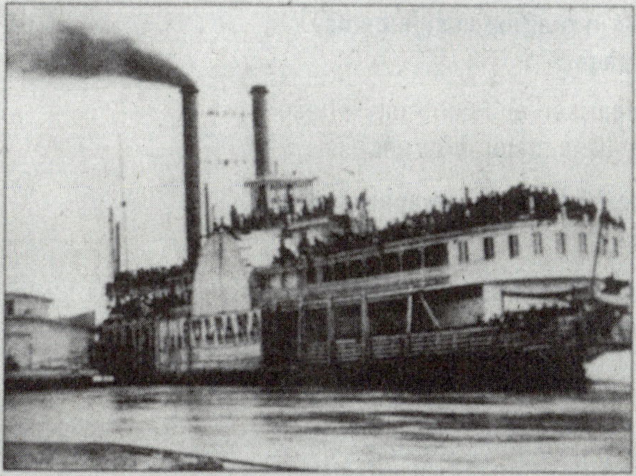

On April 25, 1865, about two weeks after the end of the Civil War, a steamboat called the *Sultana* was traveling up the Mississippi River. The ship had set out from Vicksburg, Mississippi, and was going to Cairo, Illinois. Many passengers, including hundreds of ex-prisoners of war, had boarded the ship. Since no one had taken a roll call, the exact number is not known. However, historians guess that there were about 2,300 people on board. That number is about six times as many people as the ship was built to carry. Because the *Sultana* was carrying so many people, it was going slowly.

Signal word

Cause

Effect

The load also caused the ship's steam boilers to leak several times over the next two days. The boilers were repaired, but the strain was too much. Early on April 27, the boilers exploded after the ship had sailed just a few miles north of Memphis, Tennessee. As a result of the explosion, hundreds of passengers were killed instantly. Many others drowned or died in the fire that started when hot coals burst from the boiler. Some of the victims who died in the fire were trapped below deck. Others, especially those who had been prisoners of war, were too weak to try to swim in the icy river.

In all, about 1,700 people died. That number is about 200 more than died aboard the *Titanic* 47 years later. The sinking of the *Sultana* was—and still is—the greatest seafaring disaster in American history. However, the newspapers at that time were still covering the death of Abraham Lincoln and his funeral train. Therefore, the tragedy was barely reported.

Comparison and Contrast

***Comparing* two things means showing how they are the same. *Contrasting* two things means showing how they are different. Comparisons and contrasts are often used in science and history books to make a subject clearer. Use these tips to help you understand comparison and contrast in reading assignments, such as the article on the opposite page.**

- Look for **direct statements** of comparison and contrast: "These things are similar because. . . " or "One major difference is. . . ."
- Pay attention to **words and phrases that signal comparisons,** such as *also, both, is the same as,* and *in the same way.*
- Notice **words and phrases that signal contrasts.** Some of these are *however, still, but,* and *on the other hand.*

MARK IT UP Read the essay on the opposite page. Then use the information from the essay and the tips above to answer the questions.

1. Circle the words and phrases that signal comparisons. The first one is done for you.
2. Underline the words and phrases that signal contrasts. The first one is done for you.
3. A Venn diagram shows how two subjects are similar and how they are different. Complete this diagram, which uses information from the essay to compare and contrast the United States and Bosnia. Add at least two similarities and two differences.

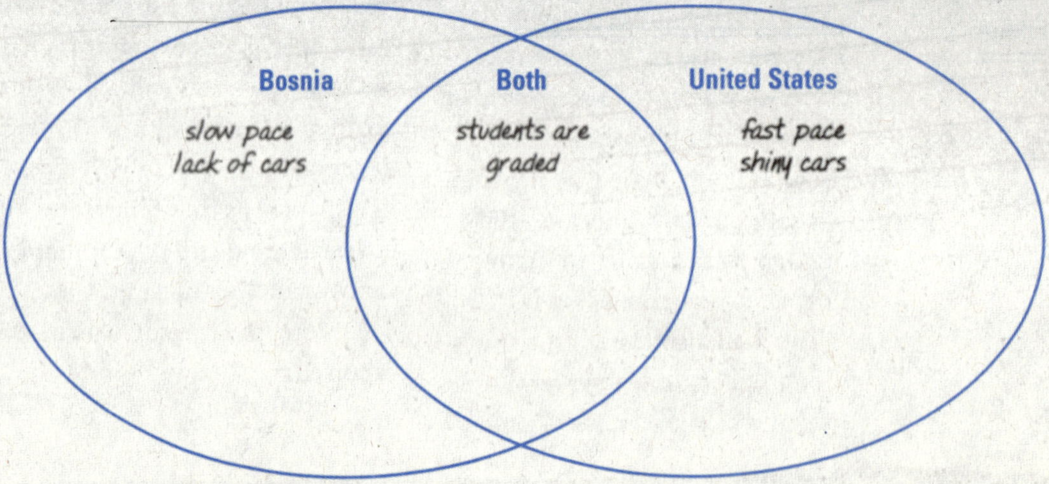

My Two Homes: Bosnia and the U.S.

by Elvisa Pandzic

My family and I came to America because of the war in Bosnia. . . . I had to catch my breath when I first set eyes on Chicago. It was spectacular—like a dream, with its tall buildings and shiny cars. Everything was moving so fast! Still, I often thought of Cazin, where I was born.

Contrast

I missed the slow pace of small-town life. That and the lack of cars. Most people had no need to travel to a place they couldn't walk to. I especially missed the mountains and hills. Nothing can replace those big beautiful meadows and the forests that took your breath away with their wonderful green smells. . . .

Comparison

Another big difference is the school system. When I started school in Chicago I was very confused—all the rules were different. In Bosnia, schools are strict and students give their teachers a lot of respect. We used to stand up when a teacher entered the classroom and when we had to answer a question. In American schools, students may talk without

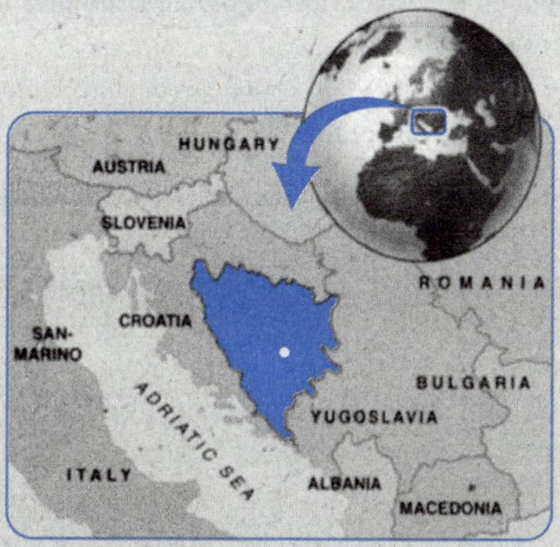

even being called on. This is not entirely bad, in my opinion. I like how students can express themselves freely. Another thing that has taken some time getting used to is the grading system. In Bosnia, all the grades are given in numbers, not letters. In Bosnia a grade of A is equal to 5, B to 4, C to 3, D to 2, and F to 1. At least the dress code in my new school is almost the same as in Bosnia. In both places you can wear blue jeans to school. . . .

I have been living in Chicago for about two years and I am adjusting well, but I still miss Bosnia, my first home. I look forward to a time of peace when I can return. I know I will never return to my "old" life, but there is one thing I do know. Wherever I end up, I will celebrate the best of both worlds.

Argument

An argument is an opinion backed up with reasons and facts. Understanding an argument will help you make informed decisions about an issue. Use the following strategies to help you understand an argument.

- Look for words that signal an opinion: *I think; I feel; they claim, argue,* or *disagree.*
- Look for reasons, facts, or expert opinions that support the argument.
- Ask yourself if the argument and reasons make sense.

MARK IT UP Read the argument on the next page, and then answer the questions below.

1. Circle the words that signal an opinion.
2. Underline the two opinions in this argument.
3. Draw a box around the statement that is not supported by reason.
4. The writer gives reasons for and against television. Fill in the chart below using the argument. One answer has been done for you.

1. *Television keeps people informed about current issues and events.*	1.
2.	2.
3.	3.
4.	4.
	5.

Television: Good or Bad?

Many people believe that life before television was happier than life today. In those days, people read books and newspapers for information. Families spent more time together. They talked, ate meals together, and shared chores. Many children used their imaginations to write and tell stories, and they participated in outdoor activities instead of spending hours in front of the television. People were not violent because they did not watch violent programs.

Others disagree. They claim that television has many advantages as an educational tool. It keeps people informed about important current events and issues. Television programs can help children learn valuable social skills such as cooperation and kindness. It can teach children how people live, work, and deal with misfortune. Some public television programs also promote activities such as visits to museums, libraries, bookstores, and zoos.

Both arguments are endless. The only thing we can say for sure is that we need more studies to show whether television is good or bad, or a little bit of both.

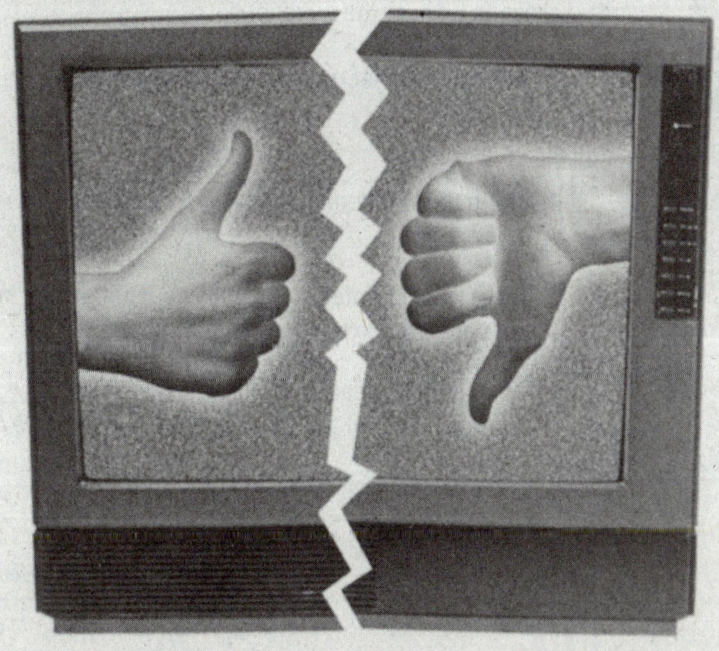

Social Studies

Your social studies textbook uses words and graphics to help you learn about people and places today and throughout history. As you read the tips below, look at the sample page on the right.

A First, look at any **headlines** or **subheads** on the page. These give you an idea of what each section covers.

B Carefully read the text and think about **ways the information is organized.** Social studies books are full of sequence, comparison and contrast, and cause and effect.

C Make sure you know the meaning of any boldfaced or underlined **vocabulary terms.** These terms often appear on tests.

D Next, look closely at any **sidebar articles** or **graphics.** Think about how they relate to the main text.

E Read any **study tips** in the margins or at the bottom of the page. These let you check your understanding as you read.

MARK IT UP The textbook page at right describes some of the effects of the Civil War on Northerners and Southerners. Use information from that page and from the tips above to answer the questions.

1. What two subjects does the page cover? ______________________

____

2. Circle the two vocabulary terms. Then underline the parts of the text that define those terms.

3. What was a Confederate soldier's monthly pay in 1864? Put a star next to the part of the page that gives you this information.

4. What does it mean to *subjugate* someone? ______________________
Put a box around the two places that *subjugate* or *subjugation* appear on the page.

5. Complete the diagram.

Cause: Many farmers were in the army.

Cause: ______________________

Cause: ______________________

→ **Cause:** Food shortages in South

A Economic Effects of the War

Many people suffered economic hardship during the war. The suffering was severe in the South, where most battles were fought, but the North also experienced difficulties.

B Food shortages were very common in the South, partly because so many farmers were fighting in the Confederate army. Moreover, food sometimes could not get to market because trains were now being used to carry war materials. The Confederate army also seized food and other supplies for its own needs.

Reading **History**
B. Analyzing Causes Why were economic problems particularly bad in the South?

E

Another problem, especially in the South, was inflation—an increase in price and decrease in the value of money. The average family food bill in the South increased from $6.65 a month in 1861 to $68 by mid–1863. Over the course of the war, prices rose 9,000 percent in the South.

Inflation in the North was much lower, but prices still rose faster than wages, making life harder for working people. Some people took advantage of wartime demand and sold goods for high prices.

Overall, though, war production boosted Northern industry and fueled the economy. In the short term, this gave the North an economic advantage over the South. In the long term, industry would begin to replace farming as the basis of the national economy.

During the war, the federal government passed two important economic measures. In 1861, it established the C first **income tax**—a tax on earnings. The following year, the government issued a new paper currency, known as **greenbacks** because of their color. The new currency helped the Northern economy by ensuring that people had money to spend. It also helped the Union to pay for the war.

Some Southerners in the border states took advantage of the stronger Union economy by selling cotton to Northern traders, in violation of Confederate law. "Yankee gold," wrote one Confederate officer, "is fast accomplishing what Yankee arms could never achieve—the subjugation of our people."

D

daily life

INFLATION IN THE SOUTH

During the Civil War, inflation caused hardship in the North and the South. But inflation was especially severe in the Confederacy, where prices could become outrageously high.

The food prices shown below are from 1864. Consider how many days it took a Confederate soldier to earn enough money to buy each of these foods.

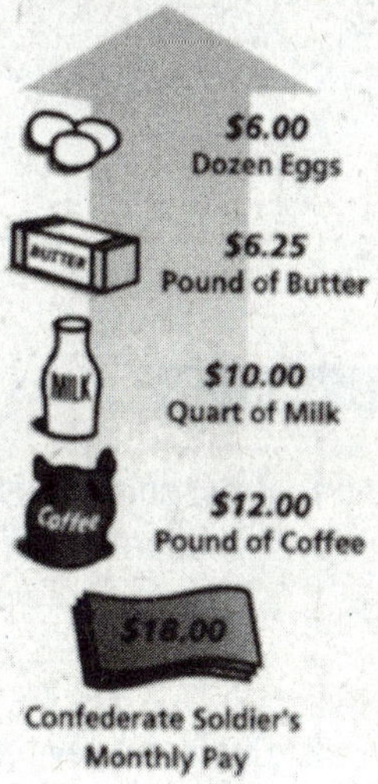

Vocabulary
subjugate: to bring under control or to conquer

E

Resistance by Slaves

Another factor that affected the South was the growing resistance from slaves. To hurt the Southern economy, slaves slowed their pace of work or stopped working altogether. Some carried out sabotage, destroying crops and farm equipment to hurt the plantation economy. When white

Science

Reading in science will be easier when you understand how the explanations, drawings, and special terms work together. Use the strategies below to help you better understand your science textbook. Look at the examples on the opposite page as you read each strategy in this list.

A Preview the **title** and **headings** on the page to see what science concepts will be covered.

B Look for **boldfaced** and **italicized** words that appear in the text. Look for **definitions** of those words.

C Many science textbooks discuss **scientific concepts** in terms of **everyday events or experiences.** Look for these places and consider how they improve your understanding.

D Look for references to numbered **figures** in the text.

E Then look in the margin for these figures, which are **diagrams** or **pictures** with **captions.** See how they illustrate and explain the text.

MARK IT UP Use the sample science page to help you answer the following questions.

1. What science concept will be covered in this lesson? Where on the page did you find this information?

   ____

2. Circle the key term *light year* and underline its definition.

3. How old is the light from Polaris when it reaches the Earth? ______________

4. Draw a star next to the reference to Figure 6-9.

5. In the third paragraph, circle the everyday experience used to help explain parallax.

6. Read the discussion of parallax in the text and look at Figure 6-9. What appears to happen to the close star's position between July and January? What actually happens to the star's position during that time?

   ____

Figure 6-8 The stars in the Big Dipper appear to be the same brightness. Does this mean that all of these stars are the same distance from Earth?

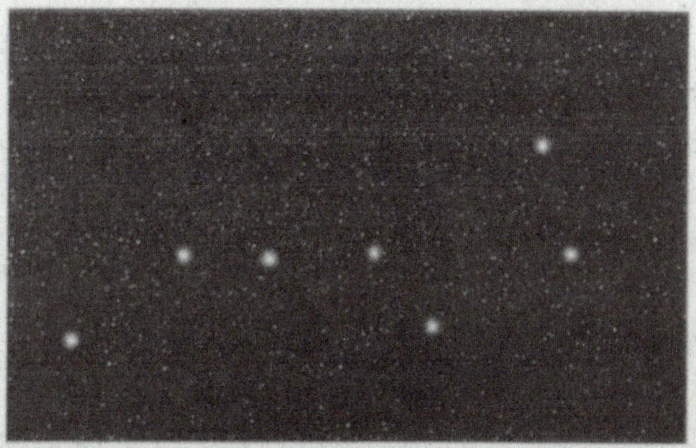

A Star Distances

All of the stars that you see at night are part of the Milky Way galaxy. The Milky Way contains about 200 billion stars. On a clear night, you might think that you can see millions of stars. Actually, you see only about 3000 stars with your C unaided eye. To understand why so few stars are visible, think about how you see a flashlight from a distance. At 1 meter, the flashlight is bright. At 50 meters, it appears dimmer. If the flashlight were far enough away, it would be too faint to see. For the same reason, you cannot see most of the stars in the Milky Way because they are too far away.

Astronomers measure distances to stars using the speed of light. Light travels at 300 000 kilometers per second. At this rate, sunlight takes 8 minutes to reach your eyes. Thus, the distance to the sun is 8 light-minutes. Distances to stars are measured in light-years. A **light-year** is the distance that B light travels in one year, about 9.5 trillion kilometers. The nearest star, Proxima Centauri, is 4.2 light-years from Earth. The distance to Polaris is 680 light-years. When you look into space, you look into the past. The light you see from Polaris left the star long before Columbus set sail for America.

D Figure 6-9 shows how to measure distance to a star by measuring its parallax. **Parallax** is the apparent shift in an object's position that is caused by the motion of the observer. You can see the parallax of your finger if you look at it only with your left eye and then only with your right eye. Your finger seems to move compared to the background. Try observing the parallax again with your finger closer to your eyes. How does the parallax change? You can observe the parallax of nearby stars with a telescope. The closer a star is, the greater is its parallax.

E Figure 6-9 In January, the close star appears to be at point A. Six months later, when Earth is at the opposite end of its orbit, the close star seems to be at point B. This apparent shift is called parallax.

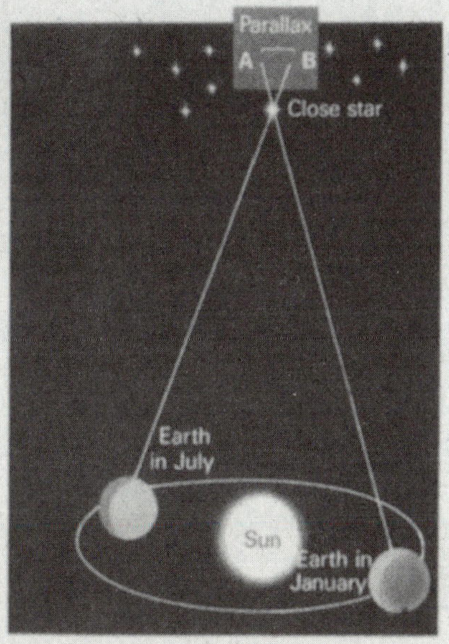

Mathematics

Reading a math textbook requires different skills than reading history, literature, or science. The tips below can help you learn these skills. As you read the tips, look at the sample math page on the right.

A First, look at the lesson **title** and any **subheads** on the page, so you know what topics will be covered.

B Find the **goals** or **objectives** for the lesson. These will tell you the most important points to know.

C Read **explanations** carefully. Sometimes the same concept is explained in more than one way to make sure you understand it.

D Look for **special features** such as study or vocabulary tips. These provide more help or information.

E Study any **worked-out solutions** to sample problems. These are the key to understanding how to do the homework assignment.

MARK IT UP Use the sample math page and the tips above to help you answer the following questions.

1. How is a multi-step equation solved? ______________________________ ______________________________ On the math page, draw a circle around the answer.

2. Draw a box around the vocabulary words that will be studied in this lesson.

3. Where will the question "How hot is Earth's crust?" be answered? ______________ Put a star next to the part of the page that answers this question.

4. How many steps are required to solve and check a linear equation? ______________

5. In Example 1, how do you isolate the variable? ______________________________ ______________________________ Underline the sentence that answers this question.

A

3.3 Solving Multi-Step Equations

B **Goal**

Use two or more steps to solve a linear equation.

Key Words

- like terms
- distributive property

How hot is Earth's crust?

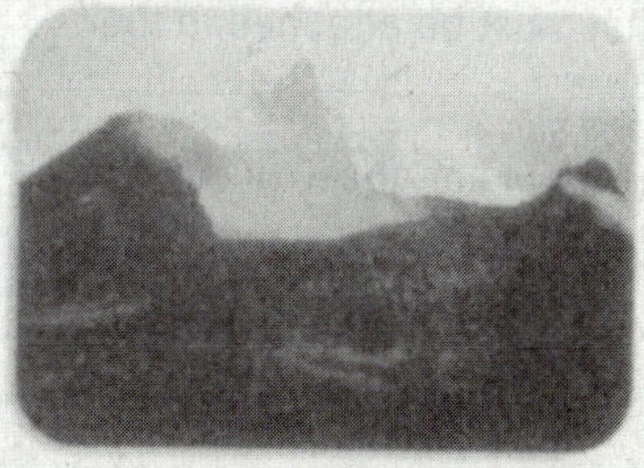

Temperatures within Earth's crust can get hot enough to melt rocks. In Example 2 you will see how a multi-step equation can be used to predict the depth at which the temperature of Earth's crust is 114°C.

C Solving a linear equation may require more than one step. Use the steps you already know for transforming an equation. Simplify one or both sides of the equation first, if needed. Then use inverse operations to isolate the variable.

Student Help

D ▶ **VOCABULARY TIP** The prefix *multi-* means "more than one". A multi-step equation is solved by transforming the equation more than one time.

A **EXAMPLE 1** *Solve a Linear Equation*

Solve $3x + 7 = -8$.

Solution

To isolate the variable, undo the addition and then the multiplication.

E $3x + 7 = -8$ Write original equation.

$3x + 7 - 7 = -8 - 7$ Subtract 7 from each side to undo the addition. (Subtraction Property of Equality)

$3x = -15$ Simplify both sides.

$\frac{3x}{3} = \frac{-15}{3}$ Divide each side by 3 to undo the multiplication. (Division Property of Equality)

$x = -5$ Simplify.

CHECK ✓ Check by substituting -5 for x in the *original* equation.

$3x + 7 = -8$ Write original equation.

$3(-5) + 7 \stackrel{?}{=} -8$ Substitute -5 for x.

$-15 + 7 \stackrel{?}{=} -8$ Multiply.

$-8 = -8$ ✓ Solution is correct.

Checkpoint ✓ *Solve a Linear Equation*

Solve the equation. Check your solution in the original equation.

1. $6x - 15 = 9$ **2.** $7x - 4 = -11$ **3.** $2y + 5 = 1$

Reading an Application

Reading and understanding an application will help you fill it out correctly and avoid mistakes. Use the following strategies to help you understand any application. Look at the example on the next page as you read each strategy.

A Begin at the top. Scan the application to see what the different sections are.

B Look for special instructions for how to fill out the application.

C Notice any request for materials that must be attached to the application.

D Watch for sections you don't have to fill in or questions you don't have to answer.

E Look for difficult or confusing words or abbreviations. Look them up in a dictionary or ask someone what they mean.

MARK IT UP Imagine that you want to participate in the student science fair. Read the application on the next page. Then answer the following questions.

1. On the application, number the four different sections.

2. What grade levels must students be in to participate in the science fair?

   ____

3. Underline all requests for materials that must be submitted along with the application.

   What are they? ______________________________

4. In the last section, which category number would you write if you had a botany project?

   ____

5. **ASSESSMENT PRACTICE** What name should be written in the Team Member Information section?
   A. your name
   B. your teacher
   C. a competing student
   D. your project partner

6. Invent an idea for a science project. Then fill out the application as best you can.

A CHICAGO PUBLIC SCHOOLS STUDENT SCIENCE FAIR, INC.

2000 STUDENT SCIENCE FAIR

Official Entry Form for Region and City Science Fairs

D DO NOT WRITE IN THIS SPACE

ENTRY NUMBER

DO NOT WRITE IN THIS SPACE

B Fill in the information below. The information must be typewritten or legibly printed (see handbook). Note: information requested for a team member refers to the second pupil on an elementary school project. Students must be in the 7th grade, 8th grade, or high school to participate in the city fair. Age requirements for participation in the state fair are determined by the rules of the Illinois Junior Academy of Science. **A COPY OF THE ABSTRACT MUST BE ATTACHED TO THIS ENTRY FORM.** C

ENTRANT INFORMATION

Entrant Name: Last First

Age: **Sex:** **Phone:** - - **Birth Date:** 1 9 Month Day Year

Address: Apartment Number Zip Code

Student Social Security Number: - - **Name of Parent or Guardian:** ____

TEAM MEMBER INFORMATION

Name: Last First

Age: **Sex:** **Phone:** - - **Birth Date:** 1 9 Month Day Year

Address: Apartment Number Zip Code

Student Social Security Number: - - **Name of Parent or Guardian:** ____

SCHOOL INFORMATION

Grade Unit Number Region School M.R.#

PROJECT INFORMATION

Electricity Required? Y N **Check Type of Endorsement(s) Attached*:** Human Vertebrate Animal Microbiology Recombinant DNA 8th Grade Recognition Luncheon Only

Organism(s) Used in Experiment: ____

E *** A COPY OF THE ENDORSEMENT(S) AND ABSTRACT MUST BE ATTACHED TO THIS ENTRY FORM.**

INSERT THE CORRESPONDING SET OF NUMERALS AND CATEGORY NAME IN THE BOXES PROVIDED.

01 Aero-Space Science
02 Behavioral Science
03 Biochemistry
04 Botany
05 Chemistry
06 Computer Science
07 Earth Science
08 Electronics
09 Engineering Science
10 Environmental Science
11 Health Science
12 Material Science
13 Mathematics
14 Microbiology
15 Physics
16 Zoology

Category Number: **Category Name**

Exhibit Title: Cannot Exceed 45 Spaces

Teacher/ Sponsor Name: Last First

Check here if an interpreter is needed. Indicate which language: ____

CERTIFICATION:

I hereby certify that this project has been personally inspected and that it fulfills all requirements as described in the Handbooks, including endorsements if applicable.

I hereby certify that I have read all of the above information and that it is accurate.

Region Science Fair Coordinator Signature ____ Date ____ Entrant's Signature ____ Date ____

83

Reading a Public Notice

Public notices can tell you about events in your community and give you valuable information about safety. When you read a public notice, follow these tips. Each tip relates to a specific part of the notice on the opposite page.

A Read the notice's **title,** if it has one. The title often gives the main idea or purpose of the notice.

B Ask yourself, **"Who should read this notice?"** If the information in it might be important to you or someone you know, then you should pay attention to it.

C Look for **instructions**—things the notice is asking or telling you to do.

D See if there is a logo, credit, or other way of telling **who created the notice.**

E See if there are details that tell you how you can **find out more** on the topic.

F Look for **special features** designed to make the notice easier to understand, such as instructions in more than one language.

MARK IT UP The notice on the opposite page is from the Web site of a public library. Read it carefully and answer the questions below.

1. Whom is this notice for?

   ____

2. What does the notice ask readers to do?

   ____

3. Underline the part of the notice that explains what "netiquette" is.

4. Circle the parts of the notice that tell who created it.

5. Put a star next to the part that tells where the library is located.

6. **ASSESSMENT PRACTICE** According to the notice, people who do not follow the library's rules for Internet use will

   A. be banned from the library
   B. lose their Internet privileges
   C. receive "flames" from other Internet users
   D. both A and C

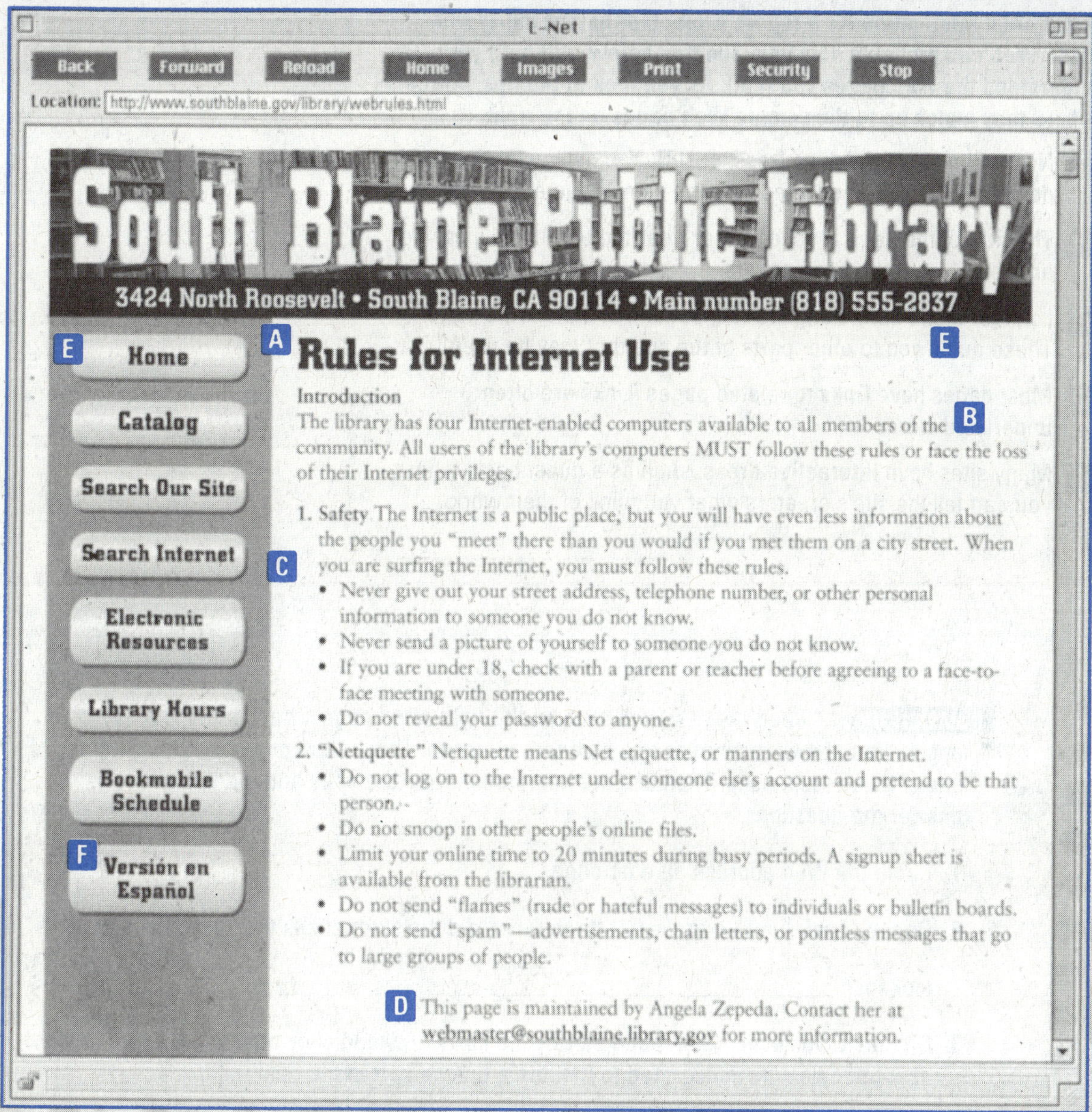
L-Net

Back | Forward | Reload | Home | Images | Print | Security | Stop

Location: http://www.southblaine.gov/library/webrules.html

South Blaine Public Library

3424 North Roosevelt • South Blaine, CA 90114 • Main number (818) 555-2837

E Home
Catalog
Search Our Site
Search Internet
Electronic Resources
Library Hours
Bookmobile Schedule
F Versión en Español

A **Rules for Internet Use** E

Introduction

The library has four Internet-enabled computers available to all members of the B community. All users of the library's computers MUST follow these rules or face the loss of their Internet privileges.

1. Safety The Internet is a public place, but you will have even less information about the people you "meet" there than you would if you met them on a city street. When C you are surfing the Internet, you must follow these rules.
   - Never give out your street address, telephone number, or other personal information to someone you do not know.
   - Never send a picture of yourself to someone you do not know.
   - If you are under 18, check with a parent or teacher before agreeing to a face-to-face meeting with someone.
   - Do not reveal your password to anyone.
2. "Netiquette" Netiquette means Net etiquette, or manners on the Internet.
   - Do not log on to the Internet under someone else's account and pretend to be that person.
   - Do not snoop in other people's online files.
   - Limit your online time to 20 minutes during busy periods. A signup sheet is available from the librarian.
   - Do not send "flames" (rude or hateful messages) to individuals or bulletin boards.
   - Do not send "spam"—advertisements, chain letters, or pointless messages that go to large groups of people.

D This page is maintained by Angela Zepeda. Contact her at webmaster@southblaine.library.gov for more information.

Reading a Web Page

If you need information for a report, project, or hobby, the World Wide Web can probably help you. The tips below will help you understand the Web pages you read. As you look at the tips, notice where they match up to the sample Web pages on the right.

A Notice the page's **Web address,** or URL. You may want to write it down in case you need to access the same page at another time.

B The **title** of the page is usually at or near the top. It will give you an idea of what the page covers.

C Look for **menu bars** along the top, bottom, or side of the page. These guide you to other parts of the site that may be useful.

D Most pages have **links** to related pages. Links are often underlined words.

E Many sites have **interactive areas,** such as a guest book, where you can tell the site's creators what you think of their work.

MARK IT UP Read the two Web sites on the right-hand page. The top one is a search engine that shows responses to a student's question. The bottom one is a site linked to one of those responses. Then use the information from the sites and the tips above to answer the questions.

1. Circle the Web address on both pages.
2. On the "LookQuick" page, what three terms did the student ask the search engine to look for? ______________________
3. On the "Gold Fever!" site, put a star by the link you would click on if you wanted to learn about people who immigrated to California to take part in the gold rush.
4. Put a box around the link you would click on to tell the creators of "Gold Fever!" your opinion of their site.
5. **ASSESSMENT PRACTICE** Choose the sentence that best summarizes the "Gold Fever!" site.
   A. It describes a dangerous illness called gold fever.
   B. It explains how you can mine for gold in your own backyard.
   C. It is an online museum exhibit about the California gold rush.
   D. none of the above

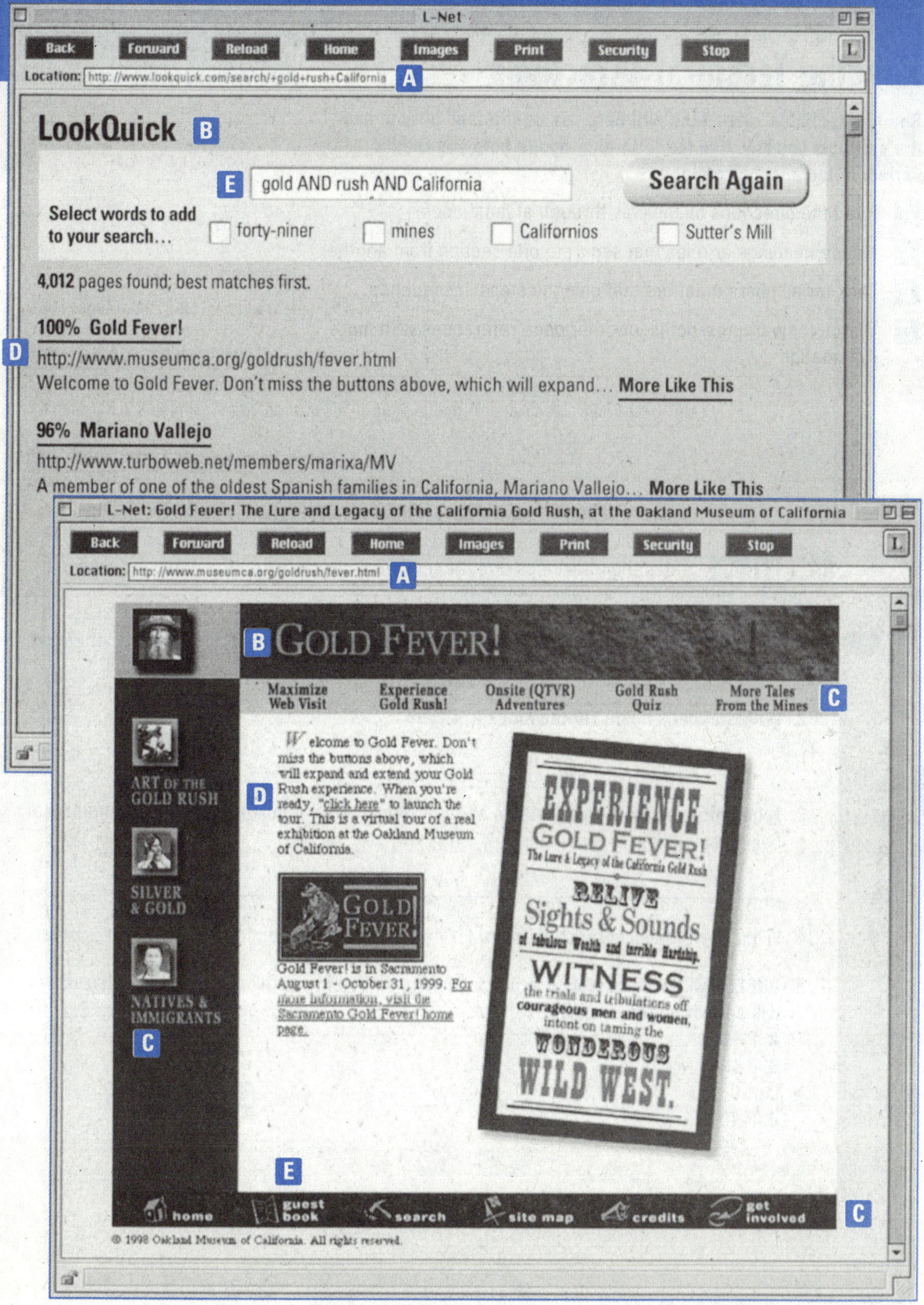
L-Net
Back
Forward
Reload
Home
Images
Print
Security
Stop
Location: http://www.lookquick.com/search/+gold+rush+California
A
LookQuick
B
E
gold AND rush AND California
Search Again
Select words to add to your search...
forty-niner
mines
Californios
Sutter's Mill
4,012 pages found; best matches first.
100% Gold Fever!
D
http://www.museumca.org/goldrush/fever.html
Welcome to Gold Fever. Don't miss the buttons above, which will expand... More Like This
96% Mariano Vallejo
http://www.turboweb.net/members/marixa/MV
A member of one of the oldest Spanish families in California, Mariano Vallejo... More Like This
L-Net: Gold Fever! The Lure and Legacy of the California Gold Rush, at the Oakland Museum of California
Back
Forward
Reload
Home
Images
Print
Security
Stop
Location: http://www.museumca.org/goldrush/fever.html
A
B
GOLD FEVER!
Maximize Web Visit
Experience Gold Rush!
Onsite (QTVR) Adventures
Gold Rush Quiz
More Tales From the Mines
C
ART OF THE GOLD RUSH
SILVER & GOLD
NATIVES & IMMIGRANTS
C
D
Welcome to Gold Fever. Don't miss the buttons above, which will expand and extend your Gold Rush experience. When you're ready, "click here" to launch the tour. This is a virtual tour of a real exhibition at the Oakland Museum of California.
GOLD FEVER
Gold Fever! is in Sacramento August 1 - October 31, 1999. For more information, visit the Sacramento Gold Fever! home page.
EXPERIENCE
GOLD FEVER!
The Lure & Legacy of the California Gold Rush
RELIVE
Sights & Sounds
of fabulous Wealth and terrible Hardship.
WITNESS
the trials and tribulations of courageous men and women, intent on taming the
WONDEROUS
WILD WEST.
E
home
guest book
search
site map
credits
get involved
C
© 1998 Oakland Museum of California. All rights reserved.

Reading Technical Directions

Reading technical directions will help you understand how to use the products you buy. Use the following tips to help you read a variety of technical directions.

A Read the directions all the way through at least once.

B Notice headings or rules that separate one section from another.

C Look for numbers or letters that give the steps in sequence.

D Watch for warnings, notes, or other page references with more information.

MARK IT UP Use the above tips and the technical directions on the opposite page to help you answer the following questions.

1. What is the first thing you must do to set the clock? Underline your answer on the next page.

2. What happens if you set the clock at 14:30?

   ____

3. What information can you find on another page? Draw a box around the statement that helps you answer this question.

   ____

4. What power level is recommended for defrosting or thawing food? Circle your answer.

5. **ASSESSMENT PRACTICE** If you are cooking something at full power, which characters will appear on the display?
   A. P-100
   B. P-HI
   C. P-0
   D. P-10

A **Microwave Instructions**

B Before Operating

1 Plug the power cord into a three-pronged electrical outlet.

C 2 Display panel will light up and flash 88:88.
Touch Stop/Clear pad.

3 Set the clock.
Touch Stop/Clear pad when the oven is first plugged in, or after the electrical power has been interrupted.

Setting the Clock

Procedure

1 Touch Clock pad

2 Enter time of day. For example, if it is 10:30, touch the number pads 1030 and "10:30" will appear.

3 Press the Clock pad again to set the time.

D **Note** You can select any time of the day from 1:00–12:59. To reset Clock, repeat steps 1 through 3 above. If incorrect time (for example, 8:61 or 13:00, etc.) is entered "EE" will appear on display. Touch Stop/Clear pad and program correctly.

Cancelling a Program

- To reset, or cancel, a cooking program as it is being entered, touch Stop/Clear pad once.
- To stop the oven while it is operating, touch Stop/Clear pad once. Do not open the door without pressing Stop/Clear pad.
- An entire cooking program (one stage or multiple stages) can be canceled after the oven has started cooking. This can be done by touching Stop/Clear pad twice.

Note See page 10 to create your own cooking programs.

Power Levels

Most foods can be cooked at full power (P-HI). However, for best results, some foods require a lower cooking power. Some foods such as tender cuts of meat can only be cooked with a lower power. Before setting any power level, the Power Level pad must be touched, followed by desired number. See chart.

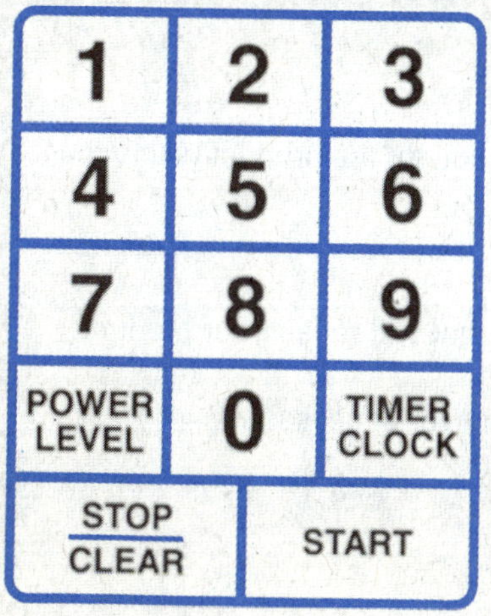

POWER	Touch Power Level pad, then	Display
100%	Touch Power Level pad once more.	P-HI
90%	Touch number pad 9.	P-90
80%	Touch number pad 8.	P-80
70%	Touch number pad 7.	P-70
60%	Touch number pad 6.	P-60
50%	Touch number pad 5.	P-50
40%	Touch number pad 4.	P-40
30%	Touch number pad 3.	P-30
20%	Touch number pad 2.	P-20
10%	Touch number pad 1.	P-10
0%	Touch number pad 0.	P-0

Note Choose P-30 for thawing or defrosting foods.

Product Information: Warranties

A warranty is a promise that the manufacturer will repair a product for free within a certain time period and under certain conditions. Learning to read a warranty will help you take advantage of the services you're entitled to. Look at the sample limited warranty as you read each strategy below.

A This section explains the services the manufacturer will carry out and the length of time they will be available. "Accessories" are items that are not part of the main product. Accessories that accompany a television may include cables and an antenna.

B In this section, the manufacturer explains the conditions under which the company is not responsible for repairing the product. Note that "acts of God" refers to such natural disasters as floods, earthquakes, and fires.

C The manufacturer may include requirements you must meet to obtain warranty service.

D Manufacturers usually include the phone number and address of their service center. You can contact the service center to find a store that will repair your product.

LIMITED WARRANTY Color TV

West Electronics Inc. ("West") warrants this Product (including any accessories) against defects in material or workmanship, subject to any conditions set forth as follows:

A A. LABOR: For a period of 90 days from the date of purchase, if this Product is determined to be defective, West will repair or replace the Product, at its option, at no charge, or pay the labor charges to any West authorized service facility. After the Warranty Period, you must pay for all labor charges.

B. PARTS: In addition, West will supply, at no charge, new or rebuilt replacements in exchange for defective parts for a period of one (1) year (color picture tube-two (2) years). After 90 days from the date of purchase, labor for removal and installation is available from West authorized service facilities or a West Service Center at your expense.

C. ACCESSORIES: Parts and labor for all accessories are for one (1) year.

B This warranty does not cover cosmetic damage or damage due to acts of God, accident, misuse, abuse, negligence, commercial use, or modification of, or to any part of the Product, including the antenna.

C Proof of purchase in the form of a bill of sale or receipted invoice which is evidence that the unit is within the Warranty period must be presented to obtain warranty service.

To locate the servicer or dealer nearest you, call:

D **West Service Center**
1-(800)-111-1111
or write to:
West Service Center
1234 Main St.
Westtown, CA 90000

MARK IT UP Read the warranty to help you answer these questions.

1. For how many days after purchase is labor free? ______________

2. Underline the conditions not covered by the warranty.

3. What do you need to provide in order to prove that you bought the product within the warranty period? ______________________________

4. Circle the phone number you should call to find a store that will repair your product.

5. **ASSESSMENT PRACTICE** How long does the warranty cover accessories?
   A. 90 days
   B. 2 years
   C. 60 days
   D. 1 year

Reading a Train Schedule

Knowing how to read a schedule accurately will help you get to places on time. Look at the example as you read each strategy on this list.

A Scan the **title** to know what the schedule covers.

B Look for **labels** that show **dates** or **days of the week** to help you understand how the weekly or daily schedule works.

C Study **place labels,** such as station names, to help you understand the stopping points on the schedule.

D Look for **expressions of time** to know what hours or minutes are listed on the schedule.

E Look for **train numbers** to help you determine which train stops at certain stations.

A **Kenwood to Turner City—Monday through Friday** **B**

E	300	302	304	306	308	310	312	314	316	318	320	322
STATIONS	A.M.	A.M.	A.M.	A.M.	A.M.	A.M.	A.M.	—	A.M.	A.M.	A.M.	A.M.
C Kenwood LV:	—	—	—	5:55	—	6:17	—	—	6:53	—	—	7:15
North Springs	—	—	—	6:03	—	6:25	—	—	7:02	—	—	7:23
Hollow Lake	—	—	—	6:07	—	6:30	—	7:09	7:06	—	—	7:28
Grant St.	4:58	5:28	5:54	6:17	—	6:39	—	7:12	7:15	7:20	—	7:37
Central St. D	5:01	5:31	5:58	6:19	—	6:43	—	7:16	↓	7:24	—	7:42
Main St.	5:05	—	6:02	—	—	6:46	—	—	↓	7:27	—	—
Ft. Peck	5:10	5:37	6:06	6:26	—	6:50	—	7:23	7:24	7:32	—	7:49
River Valley	5:13	5:40	6:10	6:30	—	6:54	—	↓	—	7:36	—	7:54
Columbus St.	5:16	5:44	6:14	6:35	—	6:59	—	↓	7:32	7:40	—	7:59
Allen Square	5:19	5:47	6:17	6:38	—	7:02	—	7:31	7:36	7:43	—	—
River Falls	5:22	5:50	6:20	6:41	—	7:05	—	7:35	—	7:46	7:53	8:05
Hudson City	5:25	5:53	6:23	6:45	—	7:09	—	↓	7:41	↓	7:57	↓
Santa Ana	—	—	—	—	—	—	—	↓	—	↓	—	↓
Lake Pawnee	5:27	5:55	6:25	6:48	—	7:12	—	7:39	7:43	↓	7:51	↓
Erie Falls	5:30	5:58	6:28	6:51	—	7:15	—	7:42	—	7:52	8:01	↓
Turner City AR:	5:33	6:01	6:31	6:54	—	7:18	—	|	7:48	—	8:06	↓

MARK IT UP Answer the following questions using the train schedule and strategies on this page.

1. Where do the trains on this schedule go? ______________________

2. What days does this schedule cover? ______________

3. Circle three stations where train 304 does not stop.

4. **ASSESSMENT PRACTICE** If you board train 316 from Grant St., what will be the first stop the train will make?
   A. Central St.
   B. Main St.
   C. Ft. Peck
   D. Columbus St.

Reading Test Model

LONG SELECTIONS

DIRECTIONS **Here is a selection entitled "Dolphinspeak" by Aline Alexander Newman. Read the selection carefully. The notes in the side columns will help you prepare for the kinds of questions that are likely to follow readings like this. You might want to preview the questions on pages 38 and 39 before you begin reading.**

Reading Strategies for Assessment

Think about the title. Titles often offer clues about the topic of a selection. Write what you think this article will be about.

Consider the author's purpose. What do these questions suggest about the author's motive for writing this article?

Look for cause-and-effect relationships. Why do scientists believe dolphins can communicate with each other? Circle the reason.

Dolphinspeak

The Incredible Ways Dolphins Communicate with Each Other—and with Us

by Aline Alexander Newman

"Psst, listen up."

A female dolphin was being trained to push paddles to get food. Although she couldn't see her partner, a male dolphin in a separate tank, she kept whistling and chirping to him. Soon he started pushing paddles, too. Did the female "tell" him how to do it?

Squawks, whistles, chirps, and clicks—the racket is earsplitting as groups of bottlenose dolphins zoom around beneath the waves. Scientists have been aware of the dolphins' noisemaking for years. But are the animals talking to each other? If they are, what are they saying?

Where there are dolphins, there are humans who are curious about them. There are dozens of species of dolphins, and they live in oceans all over the world, as well as in some rivers. They live in groups. The ultimate team players, some kinds of dolphins work together to herd fish and then take turns eating their catch. They speed through the water side by side, sometimes making sounds as they swim They zip along without bumping or banging into each other. Scientists believe the only way dolphins could work together so well and in so many ways is if they're "talking."

That's why marine biologist Kathleen Dudzinski has been eavesdropping on dolphin "conversations" for ten years. By carefully observing dolphin behavior, she hopes eventually to learn their "language." That may take a while. Dolphins are mammals, so they have lungs and must breathe air at the water's surface. But they spend 99 percent of their lives underwater, making them hard to find and study. "It's like trying to put together a giant jigsaw puzzle when you've lost the box lid with the puzzle's picture on it," says Dudzinski.

Dudzinski studies wild dolphins around the world. She films them using a custom-made video camera and recording system. When Dudzinski plays back her tapes, she makes notes of what she sees and hears.

Dolphin communication includes many different kinds of signals: touching each other, body position, movement such as leaping and rolling, and sounds. Sometimes signals are used alone, sometimes in combination. For example, making clicking noises toward each other and then rubbing fins might be the dolphin way of saying "hi."

There is evidence that dolphins call each other "by name." Vincent Janik, a zoologist from the United Kingdom, says that each individual dolphin develops a personal whistle. When the water is so murky that they can't see each other, the dolphins whistle those personal names to stay in touch.

Dudzinski's biggest discovery was recognizing the differences in communication when dolphins play and fight. It was confusing at first, because dolphins whistle loudly and bite each other in both situations. But one day after watching some puppies tumbling about, she realized that the playful dolphins usually do the same thing. They romp and roll and rub each other. Dolphins that are fighting don't do any rubbing, and they tend to get right in each other's faces.

While Dudzinski and Janik do research in the wild, other scientists study captive animals. One pair of captive dolphins knows 50 words in sign language. They even understand the difference between "take the Frisbee to the surfboard" and "take the surfboard to the Frisbee."

Wild dolphins often leap out of the water at the same time. Knowing that, trainers use signals to tell captive dolphins to plan their next move. The animals submerge, "discuss" what they're going to do, and do it—in perfect unison! And that's what humans call cool!

Analyze supporting details. Reread this paragraph to find the details that support the jigsaw puzzle comparison.

Look for clues to the main idea. This paragraph makes a general observation about dolphin communication. Write the main idea of the paragraph in your own words.

Infer meanings from word parts. Circle the word you can see in *zoologist*. Use its meaning to figure out a possible definition for *zoologist*.

Notice comparisons and contrasts. The paragraph that begins, "Dudzinski's biggest discovery . . ." compares and contrasts the behavior of fighting dolphins with that of playing dolphins. Underline the differences she discovered.

Analyze the author's perspective. Circle words that show the author's attitude toward her subject. Are they positive or negative words?

Answer Strategies

Determine author's purpose. The key words in this question are *major purpose.* They tell you that the correct answer will refer to the author's main reason for writing the article, not her reason for including some particular facts.

Look for causes and effects. The word *why* signals that the question involves cause and effect. Find the quoted word in the article. Then choose the answer that matches the reason stated in the text.

Infer meanings. Locate the quoted sentence in the passage. Reread the surrounding paragraphs to help you infer the meaning of *zoologist.*

Find contrasts. The question asks for a difference between fighting and playing dolphins. Locate and reread the paragraph that compares and contrasts dolphins' behavior in these two situations.

Identify the main idea. Think about how you would sum up the main idea of the selection in a sentence. Remember that the title often relates to the main idea. Which choice comes closest to your summary?

Answers:
1. B, 2. G, 3. A, 4. G, 5. C

Now answer questions 1 through 8. Base your answers on the article "Dolphinspeak." Then check yourself by reading through the side-column notes.

1. The author's major purpose in writing this article is to

   A. compare dolphins with other mammals.
   B. describe how dolphins communicate.
   C. get people interested in training dolphins.
   D. explain how dolphins play.

2. Why do scientists believe that dolphins "talk"?

   F. They are mammals.
   G. They are able to live in oceans all over the world.
   H. They work together well in many ways.
   I. They make many different kinds of noises.

3. Read the following sentence from the article.

   Vincent Janik, a zoologist from the United Kingdom, says that each individual dolphin develops a personal whistle.

   What is the meaning of the word *zoologist*?

   A. a scientist who studies animals
   B. someone from a foreign country
   C. someone trained to identify whistles
   D. a person who works with captive dolphins

4. What do fighting dolphins do that is different from what playing dolphins do?

   F. Fighting dolphins whistle loudly.
   G. Fighting dolphins rub each other.
   H. Fighting dolphins get in each other's faces.
   I. Fighting dolphins bite each other.

5. Which statement best summarizes the information in this article?

   A. Dolphins are very noisy mammals.
   B. Dolphins are smarter than people.
   C. Dolphins have a complicated communication system.
   D. We will never understand dolphins.

6 If the article needed a new title, which would be best?

F. "Dolphins Call Each Other by Name"
G. "Marine Biologist Kathleen Dudzinski"
H. "Under the Sea"
I. "Can Dolphins Communicate?"

Revisit the title. Consider how the current title reflects the main idea of the article. Eliminate answer choices that are too narrow or too broad. Select the one that is closest in meaning to the actual title.

7 With which statement would the author of "Dolphinspeak" most likely agree?

A. Dolphins are solitary animals.
B. Dolphins should be studied further.
C. Fish can also communicate with each other.
D. Scientists spend too much time studying dolphins.

Identify author's perspective. First eliminate answers that are obviously wrong or irrelevant (A and C). The remaining choices, B and D, express opposite opinions about studying dolphins. Which opinion matches the author's perspective?

READ THINK EXPLAIN

Short Response: Use details and information from the reading to explain your answer.

8 Read the following sentence from the article.

> **"It's like trying to put together a giant jigsaw puzzle when you've lost the box lid with the puzzle's picture on it," says Dudzinski.**

Explain the meaning of this statement in your own words. Be sure to tell what the scientist is comparing to putting together a jigsaw puzzle and in what ways the two activities are alike.

Plan your response. Underline what the question is asking you to do and what you must include. Then go back to the selection and draw stars next to details that support and develop your answer.

Sample short response for question 8:

The scientist in the article is comparing putting together a jigsaw puzzle to learning about dolphins. She is saying that it's hard to figure out where the pieces of a puzzle go when you don't know what it's supposed to look like. Trying to figure out what dolphins are doing is hard and frustrating in the same way because they spend almost all their time underwater.

Study the response. Notice how the writer states what is being compared in the first sentence. The explanation is then developed with the writer's own thoughts as well as details from the selection.

Answers: 6 H 7 B

Reading Test Practice

LONG SELECTIONS

NOTES

DIRECTIONS Now it's time to practice what you've learned about reading test items and choosing the best answers. Read the following selection, "Finding a Bit of History" by Shirley Neitzel. Use the side columns to make notes about the important parts of this selection: main ideas, cause and effect, comparisons and contrasts, difficult vocabulary, supporting details, and so on.

Finding a Bit of History

by Shirley Neitzel

Less than a quarter mile into Maldonado Bay from the dock at Punta del Este, Uruguay, Hector Bado rechecked his instruments and charts. Then he and his crew anchored his ship, the *Surveyor.* This was the place: through earlier exploration he knew what lay on the ocean's bottom here—the remains of the Spanish freighter *Salvador.*

Even though his crew was highly experienced, excitement rippled through them as divers with underwater cameras prepared to enter the murky bay. The divers could see only a few feet through the swirling sand and debris. Maldonado Bay is part of the Río de la Plata, and its sediment has slowly been burying the *Salvador* over 186 years.

In the late 1700s and early 1800s, Spain, Portugal, England, and France waged wars to expand their empires. Spain's South American colonies were occupied at different times by Portuguese and English troops. The colonists were dissatisfied with the rule of their distant king, and in 1810 José Gervasio Artigas led Uruguay in a revolution.

Spain reacted by sending in troops. In April 1812, a battalion of trained soldiers boarded the *Salvador* at Cadiz, Spain, with orders to put down the revolutionaries. On 31 August the ship arrived at the mouth of the Río de la Plata. From there a local naval pilot was to guide it through the treacherous waters into the port of Montevideo. But a *pampero,* a strong wind, was building from the southwest, so the pilot sailed the ship into Maldonado Bay for protection from the storm. The bay proved too shallow for such a large

NOTES

ship, and the *Salvador* struck bottom. The captain was able to free it, but a short time later it struck bottom again.

Although the crew hoped to ride out the storm, the winds were too strong. Sturdy oak planks splintered as each wave smashed the ship's keel onto the bottom of the bay. The *Salvador* listed and heaved. On deck, cannons broke loose from their mounts. Soldiers and crew panicked as the bronze behemoths careened among them. To keep the ship from capsizing, the crew cut the masts. The sails fell, trapping men in the heavy canvas and rigging.

Few of the seven hundred people on board knew how to swim, so they stayed with the ship. Had they known they were only about three hundred meters from shore, more of them might have been able to save themselves. But in the darkness, confusion reigned. The next morning, the *Salvador* lay on the bottom of Maldonado Bay, and most of her troops had gone down with her. Without these soldiers, the Spanish effort to crush the revolution was weakened. By 1816 Spain had lost Uruguay forever.

One of the few survivors of the wreck of the *Salvador* was Antonio De Acosta y Lara, an assistant to the coastal pilots in Montevideo. His handwritten account of that terrible night was found in 1993 by a historian studying in the Naval Archives near Madrid, Spain.

At almost the same time, Hector Bado, diving near Punta del Este, discovered the wreck. The *Salvador* was a wooden sailing vessel, and much of it had rotted away long ago. What's left no longer resembles a ship, and an inexperienced diver might easily have ignored the piles of mussel-covered rubble. But Bado knew the shells could be hiding something interesting. Mussels don't cling to bronze, so with a little investigation, he discovered cannons looking much as they did when the *Salvador* sank. Bado obtained permits from the government of Uruguay to salvage the ship. By the fall of 1998 he was ready.

Most of the items once on board the *Salvador* were hidden by sand and clay. Digging can destroy delicate artifacts, so divers must loosen the sediment by waving their hands like

NOTES

fish tails. It's slow work, but lucky divers may uncover a button, a coin, a bottle, a telescope, or something else from the ship.

A marine archaeologist oversees the salvage. Divers create a grid of string over the wreck site, then carefully explore each square of the grid. Every artifact must be cataloged, cleaned, tagged, photographed, preserved, and stored. A three-dimensional drawing shows where each artifact was found.

On 30 October 1998, the first items—four bronze cannons—were raised from the wreck site. The admiral of the Uruguayan navy, the director of the Historical Museum of Uruguay, and many other officials joined the crew of the *Surveyor* for this historic event, and a navy ship fired a twenty-one-gun salute to the people who died on the *Salvador*.

On the dock at Punta del Este, hundreds of people clapped and cheered as the 1,400-pound cannons were lifted from the *Surveyor*. Each cannon had been cast with its name. These were *Rafael, Piedad, Miguel,* and *Graviel.* Children and adults surrounded the crew of the *Surveyor* and followed the cannons as they were taken by forklift to their preservation site. The salvage of the *Salvador* acknowledges a step toward the formation of the country of Uruguay, and the crowd was eager to see this piece of their history. One old man reached out and touched a cannon, then kissed his fingers. A woman touched a cannon, crossed herself, and fell to her knees.

Afterward, the crew of the *Surveyor* returned to the business of excavating the rest of the wreck. Muskets and swords littered the shallow water, as well as two brass-and-ebony sextants used by the *Salvador*'s navigators to determine their position at sea. Divers also uncovered a tooth extractor, splints, medicine vials, and the surgical tools of the ship's doctor. They found needles, scissors, and thimbles belonging to the ship's tailor, as well as cartons of buttons and bolts of fabric for military uniforms. Careful fanning revealed coins, religious medals, and other personal belongings of the soldiers and crew.

Items uncovered from the shipwreck are being shared equally between the salvage company and the government of Uruguay. Some of the artifacts will go to museums; others

NOTES

will be sold to private collectors. Hector Bado hopes to have any human remains reburied and a memorial erected, either in Uruguay or Spain.

"There are big differences between divers who hunt for treasure and those who are motivated by a desire to learn about naval history and to preserve it," said Bado. "The important thing is to salvage this bit of history."

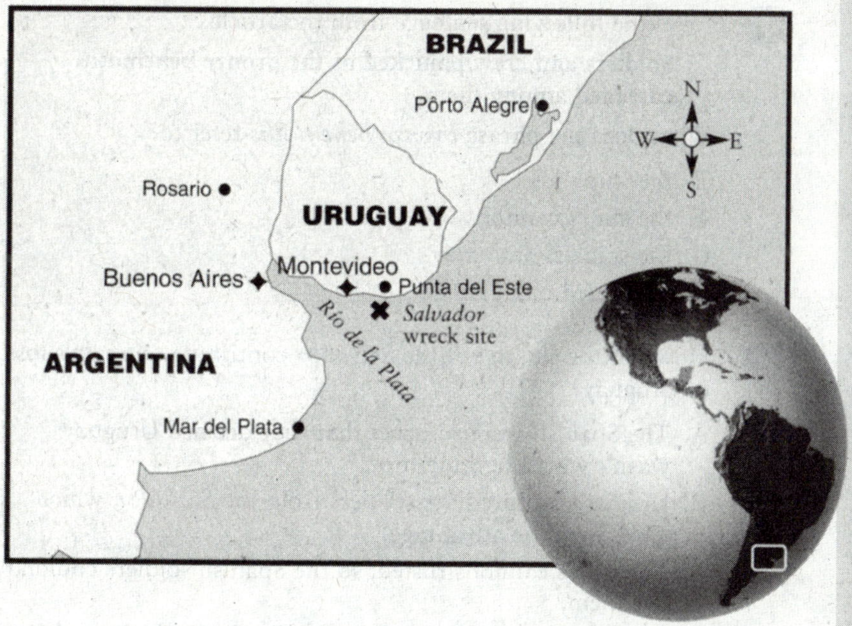

Now answer questions 1 through 10. Base your answers on the article "Finding a Bit of History."

1. What is the author's main purpose in writing this article?
   - **A.** to persuade people to study history
   - **B.** to explain how the *Salvador* sank in 1812
   - **C.** to describe the history and recovery of the *Salvador*
   - **D.** to teach people how to dive for sunken treasure

2. The Spanish ship *Salvador* sailed to Uruguay in 1812 to
   - **F.** put down a revolution by the colonists.
   - **G.** teach Spanish soldiers about life in the colonies.
   - **H.** trade with the colonists.
   - **I.** see how the ship would handle in shallow water.

NOTES

3 Using the text and the map, decide which direction the shipwreck was from Montevideo, where the *Salvador* was headed.

A. west
B. east
C. southeast
D. northwest

4 Read the following sentence from the article.

Soldiers and crew panicked as the bronze behemoths careened among them.

What does the phrase *bronze behemoths* refer to?

E. the ship's keel
F. the ship's cannons
G. the soldiers and crew
H. splintered oak planks

5 How did the sinking of the *Salvador* contribute to Spain's loss of Uruguay?

A. The Spanish were so upset that they decided Uruguay wasn't worth fighting for.
B. Uruguay captured the soldiers from the *Salvador,* which gave them the advantage.
C. The ship's cannons rusted, so the Spanish soldiers couldn't fire them.
D. Most of the soldiers on the *Salvador* died, which weakened the Spanish fighting force.

6 What organizational pattern does the author use for the third through the eighth paragraphs?

E. fact and opinion
F. problem and solution
G. chronological order
H. spatial order

NOTES

7. Which of the following statements best supports the idea that Bado is carefully preserving the *Salvador* artifacts?

   A. Bado's crew works slowly and keeps records of where each item was found.

   B. Bado's crew has found surgical tools used by the ship's doctor.

   C. A historian found a handwritten account of the *Salvador*'s sinking.

   D. The first items to be raised from the site were four bronze cannons.

8. The information in the article "Finding a Bit of History" could best be used for a student research project on

   F. mussels and other animals that live in the ocean.

   G. uncovering lost historical artifacts.

   H. how to avoid being shipwrecked.

   I. the modern government of Uruguay.

9. Read these sentences from the article.

   One old man reached out and touched a cannon, then kissed his fingers. A woman touched a cannon, crossed herself, and fell to her knees.

   What did the cannons from the *Salvador* mean to these people?

   A. recovery of the lost history of their country

   B. proof that Uruguay can never be defeated by Spain

   C. a wealth of precious bronze metal

   D. pride in the skill of their divers and marine archaeologists

READ THINK EXPLAIN

Short Response: Use details and information from the reading to explain your answer.

10. Explain how using a grid of string helped divers recover items from the wreck of the *Salvador*.

THINKING IT THROUGH

The notes in the side columns will help you review your answers on pages 44 and 45. Then see the key at the bottom of the page. How well did you do?

Keep in mind the key words *main purpose*. Do not be distracted by statements that refer to only one part of the passage.

1 What is the author's main purpose in writing this article?

A. to persuade people to study history
B. to explain how the *Salvador* sank in 1812
C. to describe the history and recovery of the *Salvador*
D. to teach people how to dive for sunken treasure

Use the question to help you find the answer. Scan the passage for the date 1812. That is where you will find the reason for the ship's sailing.

2 The Spanish ship *Salvador* sailed to Uruguay in 1812 to

F. put down a revolution by the colonists.
G. teach Spanish soldiers about life in the colonies.
H. trade with the colonists.
I. see how the ship would handle in shallow water.

Try rephrasing the question as a fill-in-the-blank statement to be sure you understand what it is asking. "The wreck is located ______ of Montevideo."

3 Using the text and the map, decide which direction the shipwreck was from Montevideo, where the *Salvador* was headed.

A. west
B. east
C. southeast
D. northwest

Find this sentence in the selection. Read the sentence preceding it to identify the part of the ship to which *bronze behemoths* refers.

4 Read the following sentence from the article.

Soldiers and crew panicked as the bronze behemoths careened among them.

What does the phrase *bronze behemoths* refer to?

F. the ship's keel
G. the ship's cannons
H. the soldiers and crew
I. splintered oak planks

Answers:
1. C, 2. E, 3. C, 4. F

5 How did the sinking of the *Salvador* contribute to Spain's loss of Uruguay?

A. The Spanish were so upset that they decided Uruguay wasn't worth fighting for.

B. Uruguay captured the soldiers from the *Salvador*, which gave them the advantage.

C. The ship's cannons rusted, so the Spanish soldiers couldn't fire them.

D. Most of the soldiers on the *Salvador* died, which weakened the Spanish fighting force.

Narrow your choices to those that you know contain accurate facts. Then refer back to the passage to determine which one is valid.

6 What organizational pattern does the author use for the third through the eighth paragraphs?

F. fact and opinion

G. problem and solution

H. chronological order

I. spatial order

Skim the paragraphs listed. What does the frequent use of dates and time-order transitions indicate about the organization?

7 Which of the following statements best supports the idea that Bado is carefully preserving the *Salvador* artifacts?

A. Bado's crew works slowly and keeps records of where each item was found.

B. Bado's crew has found surgical tools used by the ship's doctor.

C. A historian found a handwritten account of the *Salvador*'s sinking.

D. The first items to be raised from the site were four bronze cannons.

The words *carefully preserving* tell you to eliminate choices that merely state what has been found in the ship or how people learned about the ship.

8 The information in the article "Finding a Bit of History" could best be used for a student research project on

F. mussels and other animals that live in the ocean.

G. uncovering lost historical artifacts.

H. how to avoid being shipwrecked.

I. the modern government of Uruguay.

Choose the answer most closely related to the central focus of the article as a whole.

Answers:
5.D, 6.G, 7.A, 8.F

Find these sentences in the passage. What reason for these actions is given in the preceding sentence?

9 Read these sentences from the article.

One old man reached out and touched a cannon, then kissed his fingers. A woman touched a cannon, crossed herself, and fell to her knees.

What did the cannons from the *Salvador* mean to these people?

A. recovery of the lost history of their country

B. proof that Uruguay can never be defeated by Spain

C. a wealth of precious bronze metal

D. pride in the skill of their divers and marine archaeologists

READ
THINK
EXPLAIN

Short Response: Use details and information from the reading to explain your answer.

This response received a top score because it

- explains two uses of the grid.
- uses details from the passage to support the explanation.
- is clearly written.

10 Explain how using a grid of string helped divers recover items from the wreck of the *Salvador.*

Using a grid of string had a two-fold purpose. First, divers could concentrate on one particular square and thoroughly search it before moving on to the next section of the wreck. In this way, they could be sure they explored the entire area. Second, the grid allowed the divers to keep accurate records of the original location of each artifact. A three-dimensional drawing now shows where each artifact was found.